CAREER OPPORTUNITIES IN AVIATION AND THE AEROSPACE INDUSTRY

CAREER OPPORTUNITIES IN AVIATION AND THE AEROSPACE INDUSTRY

Susan Echaore-McDavid

Checkmark Books®
An imprint of Facts On File, Inc.

Career Opportunities in Aviation and the Aerospace Industry

Checkmark Books
An imprint of Facts On File, Inc.
132 West 31st Street
New York NY 10001

Library of Congress Cataloging-in-Publication Data
Echaore-McDavid, Susan.
Career opportunities in aviation and the aerospace industry/Susan Echaore-McDavid.
p. cm.
Includes bibliographical references and index.
ISBN 0-8160-4649-2 (hc : alk. paper)—ISBN 0-8160-4650-6 (pb : alk. paper)
1. Aeronautics, Commercial—Vocational guidance. I. Title.
HD8039,A23E285 2004
387.7′.023—dc22 2004004863

Checkmark Books are available at special discounts when purchased in bulk quantities for businesses, associations, institutions, or sales promotions. Please call our Special Sales Department in New York at (212) 967-8800 or (800) 322-8755.

You can find Facts On File on the World Wide Web at http://www.factsonfile.com

Cover design by Nora Wertz

Printed in the United States of America

VB Hermitage 10 9 8 7 6 5 4 3 2 1

This book is printed on acid-free paper.

Dedicated to
Santiago D. Echaore
(1905–1982)
and
James E. McDavid
(1918–2004)

CONTENTS

AVIATION CONSULTING AND SALES

AVIATION RECREATION, SPORTS, AND ENTERTAINMENT

MILITARY AVIATION

AEROSPACE MANUFACTURING INDUSTRY

SPACE FLIGHT AND EXPLORATION

APPENDIXES

ACKNOWLEDGMENTS

I could not have done this book without the help of many people who took the time out of their busy schedules to talk or correspond with me. In particular, I would like to thank the following individuals and groups:

Mark Arnold, P.E., Supervisor, Airport Engineering Section, Wisconsin Department of Transportation; Kevin K. Bailey, Aviation Maintenance Inspector, Region 4, U.S. Forest Service, Ogden, Utah; Dan Brattain, President, Cal-Ore Life Flight, Brookings, Oregon; William Broadwell, Executive Director, Aerial Firefighting Industry Association; Dan Burkhart, National Business Aviation Association Director, Regional Programs; Michael R. Callahan, Aviation Planner and Chairman, Airports Committee, American Planning Association Transportation Planning Division; Bill Cannon, President Emeritus and Founder, Professional Loadmaster Association.

Jaime Carreon, Aircraft Line, MX Control, IAH; Karen Casanovas, Executive Director, The Alaska Air Carriers Association; Jim Crouch, Director of Safety and Training, United States Parachute Association; Pat Denevan, Mission Soaring Center, Fremont, California; Stephen Dennis, Chairman, Aviation Resource Group International, Denver, Colorado; FAA, Aviation System Standards, Flight Inspection Operations Division, AVN-200; Dino Fantinato, Director of Maintenance of EADS, Socata Aircraft.

Charmiane Freeman, Flight Instructor; Jay Fuller, ALEA Safety Coordinator/NYSP Safety Officer/Pilot (Retired); Steve Gila; Mavis F. Green, Ph.D., President 2001–02, University Aviation Association; Cathy Hedglen; Chuck Kemper, Queen Bee Specialties, Rigby, Idaho; Greg Koontz, Greg Koontz Air Shows; Neil Krey, President, Magenta Line.

Paul A. Lange, Law Offices of Paul A. Lange; Robert Lattery, Senior Meteorologist, Northwest Airlines Meteorology; LCDR Christopher C. Lucas, MC (FS), USNR, Director of Academics, Naval Aerospace Medical Institute, Pensacola, Florida; Robert Malesza, Region III Assistant, Professional Airways Systems Specialists; Claudia McMullin, Aviation Weather Service, National Weather Service, Kansas City, Missouri; Matt Miller, Account Executive, Aero Insurance, Inc.; Gary J. Northam, Ph.D., Chair, Department of Aviation Science, Parks College of Engineering and Aviation, Saint Louis University, St. Louis, Missouri.

Tom O'Hara, Curator/General Manager, Flying Leatherneck Aviation Museum, Marine Corps Air Station Miramar, San Diego, California; Barbara Platt, Communications Department, Logan Airport; Mark E. Raymond, CMSgt, USAF, Retired Loadmaster; San Francisco Hang Gliding Center; LT Andrew Sikkenga, Navy ROTC, Prairie View A&M University, Prairie View, Texas; Chuck Siragusa, National Assistant, Professional Airways Systems Specialists; Dave Sorlie; Vicky Spediacci, Director of Operations, REACH Air Ambulance, Santa Rosa, California.

Drew Steketee, President and CEO, General Aviation Team 2000, Inc., BE A PILOT Foundation, Washington D.C.; Walt Strach, Meteorologist-in-Charge, Oakland Center Weather Service Unit, Oakland, California; Clifton Stroud, Director of Communications, National Air Transportation Association; Michael W. Wiemers D.O., CAPT (FS), USPHS, Chief of Operational and Clinical Medicine, U.S. Coast Guard Headquarters, Washington, D.C.; Eric A. Wildgrube, Senior Meteorologist, Northwest Airlines; and Dawn Warren Wright.

I also want to extend my gratitude to James Chambers, my editor, for his confidence and trust that I would actually see the light at the end of the tunnel.

Finally, my many thanks to Richard McDavid, my husband, for reading over my manuscript and helping me get to the end of another long tunnel.

HOW TO USE THIS BOOK

In *Career Opportunities in Aviation and the Aerospace Industry,* you will learn about 80 professions. You will learn about many types of pilot occupations as well as about various nonpilot jobs, including flight crew members, aircraft maintenance technicians, aviation safety inspectors, protective services personnel, managers, educators, engineers, and scientists. In addition, you will learn about a variety of career options that are available in a range of work settings, from airlines and airports to government agencies, the military, law enforcement, businesses, manufacturers, academic institutions, and publishing houses.

Career Opportunities in Aviation and the Aerospace Industry provides basic information about the different professions described in this book. You'll read about what the occupations are like and which job requirements are needed. You'll also get a general idea of the salaries, job markets, and advancement prospects for each occupation.

Sources of Information

The information presented in *Career Opportunities in Aviation and the Aerospace Industry* comes from a variety of sources—pilots, professionals in the different aviation fields, educators, professional societies, trade associations, government agencies, and so on. In addition, books and periodicals related to the different occupations were read along with materials created by professional associations, federal agencies, businesses, and other organizations. Job descriptions, work guidelines, and other work-related materials for the different occupations were also studied.

The World Wide Web was also a valuable source. A wide range of Web sites were visited to learn about each of the occupations that are described in this book. These Web sites include professional societies, trade associations, government agencies, academic institutions, airports, airlines, aerospace companies, aviation businesses, online periodicals, and so forth.

How This Book Is Organized

Career Opportunities in Aviation and the Aerospace Industry is designed to be easy to use and read. Altogether there are 80 profiles in 14 sections. A section may have as few as four profiles or as many as 11. The profiles are usually two or three pages long. The profiles all follow the same format so that you may read the job profiles or sections in whatever order you prefer.

Section one describes several pilot opportunities in both the private and public sectors. Sections two and three cover occupations found in flight operations and customer service, while section four discusses some careers in aviation maintenance. Sections five and six describe several opportunities found in aviation safety, aviation security, or aviation law.

Section seven discusses some careers in aviation management, and section eight goes over a few opportunities available in airport engineering, planning, and maintenance. In sections nine and 10, aviation opportunities in the fields of education, communications, and business are described. Section 11 covers some occupations in the sports and recreational segment of aviation, and section 12 discusses a few aviation opportunities in the military. The last two sections describe diverse opportunities in the aerospace manufacturing industry as well as in the area of space exploration.

The Job Profiles

The job profiles give you basic information about 80 career opportunities. Each profile starts with the *Career Profile,* a summary of a job's major duties, salary, job outlook, and opportunities for promotion. It also sums up general requirements and special skills needed for a job, as well as personality traits that successful professionals may share. The *Career Ladder* section is a visual presentation of a typical career path.

The rest of each occupational profile is divided into the following parts:

- The "Position Description" details major responsibilities and duties of an occupation. Some profiles discuss several options that are available within a profession.
- "Salaries" presents a general idea of the wages that professionals may earn.
- "Employment Prospects" provides a general idea of the job market for an occupation.
- "Advancement Prospects" discusses possible ways that individuals may advance in their careers.
- "Education and Training" describes the type of education and training that may be required to enter a profession.
- "Special Requirements" covers any professional license, certification, or registration that may be required for an occupation. (Note: Not all job profiles have this section.)
- "Experience, [Special] Skills, and Personality Traits" generally covers the job requirements needed for entry-level

positions. It also describes some basic employability skills that employers expect job candidates to have. In addition, this part describes some personality traits that successful professionals have in common.

- "Unions and Associations" provides the names of some professional associations and labor unions that professionals are eligible to join.
- "Tips for Entry" offers general advice for gaining work experience, improving employability, and finding jobs. It also provides suggestions for finding more information on the World Wide Web.

The Appendixes

At the end of the book are five appendixes that provide additional resources for the occupations described in *Career Opportunities in Aviation and the Aerospace Industry.* Appendix I presents the requirements for the various pilot certificates and ratings that are issued by the Federal Aviation Administration (FAA). Appendix II provides Web resources to learn about educational programs for some of the professions described in this book. Appendix III provides contact information about professional organizations, while Appendix IV lists some federal government agencies that are involved in aviation or space exploration. In Appendix V, you will find a listing of resources on the World Wide Web, which can help you learn more about the aviation and aerospace fields.

You will also find a glossary and a bibliography at the end of the book. The glossary defines some of the abbreviations and terms that are used in this book. The bibliography provides a listing of books, periodicals, and online sources for the various occupations in this book.

The World Wide Web

Throughout *Career Opportunities in Aviation and the Aerospace Industry,* Web site addresses for various resources, such as professional associations, are provided so that you can learn more on your own. All the Web sites were accessible as the book was being written. Please be aware that Web site owners may change Web site addresses, remove the Web pages to which you have been referred, or shut down their Web sites completely. Should you come across a URL that is unavailable, you may still be able to find the Web site by entering the Web site title in a search engine.

INTRODUCTION

Did you ever see an airplane fly overhead and wonder if you could make a living as a pilot? Have you ever walked through an airport and thought you might like to work there? Have you ever watched or read about the latest space discoveries and thought it would be fun to work at NASA?

In this book, you will learn about many career opportunities that are available in aviation and space exploration. You may be surprised by some of the options. In addition to the more common occupations—airline pilot, flight attendant, aircraft mechanic, air traffic controller, airport manager, aerospace engineer, and astronaut—you'll learn about professions that are not so familiar. Charter pilot, air tanker pilot, airspace system inspection pilot, hot-air balloon pilot, and test pilot are just a few of the many pilot occupations. Some nonflying jobs include maintenance controller, air cargo agent, avionics technician, aircraft dispatcher, aviation medical examiner, aviation lawyer, airport police officer, airport planner, aviation curator, aviation broker, NASA flight controller, aerospace machinist, quality specialist, technical communicator, aviation education specialist, research scientist, and computer engineer.

Aviation careers are found in many settings in both the public and private sector. In addition to working for airlines and the airports, pilots and others work for government agencies (such as NASA and the FAA), the military, educational institutions, research institutes, law enforcement agencies, medical facilities, insurance companies, manufacturing firms, corporate flight departments, and other organizations.

As you will find, the occupations in the field of aviation are extensive. In *Career Opportunities in Aviation and the Aerospace Industry,* you will learn about 80 occupations, one of which may be right for you.

The Aerospace Industry

The first successful human flight is attributed to Orville and Wilbur Wright, two brothers, who flew their homemade plane several hundred feet on December 17, 1903, in Kitty Hawk, North Carolina. Their amazing feat has led to a wide range of complex activities in aviation and the aerospace industry today, such as:

- daily worldwide air transportation for millions of passengers and multiple tons of cargo
- the use of aircraft in firefighting, medical transportation, search-and-rescue missions, war operations, and other applications
- the construction and deployment of satellites into orbit around the Earth for communication, navigation, scientific research, and other purposes
- human spaceflight orbit around the Earth, as well as to the moon and back
- exploration of the universe by unmanned space probes

The future of aviation and the aerospace industry will continue to offer many exciting and challenging discoveries, inventions, and technologies. Furthermore, a wide range of qualified pilots, engineers, scientists, technicians, machinists, managers, air traffic controllers, sales representatives, educators, and others will be continually needed to fill the jobs.

Job Outlook

The aerospace industry is one of the largest employers in the United States. In general, the job growth in the U.S. aerospace industry fluctuates with the health of the nation's economy. When the economy is in a downturn, many employers lay off workers and hire fewer employees. In recent years, thousands of jobs in the airlines and aerospace manufacturing firms have been lost because of a poor economy.

Unexpected events also both negatively and positively affect the job market in the aerospace industry. For example, after the terrorist attacks in the United States on September 11, 2001, the major airlines experienced a sudden decline in sales, which caused many of them to lay off employees and a few air carriers to file for bankruptcy. On the other hand, an increase in sales was experienced by regional airlines and a surge of growth was enjoyed by business aviation, the segment that serves corporate flight departments.

Additionally, the increasing competition from non-U.S. companies for the commercial aerospace market, coupled with the trend of outsourcing of jobs to other countries where labor is less expensive, can impact job opportunities.

However, even during the periods when the job outlook seems poor, opportunities will continue to be available in the aerospace industry. In fact, some occupations are expected to be in demand in the coming years because of the large number of workers soon reaching retirement age and because of the smaller number of students seeking entry into those occupations. Some of these professions include aviation maintenance technicians, scientists, engineers, aviation managers, and airline pilots.

Start Exploring Your Options

Career Opportunities in Aviation and the Aerospace Industry provides you with basic information about 80 professions in various fields. When you come across occupations that look intriguing, take the time to learn more about them. The references mentioned throughout the book and in the appendixes can help you further research aviation or aviation-related careers that interest you. In addition, here are a few other things you might do to explore a profession or field in more depth:

- Read books about the profession or field.
- Read professional and trade magazines, journals, newspapers, and other print and online periodicals.
- Visit Web sites for professional societies, trade associations, and other organizations related to your desired occupation.
- Talk with professionals—such as pilots, aircraft mechanics, or public relations specialists—who work in those jobs that interest you.
- Visit different workplaces, such as an airport, a flight service station, or an aerospace company.
- Enroll in courses related to the profession.
- Browse through career resources that are available at libraries and career centers.
- Obtain part-time, seasonal, volunteer, or internship positions at private companies or other organizations that interest you.

As you explore various occupations, you will discover the kind of careers you might like—and don't like. You will also be gaining valuable knowledge and experience. Furthermore, you will be building a network of contacts who may be able to help with your next steps—obtaining further education and training, as well as future jobs.

May you have the best of luck in the pursuit of your career goals and dreams!

COMMERCIAL AND PUBLIC SERVICE PILOTS

AIRLINE PILOT

CAREER PROFILE

Duties: Responsible for the safe operation of scheduled flights for commercial airlines; perform preflight, flight, and postflight duties; perform other duties as required

Alternate Title(s): Captain; Pilot-in-Command; First Officer; Flight Engineer; Second Officer

Salary Range: $41,000 to $147,000+

Employment Prospects: Good for pilots; poor for flight engineers

Advancement Prospects: Fair

Prerequisites:

Education or Training—High school diploma; college degree or training may be preferred; completion of airline training program

Experience—Meet an employer's minimum flight and work experience requirements

Special Skills and Personality Traits—Communication, critical thinking, interpersonal, and teamwork skills; calm, patient, positive, enthusiastic, persistent, goal-oriented, self-motivated

Special Requirements—Commercial pilot or airline transport pilot (ATP) certificate with appropriate ratings; FAA medical certificate

CAREER LADDER

Captain

First Officer

Second Officer

Position Description

Airline Pilots are responsible for the safe and economical operation of huge, expensive aircraft from takeoffs to landings and while they cruise at high speeds through the sky at such altitudes as 30,000 to 45,000 feet. Each year, these highly experienced pilots transport millions of passengers and tons of mail and cargo on scheduled flights throughout the world for various commercial airlines.

The airline industry includes small and large commercial airlines that offer scheduled flights over fixed routes to specific locations around the world. Airline Pilots are responsible for keeping these flights on schedule. Most airlines transport both passengers and cargo, but a few air carriers specialize in transporting cargo. Commercial airlines operate under Part 121 of the federal aviation regulations. Airline Pilots are responsible for ensuring that their flights are in compliance with these federal regulations as well as with company policies and protocols.

A Part 121 air carrier is generally categorized as a major, national, regional, independent, or international airline, depending on such factors as their volume of annual sales, the types of aircraft flown, and the markets they serve. For example:

- Major airlines generate more than a billion dollars in sales each year; their Pilots operate jet aircraft on scheduled flights to large cities throughout the world.
- National airlines earn less than a billion dollars annually and offer scheduled flights for just domestic routes; their pilots operate jet or nonjet aircraft.
- Regional airlines are small air carriers, which offer scheduled flights that connect smaller cities to the large cities

out of which major airlines fly; their pilots usually operate aircraft that carry between 19 and 70 passengers.

Most airline flight crews are composed of two pilots—a captain (or pilot-in-command) and a copilot. The captain is responsible for making all final decisions that affect the overall safety and success of a flight. In addition, the captain is in charge of supervising and instructing the flight crew, including all flight attendants.

The copilot is known as the first officer. He or she assists the captain with all preflight, flight, and postflight duties. For example, the copilot helps the captain perform preflight checks, monitor flight instruments, handle radio communications, and fly the aircraft during the flight phase.

Some aircraft require a third crew member known as the flight engineer, or second officer. The flight engineer is also a pilot but does not do any flying. This crew member assists with flight operations and performs such duties as conducting preflight and postflight checks, computing aircraft load weights and fuel distribution, monitoring aircraft systems in flight, and troubleshooting equipment problems.

Airline Pilots generally follow the same procedures with each flight. Pilots report to duty at least one hour before a flight is scheduled to depart. They review weather reports, weather forecasts, advisories, notices, navigational charts, and other essential flight information. They also conduct thorough preflight checks on their aircraft: They inspect the outside of the aircraft as well as check all equipment and instruments in the cockpit to ensure that the aircraft is safe to operate.

The captain of each flight reviews the flight plan that a dispatcher has prepared. The flight plan outlines the departure and destination airports, the alternative airports that would be used in case of an emergency, the flight route, the altitude and speed at which an aircraft would be flown, and so on. For commercial air carriers, both the flight captain and dispatcher are responsible for the flight operations; thus, they must jointly agree on a flight plan before an aircraft can depart.

The captain is also responsible for briefing flight attendants about the flight plan, flight conditions, and other important matters.

A flight is divided into three phases: takeoff, cruise, and landing. The Pilots are in constant communication with each other, especially during the takeoff and landing phases. Throughout their flight, pilots are constantly alert for obstacles and other aircraft. They monitor warning devices and instrument panels for the condition of their engines, aviation systems, and fuel supply. They also check weather conditions on a regular basis, particularly any forecasts of bad or severe weather. In addition, they maintain communication with air traffic controllers and aircraft dispatchers from the beginning to the end of their flights.

All Airline Pilots are responsible for the overall safety of their passengers, crew, and cargo. As emergency situations occur, pilots must make critical decisions quickly and in a calm and professional manner. For example, Airline Pilots might have to handle such urgent problems as severe storms, violent acts of passengers, and mechanical malfunctions.

Some Airline Pilots—on passenger and cargo air carriers—are volunteer Federal Flight Deck Officers (FFDOs). They have been deputized as federal law enforcement officers to defend aircraft against acts of criminal violence or air piracy. They may carry and use firearms, but only within the jurisdiction of the cockpit, or flight deck, of their aircraft. To become an FFDO, Airline Pilots must pass a psychological exam and successfully complete a training program, which includes firearms instruction. (The FFDO program is run by the Transportation Security Administration, an agency in the U.S, Department of Homeland Security.)

When flights are completed, Airline Pilots are responsible for completing flight reports, pilot logbooks, and other required paperwork.

Most Airline Pilots average about 75 to 80 flight hours a month. They are limited by law to a maximum number of flight hours each month and in a year. (In 2003, federal aviation regulations stated that Airline Pilots could not fly more than 100 hours a month or more than 1,000 hours a year.) Airline Pilots are also required by law to have a minimum number of hours of rest between consecutive flight duties.

Many Airline Pilots average about 15 to 20 duty days a month. Their schedules vary, which may include working nights, weekends, or holidays. They may be scheduled to take every few days off or a whole week off at a time. Their flight assignments also vary; for example, an Airline Pilot might be assigned to fly the same scheduled flights to certain cities, while another pilot might be assigned to fly different flights to different regions of the United States. Some flights require a layover of one or more nights. Airlines usually provide their flight crews with hotel accommodations and ground transportation between the airport and lodgings as well as an allowance for meals and expenses.

Each month, Airline Pilots receive new work schedules, which are based on such factors as their bids (or choices) for flights, and their seniority. As Airline Pilots gain seniority, they are more likely to be assigned their first choices.

New Airline Pilots usually start as reserve pilots, regardless of how much flight experience they have. They substitute for pilots who are on vacation or on leave, ill, or reassigned to other flights. Reserve pilots must be ready to fly any assignment at a moment's notice.

Airline Pilots are required to wear uniforms while on duty. They are assigned to a home base (also known as a domicile), where they usually begin and end their flight duty. Some Airline Pilots live in another city and commute by air to their home base several times a month. Depending on their flight schedules, Pilots may be away from their homes for several days or weeks at a time.

Salaries

Annual salaries for Airline Pilots vary, depending on various factors such as a pilot's position and seniority, the size and type of aircraft flown, and the type of airline. Major airlines pay the highest salaries. Some senior airline captains at major airlines earn salaries of $250,000 or more. According to the May 2003 *Occupational Employment Statistics* survey by the U.S. Bureau of Labor Statistics, the estimated annual salary for most Airline Pilots and flight engineers ranged from $40,530 to $145,600.

Employment Prospects

The competition for pilot jobs is fierce, especially with the major airlines. Job openings are expected to increase within the next few years due to the large number of pilots who will be reaching retirement age. Some industry experts predict growth in the regional airlines to increase faster than other segments in the airline industry, which may create additional openings for pilots.

Opportunities for flight engineer positions are expected to decrease through the years. This position may be eventually eliminated due to the installation of computerized flight management systems on new aircraft.

Keep in mind that job prospects in the airline industry generally fluctuate with the health of the economy. For example, when the economy is experiencing a downturn, the demand for air transportation typically falls; therefore, fewer Airline Pilots are hired, and airlines may lay off some of their pilots.

Advancement Prospects

Airlines use a seniority system. Pilots move up on the seniority list as new Airline Pilots are hired and senior pilots retire or resign. All pilots, regardless of position or experience when hired, begin at the bottom of the seniority list. With time, they build up their seniority, which results in being promoted to a higher position, earning higher pay, receiving route assignments of their choice, being assigned to flying new aircraft, and other privileges.

Airline Pilots are required by federal law to retire by the age of 60. Flight engineers may retire at age 65.

Education and Training

Airline Pilots must possess a high school diploma or high school equivalency diploma. Some airlines also require that Airline Pilots have at least two years of college training, with courses in advanced math, English, science, aeronautical engineering, and other aviation subjects. Some airlines prefer to hire candidates with a bachelor's degree in aeronautics, aviation, or any other field.

Airlines provide all new hires with a formal training program that covers a curriculum approved by the Federal Aviation Administration (FAA). Trainees study such topics as federal aviation regulations, company policies, airline operations, the type of aircraft they would be flying, and aircraft systems. Trainees also receive simulator training and practical instruction. Upon completion of their flight training, they must pass an FAA knowledge and practical examination. Pilots complete the same training procedures for every new aircraft they are assigned to fly.

Airline Pilots receive recurrent training on a regular basis to maintain their piloting skills.

Special Requirements

Minimally, Airline Pilots must hold a commercial pilot certificate with an instrument rating, which is granted by the FAA. An airline transport pilot (ATP) certificate is required for captain (or pilot-in-command) positions, but many airlines also prefer to hire first officers with ATP certificates.

In addition, Airline Pilots must hold appropriate ratings for each type of aircraft they operate. They must also possess a first-class FAA medical certificate.

Airlines require that applicants be U.S. citizens or have the necessary documents for working in the United States.

Experience, Special Skills, and Personality Traits

All airlines set their own requirements for flight experience and work experience for the captain, first officer, and flight engineer positions. Typically, Airline Pilots must have completed the minimum number of flight hours required by an airline before they are eligible to apply. Regional airlines usually require fewer hours of flight time than the major airlines. For example, a regional airline may require that applicants have completed 1,000 hours of flight time while a major airline may require 5,000 hours.

Many Airline Pilots have built up their flight hours through a succession of pilot jobs that may have included flying for air charter companies, air-taxi services, freight companies, corporate flight departments, and the military. Many Airline Pilots also gained experience performing various flight jobs in general aviation, such as crop dusting, reseeding forests, towing banners, carrying skydivers, transporting patients, aerial firefighting, and teaching others to fly. It generally takes most pilots five to six years to build sufficient flight time to be eligible for airline positions.

Airline Pilots must have strong communication skills, as they must be able to communicate clear, accurate, and succinct instructions to crew members. It is also essential that they have excellent critical thinking, interpersonal, and teamwork skills.

Being calm, patient, positive, enthusiastic, persistent, goal-oriented, and self-motivated are some personality traits that successful Airline Pilots have in common.

Unions and Associations

Most Airline Pilots belong to a union, such as the Air Line Pilots Association International or the Allied Pilots Association, which represents them in contract negotiations with their employers. The union seeks to get the best contract terms in regards to pay, benefits, and working conditions. It also handles any grievance that Airline Pilots have against their employers.

Many Airline Pilots belong to professional associations that offer professional services and resources such as networking opportunities, education programs, professional publications, and job listings. The Aircraft Owners and Pilots Association, the International Society of Women Airline Pilots, and the Organization of Black Airline Pilots are a few professional associations that serve the interests of various Airline Pilots.

Tips for Entry

1. Increasingly, airlines are requiring that candidates have bachelor's degrees. Some colleges offer degree programs in aviation that include flight training.
2. Do research on the airlines where you would like to work. In addition to finding out about pilot requirements and the job selection process at a company, learn about the company's history and its financial status. Ask a librarian for help with finding reference materials on the library's shelves as well as on the Internet. Also talk with Airline Pilots to get an idea of what it is like to work for the company.
3. Develop a network of contacts in the aviation industry that you can use to help you during your job searches.
4. Prospective employers will review your pilot logbooks when considering you for a position, so take the time to keep neat, orderly, and accurate records.
5. Learn more about Airline Pilots on the Internet. One Web site you might visit is for the Air Line Pilots Association, International, http://www.alpa.org. To find other Web sites, enter the keywords *airline pilots* into a search engine.

COMMERCIAL PILOT (GENERAL AVIATION)

CAREER PROFILE

Duties: Responsible for safe and efficient flight operations for aviation firms, public service agencies, or private companies that own aircraft for business purposes; perform preflight, flight, and postflight duties; perform other duties as required

Alternate Title(s): First Officer; Captain; Pilot-in-Command; a title that reflects a particular occupation, such as EMS Pilot, Agricultural Pilot, or Corporate Pilot

Salary Range: $26,000 to $102,000

Employment Prospects: Fair

Advancement Prospects: Fair

Prerequisites:

Education or Training—High school diploma; completion of employer's training programs

Experience—Meet an employer's requirements for flight experience and work experience; be knowledgeable about geography, public safety, and aviation security

Special Skills and Personality Traits—Math, writing, computer, communication, interpersonal, critical-thinking, and self-management skills; cooperative; calm; level-headed, flexible, focused, precise, self-reliant

Special Requirements—Commercial pilot or ATP certificate with appropriate ratings; FAA medical certificate; flight instructor certificate, if teaching

CAREER LADDER

Pilot-in-Command or Captain

Commercial Pilot

Private Pilot

Position Description

Pilots who provide flight services in general aviation as employees or independent contractors are generally known as Commercial Pilots. (General aviation includes all areas of flight operations except for military aviation and commercial airlines.) Many Commercial Pilots are involved in transporting passengers, mail, and cargo. Some are hired to perform specific tasks with their aircraft, such as dusting crops, towing banners, giving sightseeing tours, putting heavy equipment on top of buildings, monitoring freeway traffic, or putting out fires. Depending on their jobs, they might fly helicopters, single-engine planes, multiengine planes, turboprop planes, or jet planes.

Commercial Pilots work for a wide range of employers in different industries. Some of them work directly for government agencies or private companies. Others work for aviation services that offer one or more types of flight services, such as air-charter services, sightseeing tours, crop dusting, and flight lessons. The following are just a few of the different types of pilot positions that are available:

- Agricultural pilots apply fertilizer or pesticides to farmlands, or sow seeds in fields and forests.
- Air-taxi pilots provide on-demand flight services to customers; they fly to any location and whenever customers wish to travel or to have cargo delivered.
- Charter pilots fly both on-demand and scheduled flights for air charter companies.
- Ferry pilots fly new aircraft from manufacturing plants to customers' home airports or to aviation dealers' showrooms.
- Corporate pilots operate aircraft that private companies own and use for business transportation. They fly execu-

tives, managers, staff, and customers between company facilities, as well as to other locations for meetings, conferences, and other business purposes.

- Cargo pilots work for freight companies. They haul items such as mail, bank checks, perishable food items, photographic film, packages, and other freight that need to reach a certain location by a specific time.
- Tour, or sightseeing, pilots fly tourists on scenic rides over wildernesses or scenic attractions.
- Patrol pilots usually work for oil pipeline or utility companies. They fly along pipelines and power lines to check for signs of vandalism, damage, or other conditions that may require repair.
- Electronic News Gathering (ENG) pilots fly reporters to scenes to gather news for radio and TV stations. They operate helicopters equipped with cameras and broadcast equipment that can provide live transmissions to radio or TV stations.
- Photogrammetry pilots are aerial photographers who take photographs of the Earth's surface for mapping and other photogrammetric purposes.

Commercial Pilots are also flight instructors, providing ground and flight instruction to students who are seeking recreational, private, commercial, or air transport pilot (ATP) certificates from the Federal Aviation Administration (FAA). Flight instructors may be independent contractors or work for flight schools.

Some Commercial Pilots are involved in public service, working for local, state, and federal agencies. For example, they may be involved in firefighting, law enforcement, providing air transportation of rescue victims, conducting search-and-rescue missions, or performing aerial research.

Many Commercial Pilots perform a variety of flying jobs, as employees or independent contractors. For example, a Commercial Pilot might be an aerial firefighter during the fire season, and be an air-taxi pilot and flight instructor during the rest of the year.

Commercial Pilots, regardless of their jobs, are responsible for safe and efficient flight operations. Flight crews are usually composed of either two pilots or solo pilots. The pilot in command of a flight is called the captain. He or she is responsible for making all final decisions regarding the flight. The captain also provides supervision and guidance to any and all flight crew members.

Commercial Pilots perform various preflight, flight, and postflight duties. Some of their tasks include:

- planning flight plans, which outline their routes, departure and destination airports, and estimated times of departure and arrival
- filing flight plans with air traffic controllers
- gathering and analyzing weather forecasts for routes and areas where they plan to fly; also monitoring weather conditions during their flights
- calculating the amount of fuel needed for completing flights
- performing preflight and postflight checks to ensure that the aircraft and all its systems are in proper working order
- obtaining clearance and instructions from air traffic controllers for takeoffs and landings
- monitoring instruments, aircraft systems, and fuel during flights
- completing flight reports, pilot logbooks, and other required paperwork
- complying with all federal aviation regulations as well as their company's policies and protocols

Commercial Pilots also perform various nonflight duties, which vary with the different positions. For example, charter and corporate pilots might load and unload baggage, clean the interior of their aircraft, stock the aircraft with refreshments, and greet passengers.

Sometimes pilots are assigned to flights that require a layover of one or more nights. For example, a corporate pilot might be assigned to fly company salespeople to a weekend retreat in another state, and be required to stay there until they are ready to fly back.

Some Commercial Pilots own their businesses, which require following the appropriate federal aviation regulations that govern their operations. They are also responsible for a variety of business tasks, such as keeping records, paying bills and taxes, ordering supplies, generating new business, and supervising and training staff. In addition, they continually assess their business sales figures and customers' needs to determine what services and products they should add or remove from their operations.

Commercial Pilots work part time or full time. Their jobs may require them to work nights, weekends, or holidays. Some Commercial Pilots are on call 24 hours a day.

Salaries

Salaries vary, depending on such factors as position, experience, employer, and geographical location. According to the May 2003 *Occupational Employment Statistics* survey (by the U.S. Bureau of Labor Statistics), the estimated annual salary for most Commercial Pilots ranged between $26,470 and $101,890.

Employment Prospects

Airplane and helicopter pilots are employed in all 50 states by individuals, companies, nonprofitable organizations, government agencies, and so on. Typically, job openings occur when pilots retire, transfer to other positions, or leave the workforce. Many pilots use their jobs in general aviation to build up flight time for airline positions; thus, opportunities with an employer become available from time to time. Employers also create additional positions to meet their growing needs.

The aviation industry is strongly affected by the health of the economy. When the economy is on a downturn, fewer pilot jobs are available.

Advancement Prospects

At most companies, Commercial Pilots can advance through the ranks as copilots, pilots-in-command (or captains), assistant chief pilots, and chief pilots. Those with entrepreneurial ambitions may seek to become independent contractors or business owners who offer aviation services.

For many Commercial Pilots, the ultimate goal is a job with the major airlines. They work at their jobs to build up enough flight time to qualify for positions with major airlines. Many pilots start their journey as certified flight instructors. After gaining 1,000 or more flight hours, they seek positions with charter companies, freight companies, or corporate flight departments. After building sufficient flight time, many pilots apply for positions with regional airlines. Pilots are usually qualified for positions with major airlines after having 18 to 24 months of flight experience as a pilot-in-command. Altogether, it takes about five to six years to build up sufficient flight time to become eligible to apply for pilot positions with major airlines.

Education and Training

Minimally, professional pilots must possess a high school diploma or a general equivalency diploma. Depending on the employer, applicants may be required to have some college training. Some employers prefer to hire candidates with an associate's or bachelor's degree in aeronautics or another field.

Employers generally provide new hires with training that covers such topics as federal aviation regulations, company policies, and job procedures. They also provide ground and flight instruction on the type of aircraft the pilots would be operating.

Training for the commercial pilot certificate includes several weeks of ground school and simulator training, as well as many hours of practical lessons in the air. Pilots can obtain training for their commercial pilot certificate from FAA-certified flight schools or FAA-certified flight instructors. Qualifying pilot training is also available through the military.

Special Requirements

Commercial Pilots must possess either the commercial pilot certificate or the airline transport pilot (ATP) certificate, granted by the FAA. Additionally they must have an instrument rating as well as appropriate ratings for the category (airplane or helicopter), class (single-engine or multi-engine), and type (make and model) of aircraft that they operate for their jobs. They must also hold either a first-class or second-class FAA medical certificate.

Individuals who plan to teach flying lessons must obtain an FAA flight instructor certificate.

Experience, Special Skills, and Personality Traits

Job qualifications vary for the various occupations as well with the different employers. Typically, employers look for candidates who have experience operating the type of aircraft they would be flying and have completed a minimum number of flight hours to qualify for a position. For example, an air charter company might require that applicants have flown a total of 1,200 hours, which includes at least 50 hours flying multiengine aircraft.

Commercial Pilots are knowledgeable about geography, public safety, and aviation security. They should have good math, writing, and computer skills, as well as effective communication and interpersonal skills. In addition, they need strong critical thinking and self-management skills, such as being able to work independently, handle stressful situations, organize and prioritize tasks, and follow directions.

Being cooperative, calm, level-headed, flexible, focused, precise, and self-reliant are some personality traits that successful Commercial Pilots share.

Unions and Associations

Various professional organizations serve the interests of different Commercial Pilots. By joining local, state, or national associations, pilots can take advantage of networking opportunities, education programs, professional publications, and other professional services and resources. Some national associations that serve the general interests of Commercial Pilots are the Aircraft Owners and Pilots Association; the Professional Helicopter Pilots Association; Women in Aviation, International; and Black Pilots of America.

The National Agricultural Aviation Association, the National Association of Flight Instructors, the National EMS Pilots Association, and the Airborne Law Enforcement Association are a few professional societies that serve the particular interests of Commercial Pilots.

Tips for Entry

1. As a high school student, join a youth aviation program, such as the Civil Air Patrol cadet program, that may be available in your community.
2. Many organizations offer scholarships to young people who are interested in a career in aviation. If you are a high school student, talk to your guidance counselor for help finding information. If you are a college student, seek help at your college career center. You might also obtain scholarship information from professional associations; for example, The Ninety-Nines Inc., an international organization of women pilots, has a listing for scholarships on its Web site (http://www.ninety-nines.org/aemsf.html).
3. Talk with various professional pilots to learn about the different flight jobs that are available in general aviation.
4. To build up flight time for your commercial pilot certificate, you might volunteer your services to a community organization that conducts search-and-rescue

operations or a humanitarian flight organization that provides air transportation to people who need non-critical medical treatment at other hospitals.

5. Use the Internet to learn more about becoming a Commercial Pilot. Some Web sites you might visit are: The Student Pilot Network, http://www.studentpilot.net; General Aviation: Serving All Americans, http://www.gaservingamerica.org; and The 99s Pilot Careers Resource http://www.ninety-nines.org/careers/index.html.

CORPORATE PILOT

CAREER PROFILE

Duties: Responsible for the safe operation of business aircraft flown for business purposes; perform flight and nonflight duties; perform other duties as required

Alternate Title(s): Business Pilot; Executive Pilot

Salary Range: $25,000 to $120,000+

Employment Prospects: Good

Advancement Prospects: Fair

Prerequisites:

Education or Training—College degree or some college training; completion of employer's training programs

Experience—Meet an employer's minimum flight and work experience requirements

Special Skills and Personality Traits—Interpersonal, communication, customer service, and teamwork skills; cooperative, patient, confident, decisive, flexible

Special Requirements—Commercial pilot or air transport pilot (ATP) certificate with appropriate ratings; FAA medical certificate

CAREER LADDER

Chief Pilot

Captain, or Pilot-in-Command

Copilot

Position Description

Corporate Pilots are responsible for the safety of flight operations in business aviation, which is a segment of general aviation. It is composed of self-employed people, small companies, and large corporations that own and use aircraft solely for business transportation. All corporate flight operations are governed under Part 91 of the federal aviation regulations.

Corporate Pilots are employees of a business or company. They fly business aircraft for a variety of purposes, including:

- flying executives, managers, and staff members to business meetings and conferences at different company facilities, customer sites, or other locations
- transporting mail, packages, supplies, equipment, and other freight to different company facilities or other locations
- carrying customers, press, or other interest groups to company facilities for tours or product demonstrations
- performing an act of charity for their employer, such as transporting patients for medical treatments to a hospital in another city or state

Corporate Pilots generally provide on-demand flight services. They fly whenever their employers need passengers, mail, or cargo transported to a specific location. They fly to nearby communities as well as to locations in other regions, states, or countries. Some Corporate Pilots fly company shuttles between facilities on a regular schedule.

Corporate Pilots may be assigned to fly airplanes, seaplanes, helicopters, or jets. They usually transport 30 or fewer passengers. Business aircraft are often equipped with telephones, computers, facsimile machines, and other office equipment, as passengers often conduct business meetings, make sales presentations, or perform other tasks.

Every flight has a captain, or pilot-in-command, who makes all flight decisions and is in charge of the flight crew, including flight attendants. (Typically, larger companies operate aircraft that are flown by a two-person flight crew.) The captain is also responsible for the planning and safe operations of the flight. Furthermore, the captain has the final authority in determining whether a flight should be delayed or canceled because of bad flying conditions.

Corporate Pilots are responsible for various preflight, flight, and postflight duties. Their tasks vary, depending on such factors as their position (captain or copilot) and the size of the flight department. The following are some tasks that Corporate Pilots might perform:

- prepare flight plans, which involves gathering and analyzing weather forecasts along flight routes as well as at the departure and destination airports
- file flight plans with air traffic controllers
- perform preflight and postflight inspections of the aircraft and its systems to make sure everything is working properly
- obtain current updates of weather conditions and forecasts
- maintain contact with air traffic controllers during takeoffs and landings and throughout the flight
- provide passengers with safety instructions, such as using safety belts, emergency procedures, and nonsmoking rules
- complete flight reports, pilot logbooks, and other required paperwork

Corporate Pilots also perform various nonflight duties. For example, they might load and unload baggage and cargo; arrange for inflight meals; and coordinate ground transportation for passengers at their destinations. Some Corporate Pilots are responsible for getting an aircraft ready for flight. They might perform such tasks as cleaning the interior; filling the aircraft with fuel; deicing the aircraft; and stocking the aircraft with snacks, current magazines, and other supplies for the passengers.

On occasion, flights require a layover of one or more days. During layovers, pilots often have time to spend on their own. Their lodging, meals, and ground transportation are usually paid by their employers.

Corporate Pilots have a varied work schedule, which generally changes every day. Many are on-call 24 hours a day. Those who fly shuttles usually have a regular work schedule.

Salaries

Salaries vary for Corporate Pilots, and depend on such factors as their experience, their employer, the type of aircraft flown, their position, and geographical location. Annual salaries for Corporate Pilots generally range between $25,000 to $75,000, according to the Student Pilot Network (http://www.studentpilot.net).

Highly experienced pilots with large corporations can expect to earn an annual salary of $120,000 or more.

Employment Prospects

Corporate Pilots are hired by small businesses, start-up companies, and established corporations in such industries as banking, insurance, real estate, retail trade, utilities, communications, technology, transportation, mining, and construction. Additionally, pilots interested in working in business aviation can find employment with air charter companies that offer services to businesses and companies. Another source of employment includes aviation firms that offer and manage fractional ownership programs, in which companies hold part ownership in an aircraft. Some Corporate Pilots work as independent contractors.

Opportunities for Corporate Pilots have been steadily growing since the early 1990s and are expected to continue growing as more companies realize the economic benefits of owning business aircraft. In recent years, fractional ownership programs have experienced substantial growth.

Advancement Prospects

Corporate Pilots pursue advancement according to their interests and ambitions. The top goal for some Corporate Pilots is to become corporate captains, independent contractors, or consultants in business aviation. Pilots with managerial ambitions seek to become chief pilots or aviation managers of corporate flight departments. Some pilots pursue management positions in other departments within their companies.

Education and Training

Some employers require or prefer to hire pilots with a college degree or with two or more years of college training. Pilots may have a college background in aeronautics or any other field.

Employers provide new pilots with training programs that cover federal aviation regulations, company policies, and flight instruction. In addition, Corporate Pilots are expected to undergo recurrent training to maintain and refine their skills.

Special Requirements

Minimally, Corporate Pilots hold a valid commercial pilot's certificate with instrument and mullet-engine ratings. Some companies require that pilots have an air transport pilot (ATP) certificate. Corporate Pilots also hold ratings in the category, class, and type of aircraft they operate. In addition, Corporate Pilots are required to hold a first-class or second-class FAA medical certificate.

Experience, Special Skills, and Personality Traits

To qualify for a corporate captain or first officer position, candidates must have completed a minimum number of total flight hours, which varies from employer to employer. For example, different employers may require that candidates for captain positions have between at least 1,500 to 3,000 total flight hours. Many employers also look for candidates who have experience working as part of a two-person flight crew. In addition, employers seek candidates who demonstrate the ability to fit into a corporate culture.

Corporate Pilots typically gained their flight experience through a combination of previous jobs such as flight instructors, commercial pilots, or airline pilots.

Corporate Pilots must have strong interpersonal, communication, and customer service skills, as they must be able to handle executives, business professionals, and customers.

They also need excellent teamwork skills. Being cooperative, patient, confident, decisive, and flexible are some personality traits that successful Corporate Pilots share.

Unions and Associations

Many Corporate Pilots join professional associations to take advantage of networking opportunities, career services, publications, and other professional services and resources. The Aircraft Owners and Pilots Association and the Women in Aviation, International are two national organizations that serve the interests of Corporate Pilots.

Tips for Entry

1. The National Business Aviation Association offers scholarships to college students who are interested in pursuing corporate pilot careers. For more information, visit its Web site at http://www.nbaa.org.
2. Network with Corporate Pilots to learn about job openings in their companies. Also check out classified ads in trade and professional publications.
3. Contact flight departments or human resources departments at companies where you would like to work.
4. Use the Internet to learn more about Corporate Pilots and business aviation. To get a list of relevant Web sites, enter the keywords *corporate pilots, business aviation,* or *corporate flight department* into a search engine.

CHARTER PILOT

CAREER PROFILE

Duties: Responsible for the safe operation of private flights chartered by individuals, businesses, and others; perform preflight, flight, and postflight duties; perform other duties as required

Alternate Title(s): Air-Taxi Pilot

Salary Range: $15,000 to $72,000

Employment Prospects: Good

Advancement Prospects: Good

Prerequisites:

Education or Training—High school diploma; completion of employer's training programs

Experience—Meet an employer's minimum flight and work experience requirements

Special Skills and Personality Traits—Communication, interpersonal, and self-management skills; self-motivated, friendly, cooperative, flexible

Special Requirements—Commercial pilot or air transport pilot (ATP) certificate with appropriate ratings; FAA medical certificate

CAREER LADDER

Chief Pilot or Charter Company Owner

Pilot-in-Command

Copilot or Pilot-in-Command

Position Description

Charter Pilots are responsible for the safety of private flights that customers hire from air-taxi operators. These pilots fly airplanes and helicopters that carry 30 or fewer passengers and have a payload capacity of 7,500 pounds or less. They make short trips to nearby communities as well as overnight trips to locations across a state or in other states or countries.

Air-taxi operators are more commonly known as air-taxi or air charter companies, and are usually based at general aviation airports. They are also known as Part 135 operators, as they are governed under Part 135 of the federal aviation regulations.

Most air-taxi operators have no defined flight routes or schedules. They offer unscheduled and on-demand flight services to customers who wish to hire aircraft for transporting passengers or cargo. The customers determine the locations and times for departure and arrival. Charter Pilots often fly to cities and towns that the scheduled airlines do not service.

Individuals, companies, and others charter private flights for personal and business purposes. Charter Pilots, for example, have flown private flights for individuals, families, student groups, church groups, athletic teams, professional musicians, movie studios, resort casinos, nonprofit organizations, government officials, political candidates, hospital patients, wildland firefighters, and airline mechanics. Charter Pilots have also flown chartered flights to deliver packages, freight, heavy equipment, high-tech equipment, medicines, human organs, and so on.

Some air-taxi operators offer scheduled flights to communities that are not serviced by scheduled airlines. Some operators also provide scheduled service between communities and cities where travelers need to make connecting flights with an airline.

Depending on the aircraft, flight crews may be composed of one or two pilots. On long-distance flights, such as international flights, there may be three or four pilots onboard to relieve each other. The captain is responsible for making all decisions in addition to being in charge of the flight crew, including flight attendants.

Charter Pilots are responsible for planning their flights. They begin by gathering and analyzing weather reports and forecasts for weather conditions along possible routes as well as at the departure and destination airports. They also consult various charts to plan the safest flight routes.

Charter Pilots are responsible for filing their flight plans with air traffic controllers. Flight plans include information about the aircraft, the number of passengers and crew members on board, the departure and destination airports, flight route, and the estimated time of departure and arrival.

Before departure, Charter Pilots perform a preflight check on their aircraft. They make sure that all aviation systems are operating properly. They also contact air traffic control to "open" their flight plans. In other words, the pilots will be flying according to flight plans they had filed earlier with air traffic control.

Throughout their flights, pilots monitor their progress and make sure they are following federal aviation regulations as well as company policies and protocols. Pilots maintain a safe distance away from other aircraft as well as from any obstructions such as tall buildings. Pilots are also alert for sudden changes in weather and report any weather hazards to air traffic controllers.

Charter Pilots maintain communications with air traffic controllers throughout their flights. Air traffic controllers guide pilots during takeoffs and landings. They also provide pilots with updated reports on weather and other pertinent flight information.

After their flights, Charter Pilots complete flight reports, pilot logbooks, and other required paperwork. They must also contact air traffic control to close their flight plans within 30 minutes of landing. Otherwise, air traffic control must assume the pilots are lost and begin search-and-rescue procedures for the aircraft.

On occasion, Charter Pilots fly charters that involve a layover of one or more nights. They usually receive free lodging and ground transportation during the layovers.

Many Charter Pilots have nonflying duties that may include stocking aircraft with refreshments, loading and unloading baggage and cargo, cleaning the interior of the aircraft, providing aircraft maintenance, and booking charters.

Some Charter Pilots work for companies such as FBOs (flight base operators) that offer various aviation services. At these companies, Charter Pilots may perform other types of flying jobs. For example, they might also teach flying lessons, dust crops, haul skydivers, tow banners, conduct search-and-rescue missions, or fly firefighting missions.

Some Charter Pilots are independent contractors. Other Charter Pilots are owners of air-taxi or charter operations. Still other pilots have the proper certification to operate aircraft repair stations. As independent contractors or business owners, they are responsible for various business duties, such as keeping records, paying bills and taxes, generating new business, and maintaining facilities. Business owners are also responsible for hiring, supervising, and training staff.

Charter Pilots work irregular hours and may be scheduled to work on weekends and holidays. Many of them are on call 24 hours a day. They may be required to be available within 20 to 60 minutes after being called.

The Federal Aviation Administration (FAA) limits the number of duty and flight hours that Charter Pilots can complete. (Duty hours refers to the time they begin their work assignment on the ground to the time they end their day's assignment.) As of 2003, they may only work 14 duty hours and fly a maximum of 10 flight hours per day. They are required to have 10 hours of rest in a 24-hour period. The FAA also mandates that Charter Pilots cannot exceed a total of 500 flight hours in a calendar quarter (3 months), or 800 hours in two consecutive quarters, or 1,400 flight hours in a year.

Salaries

Charter Pilots may earn a salary or be paid by the hour, per day, or by the trip. Wages vary for Charter Pilots, depending on such factors as their experience, the type of aircraft being flown, their employer, and their geographical location.

The Student Pilot Network (http://www.studentpilot.net) reports that the starting salaries at charter companies range between $15,000 to $20,000; salaries for captains or chief pilots generally range between $30,000 and $50,000. According to the 2002 salary survey of helicopter pilots by *Rotor & Wing,* the average salary for respondents who worked as Charter Pilots ranged from $24,333.33 to $71,500.00.

Employment Prospects

In general, opportunities for Charter Pilots are good due to the turnover of pilots who seek airline pilot positions upon reaching the minimum number of flight hours required by airlines. Since the terrorist attacks in the United States on September 11, 2001, the demand for air-taxi and charter services has been steadily increasing, as more travelers and businesses are learning that tailor-made flights offer greater security, as well as flexibility and control in their travel arrangements.

Advancement Prospects

Charter Pilots can advance through the ranks as second-in-command, pilot-in-command, assistant chief pilot, and chief pilot. Those with entrepreneurial ambitions may seek to be air-taxi or charter company owners.

Many Charter Pilots stay in the business long enough to build up sufficient flight time to qualify for pilot positions with commercial scheduled airlines.

Education and Training

Minimally, Charter Pilots must possess a high school diploma or general equivalency diploma. Many of them also hold either an associate's or bachelor's degree.

Newly hired pilots complete a training program that generally covers such topics as company policies, federal aviation regulations, and flight procedures. They also receive instruction in the type of aircraft they would be operating. Whenever pilots are assigned to fly a new type of aircraft, they must receive the appropriate training. Employers are required to provide their pilots with recurrent training each year.

Special Requirements

To hold the pilot-in-command position, Charter Pilots must possess the air transportation pilot (ATP) certificate, granted by the FAA. Those pilots in the copilot position must hold the commercial pilot certificate with an instrument rating. Additionally, Charter Pilots must hold the appropriate ratings for all aircraft that they operate. Pilots are also required to hold either the first class or second class FAA medical certificate.

Charter Pilots who own air-taxi operations must also obtain the proper FAA certifications.

Experience, Special Skills, and Personality Traits

Work experience requirements vary from employer to employer. Employers generally consider applicants who have met their minimum flight requirements. For example, one employer might require that candidates have at least 1,500 flight hours with 500 hours flying turbine-engine aircraft, while another employer might require a total of 3,000 flight hours, with at least 1,000 hours flying multi-engine airplanes. Many employers do not require that candidates have experience flying the particular aircraft in their fleets.

To perform their work effectively, Charter Pilots should have strong communication and interpersonal skills. Additionally, they need excellent self-management skills, which include the ability to work independently, handle stressful situations, meet deadlines, and organize and prioritize multiple tasks. Being self-motivated, friendly, cooperative, and flexible are a few personality traits that successful Charter Pilots have in common.

Unions and Associations

Charter Pilots might join professional associations to take advantage of networking opportunities, education programs, and other professional services and resources. Some pilot societies that Charter Pilots might join are the Aircraft Owners and Pilots Association; Women in Aviation, International; Helicopter Association International; and Seaplane Pilots Association.

Tips for Entry

1. You can gain work experience with air-taxi operations as you complete your pilot training. For example, you might obtain a job in ramp service, fleet service, customer service, mechanic work, or another area.
2. Contact employers for whom you'd like to work about job openings. If you plan to visit their offices, bring your résumé to leave with them. Also be prepared to complete job applications and to be interviewed for a job.
3. The willingness to relocate for a job may enhance your chances of finding work.
4. Before applying or sending in your résumé for a pilot's position, first learn what the qualifications are for the job. Make sure you have met those requirements. Employers normally reject applicants who have not met their minimum requirements for a pilot position.
5. Check out the different services offered by various air-taxi and charter operations on the Internet. Enter the keywords *air taxi services* or *air charter services* into a search engine to get a list of relevant Web sites to visit.

LAW ENFORCEMENT PILOT

CAREER PROFILE

Duties: Responsible for the safe operation of aircraft used in preventing, deterring, and suppressing crime; perform preflight, flight, and postflight duties; perform law enforcement duties; perform other duties as required

Alternate Title(s): Police Officer; Deputy Sheriff; Border Patrol Agent/Pilot; Game Warden Pilot, or other title that reflects a law enforcement occupation

Salary Range: $25,000 to $100,000

Employment Prospects: Fair

Advancement Prospects: Fair

Prerequisites:

Education or Training—Educational requirements vary with the different law enforcement agencies; completion of initial and recurrent aviation training programs; completion of recurrent law enforcement training

Experience—One to five years of law enforcement experience is required; meet a minimum number of total flight hours

Special Skills and Personality Traits—Self-management, teamwork, writing, communication, map-reading, and critical-thinking skills; honest, determined, precise, self-motivated

Special Requirements—Commercial pilot certificate with appropriate ratings; FAA medical certificate

CAREER LADDER

Lead or Supervisory Pilot

Law Enforcement Pilot

Law Enforcement Officer

Position Description

Many local, state, and federal agencies have aviation units to provide air support in various types of law enforcement missions. From a vantage point in the air, officers can oversee, coordinate, and support the operational activities of those officers on the ground. Almost all the pilots who operate aircraft in these missions are law enforcement officers. They are responsible for the safe operation of helicopters and fixed-wing airplanes in preventing, deterring, and suppressing crime.

Law Enforcement Pilots are first and foremost law enforcement officers. They may be police officers, state police troopers, FBI agents, customs officers, game wardens, and so on. Their service in aviation units is on a voluntary basis.

As sworn officers, Law Enforcement Pilots enforce laws and protect lives and property within their jurisdictions. They have the power to arrest suspected criminals and the authority to carry firearms. As members of their agency's aviation unit, they provide tactical support from the air to events that are happening on the ground. For example, they may be involved in tracking, pursuing, or intercepting suspected criminals; conducting airborne surveillance; or searching for stolen vehicles.

Some Law Enforcement Pilots are assigned to air patrol duty. State trooper pilots monitor highways and freeways to enforce speed limits, to help motorists in trouble, and to help reduce traffic jams during commute hours. Pilots with the federal agencies, such as the U.S. Customs and Border Protection, fly along U.S. borders to ensure that people are not entering or leaving the country illegally or bringing in drugs or other illegal goods.

Law Enforcement Pilots also assist in various emergencies. They rescue persons from rooftops, hillsides, or canyons. They evacuate individuals who are in danger or are the victims of fire, floodwaters, hazardous waste spills, or other disasters. Many of these pilots also participate in search-and-rescue missions, seeking out lost or missing persons in wilderness areas, along waterways, or in bodies of water.

From time to time, Law Enforcement Pilots are asked to provide aerial assistance to other law enforcement units within their agency as well as to other government departments. For example, they might:

- take aerial photographs of crime scenes
- deliver physical evidence to crime labs, law enforcement agencies, or other distant locations
- deliver prisoners to jails, prisons, or courts
- search for escaped prisoners and aid in their apprehension
- assist with riot control
- transport law enforcement personnel, public officials (such as governors) or staff from other government agencies to court, crime scenes, or civil disasters
- help put out fires by delivering water, foam, or fire retardant to designated targets
- transport blood products, donor organs, equipment, or supplies needed for medical emergencies

Law Enforcement Pilots perform missions that specifically support the goals and objectives of their agencies. For example, Law Enforcement Pilots in a wildlife agency might conduct biological surveys, such as counting bird nests, or they might stock lakes with fish. On occasion, Law Enforcement Pilots provide air support to other law enforcement agencies, whether they are local, state, or federal agencies.

Furthermore, pilots perform duties related to their position (such as police, deputy sheriff, or special agent), as well as their rank (such as sergeant, detective, or supervisory special agent). For example, as law enforcement officers, their activities include interrogating suspects, interviewing witnesses, seizing contraband, serving search warrants, collecting physical evidence, testifying in court, and preparing reports.

Pilots are involved in both day and night operations. Their tasks may require them to maneuver their aircraft at low altitudes of 500 to 800 feet. Helicopter pilots must sometimes land their aircraft in confined locations such as on roadways or near cliffs. Like all other pilots, Law Enforcement Pilots are responsible for determining if flight assignments are safe to be executed. Some of their preflight, flight, and postflight duties include:

- preparing flight plans, which involve analyzing weather forecasts and determining the safest and most efficient routes to fly
- filing flight plans with air traffic controllers
- conducting preflight and postflight inspections of the aircraft and its systems to ensure everything is working properly
- monitoring weather conditions before and during their flights
- maintaining constant communication with air traffic controllers
- making sure the aircraft has sufficient fuel
- completing flight reports, records, logs, and other required paperwork
- maintaining pilot certifications and ratings

Law Enforcement Pilots usually work as part of a two-person team. The other crew member is called the observer and is also a law enforcement officer. Observers are responsible for coordinating the ground activity, operating radios and equipment, and communicating with the dispatcher. They assist pilots with navigation and the spotting of obstacles such as wires, tall trees, and towers.

Law enforcement officers are scheduled to work 40 hours a week but often work overtime. Most of them are assigned to rotating shifts, which may include working nights, weekends, and holidays. Depending on the size and needs of their agencies, officers are assigned full time or part time to their aviation units. Law Enforcement Pilots may be subject to on-call status 24 hours a day.

Law Enforcement Pilots may be expected to live near the airports or helipads where aircraft are stored so they can respond to a call in a minimum amount of time. Federal officers may be required to travel away from their homes for several days or weeks at time.

Salaries

Law Enforcement Pilots earn a salary according to their rank and seniority. Salaries also vary, depending on the law enforcement agency, geographical location, and other factors. Most pilots receive additional compensation for being part of their aviation units.

Since most Law Enforcement Pilots already have some seniority, annual salaries generally range between $25,000 and $100,000. According to a 2002 salary survey by *Rotor & Wing,* the average annual salary for respondents (helicopter pilots) who worked in the area of law enforcement ranged from $55,322.34 to $77,866.67.

Employment Prospects

At the local and state levels, Law Enforcement Pilots work in police departments, sheriff's offices, state police (or highway patrol) departments, and wildlife (or natural resources) departments. At the federal level, the Federal Bureau of Investigation, the Drug Enforcement Administration, and the U.S. Customs and Border Protection are some agencies that employ Law Enforcement Pilots.

Law enforcement agencies usually select candidates for pilot positions from their ranks. Occasionally, a law enforcement agency may hire civilian pilots.

In general, opportunities become available as Law Enforcement Pilots retire or transfer to other positions. Law enforcement agencies will establish or expand aviation units to meet growing needs as long as funding is available. The competition for pilot positions is high.

Advancement Prospects

Law enforcement officers have the flexibility to develop a career commensurate with their personal interests and ambitions. Volunteering for service in special units, such as the aviation unit, broadens their experience and serves as a stepping stone in their careers. In addition to taking on special assignments, officers can pursue promotions in rank within their agencies. For example, police officers can rise through the ranks as detectives, sergeants, lieutenants, captains, and so on. Individuals generally have to leave the aviation section to achieve higher ranks.

Administrative and managerial opportunities within the air support detail are limited to lead or supervisory pilots, chief pilots, and unit commanders. Depending on the agency, officers with administrative and managerial duties may be limited in their capacity to fly missions.

In many agencies, law enforcement officers may retire with a pension after 20 or 25 years of service. Many retired officers pursue a second career in law enforcement, security, private investigation, consultation, teaching, or another area that interests them.

Education and Training

Local and state law enforcement agencies require that their officers possess a high school diploma or general equivalency diploma. Some agencies require that officers have some college training, or possess an associate's or bachelor's degree in police science, criminal justice, or a related field. Federal law enforcement agencies usually require that special agents possess a bachelor's degree in criminal justice, corrections, or a related field.

Law Enforcement Pilots receive initial and recurrent training in federal aviation regulations, aircraft, equipment, and airborne operations. Many agencies also provide flight training so that pilots can obtain additional aircraft ratings to meet the needs of the organization. Furthermore, pilots complete annual training sessions to maintain and update their law enforcement skills.

Special Requirements

Law Enforcement Pilots must possess commercial pilot certificate with an instrument rating, granted by the Federal Aviation Administration (FAA). They must also possess appropriate ratings for operating each type of aircraft that they fly. In addition, they must hold a second-class medical certificate, granted by an FAA medical examiner. (Some agencies require that pilots have a first-class medical certificate.) Pilots are responsible for keeping their pilot and medical certificates up to date to remain qualified for the aviation unit.

Experience, Special Skills, and Personality Traits

Usually, law enforcement officers must have served one to five or more years before they can apply for a pilot vacancy in their agency's airborne unit. Some agencies allow college training or military service to be substituted for required experience.

Officers usually have piloting experience and have met the minimum number of total flight hours required by a law enforcement agency. For example, a sheriff's department may require 1,000 minimum flight hours, whereas a federal agency may require 1,500 minimum flight hours. In addition, an agency may require candidates to have a minimum number of flight hours as a pilot-in-command for flying at night or for flying at low altitudes.

To perform well in their work, Law Enforcement Officers need excellent self-management skills, such as the ability to handle dangerous and stressful situations, understand and follow directions, and organize and prioritize tasks. They must also have effective teamwork, writing, and communication skills. Additionally, they need strong map-reading and critical-thinking skills. Having good hand-eye coordination is also important.

Some personality traits that successful Law Enforcement Pilots share are being honest, determined, precise, and self-motivated.

Unions and Associations

Professional organizations are available at the local, state, and national level to serve the interests of law enforcement officers. They provide professional services and resources such as networking opportunities, education programs, and union representation. Some organizations at the national level are the American Federation of Police, the Fraternal Order of Police, the American Deputy Sheriffs' Association, the North American Wildlife Enforcement Officers Association, and the Federal Law Enforcement Officers Association. The Airborne Law Enforcement Association serves the specific interests of Law Enforcement Pilots.

Many law enforcement officers are members of a union, which represents them in contract negotiations with their employers. The union seeks to get the best contract terms in regards to pay, benefits, and working conditions. It also handles any grievances that officers have against their employers.

Tips for Entry

1. Young people might join the Law Enforcement Explorer Scouts and/or the Civil Air Patrol to gain experience in law enforcement and aviation.
2. As a law enforcement officer, let the commander of the air support unit know about your interest in joining the unit, especially before a position becomes available.
3. Law enforcement agencies require that applicants be U.S. citizens. Additionally, agencies have a minimum age qualification. For federal positions, applicants must be between 21 and 37 years old. For specific entry requirements, contact the law enforcement agencies where you are interested in working. To see if an agency has a Web site, enter its name in a search engine.
4. Some larger air support units may train law enforcement officers without any flight experience to become pilots.
5. Use the Internet to learn more about different law enforcement air support units. Enter the keywords *police air support unit* or *police aviation unit* into a search engine to get a list of relevant Web sites.

EMERGENCY MEDICAL SERVICE (EMS) PILOT

CAREER PROFILE

Duties: Responsible for the safe and efficient operation of emergency medical flights; transport patients and rescue victims from hospitals or emergency sites to medical facilities; perform preflight, flight, and postflight duties; perform other duties as required

Alternate Title(s): Air Medical Pilot; Medevac Pilot; Air Ambulance Pilot

Salary Range: $30,000 to $60,000

Employment Prospects: Good

Advancement Prospects: Fair

Prerequisites:

Education or Training—High school diploma; completion of employer's training programs

Experience—Meet an employer's minimum flight and work experience requirements; most employers require a total of 3,000 flight hours; have low-level, mountainous, and night-flying experience

Special Skills and Personality Traits—Communication, interpersonal, teamwork, critical-thinking, self-management skills; observant, cooperative, decisive, persistent

Special Requirements—Commercial or airline transport pilot (ATP) certificate with appropriate ratings; FAA medical certificate

CAREER LADDER

Chief Pilot

EMS Pilot-in-Command or Copilot

EMS Pilot Trainee

Position Description

EMS (emergency medical service) Pilots are responsible for the safe and successful operation of aircraft used for air ambulance services. They deliver critically ill and injured patients who require immediate urgent care to trauma centers, hospitals, and other medical facilities. They may be transporting patients between medical facilities, or they may be rushing rescue victims to hospitals from emergency sites.

Medical facilities and emergency services agencies use air transportation when that is the most efficient and quickest way to deliver critically ill patients to medical facilities. Air ambulances are especially used in rural areas. Pilots might drop off patients or rescue victims directly at hospitals or at airports, where they are carried by ground ambulances to medical facilities. They also fly patients to medical facilities in another community, county, or state.

EMS Pilots are dispatched at any time of day or night and in all types of weather. They fly aircraft—helicopters and airplanes—that are equipped with medical equipment and supplies to handle all types of patients. Some air ambulances are large jets, such as Boeing 747s, which have been retrofitted to act as mobile medical facilities with intensive care units and pharmacies.

Flights that involve helicopters and small airplanes are usually commanded by single pilots. Midsize planes and jets are manned by two pilots, whereas large jets may have three pilots. Helicopters are more often used for responding to emergency scenes, whereas airplanes and jets are used for transporting patients over long distances and in all types of weather.

A flight medical crew is also on board the flights to provide patient care. The medical crew consists of one or more flight nurses, paramedics, or emergency medical technicians. Some medical crews also include a medical doctor. To ensure the success of a mission, EMS Pilots and the medical crew continually communicate with each other. However, EMS Pilots make all final decisions regarding flight operations. For example, if a pilot believes the weather is too severe, she or he may choose to cancel or delay the flight.

Because they handle different types of medical situations, EMS Pilots make sure they are in compliance with federal aviation regulations as well as with company procedures and protocols. For example: At accident sites, EMS Pilots might land on freeways, near cliffs, on hillsides, in neighborhoods, and other confined areas. The first responders (the police and fire units) are responsible for identifying and securing a suitable landing area for the pilots. Ideally, they choose sites that are flat and clear of obstacles (such as wires, trees, buildings, and people) and with approach and departure paths that are clear. Before landing, EMS Pilots perform reconnaissance passes to make sure it is safe to land on a site, as well as look for an emergency landing site. Pilots may choose another landing site or refuse to land until certain conditions, such as crowds, are in control.

EMS Pilots perform various routine preflight, flight, and postflight duties. Some of these tasks include:

- preparing flight plans
- performing preflight and postflight checks to ensure that the aircraft and its systems are working properly
- maintaining communications with air traffic controllers
- completing FAA reports, pilot logbooks, and other required paperwork
- maintaining their pilot certifications

Because EMS Pilots may be dispatched at any moment, they monitor the weather around their area on a regular basis. They also make sure their aircraft are filled with fuel and properly serviced so that they are ready to go.

Many flight crews are assigned to home bases located at airports or heliports. Some crews are based at helipads at or near hospitals.

EMS Pilots work long shifts, with many of them working 12-hour shifts. (The Federal Aviation Administration, FAA, mandates that EMS Pilots can work no longer than 14 hours per shift.) Much of their time is spent waiting at their home bases to be dispatched for missions.

Most pilots are assigned to rotating shifts, which may include working nights, weekends, and holidays. They usually are assigned to work three to seven days, followed by the same number of days off.

Salaries

Salaries for EMS Pilots vary, depending on such factors as their experience, employer, and geographical location. EMS Pilots usually earn annual salaries between $30,000 and $60,000. According to a 2002 salary survey by *Rotor & Wing,* the average annual salary for respondents (helicopter pilots) who worked in emergency medical services ranged from $46,761.90 to $54,300.00

Employment Prospects

EMS Pilots are employed by emergency medical services, medical facilities, and air medical companies. Some EMS Pilots work for air charter companies that provide contractual air ambulance services. The opportunities, in general, are strong for pilots in the air medical industry. Positions usually become available to replace EMS Pilots who are retiring or transferring to other positions. Employees will create additional positions to meet growing needs, as long as funding is available.

Advancement Prospects

EMS Pilots with administrative and managerial ambitions can advance to the position of Chief Pilot or manager of flight operations. Opportunities are limited and usually require seeking such positions with other employers.

Education and Training

Minimally, EMS Pilots must have a high school diploma or general equivalency diploma. Some employers require, or strongly prefer, that candidates hold a bachelor's degree, which may be in any field.

New hires receive initial training in company policies, FAA and National Transportation Safety Board regulations, navigation, biohazards, basic medical procedures and protocols, and stress and fatigue management. They also receive ground and flight instruction for the type of aircraft they would be operating on EMS missions.

Employers provide EMS Pilots with recurrent ground and flight training to update and maintain their skills.

Special Requirements

EMS Pilots must possess a FAA commercial pilot certificate with an instrument rating and proper ratings in the category (helicopter or airplane), class (single-engine or multiengine), and type (make and model) of aircraft which they are operating. In addition, EMS Pilots must hold either a first-class or second-class FAA medical certificate.

Some employers may require that pilots possess the airline transport pilot (ATP) certificate with appropriate ratings.

Experience, Special Skills, and Personality Traits

Requirements for flight experience and work experience vary with different employers. Most employers require at least 3,000 hours of total flight time, which also includes a minimum number of hours flying the type of aircraft they would be operating. Employers also require pilots to meet a minimum number of hours as a pilot-in-command.

Employers also look for pilots who have experience flying cross-country and in such situations as flying at night, at low altitudes, and over mountainous terrain. Many EMS Pilots gained appropriate flying experience in the military or in such areas as agriculture, law enforcement, oil and gas exploration, and search-and-rescue missions.

EMS Pilots work in critical situations and must be able to work well with medical crews, thus they need excellent communication, interpersonal, and teamwork skills. Also essential are strong critical-thinking and self-management skills (such as the ability to handle stress, prioritize tasks, and follow directions). Being observant, cooperative, decisive, and persistent are some personality traits that successful EMS Pilots share.

Unions and Associations

The National EMS Pilots Association is a professional association that serves the interests of air ambulance pilots. This organization provides various professional services and resources such as networking opportunities, publications, and education programs.

Tips for Entry

1. Gain experience working in the EMS field. For example, you might get training as an emergency medical technician and work or volunteer with EMS agencies. As a pilot, you might volunteer to transport medicines, organs, or patients to medical facilities in other cities.
2. Air medical services sometimes hire pilots part time or on an on-call basis.
3. Apply directly to companies where you would like to work. Maintain contact with the persons who are responsible for hiring new pilots. Call them periodically to update them about your skills and experiences.
4. Use the Internet to learn more about EMS Pilots. You might start by visiting the Web sites for the National EMS Pilots Association (http://www.nemspa.org) and FlightWeb (http://www.flightweb.com).

AIR TANKER PILOT

CAREER PROFILE

Duties: Responsible for safe and efficient operations of aircraft used in wildland firefighting; perform aerial firefighting duties; perform preflight, flight, and postflight duties; perform other duties as required

Alternate Title(s): Firefighter Pilot; Aerial Firefighter

Salary Range: $30,000 to $100,000

Employment Prospects: Poor

Advancement Prospects: Poor

Prerequisites:

Education or Training—High school diploma; completion of employer's training programs

Experience—Meet an employer's minimum flight and work experience requirements

Special Skills and Personality Traits—Low-level flying skills; communication, interpersonal, teamwork, and self-management skills; courteous, calm, levelheaded, flexible, dedicated, courageous

Special Requirements—Commercial pilot certificate with appropriate ratings; FAA medical certificate; Pilot Qualification Card from a federal or state wildland fire protection agency

CAREER LADDER

Air Attack Pilot

Air Tanker Captain

Air Tanker Copilot

Position Description

Air Tanker Pilots are responsible for safely and efficiently operating aircraft in firefighting missions. Each year these highly skilled pilots and aerial firefighters assist in suppressing wildfires on federal and state wildlands—forests, parks, wildernesses, and so forth. Their difficult and risky missions involve flying at low altitudes, through dense smoke, and over mountainous terrain. They operate aircraft known as air tankers that carry 400 to 3,000 gallons of water, foam, or fire retardant, which pilots drop along fire perimeters and on hot spots to stop or slow fire activity.

Air tankers are considered national assets, as they are essential tools for supporting wildland firefighters on the ground. Many of these aircraft are converted military bombers, cargo planes, and agricultural planes. Some are helicopters, also known as heli-tankers. Most of the air tankers are owned by private companies that provide air tanker services on a contractual basis to the USDA Forest Service, to the U.S. Department of the Interior, and to many state wildland fire protection agencies.

For heli-tankers and most multiengine air tankers, the flight crew is composed of two pilots: a captain (or pilot-in-command) and a copilot. Some large air tankers require a third crew member, a flight engineer, who is responsible for monitoring the aircraft systems during the missions. Single-engine air tankers are operated by solo pilots. All final decisions regarding flight operations are made by the aircraft's pilot-in-command, or captain.

The suppression of wildfires is known as air attack, and involves much planning and coordination, especially for large wildfires. Besides air tankers, other aircraft occupy the airspace above the fire to perform a wide variety of missions, such as aerial reconnaissance and the transportation of smoke jumpers. Air attack supervisors, who work for federal or state wildland fire protection agencies, are responsible for overseeing the aerial firefighting operations from the ground and the air. They make sure the operations run smoothly and effectively.

Air Tanker Pilots are stationed at air tanker bases, which are near federal and state wildlands. When they are dispatched to a fire, they are expected to be in the air, heading toward their assignment, within 15 to 20 minutes. At the fire, most Air Tanker Pilots are guided to their targets by lead planes, which usually carry air tanker coordinators. The coordinators direct Air Tanker Pilots where to drop their loads of retardant, foam, or water, and how much of their load to drop. Coordinators also provide pilots with approach and departure paths to their targets.

Some Air Tanker Pilots also fulfill the role of air attack pilots, who respond to wildfires that have just begun. They can attack the fires without the supervision of lead planes. These pilots must make quick and effective decisions to put out wildfires or get them under control until ground units can arrive.

On the ground, pilots perform various preflight and postflight duties, such as:

- monitoring weather conditions and forecasts
- preparing flight plans
- performing preflight and postflight inspections of the aircraft and its systems to ensure that everything is working properly
- fueling and servicing the aircraft—ensuring that it is ready to fly at a moment's notice
- maintaining the interior and exterior of the aircraft
- completing flight reports, pilot logbooks, and other required paperwork

Air Tanker Pilots are assigned to a tanker base, which becomes their home base during the season. When the need arises, they are temporarily assigned to other tanker bases to assist with fires in their areas.

Air Tanker Pilots are usually scheduled to work six days with one day off, which may include working weekends and holidays. Duty shifts are nine to 14 hours long. Much of their time is spent waiting to be dispatched to a fire.

Air Tanker Pilots can fly a maximum of eight hours each day. They usually do not fly after sunset. The number of flight hours that Air Tanker Pilots fulfill each year varies, depending on how light or heavy the fire season has been in their assigned areas. For example, an Air Tanker Pilot may fly 50 hours one year and 300 hours in another year.

Most Air Tanker Pilots are contractual employees who are hired for the fire season, which generally extends from February to November in the United States. They are assigned to protect the different U.S. regions during their peak fire seasons, which starts in the U.S. eastern and southern regions (from February to April), followed by Alaska and the southwest (May and June), and ends in the western United States (from June to September). Some pilots are employed year-round. Between fire seasons, most Air Tanker Pilots obtain commercial pilot jobs on a part-time, full-time, or contractual basis.

Salaries

Salaries for Air Tanker Pilots vary, depending on such factors as experience, position, and the total number of flight hours. Air Tanker Pilots earn standby pay (a fixed contractual amount for serving the fire season) as well as flight pay for each hour of flight time. In general, copilots earn between $30,000 and $60,000 per fire season, whereas captains earn between $70,00 and $100,000.

Employment Prospects

The air tanker industry is small; it is composed of 13 private companies that own and operate more than 75 single-engine, multiengine, and helicopter air tankers, according to the Aerial Firefighting Industry Association. In 2003, these companies held 44 air tanker contracts with the USDA Forest Service, the U.S. Department of the Interior, and several state firefighting agencies. The state of California owns a fleet of air tankers but contracts with a private company to provide Air Tanker Pilots and aircraft maintenance personnel.

Although the job is highly challenging and dangerous, the turnover rate for Air Tanker Pilots is low, and the competition for new positions is very high. Job openings typically become available as pilots retire, transfer to other positions, or leave the field for various reasons. New positions are created to meet firefighting agencies' needs for additional air tanker services.

Advancement Prospects

Air Tanker Pilots normally start as copilots, and usually after three to 10 years they can be promoted to captain. Those companies who use aircraft that require three crew members may start new hires as flight engineers. Captains can achieve additional ranking as air attack pilots.

Pilots with managerial interests might seek management positions with the private companies that offer air tanker services. Other career paths include aviation management positions with the state and federal wildland fire protection agencies.

Education and Training

Air Tanker Pilots must possess at least a high school diploma or general equivalency diploma.

New hires and returning pilots must complete a training program that covers instruction on such topics as fire behavior, wildland firefighting operations, tactical procedures, the use of fire retardants and suppressants, and radio communications and procedures. In addition, pilots must complete flight training on the aircraft they would be operating.

Special Requirements

Minimally, Air Tanker Pilots must possess:

- an FAA commercial pilot certificate with an instrument rating and proper ratings in the category (helicopter or airplane), class (single-engine or multiengine), and type (make and model) of aircraft they operate
- a second-class FAA medical certificate
- a current Pilot Qualification Card that certifies them as eligible to fly specific firefighting missions for the USDA Forest Service, U.S. Department of the Interior, or a state firefighting agency

Experience, Special Skills, and Personality Traits

Flight and work experience requirements for Air Tanker Pilot positions vary with different employers. Minimally, applicants should have 1,500 total hours of flight time, which includes experience flying at low levels and over mountainous terrain. They should also have flight experience as the pilot-in-command of an aircraft—at least 800 flight hours for copilot positions or 1,200 flight hours for captain positions. Candidates must also complete a minimum number of flight hours operating the type of aircraft that they would be flying on firefighting missions.

Many Air Tanker Pilots have gained and maintained their skills by working as agricultural pilots, fire patrol pilots, search-and-rescue pilots, EMS pilots, or tour guide pilots to wilderness areas.

To perform their work effectively, Air Tanker Pilots need strong communication, interpersonal, and teamwork skills. In addition, they should have strong self-management skills, such as the ability to work independently, handle stressful situations, and follow directions. Being courteous, calm, level-headed, flexible, dedicated, and courageous are some personality traits that successful Air Tanker Pilots share.

Unions and Associations

Many Air Tanker Pilots are members of the Associated Airtanker Pilots, a professional association that promotes a safe and efficient working environment for all aerial firefighters. This society also provides their members with networking opportunities as well as other professional services and resources.

Tips for Entry

1. Along with building up your aviation skills and experience, gain a basic knowledge and experience in ground firefighting. For example, you might become a paid or volunteer wildland firefighter during the fire seasons.
2. Apply for jobs early during the off-season.
3. Check with prospective employers about their preferred requirements. For example, some employers may prefer to hire Air Tanker Pilots who possess an airline transport pilot certificate with appropriate ratings and also hold a first-class FAA medical certificate.
4. Use the Internet to learn more about Air Tanker Pilots and wildland firefighting. You might begin by visiting the Web sites for the Aerial Firefighting Industry Association (http://www.afia.com), the Associated Airtanker Pilots (http://www.airtanker.com), and the National Interagency Fire Center (http://www.nifc.gov).

FLIGHT OPERATIONS

AIRCRAFT DISPATCHER

CAREER PROFILE

Duties: Manage flight operations; prepare flight plans; monitor flights; perform duties as required

Alternate Title(s): Airline Dispatcher; Flight Superintendent; Flight Control Officer; Dispatcher/Scheduler

Salary Range: $20,000 to $90,000+

Employment Prospects: Fair

Advancement Prospects: Fair

Prerequisites:

Education or Training—High school diploma; completion of a flight attendant's training program

Experience—Several years of aircraft dispatch experience preferred

Special Skills and Personality Traits—Communication, interpersonal, teamwork, organizational, and self-management skills; enthusiastic, quick-minded, calm, detail-oriented, flexible, decisive

Special Requirements—FAA aircraft dispatcher certificate

CAREER LADDER

Senior Aircraft Dispatcher

Aircraft Dispatcher

Trainee, Assistant Aircraft Dispatcher or Flight Follower

Position Description

In commercial airlines, Aircraft Dispatchers have been called the "captains on the ground" because they make sure that flights run safely and smoothly from their seats in operational centers. Federal aviation regulations require that Aircraft Dispatchers and aircraft captains be jointly responsible for scheduled commercial flights. Like the captains, Aircraft Dispatchers may make important decisions about the flights under their management. For example, if dispatchers determine that weather, equipment malfunction, or other conditions threaten the safety of passengers or of the aircraft, dispatchers may delay, terminate, or cancel flights.

Most Aircraft Dispatchers work for commercial airlines—regional, major, international, and so on—a category that includes cargo air carriers such as UPS and FedEx. Some dispatchers are employed by air charter companies, which may offer scheduled or on-demand flights. Others work for corporations that own and use aircraft solely for business transportation.

Aircraft Dispatchers are responsible for managing several flights at a time. One of their responsibilities is preparing flight plans for their assigned flights. Dispatchers gather and analyze weather conditions, air traffic flow, and other data to determine the best routes and altitudes that captains should fly their aircraft. Aircraft Dispatchers also calculate the amount of fuel that aircraft need to complete flights. Additionally, dispatchers determine to which airports flights can be diverted in case of emergencies. Furthermore, they make sure that their assigned flights are in compliance with federal aviation regulations as well as company policies and protocols.

Dispatchers forward flight plans to the captains for review and discuss any concerns. Captains sign a dispatch release form on the final flight plans. This is a legal document that gives authorization for a flight to depart. Aircraft Dispatchers and captains are both legally required to sign the dispatch release form before a flight can take off.

Aircraft Dispatchers are also responsible for monitoring each of their assigned flights, which may be flying domestically or internationally. They track the progress of flights from their points of departure to their destinations, including stops they may take in between. For example, a dispatcher might be assigned to a flight that departs from Baltimore and makes stops in St. Louis and Los Angeles, before arriving at its final destination in San Francisco.

Dispatchers provide captains with updates of conditions that may affect the successful and safe completion of their flights. For example, they warn captains of sudden changes in weather, air traffic control restrictions, or airport field conditions. When necessary, Aircraft Dispatchers recommend changes in the flight plans—such as changing altitudes or landing at different airports—for safety and economic reasons. Furthermore, Aircraft Dispatchers assist in any flight emergencies. They have the authority to divert or terminate flights if they believe the flight cannot be completed safely. When flights are diverted to an alternate airport, Dispatchers must then make new flight plans to restore the flights to their original destination.

Aircraft Dispatchers have control of their assigned flights until they have landed or gone beyond their jurisdiction. When there are flights that have not been completed by the end of a dispatcher's work shift, the dispatcher is responsible for briefing the next shift's dispatcher about those flights.

At smaller airlines, air charter companies, and corporate flight departments, Aircraft Dispatchers may be responsible for fulfilling other roles as crew schedulers, reservations agents, or load planners. However, dispatchers cannot perform any additional duties (for example, answering phones or planning crew schedules) that may be a distraction while dispatching.

Aircraft Dispatchers work in an office environment. They use calculators, computers, printers, telephones, and other office equipment. Dispatchers communicate with pilots via two-way radios or satellite communications. Many of them also communicate with pilots through a computer text-messaging system.

Their job involves daily contact with various personnel to obtain necessary information and support. Some of the people they rely on for information are pilots, meteorologists, air traffic control specialists, maintenance controllers, load planners, crew schedulers, and aircraft maintenance crew.

Most dispatch centers operate on a 24-hour basis, and Aircraft Dispatchers typically work rotating shifts that are eight to 10 hours long. Their work schedule may include weekends and holidays.

Salaries

Annual earnings for Aircraft Dispatchers vary, depending on such factors as their seniority, employer, and geographical location. Dispatchers can earn additional pay by working overtime. Major airlines usually pay the highest salaries.

Starting salaries for entry-level dispatchers generally range between $20,000 and $30,000 per year. Experienced dispatchers can earn up to $55,000 or more. Top salaries for senior dispatchers at major airlines can be as high as $80,000 to $90,000 or more.

Employment Prospects

Most opportunities become available when Aircraft Dispatchers retire, transfer to other positions, or leave the work force altogether. Employers will create additional positions as their companies expand. Keep in mind that in the aviation industry, the job market fluctuates with the economy. During economic downturns, fewer opportunities are available.

Advancement Prospects

Aircraft Dispatchers with administrative and management ambitions can seek supervisory and management positions within the dispatch department. Dispatcher training positions are also available.

Many Aircraft Dispatchers pursue career growth by first working for regional airlines and then obtaining employment with a major airline.

Aircraft Dispatchers can also follow other career paths in aviation by becoming pilots, airline station managers, airport managers, air traffic controllers, or pursuing other occupations.

Education and Training

Aircraft Dispatchers must have at least a high school diploma or general equivalency diploma. Some employers require or strongly prefer that candidates have college degrees in any major.

Aircraft dispatch programs are available from public and private postsecondary schools. These programs usually cover aircraft theory, meteorology, federal air regulations, aircraft systems, dispatch procedures, and other topics.

New hires typically complete training programs that include company orientation and formal flight dispatcher training. Trainees then receive on-the-job training under the supervision of senior Aircraft Dispatchers. Field training may last several weeks or months, depending on the employer.

Commercial airlines are required to provide a training program that meets Federal Aviation Administration (FAA) guidelines. Trainees receive instruction in basic dispatcher duties as well as in the types of aircraft that they will be assigned to dispatch.

Aircraft Dispatchers keep up with changing technologies, company policies, and FAA regulations by participating in regular training sessions in addition to self-study and enrollment in continuing education programs.

Each year, Aircraft Dispatchers are required to ride in the cockpit with flight crews for at least five hours to observe flight routes, conditions, and so forth.

Special Requirements

Aircraft Dispatchers who work for U.S. airlines that operate under Part 121 of federal aviation regulations are required by law to hold an aircraft dispatcher certificate, which is granted by the FAA. Other employers may require or strongly prefer that dispatchers possess this certificate.

To be eligible for the FAA aircraft dispatcher certificate, applicants must be at least 23 years old. They must also meet qualifying experience requirements, which may be fulfilled through experience gained as a pilot, flight navigator, meteorologist, flight dispatcher, air traffic controller, or flight service specialist. Applicants can also qualify by completing an aircraft dispatcher training program from an FAA-approved school.

Furthermore, applicants must pass both the FAA knowledge exam (formerly the written exam) and the practical examination, which is administered by an FAA-designated dispatcher examiner. The practical examination includes an oral exam and the completion of a flight plan. These tests are equivalent to the examinations that pilots must pass to obtain their Air Transport Pilot certificate.

Experience, Skills, and Personality Traits

In general, employers choose candidates who have previous dispatch experience, which may have been gained through internships or employment as dispatchers or assistant dispatchers. Many airlines prefer to hire candidates with several years of dispatch experience. An airline may hire applicants without prior dispatch work experience if they completed FAA-approved training programs and hold FAA certification.

Aircraft Dispatchers must have excellent communication and interpersonal skills, as they must be able to work with various people from different backgrounds. In addition, they need strong teamwork skills as well as organizational and self-management skills—such as the ability to manage multiple tasks, work independently, and handle stressful situations.

Some personality traits that successful Aircraft Dispatchers share are being enthusiastic, quick-minded, calm, detail-oriented, flexible, and decisive.

Unions and Associations

Many Aircraft Dispatchers are members of a union, which represents them in contract negotiations with their employers. The union seeks to get the best contract terms in regards to pay, benefits, and working conditions. It also handles any grievance that dispatchers have against their employers.

Many dispatchers join the Airline Dispatchers Federation, a professional society that serves the interests of Aircraft Dispatchers. It offers networking opportunities, education programs, job listings, and other professional services and resources.

Tips for Entry

1. If you plan to enroll in a training school for Aircraft Dispatchers, be sure to carefully research prospective schools. Find out how long they have been in business, where their graduates are currently working, about their instructors' backgrounds, and about their job placement programs. Ask the school for names of graduates whom you can contact. If possible, talk to dispatch professionals about which schools they would recommend.
2. When you turn 21 years old, you can start training to become an Aircraft Dispatcher. You are also eligible to take the exams for the FAA aircraft dispatcher certificate. If you pass, you will be issued a Letter of Aeronautical Competency and receive the aircraft dispatcher certificate upon reaching your 23rd birthday.
3. Are you uncertain whether your work experience is acceptable toward obtaining the FAA aircraft dispatcher certificate? Contact your local Flight Standards District Office for advice.
4. Find out the name of the director of the flight dispatch department where you want to work by calling up the company. Then send your application package directly to that person. On a regular basis, send the director a brief follow-up letter to remind him or her of your interest and availability. Many Aircraft Dispatchers have been hired because they contacted an airline at a time when an opening just became available.
5. Learn more about Aircraft Dispatchers on the Internet. You might start by visiting the Web site for the Airline Dispatchers Federation, http://www.flightdispatch.net.

CREW SCHEDULER

CAREER PROFILE

Duties: Plan, manage, and coordinate work schedules for pilots and flight attendants; make sure all flights are sufficiently staffed; perform duties as required

Alternate Title(s): Schedule Coordinator; Flight Coordinator/Scheduler; Scheduler/Dispatcher

Salary Range: $20,000 to $40,000+

Employment Prospects: Fair

Advancement Prospects: Fair

Prerequisites:

Education or Training—High school diploma; completion of employer's training program

Experience—One or more years of work experience in the aviation industry

Special Skills and Personality Traits—Organizational, problem-solving, communication, interpersonal, teamwork, customer service, writing, computer, and self-management skills; optimistic; calm; diplomatic; detail-oriented; self-motivated; flexible

Special Requirements—Driver's license may be required

CAREER LADDER

Senior Crew Scheduler

Crew Scheduler

Trainee or Assistant Crew Scheduler

Position Description

Crew Schedulers provide an important link between flight operation departments and flight crews—the pilots and the flight attendants. Crew Schedulers' main responsibility is to plan, coordinate, and manage flight crew schedules. They make sure all flights are staffed with the sufficient number of crew members. They are also responsible for monitoring schedules and updating crew schedules when changes occur.

Many Crew Schedulers are employed by commercial airlines. Some work for air charter companies, while some others are hired by companies that own and use aircraft for business purposes.

Crew Schedulers work in an office environment, but with varying work settings. For example, Crew Schedulers at major airlines typically work in large teams stationed in airline system control centers, while Crew Schedulers for corporate flight departments might work alone in an office shared with pilots and flight operations staff.

To ensure safe, efficient, and economical flights, Crew Schedulers consider many factors while making assignments. They take into account the seniority of crew members and their bids (or choices) for flights. They check requests by the different crew members for time off for vacation, illness, emergencies, jury duty, or other purposes.

Crew Schedulers make sure that all scheduling complies with federal aviation regulations. For example, pilots are limited by the total number of hours they can fly. In addition, schedulers check that assignments are in accordance with company policies, and with contractual agreements when crew members are unionized.

The job of Crew Schedulers involves direct communication with pilots and flight attendants, who may be company employees or independent contractors. Crew Schedulers are responsible for providing flight crews with their assignments. They also notify flight crews of any changes that occur with their assigned flights due to weather, mechanical problems, crew issues, or other matters. Crew Schedulers also handle any questions or problems that crew members may have about their assignments.

Crew Schedulers may provide other support services to crew members. Airline Crew Schedulers, for example, might coordinate ground transportation and hotel lodgings for crew members when they are on layovers. Employees with charter companies and corporate flight departments may be responsible for handling ground transportation and hotel accommodations for passengers.

Nonairline Crew Schedulers typically perform other tasks besides crew scheduling. For example, their duties might include preparing required documentation such as landing permits, planning inflight menus, and arranging for catering of meals. In some corporate flight departments, Crew Schedulers perform the role of aircraft dispatcher. Some of their dispatch responsibilities include receiving requests for air transportation, scheduling aircraft, monitoring daily flight operations, and communicating important information to pilots in flight.

Depending on the employer, Crew Schedulers may be required to work shifts including evenings, weekends, and holidays.

Salaries

Annual wages for Crew Schedulers vary, depending on such factors as their education, experience, employer, and location. In general, schedulers may earn between $20,000 and $40,000 or more per year.

Employment Prospects

Job openings usually become available as Crew Schedulers retire or transfer to other positions. In general, job prospects in the aviation industry, especially with commercial airlines, fluctuate with the health of the economy. When the economy is in a downturn, employers normally hire fewer people and sometimes lay off employees.

Advancement Prospects

Crew Schedulers with managerial ambitions can seek out supervisory and management positions in the scheduling department or advance to management positions in flight operations.

Other career paths for schedulers can include becoming crew scheduler trainers, aircraft dispatchers, or operations planners.

Education and Training

Minimally, employers require that Crew Schedulers have a high school diploma or a general equivalency diploma. Some employers prefer to hire candidates with a two-year or four-year college degree, particularly with a major or course work in air transport operations.

New schedulers typically receive training in company policies, federal aviation regulations, scheduling procedures, computer systems, and other topics. Airline schedulers may be sent to formal training programs.

Special Requirements

Many employers require that Crew Schedulers possess a valid driver's license.

Experience, Special Skills, and Personality Traits

Most employers require that applicants have one or more years of previous experience working in the aviation industry. Many Crew Schedulers entered this field with experience working as ramp agents, ticket agents, office assistants, and other positions for airlines, air charter companies, or fight departments. Some schedulers have gained experience working in aviation positions in the military.

Some employers look for candidates who have previous crew scheduling experience and are knowledgeable about federal aviation regulations.

To do their work effectively, schedulers must have excellent organizational, problem-solving, communication, interpersonal, and teamwork skills. Having basic customer service, writing, and computer skills is also important. Further, they need strong self-management skills, such as the ability to manage multiple tasks, work under stressful conditions, and understand and follow directions.

Being optimistic, calm, diplomatic, detail-oriented, self-motivated, and flexible are some personality traits that Crew Schedulers have in common.

Unions and Associations

Many airline schedulers belong to a union, which represents them in contract negotiations with their employers. The union seeks to get the best contract terms in regards to pay, benefits, and working conditions. It also handles any grievances that schedulers have against their employers.

Tips for Entry

1. If you are in high school or college, contact companies where you would like to work. Ask about their job requirements and selection process for Crew Schedulers. Also ask human resource officers or Crew Schedulers for advice on how you could break into this field.
2. To enhance your employability, obtain a working knowledge of the different types of aircraft and the various roles (such as maintenance, dispatch, and air traffic control) in flight operations.
3. Become proficient in computers and the use of various software applications such as word-processing and spreadsheet programs.
4. Use the Internet to find out about job openings available at airlines. To find a specific airline, enter its name into a search engine.

MAINTENANCE CONTROLLER

CAREER PROFILE

Duties: Plan, coordinate, and manage scheduled and emergency maintenance projects; provide technical assistance to pilots and aviation maintenance crew; perform duties as required

Alternate Title(s): Line Maintenance Controller; Systems Maintenance Controller

Salary Range: $29,000 to $107,000

Employment Prospects: Fair

Advancement Prospects: Fair

Prerequisites:

Education or Training—High school diploma; completion of employer's training programs

Experience—Highly experienced and knowledgeable in the field of aircraft maintenance, preferably with supervisory experience

Special Skills and Personality Traits—Communication, interpersonal, teamwork, writing, computer, organizational, and self-management skills; analytical, detail-oriented, flexible, decisive

Special Requirements—FAA Airframe and Powerplant (A&P) certificate

CAREER LADDER

System Maintenance Controller

Line Maintenance Controller

Lead Aircraft Maintenance Technician

Position Description

Maintenance Controllers are an essential part of flight operations for commercial airlines. They are responsible for managing scheduled and emergency maintenance projects to ensure the efficient and quick return of aircraft back into service. Maintenance Controllers are assigned to oversee the maintenance program for a particular type of fleet, such as a fleet of Boeing 727s. They plan and coordinate maintenance projects and monitor their progress. They also provide technical advice and guidance to aircraft maintenance crews as needed. Further, they make sure maintenance projects are in compliance with federal aviation regulations, company policies, maintenance manuals, and manufacturers' specifications.

Maintenance Controllers are also responsible for providing pilots with technical assistance when problems occur with aircraft in flight. If emergency repairs or maintenance are needed, Maintenance Controllers coordinate those efforts to minimize any delay in flight schedules. They contact the aircraft maintenance crew at the station where the plane will be arriving and advise them of the problem. Controllers also determine whether there are qualified mechanics to perform the job at the station, and if the proper parts and tools are available so that crew can work on the problem immediately. Maintenance Controllers also inform other appropriate personnel in flight operations (such as aircraft dispatchers and maintenance planners) and in other departments.

Maintenance Controllers perform a wide range of duties, such as:

- preparing accurate and comprehensive reports on projects
- maintaining daily logs of all maintenance activities
- coordinating the timely acquisition of materials and supplies for projects
- recommending vendors for contractual maintenance services

- notifying appropriate maintenance managers about accidents or incidents involving staff or equipment
- troubleshooting problems as they occur

Maintenance Controllers are seasoned aircraft mechanics, and usually have prior experience as lead aircraft maintenance technicians. In a management role, Maintenance Controllers work in an office environment. They use computers and different software applications to complete their various tasks. Their work also involves establishing and maintaining effective working relationships with a wide range of personnel. Throughout the day they are communicating with pilots, dispatchers, aircraft maintenance crews, ramp operations crews, vendors, and others over the phone and in person.

At major airlines, the maintenance control role is performed by line maintenance controllers and system maintenance controllers. Line controllers are assigned to one of the airports that an airline serves, and they are responsible for managing maintenance control on the flights that are destined for their airport. System controllers are often located at their airline's headquarters and are responsible for handling maintenance control on fleets that fly internationally.

Maintenance Controllers usually work rotating shifts, which may include working nights, weekends, and holidays. Airline Maintenance Controllers may work 10- to 12-hour shifts with staggered days off. For example, a Maintenance Controller might be scheduled to work three days followed by three days off, then work four days followed by four days off.

Salaries

Salaries for Maintenance Controllers vary and depend on various factors such as their experience, job duties, employer, and geographical location. Formal salary information about Maintenance Controllers is unavailable. This occupation is similar to an administrative services manager. The estimated annual salary for most administrative services managers ranged between $28,690 and $107,490 according to the May 2003 *Occupational Employment Statistics* survey by the U.S. Bureau of Labor Statistics.

Employment Prospects

Maintenance Controllers are mostly employed by airlines, cargo carriers, and corporate flight departments with large fleets. Job openings usually become available as individuals transfer to other positions, retire, or leave the job for other reasons.

Job growth in the aviation industry fluctuates with the strength of the overall economy. When the economy is in a downturn, fewer job opportunities are available.

Advancement Prospects

The position of Maintenance Controller is at the first-level of aviation maintenance management. Further advancement depends upon an individual's ambitions, interests, and workplace. Maintenance Controllers can pursue other maintenance management positions such as line maintenance planners, maintenance line managers, and maintenance managers at airports. With experience and dedication, Maintenance Controllers who desire higher-level responsibilities can pursue senior management positions in administration.

Education and Training

Minimally, Maintenance Controllers must have a high school diploma or general equivalency diploma. Employers typically provide Maintenance Controllers with initial and recurrent training programs.

Special Requirements

Maintenance Controllers must possess the Airframe & Powerplant (A&P) certificate granted by the Federal Aviation Administration (FAA).

Experience, Special Skills, and Personality Traits

Maintenance Controllers are highly experienced and knowledgeable in the field of aircraft maintenance. Employers typically look for candidates who have several years of work experience, preferably with supervisory experience. Additionally, they prefer candidates who have experience working on the types of aircraft with which they would be working. Further, some employers prefer to hire candidates who have experience working in their settings.

This job requires that Maintenance Controllers have excellent communication skills, as they must be able to relate well with people of different occupations and backgrounds. They must also have strong interpersonal and teamwork skills as well as good writing and computer skills. Additionally, they need exceptional organizational skills and self-management skills, including the ability to handle multiple tasks, meet deadlines, work independently, and deal with stressful situations.

Being analytical, detail-oriented, flexible, and decisive are some personality traits that successful Maintenance Controllers have in common.

Unions and Associations

Maintenance Controllers may join an organization, such as the Professional Aviation Maintenance Association, that serves the professional interests of the aviation maintenance field. As members of a professional association, they can take advantage of various services and resources such as networking opportunities, education programs, and career resources.

Tips for Entry

1. To enhance your employability, enroll in courses to improve your writing, communication, and computer skills.

2. Talk with Maintenance Controllers, aviation maintenance supervisors, and vocational counselors to get an idea of specific training and work experience you could accumulate to advance toward your goal of becoming a Maintenance Controller.

3. Use the Internet to learn more about the field of aviation maintenance. To get a list of relevant Web sites, enter the keywords *aviation maintenance* into any search engine.

AVIATION METEOROLOGIST

CAREER PROFILE

Duties: Prepare weather reports and forecasts that serve the needs of the aviation community; produce and issue warnings, advisories, maps, and other weather information products; perform duties as required

Alternate Title(s): Airline Meteorologist; Weather Forecaster; Weather Briefer; Weather Officer

Salary Range: $20,000 to $100,000

Employment Prospects: Fair

Advancement Prospects: Fair

Prerequisites:

Education or Training—Bachelor's degree in meteorology, atmospheric science, or a related field

Experience—General weather forecasting experience usually required; aviation forecasting experience may be required

Special Skills and Personality Traits—Math, computer, communication, writing skills, analytical, teamwork, and interpersonal skills; quick thinking, creative, flexible, enthusiastic

CAREER LADDER

Senior Meteorologist

Lead Meteorologist

Meteorologist

Position Description

Aviation Meteorologists play an important role in the success of all flight operations that occur every day throughout the world. They are operational (or synoptic) meteorologists who generate weather forecasts that serve the specialized needs of the aviation community—private pilots, commercial pilots, airlines, flight departments, airports, the Federal Aviation Administration (FAA), and so on. Accurate and up-to-date weather information is essential for planning safe, efficient, and economical flight routes. Aviation Meteorologists also influence the critical decisions that pilots and others must make in flight as well as during takeoffs and landings. Current or predicted bad weather may cause proposed flight routes to be altered or flights to be delayed or canceled.

Aviation weather forecasts are overviews of the weather conditions in a particular region or at a specific airport. Meteorologists report on current weather at a location, and predict what the weather may be like in the coming hours. They also provide forecasts of air velocity and temperature, as well as forecasts of wind direction and speed at different altitudes up to 25,000 feet or more. Additionally, they give information about such dangerous conditions as icing, turbulence, low clouds, and the eruption of volcanic ash. Furthermore, they issue warnings and advisories for severe weather—tornadoes, dust storms, thunderstorms, snow, hail, and so on.

Aviation Meteorologists work at weather facilities that are usually located at or near airports. To make their aviation weather forecasts, meteorologists gather and analyze weather data from various sources. They examine data obtained from weather instruments, such as thermometers, barometers, anemometers, and weather balloons. They also interpret data gathered by aircraft and satellites. In addition, they review observations from pilots who report about the weather conditions they are experiencing while in flight.

Meteorologists apply physical and mathematical principles and use sophisticated computer models to make short-term and long-term forecasts. They then produce reports, warning bulletins, maps, charts, computer models, and other weather information products that are issued to the aviation community. This weather information may be distributed by way of telephone, fax, radio broadcasts, and the Internet. Aviation Meteorologists may also advise pilots, flight dispatchers, air traffic controllers, and other interested parties in person or by phone. A product is updated every hour or few hours.

Along with weather forecasting, some Aviation Meteorologists are involved in conducting research studies. Their studies may involve gaining new knowledge about weather systems or developing new tools and methodologies for weather forecasting.

Aviation Meteorologists work in different settings. Some are staff members at major airlines, where they prepare weather products for pilots, aircraft dispatchers, and other personnel who need aviation weather forecasts. Some meteorologists work for private firms that offer aviation weather services on a contractual basis to airlines, flight departments, air charter companies, and others. These meteorologists may be assigned to also provide weather forecasts for other markets, such as the media and agricultural industry.

Other Aviation Meteorologists are employed by the U.S. National Weather Service (NWS). Some of them work for the Aviation Weather Center, which provides warnings and advisories for the aviation community. Some meteorologists work at NWS center weather service units (CWSU), which are located at or near airports. CWSUs are contracted to the FAA to provide weather forecasting services that meet the needs of the FAA's air traffic division. CWSU meteorologists provide air traffic controllers with detailed forecasts of weather conditions around airports several times a day, and they brief air traffic controllers about rapidly changing weather hazards.

Aviation Meteorologists usually work indoors, but may occasionally work outdoors to check weather instruments and make observations.

The aviation industry operates 24 hours a day, 7 days a week. Thus, most Aviation Meteorologists work rotating shifts, which may include working nights, weekends, and holidays. Employers may require them to work overtime when severe weather conditions occur.

Salaries

Salaries for Aviation Meteorologists vary, depending on such factors as their experience, education, employer, and geographical location. Starting salaries for entry-level positions generally range between $20,000 and $30,000. Annual salaries for entry-level NWS meteorologists start at the GS-5 level (which in 2003 ranged from $23,442 to $30,471 per year). The U.S. Bureau of Labor Statistics, in its May 2003 *Occupational Employment Statistics* survey, reports that the estimated annual salary for most atmospheric scientists ranged between $31,980 and $100,290.

Employment Prospects

The number of meteorologist positions available with the airlines are limited, as only a few major airlines have their own meteorology staff. Opportunities are generally better with weather companies that offer aviation weather services.

Job openings with the airlines, NWS, or weather companies typically become available as Aviation Meteorologists retire, resign, or transfer to other positions. However, the turnover in jobs is low, and the competition for positions is stiff.

Advancement Prospects

Meteorologists with management or administrative ambitions can advance to such positions, but it may require moving to other locations within an organization or working for a different employer.

Airline meteorologists may choose to become aircraft dispatchers or flight planners, which requires being highly knowledgeable about weather.

Aviation Meteorologists may also choose to follow a career path toward academic teaching and independent research, which usually requires obtaining master's and doctoral degrees.

Education and Training

A bachelor's degree in meteorology or atmospheric science is the usual minimum requirement for becoming an operational meteorologist. Employers may consider applicants with degrees in other fields if they have studied a minimum number of hours in meteorology, physics, and calculus.

Employers typically provide new hires with training programs that cover such topics as airport terminal forecasting, turbulence forecasting, snow prediction, thunderstorm prediction, and forecasting the wind flow in the upper atmosphere. Meteorologists also receive recurrent training to maintain and update their skills.

Experience, Skills, and Personality Traits

Airlines and private firms usually require that candidates have a few years of general forecasting experience with the military, the FAA, or the NWS. Being knowledgeable about the effects of weather on aircraft and about aviation weather forecasting is highly desired by employers. Some employers may require one or more years in the field of aviation forecasting.

Meteorologists need to have strong math and computer skills. In addition, they need excellent communication skills, and they must be able to discuss weather in language that can be understood by nontechnical audiences. They also need strong writing and analytical skills. Further, they should have strong teamwork and interpersonal skills, as they must be able to work well with various people of diverse backgrounds and with various technical levels. Some personality traits that successful Aviation Meteorologists share are being quick-thinking, creative, flexible, and enthusiastic.

Unions and Associations

Many Aviation Meteorologists join professional associations to take advantage of networking opportunities, training programs, and professional services and resources. Two national organizations that serve the interests of Aviation Meteorologists are the American Meteorological Society and the National Weather Association Aviation Meteorology Committee.

Airline meteorologists usually belong to a union, which represents them in labor negotiations with their employers for such contractual terms as pay, benefits, and working conditions. The union also handles any grievance that meteorologists have against their employers.

Tips for Entry

1. Gain experience in the field by obtaining internships with airlines, private weather firms, or the NWS. Talk with your college adviser or the college placement center for assistance with finding out about relevant internship programs in your area.
2. To improve your chances of finding a job, you may need to be willing to relocate to other cities or states.
3. To obtain information about meteorologist jobs with the federal government, contact the U.S. Office of Personnel Management. Look in your telephone book under U.S. Government for a local phone number. Or visit its Web site at http://www.usajobs.opm.gov.
4. Learn more about meteorology and aviation weather forecasting on the Internet. You might start by visiting the Web sites for the Aviation Weather Center, http://aviationweather.gov, and the NWS, http://www.nws.noaa.gov.

CUSTOMER SERVICES IN AVIATION

FLIGHT ATTENDANT

CAREER PROFILE

Duties: Ensure the safety and comfort of passengers during flight; enforce federal safety regulations and company policies; perform duties as required

Alternate Title(s): Stewardess; Steward

Salary Range: $21,000 to $92,000

Employment Prospects: Good

Advancement Prospects: Good

Prerequisites:

Education or Training—High school diploma; completion of a flight attendant's training program

Experience—Several years of work experience in customer service

Special Skills and Personality Traits—Communication, interpersonal, customer service, teamwork, dispute resolution, organizational and self-management skills; know a foreign language for international positions; patient, poised, tactful, respectful, friendly, outgoing, efficient, flexible, well-groomed

CAREER LADDER

Lead Flight Attendant

Flight Attendant

Trainee

Position Description

Flight Attendants play an important and challenging role in flight operations. They are responsible for the safety and comfort of passengers from the moment they board to the moment passengers depart a flight. The Flight Attendant's job involves the performance of tasks that are in compliance with federal aviation regulations as well as company policies and protocols. In addition, Flight Attendants are trained to handle different types of problems and emergencies that may occur in flight, such as disruptive passengers, sick passengers, severe weather conditions, fires, hijacking, and emergency landings. Flight Attendants are expected to perform their duties in a pleasant, respectful, calm, and diplomatic manner at all times.

Most Flight Attendants work for commercial airlines that offer scheduled flights along specific routes. Airline Flight Attendants are assigned to a home base (also known as a domicile) that may be any one of the airports to which their airline provides services.

Other Flight Attendants are employed by air charter companies that may provide on-demand or scheduled flights to travelers. Still other Flight Attendants are hired by private companies that own and use aircraft for business purposes. Furthermore, some Flight Attendants are self-employed, or independent contractors.

Flight Attendants work in tight and confined spaces. They stand, walk, kneel, and stoop for long periods of time. Their work routine is generally the same whether they are employed by an airline, a charter company, or a corporate flight department.

Before each flight, the captain or lead Flight Attendant briefs the Flight Attendants about the flight, expected weather conditions, safety-related issues, and any special needs for specific passengers. Flight Attendants also perform various preflight tasks. They make sure all first aid kits and emergency equipment are on board and in working order. In addition, they check that the cabin has sufficient supplies of blankets, pillows, food, beverages, and magazines for the passengers.

When passengers board a flight, Flight Attendants stand by to greet and direct passengers to their seats. They assist passengers with special needs—such as the elderly, persons with disabilities, parents with babies, or young children flying alone. They also help passengers stow their carry-on items in overhead bins or beneath seats.

Before a flight takes off, Flight Attendants go over safety information with their passengers. They instruct and demonstrate the use of safety equipment, such as oxygen masks, in case of an emergency. Flight Attendants also perform final safety checks before an aircraft takes off or lands. They go through the cabin and make sure that all passengers have fastened their seat belts. They also check that carry-on items are properly stowed and that all trays and seat backs are in an upright position.

Flight Attendants provide various services to passengers while in flight. On most flights, passengers are served complimentary refreshments. Meal service—breakfast, lunch, or dinner—is typically offered on long flights. Flight Attendants also distribute pillows, blankets, reading materials, and headphones for inflight entertainment to passengers who wish them.

Flight Attendants make flight announcements as needed throughout the trip. They answer passengers' questions and reassure passengers about any concerns they may have about weather, turbulence, or other matters regarding the flight. In addition, Flight Attendants take care of young children who are traveling alone and passengers who are feeling ill.

At the end of a flight, Flight Attendants complete any required paperwork. For example, a Flight Attendant might write a report about the first aid she administered to a passenger. Flight Attendants also inform the appropriate personnel of any problems or concerns about the cabin, galley, safety equipment, or other matters.

Many corporate Flight Attendants—those who work for corporate flight departments—perform additional duties. For example, they might plan inflight menus; coordinate the catering of meals; and order office supplies, computer accessories, food, magazines, and other items that business passengers may require. For international flights, some Flight Attendants are responsible for performing aircraft maintenance or repairs. (These Flight Attendants may be required to be aircraft mechanic–certified by the Federal Aviation Administration, or FAA.)

Some flights include layovers in another city. A layover may be several hours or several days. With layovers, companies or airlines usually pay for Flight Attendants' hotel accommodations, meals, and transportation to and from the airport.

Flight Attendants have a flexible work schedule. They might work nights, weekends, or holidays. The number of trips they make per week or month depends on their flight assignments. The number of hours they work per shift and the number of days they work each month also varies. When delays or other problems occur, Flight Attendants can expect to be on duty for up to 10 to 14 hours.

Airline Flight Attendants receive new work schedules each month, which are based on their bids (or choices) for flights in the previous month. They are given flight assignments based on their seniority.

New hires at airlines are known as reserve Flight Attendants. They are on call and fill in for Flight Attendants when they are on vacation or leave, are sick, or reassigned to other flights.

Salaries

Salaries vary for Flight Attendants, depending on such factors as their seniority, employer, and type of flights. According to the May 2003 *Occupational Employment Statistics* survey (by the U.S. Bureau of Labor Statistics), the estimated annual wage for most Flight Attendants ranged from $20,600 to $92,020.

Airline Flight Attendants are generally guaranteed a monthly salary based upon a minimum number of base hours. They usually earn extra pay for every hour that they fly beyond that base. They may also earn extra pay for working night and international flights, as well as by working on holidays. Other benefits may include free or reduced airline fares for themselves and their immediate families.

Employment Prospects

The competition for jobs is fierce because so many men and women are attracted to the glamour of working with an airline and the opportunity of traveling to various locations. Most opportunities become available as Flight Attendants resign, retire, or transfer to other occupations. Airlines, charter companies, and corporate flight departments will create additional positions to meet their growing needs.

Job prospects in the airline industry typically fluctuate with the economy. The demand for air travel decreases during a recession, so airlines may relegate Flight Attendants to part-time status or lay them off.

Advancement Prospects

In the airline industry, Flight Attendants advance by virtue of their seniority (their length of service with their company). As they gain seniority, they can obtain promotions, earn higher salaries, and receive their choices of work schedules. Reserve Flight Attendants, regardless of position or experience when hired, begin at the bottom of the seniority list. Reserves can expect to have this status anywhere from one to 10 years or more.

Administrative and managerial positions are available for Flight Attendants with those interests. For example, airline Flight Attendants can rise through the ranks as a lead Flight Attendant, supervisor, flight attendant base manager, and manager or vice president of all flight attendant bases.

Other career options include becoming a flight attendant recruiter or a flight attendant instructor. With additional education and training, Flight Attendants might follow career paths toward other areas of their companies in which they are interested, such as human resources, marketing, or finance. Another career option is to obtain training and certification to become a commercial or airline pilot.

Education and Training

Employers require that Flight Attendants possess at least a high school diploma or general equivalency diploma. Some employers prefer to hire candidates with a college degree or some college training.

New airline hires are required to complete a formal training program at an airline flight training center, which usually lasts between four and seven weeks. The program covers various topics, such as the types of aircraft the airline operates, federal aviation regulations, company policies, first aid, CPR, emergency evacuation procedures, survival tactics, security measures, and handling disruptive passengers. They also are given instruction about appearance standards, customer service skills, and in-flight meal service. Trainees receive classroom instruction and also go on practice flights. If trainees successfully complete the training program, they then become airline employees and are assigned a home base.

Flight Attendants are required to complete annual training programs to hone their skills, as well as to learn new procedures and skills required by the FAA or their employer.

Experience, Special Skills, and Personality Traits

Employers look for candidates who have several years of experience working with the public, which may have been gained through such jobs as a waiter, food counterperson, sales clerk, cashier, or customer service representative. Additionally, employers seek candidates who are able to demonstrate that they are mature, professional, and emotionally stable.

Airlines in the United States require that applicants be U.S. citizens or have the proper paperwork to work in the United States.

All airlines have a minimum age requirement, which usually varies between 18 and 21 years. Some airlines have a higher minimum age requirement. Airlines also have height requirements and require that applicants' weight be proportionate to their height.

Flight Attendants need excellent communication, interpersonal, and customer service skills. Their job also requires having strong teamwork skills. In addition, they should have good dispute resolution skills, organizational skills, and self-management skills—such as the ability to follow directions, handle stressful situations, prioritize tasks, and work independently. Those seeking positions with international airlines should be fluent in a foreign language, such as French, German, Spanish, or Japanese.

Being patient, poised, tactful, respectful, friendly, outgoing, efficient, and flexible are some personality traits that successful Flight Attendants share.

Unions and Associations

Most airline Flight Attendants belong to a union, which represents them in contract negotiations with their employers. The union seeks to get the best contract terms in regards to pay, benefits, and working conditions. It also handles any grievances that agents have against their employers.

Some unions that represent Flight Attendants include the Association of Flight Attendants, AFL-CIO, the Transport Workers Union of America, the International Brotherhood of Teamsters, and the Association of Professional Flight Attendants.

Tips for Entry

1. Airlines look for applicants who have experience working with the public. This may include any volunteer work you have done for school, church, community service programs, political campaigns, or other groups. If you have done any teaching or coaching, be sure to mention those experiences as well.
2. Many airlines post job listings and their selection process on their Web sites. Some of them also provide a file of their job application which you can download to a computer.
3. Prepare yourself for your interview. Know exactly why you want to become a Flight Attendant and be ready to share your reasons with job interviewers. In addition, pick an outfit for your interview that closely resembles what Flight Attendants wear.
4. Learn more about Flight Attendants on the Internet. Two Web sites you might visit are SkyChick, http://www.skychick.com, and Flight Attendants.org, http://www.flightattendants.org. To find other Web sites, enter the keywords *flight attendants* into a search engine.

CUSTOMER SERVICE AGENT (AIRPORT OR AIRLINE)

CAREER PROFILE

Duties: Provide direct or indirect customer service to passengers; perform duties as required

Alternate Title(s): Customer Service Representative; a title that reflects a particular job such as Skycap; Gate Agent; Passenger Service Agent; or Baggage Service Agent

Salary Range: $15,000 to $32,000+

Employment Prospects: Fair

Advancement Prospects: Fair

Prerequisites:

Education or Training—High school diploma; completion of employer's training program

Experience—Varies with the different jobs; some jobs require no work experience while others require one or more years of work experience

Special Skills and Personality Traits—Communication, teamwork, interpersonal, customer service, writing, computer and self-management skills; energetic, cooperative, efficient, outgoing, calm, courteous

Special Requirements—Driver's license may be required

CAREER LADDER

Lead Customer Service Agent

Customer Service Agent

Trainee

Position Description

Airports and airlines employ various Customer Service Agents to provide services to passengers at airport terminals. For example, different agents help passengers with their luggage, sell and issue airline tickets, provide assistance to passengers with special needs, answer questions about airport services, resolve passengers' issues, load baggage onto aircraft, or service aircraft.

Customer Service Agents may serve passengers directly or indirectly, but all work toward the same goal: making sure passengers have a pleasant, comfortable, and safe traveling experience.

Customer Service Agents work in a fast-paced and constantly changing environment. They must meet the challenge of completing their tasks within specific time frames so that flights depart on schedule.

Some of the more typical customer service personnel who work at airport terminals are described below. Many of them are entry-level positions.

Public Service Agents are airport employees who assist travelers. They may be stationed at information desks or travel throughout the airport. These agents answer questions about the airport and the restaurants, shops, and other services that are available. They direct travelers to specific locations such as the baggage claims area, departure gates, or the airline ticket counter. In addition, they provide information about ground transportation to and from the airports as well as about local accommodations, events, entertainment, and tours. Public Service Agents also handle problems or complaints that travelers may have regarding the airport. Those with bilingual skills often function as interpreters for foreign travelers.

Skycaps help passengers with their luggage. They are usually stationed at airport curbsides, where they assist arriving travelers by loading their luggage onto baggage carts and wheeling them to the appropriate airline ticket counter. Skycaps also help departing travelers by carting luggage from the baggage claim area to their vehicles, taxis, or bus stops. Skycaps may drive passengers in electric carts or push them in wheelchairs to their departure gates or other destinations in the airport. Some airlines allow skycaps to perform baggage checks.

Skycaps are employed by airlines or airports. Airline Skycaps assist passengers for their specific airlines. Airport Skycaps are usually assigned to a specific terminal, where they provide services to passengers of all airlines working out of their assigned terminal.

Ticket Agents work behind airline ticket counters at the airport. They are responsible for selling and issuing tickets for scheduled flights. Their other major responsibility is to process passengers for their flights. This includes checking in passengers and their baggage, assigning seats, issuing boarding passes, and directing passengers to departure gates.

Gate Agents work at terminal gates. They are responsible for coordinating the boarding and off-loading of passengers for their airline. Gate Agents also make boarding announcements, assign seats, handle standby passengers, and assist passengers with their questions, concerns, or needs.

Passenger Service Agents are employed by airlines to provide assistance to their passengers. They answer questions about flights and airport services. They coordinate any special assistance for passengers such as those who may need wheelchairs or who are young children traveling alone. These agents are also responsible for resolving any passenger problems or issues. Many of them perform ticket, gate, and/or ramp duties as well.

Cargo Agents are also airline employees. They work for air carriers that transport only cargo or both passengers and cargo. These agents are responsible for receiving and processing cargo and freight shipments from customers and freight forwarders (companies that handle shipments for customers). Cargo Agents also provide customers with information about an airline's cargo services, rates, packaging requirements, and so forth. They may load and unload packages, mail, and freight on and off trucks and aircraft.

Baggage Service Agents are responsible for handling airline passengers whose luggage may be missing, lost, or damaged. These agents track luggage through computer systems and other resources and inform passengers of their whereabouts. They assure passengers that their bags will be held or forwarded to them in a timely manner. Baggage Service Agents also complete required paperwork for reimbursements to passengers, as well as discuss terms of settlement for their damaged or lost luggage.

Many airline Customer Service Agents work outdoors on the ramp, or apron, where aircraft are parked while passengers board or disembark. Most of these agents rarely have direct contact with passengers, but they play a valuable role in the quality of customer service that airlines offer their customers. These agents perform different jobs, such as unloading baggage, fueling the aircraft, or replenishing food supplies in the galley. Often times, they must perform their tasks in a short period of time—sometimes as little as 20 to 30 minutes. A few of these agents are described below.

Ramp Service Agents are responsible for loading and unloading passengers' baggage, mail, and cargo; marshaling aircraft; fueling aircraft; deicing aircraft windshields; and other duties. These agents operate forklifts, baggage conveyors, baggage vehicles, and other machinery.

Fleet Service Agents clean and maintain the interior of the aircraft. Some of their tasks include washing cockpit windows, vacuuming, throwing away trash, and washing lavatories. They also refold blankets and restock items, such as safety instructions and magazines, in the cabin. In addition, some of them are responsible for washing and polishing the exterior of the aircraft.

Provisioning Agents are responsible for stocking aircraft with food, beverages, blankets, pillows, headphones, and other products that might be offered to passengers. They transport supplies from warehouses to the aircraft. Their other duties might include stocking and taking inventory of warehouse items and performing shipping and receiving functions.

Most Customer Service Agents, particularly those who are employed by the airlines, wear uniforms on the job. Depending on their position, Customer Service Agents may do a considerable amount of standing and walking. Those working outdoors are exposed to aircraft fumes and noise.

Customer Service Agents work full time or part time. Most of them work rotating shifts, which may include working nights, weekends, or holidays.

Salaries

Salaries vary for the different customer service positions. The wages for a particular occupation also vary, depending on such factors as seniority, employer, and geographical location. In general, Customer Service Agents earn between $15,000 and $32,000 or more per year.

Many airlines offer free or reduced airline tickets to agents and their immediate families.

Employment Prospects

Customer Service Agents are hired either by airlines or airports. Some of them are employed by firms that offer services, such as ramp or skycap services, to airlines or airports on a contractual basis.

Customer service jobs are available at the different types of airlines—regional, major, independent, and so on. Usually, the larger the airport, the greater variety and number of job opportunities are available. Opportunities generally become available as Customer Service Agents transfer to other positions, retire, or leave the work force, but competition for jobs is stiff.

Keep in mind that the aviation industry is influenced by the health of the economy. During economic downturns, people and businesses take fewer trips, thus causing airlines and airports to hire fewer people and oftentimes lay off personnel.

Advancement Prospects

In the airlines, Customer Service Agents earn higher wages and advance up the ranks as they gain seniority. Depending on their interests and ambitions, agents can seek managerial, administrative, or training positions within their departments. With additional education and experience, Customer Service Agents can pursue other occupations in aviation, such as a pilot, flight attendant, aviation mechanic, airport manager, air traffic controller, or airline sales representative.

Education and Training

Minimally, Customer Service Agents must have a high school diploma or a general equivalency diploma. Employers may prefer to hire candidates with college training for some occupations, such as a passenger service agent.

New hires receive training, which may include classroom training that lasts several days or weeks. They complete recurrent training to maintain and learn new skills and job procedures.

Special Requirements

Some Customer Service Agents are required to possess a valid state driver's license with a good driving record. Ramp agents may also need to have the proper licensure for driving large trucks, forklifts, and other vehicles.

Experience, Special Skills, and Personality Traits

Requirements vary for the different occupations. Some employers require no previous work experience for entry-level positions; whereas others may require that applicants have one or more years of related work experience. For example, an employer might seek candidates for passenger service agents who have two to three years of working with the public. The experience may have been gained through performing such jobs as a salesclerk, customer service representative, or receptionist.

Employers typically look for candidates who are well groomed and physically fit. For positions dealing directly with the public, candidates should have a clear speaking voice and be able to communicate in the English language. Some positions may require that agents be able to handle packages that weigh 25 or more pounds.

Employers usually require that applicants be U.S. citizens or have the proper paperwork that authorizes their eligibility to work in the United States. In addition, applicants must meet a minimum age requirement, usually between 18 and 21 years.

Customer Service Agents must have excellent communication, teamwork, interpersonal, and customer service skills to do their work effectively. They also need good writing skills, and many positions require that agents be computer literate. In addition, they need strong self-management skills, which include the ability to work independently, handle stressful situations, understand and follow directions, meet deadlines, and organize and prioritize tasks.

Being energetic, cooperative, efficient, outgoing, calm, and courteous are some personality traits that successful Customer Service Agents share.

Unions and Associations

Many Customer Service Agents are members of a union, which represents them in contract negotiations with their employers. The union seeks to get the best contract terms in regards to pay, benefits, and working conditions. It also handles any grievances that agents have against their employers.

Tips for Entry

1. To gain work experience, you might get a seasonal or temporary job with an airline or airport. Many airlines and airports need extra help during holiday and summer seasons when travel is usually higher. Contact the airlines or airports where you would like to work to learn about short-term openings. Be sure to call a few months ahead.
2. Many airlines accept applications and résumés even though there are no openings. They usually keep them on file for six months.
3. Don't assume that a job title refers to the same job in all companies. Always ask for a copy of the job description for a position in which you are interested, and read it carefully. Make sure it is the job you want and that you meet the qualifications before applying for it.
4. Use the Internet to learn more about an airline or airport where you are interested in working. Enter the name of the airline or airport into a search engine to find its Web site. (Note: Not all airlines and airports have a Web site.)

PASSENGER SERVICE AGENT

CAREER PROFILE

Duties: Sell and issue airline tickets; check in passengers and their baggage; board passengers onto flights; assist passengers with their problems; may perform security duties and/or ramp duties; perform duties as required

Alternate Title(s): Customer Service Agent; Gate Agent; Station Agent; Ticket Agent

Salary Range: $17,000 to $45,000

Employment Prospects: Good

Advancement Prospects: Fair

Prerequisites:

Education or Training—High school diploma; completion of employer's training program

Experience—One or more years of previous work experience in customer service

Special Skills and Personality Traits—Be fluent in English; fluency in a foreign language may be required; communication, interpersonal, customer service, problem-solving, computer, writing, math, and self-management skills; helpful, friendly, enthusiastic, polite, diplomatic, energetic, flexible

Special Requirements—Driver's license

CAREER LADDER

Lead Passenger Service Agent

Passenger Service Agent

Trainee

Position Description

Passenger Service Agents are responsible for providing customer service to passengers at the airports that their airlines serve. They work at an airline's ticket counters and at the gates where passengers board onto and disembark from aircraft.

At ticket counters, Passenger Service Agents sell airline tickets, make reservations, and issue airline tickets for scheduled flights. They collect payments and keep accurate records of sales. Those agents who work exclusively at ticket counters are known as ticket agents.

Passenger Service Agents also check in passengers at the airline ticket counters. They verify names on passenger lists, examine passengers' identification, assign them flight seats, and issue boarding passes that authorize passengers to board their flights. Agents also check in passengers' luggage for shipment in the cargo section of the aircraft. Further, they direct passengers to the gates where they will board their flights.

At the gates, Passenger Service Agents coordinate the boarding of passengers as well as the arrival of passengers and crew from inbound flights. To ensure that the process is done smoothly and efficiently, agents are in constant communication with staff members at the ticket counter, operations center, ramp services, and other areas. Those who work exclusively at the gate counters are called gate agents.

Gate agents also assist departing and arriving passengers. They answer questions and direct passengers to places in the airport such as the baggage claims area. They also coordinate special assistance services for passengers such as the disabled, elderly, parents with infants, and young children who are traveling alone. For example, agents make sure wheelchairs or electric carts are waiting at gates for arriving passengers who require them. In addition, gate agents are responsible for informing inflight crews about any special needs and requests of passengers.

Passenger Service Agents open gate doors when it is time for boarding. They check tickets or boarding passes to make sure passengers are authorized to board a flight. Agents also control the flow of traffic, so the boarding is done in a smooth and orderly manner. In addition, they monitor the number and size of carry-on bags that passengers have, and if necessary, check in luggage into cargo.

Furthermore, Passenger Service Agents resolve passengers' complaints or problems. For example, an agent might help passengers obtain seats on another airline when they missed their connecting flight.

Some Passenger Service Agents assist in the maintenance of the safety and security of their airlines. Following company policies and procedures, agents screen passengers and luggage for prohibited items such as firearms, sharp objects, flammable items, and explosive materials. Agents might perform hand-wand or pat-down inspections on passengers. They might also open and examine passengers' luggage.

At smaller airports, Passenger Service Agents might perform ramp duties. Their tasks may include loading and unloading baggage, mail and cargo; marshaling aircraft; operating ground service equipment; deicing aircraft; and calculating the weight and balance of aircraft.

Some Passenger Service Agents may also work in airline ticket offices, which are usually located in downtown areas of large cities. They sell and issue tickets directly to customers. They answer general inquiries about flight schedules and fares in person or over the telephone. In addition, these agents promote special travel packages offered by their airline.

Agents' work can oftentimes become stressful, particularly during busy periods such as holidays, and when flights are delayed or canceled due to severe weather, mechanical problems, or for other reasons. Passenger Service Agents are expected to handle frustrated, angry, or upset passengers with a professional, calm, and friendly demeanor.

Passenger Service Agents usually work rotating shifts, which may include working nights, weekends, or holidays. On occasion, they are required to work overtime. Agents may be employed full time, part time, or on a temporary basis.

Salaries

Salaries for airline Passenger Service Agents vary, depending on such factors as their position, seniority, employer, and geographical location. The U.S. Bureau of Labor Statistics, in its May 2003 *Occupational Employment Statistics* survey, reports that the estimated annual salary for most transportation ticket agents ranged from $17,270 to $44,660.

Employers may provide agents with free or discounted airline tickets for themselves and their immediate families, as part of their fringe benefits.

Employment Prospects

Most Passenger Service Agents work in major metropolitan areas where large airports are located. Passenger Service Agents are employed by the different types of commercial airlines—regional, major, international, and so on. Some agents are employed by companies that perform customer services for airlines on a contractual basis.

Opportunities generally become available as Passenger Service Agents resign, transfer to other positions, or retire. A recent trend among many airlines is to hire temporary agents or permanent part-time agents.

Keep in mind that the airline industry fluctuates with the health of the economy. Usually, during recessions, airlines tend to lay off personnel as well as hire fewer new employees.

Advancement Prospects

Passenger Service Agents can be promoted to supervisory and management positions as well as training instructor jobs. Many agents use this job to advance to other positions in sales, customer service, and flight operations departments.

Education and Training

Passenger Service Agents are required to possess a high school diploma or a general equivalency diploma. Some employers require or strongly prefer that candidates have one or two years of college training.

New agents typically attend several weeks of a formal training program, which covers such topics as company policies, federal aviation regulations, ground operations, and computerized reservations systems.

Special Requirements

Applicants may be required to possess a valid driver's license.

Airlines typically require that applicants be U.S. citizens or have authorized paperwork that allows them to work in the United States. In addition, applicants must meet a minimum age requirement, usually between 18 and 20 years.

Experience, Special Skills, and Personality Traits

Most employers require that Passenger Service Agents have one or more years of previous customer service experience, which may have been gained as reservation agents, ticket agents, salesclerks, or in other positions.

Airlines typically choose candidates who are well groomed and physically fit. It is usually required that applicants' weight be in proportion to their height. They must maintain that requirement throughout their employment as Passenger Service Agents. Airlines also look for candidates who can speak and understand English fluently. International airlines may require candidates to be fluent in a foreign language such as Spanish or French.

Passenger Service Agents need excellent communication, interpersonal, customer service, and problem-solving skills, as they are dealing constantly with customers from diverse backgrounds. They also need good computer, writing, and math skills. Further, they should have strong self-management skills, including the ability to handle stressful situations, meet deadlines, organize and prioritize tasks, and work independently.

Being helpful, friendly, enthusiastic, polite, diplomatic, energetic, and flexible are some personality traits that successful Passenger Service Agents share.

Unions and Associations

Many Passenger Service Agents are members of a union, such as the Communications Workers of America, which represents them in contract negotiations with their employers. The union seeks to get the best contract terms in regards to pay, benefits, and working conditions. It also handles any grievances that agents have against their employers.

Tips for Entry

1. Talk with various Passenger Service Agents to learn more about their work and how they obtained their jobs.
2. You can sometimes obtain job applications at airline ticket counters or offices.
3. Many airlines hold job fairs (or group sessions) to inform applicants about Passenger Service Agent positions as well as to screen for potential candidates. Dress and act appropriately when going to a job fair. Also be ready to provide a résumé and handle an interview.
4. Learn as much as you can about an airline before you go to your job interview. Most airlines have a Web site that provides information about the company. Enter an airline's name into a search engine to find the Web site. Check out every link on its Web site.

AIRLINE RESERVATIONS AGENT

CAREER PROFILE

Duties: Provide customers with information about flight schedules, rates, and availability of seats; make reservations; help customers complete their travel plans; perform additional duties as required

Alternate Title(s): Reservation Sales Agent; Sales Associate; Airline Reservationist; Customer Service Agent

Salary Range: $17,000 to $45,000

Employment Prospects: Good

Advancement Prospects: Fair

Prerequisites:

Education or Training—High school diploma; completion of employer's training program

Experience—One or more years of sales, telemarketing, public relations, or other job working with the public

Special Skills and Personality Traits—Fluency in English; communication, interpersonal, customer service, spelling, keyboarding (or typing), computer, and self-management skills; friendly, courteous, calm, detail-oriented, accurate, dependable, efficient

CAREER LADDER

Lead Reservations Agent

Reservations Agent

Trainee

Position Description

Most, if not all, airlines offer customers the opportunity to purchase their tickets for scheduled flights directly over the telephone. Reservations Agents are responsible for making these telephone sales and for booking seats for customers. The customers will then receive confirmation of their booked flights through the U.S. postal service, by e-mail, or by overnight delivery services. Reservation Agents are also responsible for confirming and changing reservations for customers.

Reservations Agents usually work in large phone centers at airline offices. (A few airlines allow their agents to work at home.) Most of their day is spent answering telephones and working at computers. To complete customer transactions, Reservations Agents access automated reservations systems. When computer systems are down, agents rely on airline guides, company manuals, and other materials to determine routes and fares. All reservations made during this time are documented on paper.

Airline Reservations Agents are responsible for knowing the policies of their company and the airline industry. In addition, they are familiar with flight safety procedures and federal aviation regulations.

Reservations Agents often help customers complete their business or personal travel plans. Customers tell agents where and when they wish to travel and how many people are in their traveling party. Then Reservations Agents perform a search in the airline's computer reservation system to find scheduled flights that meet customers' particular travel requirements.

Agents provide customers with information about flight schedules, which may be nonstop flights or flights that involve one or more connecting flights. They try to match departure and return times as closely as possible to customers' needs. The agents inform customers of the availability of seats and quote fares, including any discounted rates for which customers may qualify. Reservations Agents may recommend routes and schedules with other airlines if their own airlines do not fit customers' particular needs.

Reservations Agents also describe any specials that their airline may be offering for a limited time period. For example, an airline might offer discounts on flights to certain cities or travel packages that include air transportation, car rental, and hotel accommodations. At some airlines, Reservations Agents are able to provide customers with information about lodging and car rental rates and may make those reservations for customers.

When customers decide on an itinerary, Reservations Agents reserve seats on those flights for them. If a trip involves connecting flights on different airlines, such as an international flight, Reservations Agents usually complete reservations for the entire trip. Customers make payments for their tickets by providing agents with their credit card information. Reservations Agents make sure they have inputted customers' information correctly and accurately into the computer by confirming spellings, addresses, times, amounts, and so forth.

Although unseen by the public, Reservations Agents are usually the first contact that customers have with airlines. They are expected to speak clearly and in a professional, efficient, and friendly manner at all times. This can sometimes be challenging when they are met with customers who may be demanding, indecisive, hostile, or overly talkative.

These agents' job can also become stressful during busy periods of holiday travel or when computer systems are down. In addition, Reservations Agents may become stressed when they are flooded with calls from customers about flights that are delayed or canceled because of weather or problems with aircraft.

To ensure the quality of agents' job performance, their telephone conversations with customers may be monitored.

Reservations Agents work full time or part time. Some airlines hire Reservations Agents on a temporary basis. They are usually assigned to rotating shifts and may be scheduled to work nights, weekends, or holidays.

Salaries

Salaries for airline Reservations Agents vary, depending on such factors as their seniority, employer, and geographical location. Agents typically earn an hourly rate, with those working afternoon and evening shifts generally earning more. According to Avjobs.com, the annual salary range for airline Reservations Agents ranged between $12,000 to $38,600. The U.S. Bureau of Labor Statistics reports, in its May 2003 *Occupational Employment Statistics* survey that the estimated annual salary for most reservationists (in all industries) ranged from $17,270 to $44,660.

Employers may provide agents with free or discounted airline tickets for themselves and their immediate families, as part of their fringe benefits.

Employment Prospects

Reservations Agents are employed by the different types of commercial airlines—regional, national, major, and so on. Some agents are employed by companies that perform customer service for airlines on a contractual basis.

Job openings for Reservations Agents usually become available as replacements are needed for those who retire, transfer to other positions, or leave the workforce.

Employment in the airline industry fluctuates with the health of the economy. During recessions, airlines tend to lay off personnel as well as hire fewer employees.

Advancement Prospects

Reservations Agents earn promotions and choices of work shifts, according to their seniority.

The position of Reservations Agent is an entry-level position. Advancement prospects within the reservations departments are limited to lead or supervisory positions. Depending on an individual's interests and ambitions, Reservations Agents can also seek occupations in another airline department, such as training, passenger service, sales, or office administration.

Education and Training

The minimum educational requirement for Reservations Agents is a high school diploma or a general equivalency diploma. Some employers require or prefer to hire candidates who have completed one or two years of college training, particularly in airline operations.

New Reservations Agents complete a formal training program that covers company policies, computer systems, reservations procedures, telephone skills, federal aviation regulations, and other topics. After their classroom instruction, agents receive on-the-job training while working under the supervision of experienced Reservations Agents.

Before they can be hired, prospective candidates must pass a selection process that may include a drug screen testing, security check, and background investigation.

Experience, Special Skills, and Personality Traits

Depending on the employer, candidates may be required to have one or more years of experience working directly with the public. Many employers prefer to hire candidates who have sales, customer service, or other public relations work experience.

Airlines typically require that applicants be U.S. citizens or have the proper paperwork that authorizes their ability to work in the United States. In addition, applicants must meet a minimum age requirement, usually between 18 and 20 years.

Reservations Agents must have a clear speaking voice and be able to speak and understand English fluently. Having excellent communication, interpersonal, and customer service skills is essential. They should also have competent spelling and keyboarding (or typing) skills as well as basic computer skills. Further, Reservations Agents need strong self-management skills, such as being able to work independently, handle stressful situations, and organize and prioritize tasks.

Being friendly, courteous, calm, detail-oriented, accurate, dependable, and efficient are some personality traits that successful Reservations Agents share.

Unions and Associations

Many Reservations Agents are members of a union, such as the Communications Workers of America, which represents them in contract negotiations with their employers. The union seeks to get the best contract terms in regards to pay, benefits, and working conditions. It also handles any grievances that agents have against their employers.

Tips for Entry

1. During peak travel seasons, airlines sometimes hire Reservations Agents for part-time or temporary positions.
2. Contact an airline's human resources office for information about current job opportunities, job requirements, and their selection processes.
3. Many airlines prefer to hire applicants who live in or near cities where their reservations centers are located.
4. To enhance your employability, you might consider enrolling in one or more courses in airline operations at a travel school or community college.
5. You can learn about different airlines on the Internet. If an airline has a Web site, you can usually find it by entering its name into any search engine.

AIR CARGO AGENT

CAREER PROFILE

Duties: Receive and process packages and freight shipments; perform customer service duties; perform other duties as required

Alternate Title(s): Air Freight Agent; Customer Service Representative

Salary Range: $19,000 to $52,000

Employment Prospects: Fair

Advancement Prospects: Fair

Prerequisites:

Education or Training—High school diploma; completion of a flight attendant's training program

Experience—One or more years of experience in customer service and shipping operations is preferred

Special Skills and Personality Traits—Communication, interpersonal, customer service, math, telephone, computer, and self-management skills; energetic, friendly, calm, courteous, organized, decisive, detail-oriented

Special Requirements—Driver's license may be required

CAREER LADDER

Lead Air Cargo Agent

Air Cargo Agent

Trainee

Position Description

Air Cargo Agents are responsible for providing efficient and friendly customer service for commercial airlines that offer air cargo services. Their major duties include providing information about air cargo services, receiving and processing shipment orders, and helping customers with their orders. They are employed by air carriers that carry only cargo, as well as those that transport both passengers and cargo.

Millions of tons of air cargo are shipped each year throughout the world on commercial airlines. Individuals, businesses, companies, institutions, and other organizations ship packages, mail, and freight for personal and business purposes. These include perishable and nonperishable food; animals and livestock; gems, money, and other valuables; textiles; paper products; engineering goods; chemical and pharmaceutical products; human remains; and so forth. Air Cargo Agents are responsible for knowing airline requirements, as well as federal, state, and international regulations regarding acceptable and forbidden air cargo.

Air Cargo Agents work in offices at or near airports, and much of their job involves the operation of telephones, computers, and calculators. (They often are the only contacts that customers have with an airline.) Cargo Agents handle shipment orders directly from individuals, businesses, organizations, and so on. They also take care of shipment orders from freight forwarders, which are businesses that arrange air transportation of cargo or freight belonging to others.

These Agents generally perform the same tasks when receiving packages and freight shipment orders. They check that the orders are properly packaged and, if warranted, inspect them for security purposes. They weigh packages or freight, and determine shipping costs according to weight, type of delivery service (such as overnight delivery or two-day service), destination, tariffs, and other charges that may apply. They then quote rates to customers. Air Cargo Agents usually accept payment in the form of cash, check, or credit card from customers.

Air Cargo Agents are also responsible for the processing of all required documentation that goes with each shipment. They review cargo airway bills that accompany shipments to ensure that the customers have provided all shipping information. The agents make sure they enter each airway bill number accurately into their company's computer system, which is used for tracking and other purposes. Air Cargo Agents also verify that customs paperwork for international shipments is in order.

In addition, Air Cargo Agents determine the best route and flights to send shipments in order to reach their destinations within the time frame requested by customers.

Some Air Cargo Agents are involved in assembling cargo according to their destinations, and preparing accompanying manifests. Depending on the size of the operation, Air Cargo Agents may load items onto trucks that haul the cargo to departing flights. They may also unload shipments from incoming trucks.

Air Cargo Agents perform various other customer service tasks. For example, they might:

- provide the public with general information about their airline's air cargo services, such as flight schedules, rates, and packaging instructions
- notify customers of the arrival of shipments and make arrangements for pickup or delivery
- provide information to customers about the status of their incoming or outgoing shipments
- track and locate shipments for customers
- notify customers of delays in the departure of their shipments

Furthermore, Air Cargo Agents are responsible for maintaining accurate records about cargo shipments. For example, they log missing items, report conditions of damaged goods, and keep files on dangerous goods that have been shipped. Some agents are also responsible for completing reports on outbound cargo.

Air Cargo Agents may be employed part time or full time. Many of them work rotating shifts, which may include working nights and weekends.

Salaries

Salaries for Air Cargo Agents vary, depending on factors such as their seniority, employer, and geographical location. According to the May 2003 *Occupational Employment Statistics* survey (by the U.S. Bureau of Labor Statistics), the estimated annual salary for most cargo agents (in all industries) ranged between $19,080 and $51,750.

Employment Prospects

Most opportunities for Air Cargo Agents become available as agents retire, transfer to other positions, or leave the workforce altogether. Employers may create additional positions as their companies expand.

Advancement Prospects

With additional experience, Cargo Agents may advance to lead agent, ramp service planner, and supervisor positions. They can also follow career paths that lead to air cargo management or sales.

Education and Training

Minimally, Air Cargo Agents must hold a high school diploma or a general equivalency diploma.

New hires must successfully complete a formal training program provided by their employers. The program covers such topics as company policies, federal aviation regulations, security precautions, job procedures, airway bill preparation, tariffs, and hazardous material guidelines. Agents receive recurrent training to maintain and update their skills.

Special Requirements

Employers usually require that applicants possess a valid driver's license, with a good driving record. Applicants must be U.S. citizens or possess the proper authorization to work in the United States. In addition, applicants must meet a minimum age requirement, which usually varies between 18 and 21 years.

Before they can be hired, prospective candidates must pass a selection process that may include a drug screen testing, security check, and background investigation.

Experience, Special Skills, and Personality Traits

Employers prefer to hire candidates who have one or more years of experience in customer service and shipping operations. Being physically strong is also essential.

Air Cargo Agents must have strong communication, interpersonal, and customer service skills. Their job also requires that they have good math, telephone, and computer skills. In addition, they have strong self-management skills, which include the abilities to work independently, manage several tasks at the same time, meet deadlines, and handle stressful situations.

Some personality traits that successful Air Cargo Agents share are being energetic, friendly, calm, courteous, organized, decisive, and detail-oriented.

Unions and Associations

Many Air Cargo Agents are members of labor unions, which represent them in contract negotiations with their employers. Unions seek to get the best terms in regards to pay, benefits, and working conditions. They also handle any grievances that agents may have with their employers.

Tips for Entry

1. Enroll in such high school courses as math, computers, English, and speech to help you prepare for a career as an Air Cargo Agent.
2. To gain entry into the field, you might start by obtaining a position as a cargo handler with an air carrier. Employment as a warehouse worker, shipping clerk,

or inventory clerk and similar occupations also provide valuable experience.

3. Contact airlines directly to learn about job vacancies and their job selection process.
4. Ask a job counselor or friend to help you prepare for a job interview. Practice answering such questions as Why are you qualified for this position? Why should you be hired? What are your best strengths? What are your weaknesses? What do you expect to be doing in five years? What experiences do you have that qualify you for this job?
5. Learn more about the air cargo industry on the Internet. To get a list of relevant Web sites, enter the keywords *air cargo services* into any search engine.

RAMP SERVICE AGENT (AIRLINES)

CAREER PROFILE

Duties: Load and unload baggage, mail, and cargo; marshal aircraft in and out of terminal gates; fuel and service aircraft; clean and maintain the interior and exterior of aircraft; perform other duties as required

Alternate Title(s): Ramp Clerk; Ramp Agent; a title that reflects a specific position such as Baggage Handler; Aircraft Fueler; or Fleet Service Agent

Salary Range: $15,000 to $31,000

Employment Prospects: Fair

Advancement Prospects: Fair

Prerequisites:

Education or Training—High school diploma; completion of a flight attendant's training program

Experience—Previous experience in ramp services preferred

Special Skills and Personality Traits—Have a mechanical aptitude; physically fit; able to read and write English; teamwork, interpersonal, communication, self-management, and problem-solving skills; energetic; dedicated, detail-oriented, reliable, self-motivated

Special Requirements—Driver's license

CAREER LADDER

Lead Ramp Service Agent

Ramp Service Agent

Trainee

Position Description

Airlines use their aircraft to fly several scheduled flights each day. Getting an aircraft ready for the next flight is known as turning the aircraft around. Those in charge of seeing that the turnaround is done quickly and efficiently are the Ramp Service Agents. From the moment an aircraft pulls onto the ramp at the terminal gate until the moment it is pushed back from the gate, various Ramp Service Agents are working in sync to complete a variety of tasks. They service and clean the aircraft, as well as unload and load passengers, baggage, mail, and cargo. It is not uncommon for the ramp crew to have 15 to 45 minutes to turn an aircraft around in order for a flight to stay on schedule.

Here is what generally happens on a turnaround for aircraft that transport both passengers and cargo: Before an aircraft arrives at its assigned gate, the Ramp Service Agents prepare for its arrival by having all necessary supplies and machinery in place and ready to go. When the aircraft reaches the gate, Ramp Service Agents use orange wands to make appropriate hand signals to guide the pilot to a parking position.

When the aircraft has stopped, agents chock the wheels of the nose gear to make sure it doesn't move. Then other agents hook up the jetbridge, or jetway. This is the mobile bridge that passengers use to walk between the aircraft door and the airport terminal. Sometimes, Ramp Service Agents attach mobile stairs to the aircraft for passengers to ascend into or descend from the aircraft.

At the same time, other Ramp Service Agents open the door to the cargo bay and unload the passengers' baggage as well as mail and cargo. Ramp Service Agents sort the baggage, mail, and cargo for their next destinations, which may be connecting flights, the airport baggage claims area, or the air cargo offices. The agents also transport all items to the appropriate locations. Once the unloading is complete, other

Ramp Service Agents arrive to fill the cargo bay with baggage, mail, and cargo for the next flight.

Still other Ramp Service Agents are busy filling the fuel tank, washing cockpit windows, and performing other service jobs. During weather conditions when ice, frost, or snow can accumulate on the aircraft, especially the wings, the servicers are responsible for deicing the aircraft. They spray a special solution over an aircraft's surface to remove as well as to prevent the further accumulation of ice, frost, or snow.

Inside the aircraft, some agents are performing a variety of light housekeeping duties such as vacuuming, picking up trash, cleaning lavatories, folding blankets, restocking seat packets, refilling the drinking water supply, replenishing first-aid supplies, and so forth. Furthermore, other personnel—caterers and food and beverage agents—are loading snacks, meals, and beverages for the next flight.

When passengers are all boarded and the cargo compartments are loaded and secured, the Ramp Service Agents help the pilots prepare for departure. They pull jetway bridges or mobile stairs away from the aircraft, perform a final walk around the aircraft to make sure all doors and compartments are secured, and remove the chocks from behind the wheels. Using special equipment, the Ramp Service Agents then push the aircraft away from the gates and guide the pilots to a position where they can begin their taxiing down the runway.

Ramp Service Agents repeat this same scenario several times a day—sometimes turning around 12 flights in one work shift.

Depending on the size of the ground crew operations, a Ramp Service Agent may be responsible for one or several duties. Many Ramp Service Agents perform multiple tasks, and often hold the title *Ramp Agent.* In some operations, Ramp Service Agents perform specific roles. The following are the more common types of agents:

- *Baggage Handlers* are responsible for loading and unloading baggage, as well as sorting and distributing baggage to connecting flights or to airport baggage claim areas.
- *Cargo Handlers* are responsible for loading and unloading cargo compartments as well as for transporting cargo to connecting flights and air cargo offices. Some handlers also have the responsibility for positioning and securing the cargo in the aircraft.
- *Aircraft Fuelers* are responsible for filling aircraft with fuel and keeping fuel trucks filled with aviation fuel.
- *Fleet Service Agents* are responsible for cleaning and maintaining the interiors and exteriors of the aircraft. (They are also known as aircraft servicers, or aircraft appearance technicians.) These agents usually perform a more thorough cleaning of aircraft at night when they are out of service. They also replace carpets and seat covers, as well as touch up the paint whenever it is needed.
- *Aircraft Drivers* are responsible for driving various vehicles, such as fuel trucks and employee buses, to and from the airports. Additionally, they are responsible for operating mobile stairs, jetways, power carts, conveyors, and other machinery on the ramp.

At some airlines, Ramp Service Agents might also perform the role of gate agents. As gate agents, they help coordinate the boarding and deplaning of passengers. They also help passengers with their special needs, such as escorting disabled passengers on board. In addition, they handle passengers' problems, such as finding new flights for passengers who missed their flight connections.

Ramp Service Agents work mostly outdoors on the ramp in all kinds of weather conditions—hot, windy, rainy, icy, and so forth. At times, many of them work in confined spaces. Ramp Service Agents are typically under pressure to make deadlines. They may feel additional stress when flights arrive late or several flights arrive at the same time because of bad weather conditions or other reasons.

Ramp Service Agents are trained to be safety conscious at all times. They are exposed to moving aircraft and equipment, aircraft engine noises, gas fumes, and hazardous materials. In addition, their work is physically demanding. They are constantly climbing, bending, kneeling, crawling, and stooping in their work. They lift and move heavy items that often weigh between 75 to 100 pounds. Thus, Ramp Service Agents observe strict safety rules and follow standard procedures for performing their various tasks.

Ramp Service Agents wear uniforms on the job. They are employed part time or full time. They are usually assigned to rotating work shifts, which may include working nights, weekends, and holidays. On occasion, Ramp Service Agents may be required to work overtime.

Salaries

Wages for Ramp Service Agents vary and depend on such factors as position, experience, employer, union contract, and geographical location. The annual salaries for these agents generally range between $15,000 and $31,000. Those working late-afternoon and night shifts may earn additional pay.

Employers may provide Ramp Service Agents with free or discounted airline tickets for themselves and their immediate families, as part of their fringe benefits.

Employment Prospects

Ramp Service Agents are employed by airlines as well as by aviation service firms who perform ramp services for airlines on a contractual basis. Ramp Service Agents are also employed in general aviation, working for FBOs (fixed base operators), corporate flight departments, air charter companies, and so on. In general aviation, these agents are often known as line service technicians or similar titles.

Most job opportunities are created to replace Ramp Service Agents who are retiring, transferring to other positions, or leaving the workforce. Airlines will create additional positions as their companies grow and expand. However, keep in mind that the airline industry fluctuates with the health of the economy. Usually, during recessions, airlines tend to lay off personnel as well as hire fewer new employees.

Advancement Prospects

Ramp Service Agents earn higher wages and advance up the ranks as they gain seniority. As they gain additional experience, they can seek such positions as ramp loaders, baggage planners, and operations agents. Those interested in administrative and managerial positions may become crew leaders and supervisors in their work areas, such as in baggage handling or fleet service.

With appropriate training and experience, Ramp Service Agents can also seek another occupation in aviation such as an aviation mechanic, passenger service agent, pilot, airline sales representative, air traffic controllers, or airport manager.

Education and Training

The minimum educational requirement for Ramp Service Agents is a high school diploma or a general equivalency diploma.

Newly hired Ramp Service Agents must successfully complete a training program which covers such topics as company policies, safety measures, job procedures, and handling of equipment. Agents receive training as they are assigned to new duties, new equipment is put into service, or new job procedures are being instituted.

Special Requirements

Applicants for Ramp Service Agents must possess a valid state driver's license and a good driving record. They may also need to have the proper licensure for driving large trucks, forklifts, and other vehicles. Additionally, applicants must be U.S. citizens or have the proper authorization that allows them to work in the United States. They must also meet a minimum age requirement, which varies from 18 to 21 years.

Experience, Special Skills, and Personality Traits

Some employers hire applicants with no previous work experience, but in general, most employers prefer to hire candidates who have some experience working in ramp services. Their experience may have been gained by working as ramp personnel at other airlines or as line service technicians in general aviation settings.

Employers look for candidates who have some mechanical aptitude, such as the ability to operate machinery. Candidates should also be well-groomed and able to routinely handle items up to 70 or more pounds. In addition, employers seek candidates who can read and write English.

To do their work effectively, Ramp Service Agents must have strong teamwork, interpersonal, and communication skills. Their job also requires that they have excellent self-management skills, which include the ability to understand and follow directions, organize and prioritize multiple tasks, handle stressful situations, and work independently. Having good problem-solving skills is important too. Some personality traits that successful Ramp Service Agents share are being energetic, dedicated, detail-oriented, reliable, and self-motivated.

Unions and Associations

Airline Ramp Service Agents are usually members of a union, which represents them in contract negotiations with their employers. The union seeks to get the best contract terms in regard to pay, benefits, and working conditions. It also handles any grievances that agents have against their employers.

Tips for Entry

1. As a high school student, you may be able to start gaining experience at a local general aviation airport. Sometimes FBOs and air-taxi companies hire high school students to wash and fuel planes and perform other line service tasks.
2. Some two-year colleges and high school occupational programs offer a program in ramp operations. To enhance your employability, consider completing such a program or enrolling in one or more courses.
3. Many airlines require that you give a complete history of your employment, training, and residences when you apply for a job, often as far back as 10 years. To make sure you have all the information you need, prepare a list of your previous employers, schools, training programs, and residences. Check that all dates, addresses, phone numbers, and names are correct and accurate.
4. Many airlines post job descriptions and job vacancies at their Web sites. To find out if a particular airline has a Web site, enter its name into any search engine. At the airline's Web site, look for a link with a title such as *careers* or *employment.*

AIRCRAFT MAINTENANCE

AVIATION MAINTENANCE TECHNICIAN (AMT)

CAREER PROFILE

Duties: Perform aircraft maintenance and repairs; may be engaged in different types of assignments such as maintenance, inspections, troubleshooting, emergency repairs; perform duties as required

Alternate Title(s): Aircraft Mechanic; a title that reflects a specialty such as Airframe Mechanic; Avionics Technician; or Helicopter Mechanic

Salary Range: $28,000 to $64,000

Employment Prospects: Good

Advancement Prospects: Good

Prerequisites:

Education or Training—High school diploma; may have completed a formal AMT program; complete employer's training program

Experience—Entry-level candidates should have gained experience through formal AMT training, military AMT experience, or apprenticeship; experience with the type of aircraft or components on which they would be working

Special Skills and Personality Traits—Organizational, troubleshooting, problem-solving, communication, interpersonal, teamwork, writing, and computer skills; detail-oriented, cooperative, self-motivated, enthusiastic, energetic

Special Requirements—FAA mechanic certificate may be required

CAREER LADDER

Lead Aviation Maintenance Technician

Aviation Maintenance Technician

Trainee or Apprentice Aviation Maintenance Technician

Position Description

Aviation Maintenance Technicians (AMTs) play a very important role in aviation safety. Their job is to keep aircraft—airplanes, helicopters, and jets—in safe, efficient, and reliable working condition. They are responsible for maintaining and repairing aircraft and all their various complex parts and systems—engines, wings, landing gear, propellers, hydraulic systems, navigational systems, and so on. At all times, AMTs must make sure that their work is in compliance with governmental regulations, company policies and protocols, and manufacturers' specifications.

AMTs are more commonly known as aircraft mechanics. They work on various aircraft, but usually focus on specific types of aircraft, such as fixed-wing airplanes, helicopters, seaplanes, turboprop airplanes, or jet aircraft.

AMTs also specialize in one of the various areas of aviation maintenance. Airframe mechanics work on the parts and systems that make up the aircraft's structure—its wings, fuselage (body), tail, and landing gear. They work on every part, except for engines, propellers, and aircraft instruments. Powerplant mechanics concentrate on aircraft engines, engine systems, and other systems related to the engine.

They may also do some work on propellers. Many AMTs specialize in both airframe and powerplant areas, and are known as airframe and powerplant (A&P) mechanics.

Other AMTs are avionics technicians, who work on electrical and electronic systems and equipment that pilots use for navigation, communication, and flight. Some AMTs specialize in repairing specific aircraft components, such as radios, navigation instruments, propellers, carburetors, and hydraulic systems.

AMTs work on commercial, corporate, private, government, and military aircraft. They are employed by airlines, corporate flight departments, government agencies, air taxi operations, air ambulance services, fixed base operators, repair shops, aircraft maintenance and repair services, and so on. AMTs also are employed by manufacturing facilities where they are involved in the development and design of new aircraft, aircraft parts, or aircraft systems.

AMTs may work in hangars and other indoor areas to perform maintenance, inspection, and repairs on aircraft. Line mechanics work outdoors at airports, where they mostly perform preventative services and repairs on aircraft between flights.

AMTs may be engaged in such activities as scheduled or unscheduled maintenance, inspections, diagnostic testing, troubleshooting, emergency repairs, major repairs, corrosion control, and alterations. Their duties and responsibilities vary, depending on their experience, specialization, position, workplace, and other factors. However, all AMTs perform similar tasks, such as:

- examine components that may require maintenance or repair
- interpret diagnostic tests
- make recommendations to supervisors, customers, or others for solving mechanical or electrical problems
- make appropriate adjustments, replacements, or repairs of parts
- read manufacturers' manuals, company maintenance manuals, blueprints, and other materials to determine what tools and equipment are needed and what job procedures must be followed
- use aviation equipment to troubleshoot problems
- use various hand tools, power tools, machinery, and equipment to complete work assignments
- place orders for aircraft parts needed for maintenance or repairs
- complete required paperwork and computer records
- maintain tools, equipment, and working environment

In the United States, all maintenance, inspections, and repairs of U.S. registered aircraft must be performed by Aviation Maintenance Technicians (or by repair shops) certified by the Federal Aviation Administration (FAA). Noncertified mechanics may perform limited duties while working under the supervision of certified AMTs.

AMTs are frequently engaged in physical activity. They might climb ladders; perch on scaffolds; crawl under wings; stoop, crouch, squat, and kneel; lift or pull objects weighing up to 70 pounds or more; and so forth. AMTs work in high places as well as in confined spaces. Their working conditions include exposure to dust, chemicals, fumes, and gases as well as vibrating machinery and high levels of noise from power tools and aircraft. Those working outdoors also deal with the varying temperatures and weather conditions.

Most AMTs wear uniforms on the job and normally supply their own hand tools.

AMTs work a 40-hour week, which may include working nights and weekends. From time to time, they may be required to work overtime. At some work sites, AMTs are on call 24 hours a day.

Salaries

Salaries vary for Aviation Maintenance Technicians, depending on such factors as their experience, certification, seniority, employer, and geographical location.

According to the May 2003 *Occupational Employment Statistics* survey (by the U.S. Bureau of Labor Statistics), the estimated annual salary for most AMTs ranged between $27,550 and $63,590.

Employment Prospects

The job market for Aviation Maintenance Technicians is expected to grow between 10 and 20 percent through 2010, according to the U.S. Bureau of Labor Statistics. Most job openings will become available as AMTs retire or transfer to other positions.

Opportunities are expected to increase in the next few years due to the large number of workers becoming eligible for retirement. However, keep in mind that job opportunities in the aviation industry generally fluctuate with the health of the economy. For example, in a sluggish economy, fewer openings for Aviation Maintenance Technicians are available.

Advancement Prospects

AMTs can develop career paths in any number of ways. Some AMTs start their careers in general aviation settings with the goal of obtaining a position with a major airline. AMTs who are interested in supervisory and management positions can become lead mechanics, aviation mechanic inspectors, aircraft maintenance controllers, aircraft maintenance supervisors, and aircraft maintenance managers. FAA mechanic certifications are usually required for AMTs to obtain higher positions.

In airlines, AMTs advance according to their seniority. All AMTs, regardless of their prior position or experience, begin at the bottom of the seniority list. With time, they build up their seniority, which results in being promoted to higher positions, earning higher pay, or receiving assignments of their choice.

Education and Training

Minimally, AMTs must possess a high school diploma or general equivalency diploma.

AMTs may learn their trade through apprenticeships or on-the-job training. Increasingly, AMTs gain entry into the field by first completing an aviation maintenance program at a technical school, two-year college, four-year college, or university. Those attending colleges or universities may also earn associate's or bachelor's degrees in avionics, aviation technology, aviation maintenance management, or other field.

Students who graduate from FAA-approved aircraft mechanic schools are eligible to apply for FAA mechanic certificates.

Employers provide new hires with training programs, which may include both formal instruction and on-the-job training.

Throughout their careers, AMTs complete training and education programs to update and sharpen their skills.

Special Requirements

Employers generally prefer to hire AMTs who possess an FAA mechanic certificate with an airframe (A), a powerplant (P), a combined airframe and powerplant (A&P), or repairman (R) rating. Certified mechanics can only work in the technical areas in which they are rated.

To obtain FAA certification, AMTs must pass a series of tests to demonstrate their knowledge and skills. They must meet the following qualifications to be eligible to take these exams:

- be at least 18 years old
- be a U.S. citizen or have the appropriate paperwork to be eligible to work in the United States
- be able to read, write, and understand English
- have 18 months of practical experience for a single rating (airframe or powerplant) or have 30 months of practical experience for an A&P rating, or be a graduate from an FAA-approved mechanic school

AMTs applying for a repairman rating are recommended by their employers.

To maintain their certificates, AMTs must complete a minimum number of hours of training.

Experience, Skills, and Personality Traits

Most AMTs gain entry into this field by completing aircraft mechanic programs. Some AMTs have previous experience as military aircraft mechanics or have completed apprenticeships, usually in general aviation settings.

Employers typically seek candidates—entry-level or experienced—who have previous maintenance experience with the type of aircraft, aircraft components, or aircraft systems on which they would be working.

Skills that AMTs need to succeed at their jobs are organizational, troubleshooting, and problem-solving skills. They also should have strong communication, interpersonal, and teamwork skills. Having basic writing and computers skills is also essential.

Some personality traits that successful AMTs share are being detail-oriented, cooperative, self-motivated, enthusiastic, and energetic.

Unions and Associations

Many AMTs belong to a union, such as the International Association of Machinists and Aerospace Workers, the Transport Workers Union of America, or the International Brotherhood of Teamsters. A union represents members in negotiations with their employers for contractual terms relating to pay, benefits, and working conditions.

AMTs may join professional associations that offer networking opportunities and other professional services and resources. The Professional Aviation Maintenance Association and the Association for Women in Aviation Maintenance are two national societies that serve the interests of AMTs.

Tips for Entry

1. In high school, start gaining knowledge about the various aircraft and how they work. For example, you can read aviation books and magazines, talk to pilots and AMTs, attend air shows, and visit aviation museums. You might also obtain a part-time job as a line service worker at a local airport.
2. You may be able to get financial aid—such as scholarships or grants—to help you with your schooling. For information, talk with a high school guidance counselor or a college career counselor.
3. Contact employers directly about job vacancies. You can find phone numbers and addresses in the yellow pages of your telephone directory under such headings as *aircraft charters, airline companies, airports,* or *aircraft servicing and maintenance.*
4. To enhance your employability and prospects for advancement, obtain an FAA mechanic certificate with an A&P rating. For more information about the FAA mechanic certificate, contact a Flight Standards District Office. You can also find information at the FAA Web site, http://www.faa.gov.
5. Learn more about Aviation Maintenance Technicians on the Internet. One Web site you might visit is the Professional Aviation Maintenance Association at http://www.pama.org. To find other relevant Web sites, enter the keywords *aircraft mechanic* or *aviation maintenance technician* into a search engine.

AVIONICS TECHNICIAN

CAREER PROFILE

Duties: Perform maintenance and repairs on avionics systems and equipment; may be engaged in different types of assignments, such as maintenance, inspections, testing, troubleshooting, installations, emergency repairs, or major repairs; perform duties as required

Alternate Title(s): Avionics Specialist; Aviation Electronics Technician; Avionics Repair Technician

Salary Range: $30,000 to $58,000

Employment Prospects: Good

Advancement Prospects: Good

Prerequisites:

Education or Training—High school diploma; a certificate or associate's degree in avionics technology may be required

Experience—Entry-level candidates usually gain experience through a formal avionics training program

Special Skills and Personality Traits—Mathematics proficiency; electrical and mechanical aptitudes; problem-solving, troubleshooting, communication, interpersonal, teamwork, writing, and computer skills; detail-oriented, organized, curious, precise, flexible, cooperative

Special Requirements—FCC license and FAA mechanic certificate may be required

CAREER LADDER

Lead Avionics Technician

Avionics Technician

Trainee

Position Description

All modern aircraft are equipped with avionics (or aviation electronics) technology, which allow for safer and more efficient travel. These complex avionics systems and equipment are used by pilots for communication and navigation, as well as for such primary functions as monitoring engines, raising and lowering landing gear, flying by autopilot, detecting obstructions, controlling air conditioning systems, and recording flight data.

Avionics Technicians are responsible for ensuring that the avionics systems and equipment on board aircraft are in reliable and efficient condition. They are aircraft mechanics who have been especially trained to maintain and repair avionics instruments, devices, control panels, equipment, and systems. These include weather radar equipment, navigation systems, communication radios, global positioning systems, autopilot equipment, transponders, distance measuring equipment, flight management computers, and so on.

Technicians typically specialize in one or more areas—such as navigation systems—in avionics technology. (Their specialties may change or evolve with the development of new technology.) Many Avionics Technicians also concentrate on working with specific types of aircraft—such as general aviation airplanes, helicopters, jet airplanes, military aircraft, or spacecraft.

Avionics Technicians work alongside other aircraft mechanics. Their work assignments may entail performing routine maintenance, inspections, troubleshooting, installations, and repairs. They do a variety of tasks, such as:

- perform diagnostic tests to determine what is causing equipment to malfunction

- analyze problems and develop solutions
- recommend solutions to supervisors, customers, and others for solving problems
- make appropriate adjustments to equipment or systems
- repair or replace defective wiring, parts, or instruments
- read and interpret technical repair manuals, electrical diagrams, blueprints, and other materials to determine what tools and parts they need and what procedures they must follow
- use hand tools and electronic test instruments
- complete required paperwork and computer records
- maintain tools, equipment, and working environment

Depending on the work assignments, Avionics Technicians may work alone or in teams. They are often under pressure to meet tight deadlines. At all times, they must make sure that their work is accurate and flawless. They also ensure that their work is in compliance with federal aviation regulations, company policies and protocols, and manufacturers' specifications.

Avionics Technicians normally work indoors in hangars and repair shops in a well-lit and temperature-controlled environment. Their work involves working in the cockpit and other confined spaces. They are frequently involved in physical activity such as stooping, crouching, bending, squatting, and kneeling; climbing ladders; and pulling or lifting heavy objects up to 70 pounds.

Most Avionics Technicians wear uniforms on the job and normally supply their own hand tools.

Avionics Technicians work 40 hours a week. Many of them work shifts, which includes working nights, weekends, and holidays. Overtime is often required.

Salaries

Salaries vary for Avionics Technicians, depending on such factors as their experience, certification, seniority, employer, and geographical location.

According to the May 2003 *Occupational Employment Statistics* survey (by the U.S. Bureau of Statistics), the estimated annual salary for most Avionics Technicians ranged between $29,970 and $57,650.

Employment Prospects

Avionics Technicians are employed by airlines, corporate flight departments, government agencies, and other organizations that have their own aircraft fleets. Some other employers include repair shops, aviation maintenance firms, aircraft manufacturers, and avionics manufacturers.

Most job openings will become available as Avionics Technicians retire, advance to other positions, or transfer to other occupations. Employers will create additional positions as their companies expand and require more Avionics Technicians.

Job prospects are generally stronger for experienced Avionics Technicians who hold mechanic certificates with A&P ratings, issued by the Federal Aviation Administration (FAA).

Advancement Prospects

Avionics Technicians with supervisory and management ambitions can become lead technicians, supervisors, inspectors, aircraft maintenance controllers, and aircraft maintenance managers. FAA certifications are usually required to obtain higher positions. Those with entrepreneurial ambitions pursue goals of becoming independent consultants or owning aircraft maintenance facilities or other aviation-related businesses.

Some Avionics Technicians earn bachelor's degrees to become aviation, electrical, or communications engineers.

Education and Training

Minimally, Avionics Technicians must possess a high school diploma or a general equivalency diploma. Employers may require additional postsecondary training in aviation electronics.

Many Avionics Technicians have earned certificates or associate's degrees in avionics technology or electronics technology with an emphasis on aviation. These programs provide students with formal instruction as well as practical experience in maintaining, troubleshooting, testing, installing, and repairing avionics systems and equipment.

Students who graduate from FAA-approved programs are eligible to apply for the FAA mechanic certificate.

Employers provide new hires with training programs, which may include both formal instruction and on-the-job training.

Avionics Technicians enroll in training and education programs throughout their careers to keep up with new advances in avionics technology and to update and maintain their skills.

Special Requirements

Many employers require that Avionics Technicians possess a radiotelephone operator license, issued by the U.S. Federal Communications Commission (FCC).

Employers might also require that Avionics Technicians possess an FAA mechanic certificate with one of these ratings: an airframe (A) rating, a combined airframe and powerplant (A&P) rating, or a repairman (R) rating. Employers may hire uncertified technicians on the condition that they obtain the appropriate certification within a specified time period.

To qualify for FAA certification, individuals must pass a series of tests to demonstrate their knowledge and skills. They must meet the following qualifications to be eligible to take these exams:

- be at least 18 years old
- be a U.S. citizen or have the appropriate paperwork to be eligible to work in the United States

- be able to read, write, and understand English
- have 18 months of practical experience for an airframe rating or have 30 months of practical experience for an A&P rating, or be a graduate from an FAA-approved mechanic school

Avionics Technicians applying for a repairman rating are recommended by their employers.

To maintain their certificates, Avionics Technicians must complete a minimum number of hours of training.

Experience, Skills, and Personality Traits

Employers usually fill entry-level positions with candidates who have completed formal avionics programs, especially from FAA-approved schools. Employers also hire applicants who have previous military experience in avionics or have a few years of avionics troubleshooting and installation experience as aircraft mechanics.

Avionics Technicians must be proficient in mathematics and have electrical and mechanical aptitudes. They also need effective problem-solving and troubleshooting skills, as well as strong communication, interpersonal, teamwork, writing, and computer skills.

Being detail-oriented, organized, curious, precise, flexible, and cooperative are some personality traits that successful Avionics Technicians have in common.

Unions and Associations

Avionics Technicians may join professional associations such as the Professional Aviation Maintenance Association or the Association for Women in Aviation Maintenance. By joining such organizations, they can take advantage of networking opportunities and other professional services and resources.

Many Avionics Technicians belong to a union such as the International Association of Machinists and Aerospace Workers, the Transport Workers Union of America, or the International Brotherhood of Teamsters.

Tips for Entry

1. Some high school courses that can prepare you for a career in avionics are algebra, physics, mechanics, electricity, English, and keyboarding. For more suggestions, talk with your guidance counselor.
2. Avionics technology programs vary from school to school; therefore, carefully research the programs that interest you. Visit school campuses and talk with program advisers, instructors, and students. Also read school catalogs and brochures. Compare information about the courses, instructors, career services, costs, and so on.
3. To enhance their employability, many Avionics Technicians become cross-trained in other aviation maintenance areas, such as airframe mechanics.
4. Use your local state employment office to learn about job vacancies in your field. Many offices also teach workshops in job search skills.
5. On the Internet, learn more about Avionics Technicians. To find relevant Web sites, enter the keywords *avionics technicians* or *avionics* into a search engine.

AIRCRAFT MAINTENANCE INSPECTOR

CAREER PROFILE

Duties: Examine the quality of maintenance and repairs performed by aviation maintenance technicians; approve the return of aircraft to service; prepare reports and other required paperwork; perform other duties as required

Alternate Title(s): Avionics Inspector; Quality Control Inspector; Aviation Maintenance Safety Technician

Salary Range: $38,000 to $75,000

Employment Prospects: Fair

Advancement Prospects: Fair

Prerequisites:

Education or Training—High school diploma; a bachelor's degree may be required

Experience—Three or more years of experience as an aircraft mechanic at the journeyman level; previous experience with the type of aircraft that would be inspected

Special Skills and Personality Traits—Communication, reading, writing, observational, leadership, interpersonal skills; honest, impartial, diligent, trustworthy

Special Requirements—FAA mechanic certificate with an A&P rating; FAA Inspection Authorization (IA)

CAREER LADDER

Senior Inspector

Aircraft Maintenance Inspector

Aviation Maintenance Technician

Position Description

Aircraft Maintenance Inspectors are staff members of aviation maintenance programs that maintain and repair commercial, corporate, private, government, or military aircraft. These inspectors are highly experienced aviation maintenance technicians. Their job is to certify the airworthiness of aircraft before they are returned to service. They ensure that all maintenance, repairs, and alterations performed on aircraft meet the manufacturers' specifications, as well as conform with standard procedures for completing maintenance and repairs. In addition, Aircraft Maintenance Inspectors make sure that all work complies with federal aviation regulations and company safety policies.

Aircraft Maintenance Inspectors typically specialize in the type of aircraft that they examine—fixed-wing airplanes, seaplanes, helicopters, turboprop airplanes, jet aircraft, or other aircraft. They work in aviation maintenance programs for airlines, corporate flight departments, air charter operations, government agencies, repair shops, aircraft manufacturing facilities, and so on.

One of the inspector's major duties is checking the quality of the maintenance or repairs that have been done on any part of an aircraft—such as its wings, landing gear, engine, propeller, carburetor, or hydraulic system. Aircraft Maintenance Inspectors also examine any maintenance or repairs completed on avionics systems, or the equipment that pilots use for communication, navigation, and flight control.

Aircraft Maintenance Inspectors examine the quality of the craftsmanship of aircraft mechanics and avionics technicians, as well as the quality of any parts and materials used in the work. Their work involves performing such tasks as checking the way components fit together, testing the tightness of assembled parts, evaluating engine performance, and determining the accuracy of avionics equipment. Inspectors use hand tools, precision measuring devices (such as calipers and gauges), flashlights, and test instruments to help them accomplish their inspection jobs. Inspectors may also fly with pilots on test flights to make observations regarding the performance and airworthiness of the aircraft.

Aircraft Maintenance Inspectors have the authority to decide whether aircraft are ready to return to service. When aircraft pass inspection, they complete and sign the appropriate forms. If aircraft do not pass inspections, they must state the specific reasons for rejecting their return to service. Aircraft Maintenance Inspectors are held accountable for their decisions. If, for example, an accident occurs, the Aircraft Maintenance Inspector who had approved it as being airworthy is usually the first person contacted by a National Transportation Safety Board safety investigator.

Another major responsibility of Aircraft Maintenance Inspectors is completing required reports, logs, forms, and other paperwork as mandated by the Federal Aviation Administration (FAA). With each inspection job, inspectors prepare a report to document their findings. They make sure written or computer data are compiled accurately and entered correctly into aircraft maintenance records.

Some Aircraft Maintenance Inspectors perform the routine maintenance inspections on aircraft that are required by the FAA. For example, the FAA requires that all aircraft weighing 12,500 pounds or less that are flown for pleasure or business must undergo an annual inspection. Following maintenance manuals, Aircraft Maintenance Inspectors examine aircraft to determine their airworthiness and to check if any repairs are required or any parts need to be replaced.

Aircraft Maintenance Inspectors perform other duties, which vary according to their experience, job description, workplace, and other factors. For example, one inspector might be responsible for aircraft accident investigations, whereas another inspector might have the duty of assisting in the development of training programs for aircraft mechanics.

At some workplaces, Aircraft Maintenance Inspectors continue performing work assignments as aircraft mechanics. They might do maintenance, troubleshooting, testing, corrosion control, emergency repairs, or major repairs.

Aircraft Maintenance Inspectors are expected to keep up to date with federal aviation regulations, airworthiness directives, service bulletins, and technical publications. They also stay current with changing trends and developments in the maintenance and repair of the aircraft on which they work.

Aircraft Maintenance Inspectors work in high places (such as on ladders and wings) and in confined spaces. Their job involves such physical activity as climbing, crawling, stooping, crouching, kneeling, lifting, and pulling. They are exposed to dust, chemicals, fumes, and gases, as well as vibrating machinery and high levels of noise from power tools and aircraft.

They work a 40-hour week, which may include working nights and weekends. From time to time, they may be required to work overtime.

Salaries

Annual salaries vary for Aircraft Maintenance Inspectors, depending on such factors as their experience, education, employer, and geographical location. According to the 2002 salary survey by *Aviation Maintenance,* the annual salary for inspectors ranged from $37,900 to $74,500.

Employment Prospects

Most job opportunities for Aircraft Maintenance Inspectors become available as inspectors retire, advance to higher positions, or transfer to other occupations. Employers will create additional positions as their needs grow and when funding is available.

Job prospects are expected to increase in the aviation maintenance field in the next few years due to the large number of workers becoming eligible for retirement. However, keep in mind that the job opportunities in the aviation industry follow the fluctuations of the economy. During economic downturns, employers generally hire fewer employees, as well as lay off employees.

Advancement Prospects

Aircraft Maintenance Inspectors with supervisory and management ambitions might advance to such positions as aircraft maintenance controller, aircraft maintenance supervisor, or aircraft maintenance manager.

In airlines, employees advance according to their seniority. All Aircraft Maintenance Inspectors, regardless of their prior position or experience, begin at the bottom of the seniority list. With time, they build up their seniority, which results in being promoted to higher positions, earning higher pay, or receiving assignments of their choice.

Education and Training

Educational requirements vary from employer to employer. Minimally, Aircraft Maintenance Inspectors must possess a high school diploma or general equivalency diploma. Some employers also require that inspectors hold a bachelor's degree in aviation management or a related field.

Throughout their careers, Aircraft Maintenance Inspectors enroll in training seminars and education programs to sharpen and update their skills in aircraft maintenance and aviation management.

Special Requirements

Most employers hire candidates for Aircraft Maintenance Inspector positions who possess the FAA mechanic certificate with the combined airframe and powerplant (A&P) rating. In addition, they hold the FAA Inspection Authorization (IA).

Experience, Special Skills, and Personality Traits

Depending on the employer, job candidates generally need three or more years of experience as an aircraft mechanic at the journeyman level. They also have experience with the class, category, and type of aircraft that their prospective employers operate.

To perform their work effectively, Aircraft Maintenance Inspectors need strong communication, reading, and writing skills as well as excellent observational, leadership, and interpersonal skills. Some personality traits that successful Aircraft Maintenance Inspectors have in common are being honest, impartial, diligent, and trustworthy.

Unions and Associations

Aircraft Maintenance Inspectors might join a union, such as the Aircraft Mechanics Fraternal Association, which would represent them in contract negotiations for pay, benefits, and working conditions. They might also join professional associations that offer networking opportunities and other professional services and resources. Two national societies that serve the interests of aircraft maintenance professionals are the Professional Aviation Maintenance Association and the Association for Women in Aviation Maintenance.

Tips for Entry

1. Preparing paperwork and reading technical materials is an important aspect of an inspector's job; therefore, take courses in English to develop writing skills as well as reading comprehension and critical-thinking skills.
2. Minimum requirements for Aircraft Maintenance Inspector positions vary from employer to employer. Read job announcements carefully. Make sure you meet the minimum requirements before applying for a job. Employers will not consider any applicants who do not meet their minimum requirements.
3. For information about obtaining the Inspection Authorization (IA), visit or contact a nearby FAA Flight Standards District Office.
4. Use the Internet to learn more about the aviation maintenance field. To find relevant Web sites to visit, enter the keywords *aviation maintenance* into any search engine.

AIRCRAFT MAINTENANCE SUPERVISOR

CAREER PROFILE

Duties: Oversee the day-to-day management and supervision of aviation maintenance programs; provide staff direction and guidance; perform and supervise maintenance and repair work; perform administrative duties; perform other duties as required

Alternate Title(s): Aircraft Mechanic Supervisor; Aviation Maintenance Supervisor; Avionics Supervisor; Repair Shop Supervisor; Field Maintenance Supervisor; Airline Maintenance Supervisor

Salary Range: $29,000 to $76,000

Employment Prospects: Fair

Advancement Prospects: Fair

Prerequisites:

Education or Training—Trade school, vocational school, or college training required by some employers

Experience—Three or more years of experience at the journeyman level; previous supervisory experience; knowledgeable about aircraft maintenance programs and supervisory methods and practices; experience working with aircraft operated by employer

Special Skills and Personality Traits—Leadership, supervisory, management, communication, listening, interpersonal, computer, writing, critical-thinking, problem-solving, and self-management skills; decisive, fair, honest, trustworthy, respectful, friendly, consistent, dependable, self-motivated

Special Requirements—FAA mechanic certificate with A&P rating; FAA Inspector Authorization (IA)

CAREER LADDER

Aircraft Maintenance Supervisor

Lead Aviation Maintenance Technician

Aviation Maintenance Technician

Position Description

Aircraft Maintenance Supervisors are responsible for the day-to-day management and supervision of aviation maintenance programs for air carrier, corporate, general aviation, government, or military flight operations. Their job involves overseeing the maintenance and repair of aircraft to ensure their return to service in a timely manner. Aircraft Maintenance Supervisors also make sure that all work complies with federal aviation regulations, company policies and protocols, and manufacturers' specifications.

As first-line managers, Aircraft Maintenance Supervisors provide direction and guidance to a team of aviation maintenance technicians and inspectors and to contractual service providers. They also work alongside aircraft maintenance technicians while they perform maintenance, inspections, diagnostic testing, troubleshooting, corrosion control, or repairs on aircraft parts, instruments, and systems.

Aircraft Maintenance Supervisors are responsible for coordinating job orders, prioritizing jobs, and planning maintenance and inspection schedules to ensure the efficient and timely completion of jobs. They assign personnel to the various jobs and explain the work requirements and deadlines. Supervisors monitor individual workloads and, if necessary, adjust job assignments to ensure that deadlines are met.

Supervisors also resolve any problems or issues that arise with job orders, which may involve developing special tools, reviewing airworthiness directives from the Federal Aviation Administration (FAA), or researching manufacturers' manuals. Supervisors are accountable for the work performed in their unit and are therefore required to inspect and sign off on major repairs or alterations done on aircraft.

Aircraft Maintenance Supervisors also perform a variety of administrative duties. Some of these responsibilities include:

- developing short-term program goals and establishing program priorities
- designing work procedures to meet operational requirements
- administering program budgets
- preparing work schedules
- participating in the hiring process of new staff members
- providing training to staff members
- performing job evaluations of staff members
- maintaining an inventory of operating supplies and spare parts
- approving invoices and repair orders
- preparing reports, records, and required paperwork
- maintaining written and computerized maintenance records and logbooks
- monitoring the workplace to ensure compliance with appropriate local, state, and federal laws and regulations relating to employment, safety, and environmental practices.

Aircraft Maintenance Supervisors regularly meet with higher-level managers to inform them about the status of work projects as well as to discuss changes. They may discuss problems with personnel, facilities, equipment, work techniques, and so forth. Supervisors also assist managers in the development of long-range plans, department policies, and work procedures. In addition, they assist in the preparation of annual operating budgets.

Their job involves physical activity such as climbing ladders and lifting objects weighing up to 70 pounds or more. They are exposed to dust, chemicals, fumes, and gases, as well as to vibrating machinery and high levels of noise from power tools and aircraft.

Aircraft Maintenance Supervisors work a 40-hour week, which may include working nights, weekends, and holidays. On occasion, they are required to work overtime. Some supervisors are on call 24 hours a day.

Salaries

Salaries vary for Aircraft Maintenance Supervisors, depending on such factors as experience, certification, seniority, employer, and geographical location.

The U.S. Bureau of Statistics, in its May 2003 *Occupational Employment Statistics* survey, reports that estimated salary earnings for most first-line supervisors of mechanics ranged between $29,600 and $76,160.

Employment Prospects

Some employers of Aircraft Maintenance Supervisors are airlines, corporate flight departments, air charter operations, government agencies, air ambulance services, fixed base operators, repair shops, aviation maintenance firms, and aircraft and aircraft parts manufacturers. Civilian employees are also hired by the U.S. military. Most job openings will become available as supervisors retire, advance to other positions, or transfer to other occupations.

Advancement Prospects

Aircraft Maintenance Supervisors can pursue other managerial positions in aviation maintenance, such as maintenance controller and maintenance manager positions. Opportunities for higher managerial positions are generally better with major airlines and organizations with large aircraft fleets.

Many supervisors seek positions with other employers in order to obtain higher positions or earn higher pay.

Education and Training

Educational requirements vary from employer to employer. Minimally, Aircraft Maintenance Supervisors must possess a high school diploma or general equivalency diploma. Some employers may also require that supervisors have completed two years of trade or vocational school. Some others may require that supervisors hold a bachelor's degree in aviation management or a related field.

Throughout their careers, Aircraft Maintenance Supervisors enroll in training seminars and education programs to sharpen and update their skills in aircraft maintenance and aviation management.

Special Requirements

Most employers hire candidates for supervisory positions who possess the FAA mechanic certificate with the combined airframe and powerplant (A&P) rating. In addition, supervisors must hold the FAA Inspector Authorization (IA).

Experience, Skills, and Personality Traits

Depending on the employer, job candidates generally need three or more years of experience as an aircraft mechanic at the journeyman level. Many candidates have gained supervisory experience while holding the position of lead aircraft mechanic.

Employers seek candidates who are knowledgeable about aviation maintenance programs, including FAA regulations, standard practices, materials, tools, equipment, and safety practices. They are also knowledgeable about supervisory methods and practices. Candidates should also have a broad knowledge of and experience with the class, category, and type of aircraft that their prospective employers operate.

To perform their job effectively, Aircraft Maintenance Supervisors must have excellent leadership, supervisory, and management skills. In addition, they must have superior communication, listening, and interpersonal skills, as they must work well with staff members, managers, customers, vendors, and others. Other skills that are essential include computer, writing, critical-thinking, and problem-solving skills. Furthermore, they should have excellent self-management skills, including the ability to organize and prioritize tasks, meet deadlines, and handle stressful situations.

Being decisive, fair, honest, trustworthy, respectful, friendly, consistent, dependable, and self-motivated are some personality traits that successful Aircraft Maintenance Supervisors share.

Unions and Associations

Aircraft Maintenance Supervisors may join professional associations to take advantage of professional services and resources as well as networking opportunities. Two national societies that serve the interests of professionals in the aviation maintenance field are the Professional Aviation Maintenance Association and the Association for Women in Aviation Maintenance.

Tips for Entry

1. If your high school has a work experience program, see if you can be placed with a local aviation maintenance program or other aviation business to gain experience.
2. To enhance their employability as well as advancement prospects, many aircraft mechanics have earned associate's or bachelor's degrees in aviation maintenance management, aviation technology, or a related field.
3. Take advantage of various job banks on the Internet to learn about job vacancies nationwide. Two Web sites that list jobs specifically for the aviation industry are Air Jobs Online.com, http://www.airjobsonline.com; and Aviation Employment.com, http://www.aviationemployment.com.

AVIATION SAFETY

FAA AIR TRAFFIC CONTROLLER (TERMINAL AND ARTCC FACILITIES)

CAREER PROFILE

Duties: Manage air traffic so it flows safely and efficiently; provide pilots with air traffic clearance, landing, and take-off instructions; advise pilots about weather conditions, air traffic, and potential hazards; perform duties as required

Alternate Title(s): Air Traffic Control Specialist; a title that reflects a particular position such as En Route Controller or Ground Controller

Salary Range: $30,000 to $136,000

Employment Prospects: Good

Advancement Prospects: Limited

Prerequisites:

Education or Training—Appropriate college or military training in air traffic control; complete FAA training program

Experience—Three years' work experience required for those without a college degree; pilot, navigator, or military air traffic controller experience preferred

Special Skills and Personality Traits—Have a superior memory; concentration, critical-thinking, problem-solving, teamwork, interpersonal, communication, and self-management skills; alert, calm, precise, decisive, flexible

Special Requirements—FAA certification and facility rating

CAREER LADDER

Air Traffic Control Specialist

Air Traffic Controller

Air Traffic Controller—Trainee

Position Description

The U.S. air traffic control system is run by the Federal Aviation Administration (FAA), an agency in the U.S. Department of Transportation. Various Air Traffic Controllers (ATCs) are stationed in terminal facilities and air route traffic control centers to coordinate the safe and efficient flow of air traffic within the national airspace. ATCs manage and separate thousands of aircraft each day as they take off and land from airports as well as fly between departure and destination airports.

By law, ATCs are responsible for monitoring commercial, military, and general aviation flights that are operating under instrument flight rules (or IFR). In other words, pilots use their instruments to navigate their aircraft. ATCs monitor IFR flights from the time aircraft back away from terminal gates or hangars to the time they are parked at their destination airports.

ATCs control aircraft as they pass through their assigned airspace, runways, or taxiways. They use radar equipment, computer systems, and other procedures and techniques to monitor flights. They communicate directly with pilots via radio to give them important instructions, advice, and information about air traffic, weather, potential hazards, and so on. For example, ATCs advise pilots about current weather conditions at an airport, alert pilots to air traffic delays, and instruct pilots to change their altitudes in order to avoid another aircraft.

ATCs perform different duties at different facilities. ATCs stationed at airport traffic control towers coordinate the orderly flow of aircraft on the ground, using radar and their observations. These ATCs work in glass rooms at the top of control towers and are often referred to as tower controllers. They usually rotate the following positions:

- The clearance delivery controller reviews flight plans and determines whether to give pilots permission to depart from an airport.
- The ground controller oversees the traffic—including aircraft, ground vehicles, and employees—on the airport ramps and taxiways. He or she is responsible for guiding aircraft between terminal gates or hangars and runways.
- The local controller manages aircraft as they arrive at or depart from an airport. They give final clearance and instructions for pilots to take off or land at their assigned runways.

The ATCs at the terminal radar approach control (or TRACON) facilities use radar to monitor aircraft during their departure and arrival phases. These controllers serve a primary airport as well as other airports that are within 50 miles of their radar service area. They work in radar rooms, which may be located within the control tower building or in a separate building on or near an airport that they serve. The following controllers work at TRACON facilities:

- The departure controller manages aircraft upon takeoff and until they leave the TRACON airspace. They also instruct pilots on which direction, speed, and rate of ascent to take as they move along a departure route.
- The feeder controller guides aircraft that have just entered the TRACON airspace into their destination airport.
- The approach controller separates and lines up aircraft for their final destinations. The controller tells pilots what speed, altitude, and direction to fly to prepare for their landing. This controller also instructs pilots on which runways to take at their destination airports.

ATCs who monitor aircraft during their en route phase are known as en route controllers. They work in one of the 21 FAA air route traffic control centers (ARTCC) across the United States. Each facility manages air traffic within airspace that generally covers hundreds of thousands of miles. The airspace is divided into sectors. As aircraft pass into each sector, they are monitored through radar by a team of two or three en route controllers. When necessary, the controllers will communicate with pilots to advise them about bad weather conditions, airport conditions, nearby aircraft, status of military operating areas, and other potential hazards. They also instruct pilots to change speed or altitude in order to maintain a safe distance apart from other aircraft.

Some ATCs work in flight service stations across the continental United States and Alaska. They provide pilots with essential information, such as weather, to help them prepare flight plans. These ATCs are known as flight service station specialists.

Air Traffic Controllers work rotating shifts. They usually work a 40-hour week and at times may be required to work overtime.

Salaries

Salaries for Air Traffic Controllers vary, depending on such factors as their experience, job responsibilities, facility, and geographical location. According to the May 2003 *Occupational Employment Statistics* survey (by the U.S. Bureau of Labor Statistics), the estimated annual wages for Air Traffic Controllers ranged between $49,920 and $136,120.

FAA controllers usually start at the GS-7 level on the federal government pay schedule. In 2004, the basic pay rate for GS-7 employees ranged from $29,821 to $38,767. ATC recruits earn a salary while attending training programs at the FAA academy.

Employment Prospects

The majority of ATCs work for the FAA. Some ATCs are employed by private firms that provide air traffic control services on a contractual basis to the FAA. Private ATCs usually work at low-activity air traffic control towers that generally operate under visual flight rules (VFR). The military also employs some civilian ATCs.

Job vacancies typically become available as ATCs retire, transfer to other positions, or resign for other reasons. Opportunities are expected to increase in the coming years due to the large number of ATCs who will become eligible to retire. The National Air Traffic Controllers Association estimates that about half of the ATC workforce in the United States will be retiring by 2010.

Advancement Prospects

Many Air Traffic Controllers pursue career advancement by earning higher wages, receiving more responsibilities, or obtaining transfers to air traffic facilities of their choice.

ATCs can advance to supervisory and management positions within the air traffic control system, as well as to top administrative jobs in the FAA. This may require transferring to other locations. ATCs can also advance to specialist positions in which they perform support roles for their facilities, such as a quality assurance specialist or an automations specialist.

Researcher and instructor positions with the FAA are also available to ATCs who are interested in pursuing those career options.

Education and Training

Applicants may qualify for entry-level ATC positions if they have completed military training as an ATC. They may also qualify if they have earned a bachelor's degree with an emphasis in air traffic control from a college that offers FAA-certified air traffic control programs.

Applicants with qualifying work experience, or a combination of experience and college work, may also qualify for entry-level ATC positions.

Recruits undergo an intensive training program that begins with basic ATC training at the FAA Academy in Oklahoma City. Recruits for ARTCC positions complete a 12-week program, whereas those for control tower and TRACON positions complete a 15-week program. All recruits receive instruction in such areas as federal aviation regulations, the air traffic control system, ATC equipment, job procedures, and aircraft performance.

After graduation from the FAA Academy, trainees are assigned to an air traffic control facility where they continue their training on the job under a certified professional controller and in classroom and lab settings as well. Trainees with no previous work experience are called developmental controllers. Depending on the facility, developmental controllers are in training for between one and five years. Upon successful completion of their training, they become certified as full performance-level ATCs or certified professional controllers (CTCs).

Air Traffic Controllers receive recurrent training to sharpen their skills and to learn about new procedures and equipment.

Special Requirements

ATCs must obtain and maintain professional certification and facility ratings from the FAA.

To qualify for entry-level positions, applicants must meet the following requirements:

- be a U.S. citizen
- be under 31 years old when initially hired
- be able to speak, read, write, and understand English fluently
- meet vision, color vision, hearing, and other medical standards
- achieve a qualifying score on the FAA pre-qualification exam, which is an aptitude test designed to identify the cognitive skills required by ATCs

Air Traffic Controllers must pass an annual physical exam as well as a job performance examination that is given twice a year. ATCs must also pass random drug screenings in order to keep their jobs.

ATCs are required to retire when they reach the age of 56. They are eligible for retirement at age 50 if they have 20 years of service, or at any age if they have 25 years of service.

Experience, Skills, and Personality Traits

Without a bachelor's degree, entry-level applicants must have three years of general work experience that demonstrates a capacity to become Air Traffic Controllers. The FAA may also accept applicants who have qualifying experience as pilots, navigators, military controllers, or aircraft dispatchers.

ATCs must have superior memories and concentration skills. Their job also requires strong critical-thinking and problem-solving skills, with the ability to make wise decisions quickly and effectively. In addition, ATCs must have excellent teamwork, interpersonal, and communication skills. Furthermore, ATCs need good self-management skills, such as the ability to handle stressful situations, work independently, and organize and prioritize tasks.

Being alert, calm, precise, decisive, and flexible are some personality traits that successful Air Traffic Controllers share.

Unions and Associations

ATCs are members of the National Air Traffic Controllers Association, a union that represents them in negotiations for such contractual terms as pay, benefits, and working conditions. The union also handles any grievances that ATCs may have against their employers.

Many ATCs join professional societies—such as the Air Traffic Control Association and the Professional Women Controllers, Inc.—to take advantage of networking opportunities and other professional resources and services.

Tips for Entry

1. Visit different air traffic control facilities to see which environment might best suit you.
2. To learn about civilian ATC vacancies with the U.S. Department of Defense or about openings with the FAA, contact a U.S. Office of Personnel Management (OPM) office or visit the OPM Web site at http://www.usajobs.opm.gov. To learn about specific vacancies at the FAA, visit its Web site at http://www.faa.gov.
3. The FAA has special hiring policies for applicants who are former civilian or military controllers, veterans, or graduates of FAA-certified ATC programs.
4. The FAA Contract Tower Program oversees the contracting of air traffic services to private companies. For more information visit the U.S. Contract Tower Association Web site at http://www.airportnet.org/cta.
5. Use the Internet to learn more about ATCs and their work. Some Web sites you might visit include the Air Traffic Control Association, http://www.atca.org; the National Air Traffic Controllers Association, http://www.natca.org; and the FAA Academy, http://www.academy.jccbi.gov.

FLIGHT SERVICE STATION (FSS) SPECIALIST

CAREER PROFILE

Duties: Provide pilots with essential information about weather conditions, air traffic, terrain, and other aviation matters for flight planning; assist pilots in flight with aviation matters and emergency situations; perform duties as required

Alternate Title(s): FSS Controller; Air Traffic Controller

Salary Range: $50,000 to $136,000

Employment Prospects: Fair

Advancement Prospects: Limited

Prerequisites:

Education or Training—Bachelor's degree; complete FAA training program

Experience—Three years of work experience for those without a college degree; pilot, navigator, or military air traffic controller experience preferred

Special Skills and Personality Traits—Teamwork, interpersonal, communication, critical-thinking, problem-solving, and self-management skills; alert, calm, precise, decisive, flexible

Special Requirements—FAA certification and facility rating

CAREER LADDER

FSS Supervisor

FSS Specialist

Flight Service Station (FSS) Trainee

Position Description

Flight Service Station (FSS) Specialists are part of the air traffic control system that is run by the Federal Aviation Administration (FAA). They are air traffic controllers, but they do not participate in the control and separation of air traffic in the national airspace. Their role is to help pilots avoid potential flight hazards.

FSS Specialists work in flight service stations that are located at airports throughout the United States, where they primarily assist general aviation and military pilots. Specialists provide pilots with information about weather conditions, weather hazards, routes, altitudes, terrain, air traffic, and other matters that affect the safety of their flights within the area that the FSS specialists serve. Some specialists provide airport advisory services to local air traffic at airports that have no control towers.

One of the major duties that FSS Specialists perform is to assist pilots with preflight and weather briefings over the phone or in person. These briefings help pilots prepare safe and efficient flight plans. Specialists give pilots information that is tailored specifically to their proposed flight plans. For example, an FSS Specialist would advise a pilot about any hazardous weather conditions or restricted airspace along the pilot's proposed flight route.

Flight service stations are the primary source of aviation weather information for general aviation pilots. Although FSS Specialists are not meteorologists, they are trained in weather theory and interpretation. The specialists receive weather reports and forecasts from such sources as the National Weather Service (NWS), as well as weather observations from pilots in flight. The FSS specialists then translate the weather information into terms that would be understood by pilots.

Another major duty of FSS Specialists is to assist pilots while they are in flight. Pilots can contact them by radio for updated information on weather conditions, airport delays, and military activity along their flight routes and at their destination points. In addition, pilots can ask FSS Specialists for navigation assistance when they have become lost or are unsure of their surroundings.

FSS Specialists also provide assistance to pilots when they encounter emergencies. For example, if a pilot must make an emergency landing, an FSS Specialist can immediately contact local emergency services for help.

FSS Specialists also perform other duties. For example, they may be assigned to:

- process flight plans that pilots may file by radio, computer, phone, or in person
- monitor flight plans for aircraft that are overdue at their destination points
- initiate search and rescue procedures for missing or overdue aircraft
- report pilot weather observations, NWS advisories, notices to airmen, and other pertinent information to air traffic control facilities
- gather and review updated weather reports, weather forecasts, and aeronautical information and disseminate information
- complete reports, forms, and other required paperwork
- provide on-the-job training to developmental (or trainee) FSS Specialists as required

FSS Specialists are assigned to rotating shifts, which include working nights, weekends, and holidays. They generally work a 40-hour work schedule and occasionally may be required to work overtime.

Salaries

Salaries for FSS Specialists vary, depending on such factors as their experience, job responsibilities, employer, and geographical location. According to the May 2003 *Occupational Employment Statistics* survey (by the U.S. Bureau of Labor Statistics), the estimated annual wages for air traffic controllers ranged between $49,920 and $136,120.

Employment Prospects

FSS Specialists work in flight service stations throughout the United States. The majority of facilities are automated flight service stations (AFSS), which refers to the use of recorded telephone messages to provide updates on basic weather and operational information.

Most openings become available as FSS Specialists retire, resign, or transfer to other positions.

In August 2002, the FAA began a study to determine whether flight services at 58 of the flight service stations in the continental United States should be contracted out for bid from private firms. The study is expected to be completed in 2004. However, in 2003, Congress introduced legislation to keep most traffic controller positions, including FSS Specialists, as exclusively federal employees.

Advancement Prospects

Supervisory and management positions are available but limited. Many FSS Specialists pursue career advancement by earning higher wages or by receiving greater responsibilities. Some specialists use their positions as stepping stones to air traffic controller careers in air traffic control towers, terminal radar approach control facilities, or air route traffic control centers.

FSS Specialists are eligible for retirement at age 50 if they have 20 years of service, or at any age if they have 25 years of service.

Education and Training

Applicants for FSS Specialists must have bachelor's degrees, preferably in air traffic control or another related field. The FAA also accepts applicants with a combination of education and work experience.

Recruits undergo an intensive training program that begins with several weeks of basic training at the FAA Academy in Oklahoma City. They receive instruction in such areas as federal aviation regulations, the air traffic control system, job procedures, and aircraft performance. After graduation, trainees are assigned to a flight service station, where they receive on-the-job training under certified FSS Specialists. Upon successful completion of their training, they become certified as full performance-level FSS Specialists.

FSS Specialists receive recurrent training to sharpen their skills and to learn new procedures and equipment.

Special Requirements

FSS Specialists must obtain and maintain professional certification and facility ratings from the FAA.

To qualify for entry-level positions, applicants must meet the following requirements:

- be a U.S. citizen
- be able to speak, read, write, and understand English fluently
- meet vision, color vision, hearing, and other medical standards
- achieve a qualifying score on the FAA prequalification exam, which is an aptitude test designed to identify the cognitive skills required by air traffic controllers

Experience, Skills, and Personality Traits

Without a bachelor's degree, entry-level applicants must have three years of general work experience that demonstrate a capacity to become an FSS Specialist. The FAA may also accept applicants who have qualifying experience as pilots, navigators, military controllers, or aircraft dispatchers.

FSS Specialists must have excellent teamwork, interpersonal, and communication skills. In addition, they need strong critical-thinking and problem-solving skills, with the ability to make wise decisions quickly and effectively. They also need good self-management skills, such as the ability to handle stressful situations, work independently, and organize and prioritize tasks.

Being alert, calm, precise, decisive, and flexible are some personality traits that successful FSS Specialists share.

Unions and Associations

FSS Specialists are union members of the National Association of Air Traffic Specialists. The union represents them in contract negotiations with their employers, seeking the best contract terms in regards to pay, benefits, and working conditions.

FSS Specialists might join professional associations to take advantage of networking opportunities and other professional resources and services. Two national associations that they might join are the Air Traffic Control Association and Professional Women Controllers, Inc.

Tips for Entry

1. Gain experience working with the public. For example, while in school you might get a job as a customer service representative with an airline.
2. Obtain computer skills as well as skills for reading geographical maps, weather products, and aeronautical charts.
3. Incomplete job applications may disqualify you for a position. Therefore, review your application before you submit it. Have you answered all questions completely, clearly, and truthfully? Have you completed and attached other accompanying forms that are required? Have you attached all required documents, such as proof of U.S. citizenship, that the FAA is requesting?
4. Use the Internet to learn more about FSS Specialists. You might start by visiting the National Association of Air Traffic Specialists Web site, http://www.naats.org.

FAA AVIATION SAFETY INSPECTOR

CAREER PROFILE

Duties: Administer and enforce federal air regulations and standards that govern the quality, performance, operation, and safety of aircraft in civil aviation; perform duties as required

Alternate Title(s): A title that reflects a particular type of inspection such as Air Carrier Maintenance Inspector

Salary Range: $36,000 to $69,000

Employment Prospects: Fair

Advancement Prospects: Limited

Prerequisites:

Education or Training—High school diploma; complete FAA training program

Experience—Requirements vary for the different inspector positions

Special Skills and Personality Traits—Communication, interpersonal, report-writing, and self-management skills; dedicated, reliable, trustworthy

Special Requirements—Driver's license; FAA mechanic or pilot certificate with appropriate ratings may be required

CAREER LADDER

Senior Aviation Safety Inspector

Aviation Safety Inspector

Aviation Safety Inspector—Trainee

Position Description

Aviation Safety Inspectors play an important role in ensuring that the U.S. aviation system is safe for millions of travelers who fly every year. They are compliance inspectors for the Federal Aviation Administration (FAA). Their job is to administer and enforce federal air regulations and standards that govern the safety, quality, performance, and operation of aircraft in civil aviation.

Aviation Safety Inspectors are involved in evaluating the maintenance, operation, production, and modification of aircraft. Some of them specialize in inspecting large multiengine aircraft used by commercial air carriers—scheduled and supplemental air carriers, air travel clubs, and other commercial operators. Other inspectors are devoted to examining single- and multiengine aircraft (airplanes and helicopters) used in general aviation for pleasure, business, air taxi, or other purposes.

These inspectors work in four types of inspection areas, or options. One option is maintenance inspection. Air carrier or general aviation maintenance inspectors generally perform the following duties: evaluating aircraft mechanics and repair facilities for certification; examining mechanic training programs; checking aircraft and related equipment for airworthiness; and investigating accidents, incidents, or violations.

Another option is avionics (aviation electronics) inspection. Air carrier or general aviation avionics inspectors evaluate the overall avionics programs of air carrier, air taxi, or other operations. Their duties include evaluating avionics technicians and repair facilities; reviewing training programs for avionics technicians; examining the airworthiness of avionics systems and equipment; and investigating accidents, incidents, or violations.

Operations inspection is another option in which Aviation Safety Inspectors specialize. These inspectors evaluate air carrier and general aviation operations. They appraise the management of such areas as facilities, equipment, operational procedures, and training programs. They also examine pilots, dispatchers, flight instructors, and other airmen for initial and continuing certification. Further, they investigate accidents, incidents, or violations related to operations.

The fourth option for Aviation Safety Inspectors is manufacturing inspection. These inspectors monitor manufacturing facilities that produce or modify aircraft or aircraft parts. They also inspect any originally built or modified aircraft, aircraft parts, and avionics equipment. Furthermore, they issue FAA certificates for all civil aircraft, including imports, amateur-built planes, and modified planes.

Aviation Safety Inspectors have irregular work schedules, which may include working on weekends and holidays. Their job requires traveling to other geographical locations for extended periods of time.

Salaries

Salaries for Aviation Safety Inspectors vary, depending on various factors such as their experience, geographical location, and their grade and step ranking on their pay schedule. Earnings are generally higher in areas where the cost of living is higher.

Inspectors enter at the FG-9 level of their pay schedule and can advance to the FG-12 level. (Their pay schedule is equivalent to the general schedule for regular federal employees.) In 2004, the basic annual salary at the FG-9 to FG-12 level ranged from $36,478 to $68,766.

Employment Prospects

Aviation Safety Inspectors who perform avionics, maintenance, and operations inspections are stationed at FAA Flight Standards Service offices throughout the United States and Puerto Rico. Those performing manufacturing inspections are based at FAA Manufacturing Inspection offices.

Competition for Aviation Safety Inspector jobs is high; and most job opportunities become available when inspectors retire, resign, or are promoted to higher positions. The creation of additional positions depends on the agency's needs and the availability of funding.

Advancement Prospects

Supervisory and management opportunities are available, but limited. Advancement is competitive, based on the agency's needs and individual merit.

Education and Training

Minimally, Aviation Safety Inspectors must have a high school diploma or general equivalency diploma.

New employees must successfully complete a training program that includes classroom instruction and on-the-job training. This training covers such areas as FAA policies, federal air regulations, and inspection procedures.

Aviation Safety Inspectors receive recurrent training throughout their careers to upgrade and maintain their skills.

Special Requirements

To be eligible for FAA Aviation Safety Inspector positions, applicants must be U.S. citizens and possess a valid driver's license. Applicants must also speak, read, write, and understand English fluently.

Applicants for maintenance inspector positions must possess the FAA mechanic certificate with an airframe and powerplant (A&P) rating.

Applicants for operations inspector positions must hold appropriate FAA pilot certificates and rankings as well as the first-class FAA medical certificate. Furthermore, they may not have more than two FAA violations within the five years prior to application.

Experience, Skills, and Personality Traits

Requirements vary with the different positions. In general, applicants must have extensive work experience in the areas in which they are applying. For example, general aviation avionics inspectors must have experience working on the maintenance and repair of avionics systems in aircraft weighing 12,500 pounds or less.

Applicants for avionics and maintenance inspector positions are expected to have at least three years of supervisory experience as lead aircraft mechanics. They should also have performed avionics work within the last three years on the appropriate types of aircraft.

Applicants for operations inspector positions must have completed a minimum of 1,500 hours of total flight time as pilots or copilots of appropriate aircraft. Additionally, they must meet other flight and work experience requirements that are pertinent to the inspector positions for air carrier or general aviation operations.

Applicants for manufacturing inspector positions must have experience in quality control and quality assurance systems, as well as be knowledgeable about the methods and techniques in the manufacture of aircraft, aircraft engines, and other aircraft parts. Alternatively, applicants must have experience issuing certificates or approvals for the airworthiness of aircraft and aircraft parts, or in managing programs that lead to such issuance.

To perform their work effectively, all Aviation Safety Inspectors need excellent communication, interpersonal, and report-writing skills. In addition, they must have strong self-management skills, such as the ability to meet deadlines, organize and prioritize tasks, handle stressful situations, and work independently. Being dedicated, reliable, and trustworthy are some personality traits that successful Aviation Safety Inspectors share.

Unions and Associations

Aviation Safety Inspectors are members of the Professional Airways Systems Specialists, a union that conducts contract negotiations for them. It seeks the best contractual terms relating to pay, job benefits, and working conditions.

Tips for Entry

1. To obtain information about student internships, career information, and job vacancies, visit the FAA job Web site at http://jobs.faa.gov.
2. Read the instructions completely when submitting applications. Make sure you complete and attach all the forms that the FAA requires. Send only the forms that the FAA requests and nothing more.
3. If you are eligible for an avionics, maintenance, manufacturing, or operations position, the FAA will place you on its national register of eligible applicants for one year. The FAA refers to this register for possible job candidates when vacancies become available. If you are not selected for a position after a year, and still wish to be considered, you must complete another application package.
4. To learn more about aviation safety, check out the FAA's Flight Standards Service Web site at http://www.faa.gov/avr/afs. You can find contact information for regional offices at that Web site.
5. To find relevant Web sites about Aviation Safety Inspectors, enter the keywords *aviation safety inspectors* into any search engine.

AIRSPACE SYSTEM INSPECTION PILOT (ASIP)

CAREER PROFILE

Duties: Evaluate and certify air navigation facilities and flight instrument procedures; perform duties as required

Alternate Title(s): Flight Inspection Pilot

Salary Range: $53,000 to $96,000

Employment Prospects: Limited

Advancement Prospects: Limited

Prerequisites:

Education or Training—Complete FAA training program

Experience—Meet the FAA's minimum flight experience requirements

Special Skills and Personality Traits—Communication, interpersonal, teamwork, leadership, and self-management skills; analytical, flexible, precise, calm, cooperative

Special Requirements—Airline transport pilot (ATP) certificate with appropriate ratings; FAA medical certificate

CAREER LADDER

Captain or Pilot-in-Command

Copilot or Second-in-Command

Trainee

Position Description

Airspace System Inspection Pilots (ASIPs) play an essential role in maintaining the safety and efficiency of air traffic movement in the national airspace. As employees of the Federal Aviation Administration (FAA), they work in the flight inspection operations division. More commonly known as flight inspection pilots, ASIPs fly missions to inspect and certify air navigation facilities that are used for guiding or controlling aircraft in the national airspace.

Air navigation facilities include navigational aids such as ground-based navigational transmitters, instrument landing systems, radar systems, and global positioning systems (GPS). They also include communication systems, airport lighting, aeronautical light beacons, and various other types of apparatus, equipment, systems, structures, and mechanisms. ASIPs inspect the different facilities to determine whether they meet operational standards. In addition, ASIPs evaluate the quality of signals emitting from different navigational aids to ensure they are operating correctly and accurately.

ASIPs also are responsible for evaluating the safety, practicability, and airworthiness of published instrument flight procedures. Pilots are required to follow these procedures when operating under instrument flight rules (IFR). Instrument flight procedures are series of maneuvers that the FAA has designed for the different airports in the United States. These procedures allow pilots to operate their aircraft more safely while in flight and as they perform their landings and departures, particularly during periods of adverse weather.

ASIPs fly jet aircraft owned by the FAA to conduct their airborne inspections. The aircraft are specially equipped with avionics and computer equipment to serve as electronic laboratories in the sky. They perform flight inspections at civil airports throughout the United States as well as at military airports around the world. Some ASIPs also provide inspection services to foreign governments upon request.

ASIPs perform several types of flight inspections. They conduct scheduled or unscheduled flight inspections to ensure that air navigation facilities or flight instrument procedures continue to meet required operational standards. They also inspect and evaluate proposed air navigational facilities or modified flight instrument procedures. Further, they conduct flight inspections for the purpose of resolving particular problems with navigational aids or flight instrument procedures.

On occasion, ASIPs provide assistance to National Transportation Safety Board (NTSB) air safety investigators. For example, an ASIP might be asked to help with an NTSB investigation by making flight tests to evaluate navigational aids that may have been involved in an aviation accident.

The flight inspection crew is composed of two pilots and one technician. One pilot is designated the pilot-in-command (or captain) of the mission. The pilot-in-command is in charge of overseeing the flight mission and ensuring that the mission is completed in a safe, efficient, and timely manner. This pilot performs such tasks as:

- supervising and instructing crew members
- determining whether each air navigational facility or flight instrument procedure meets FAA requirements
- notifying appropriate personnel about any facility or procedure that performed unsatisfactorily
- preparing a final report of his or her findings and conclusions
- completing forms, pilot logs, and other required paperwork

ASIPs perform their inspections during the day or night in normal air traffic conditions. Their inspections often require them to fly at very low altitudes and low speeds for long periods of time.

Airspace System Inspection Pilots are full-time employees who work a 40-hour week. Their job requires travel to different locations within their assigned regions. They are sometimes assigned to complete inspection assignments in other regions.

Salaries

Salaries for Airspace System Inspection Pilots vary, depending on such factors as experience, seniority, and geographical location.

Entry-level positions are filled at the FG-12 level of the pay schedule for these FAA employees. ASIPs can advance to the FG-14 level. (Their pay schedule is equivalent to the general schedule for regular federal employees.) In 2004, the basic annual salaries at the FG-12 to FG-14 ranged from $52,899 to $96,637.

Employment Prospects

Airspace System Inspection Pilots are based at flight operations headquarters in Oklahoma City, as well as at field offices in Anchorage, Atlantic City, Battle Creek (Michigan), Sacramento, and Atlanta. (The Flight Inspections Operations Division is within the Aviation System Standards, an FAA agency.)

Opportunities are limited, and openings usually become available as pilots retire, resign, or transfer to other positions.

Advancement Prospects

Upon completion of their initial training program, Airspace System Inspection Pilots advance to the second-in-command (or copilot) position. As they gain experience and as opportunities arise, they can be promoted to the pilot-in-command position. Pilots who are interested in pursuing higher managerial positions can seek promotions to become managers of field offices.

Education and Training

New hires undergo an intensive trainee program that consists of four phases. In the first phase, trainees receive instruction in such areas as federal aviation regulations, aircraft operation, crew resource management, and flight inspection techniques. In the second phase, trainees complete a training program to become qualified as second-in-command pilots. Upon successful completion of the program, they enter phase three, in which they gain mission proficiency by flying as copilot in line operations and by training with an instructor pilot. The fourth phase involves training to upgrade to pilot-in-command status.

ASIPs receive recurrent training throughout their careers to upgrade and maintain their skills.

Special Requirements

The FAA requires that ASIPs possess an airline transport pilot (ATP) certificate. Candidates who have commercial pilot certificates with multiengine and instrument ratings may be hired on the condition that they pass the ATP written examination within 60 days after they begin working. Pilots must also possess appropriate ratings for each type of aircraft they operate. Additionally, they must hold and maintain the first-class FAA medical certificate.

Experience, Skills, and Personality Traits

To be eligible for entry-level positions, applicants must have completed a minimum of 1,500 hours of total flight time. They must also meet other minimum flight-hour requirements, such as the number of hours of recent flight experience, night flying, and acting as the pilot-in-command of flights. Candidates may have gained their flight experience as pilots for commercial airlines, as military pilots, or as general aviation pilots.

To perform their tasks effectively, Airspace System Inspection Pilots should have excellent communication, interpersonal, teamwork, and leadership skills. In addition, they need strong self-management skills, such as the ability to meet deadlines, organize and prioritize tasks, work independently, and handle stressful situations. Being analytical, flexible, precise, calm, and cooperative are a few personality traits that successful ASIPs share.

Unions and Associations

Airspace System Inspection Pilots are members of the Professional Airways Systems Specialists, a union that represents them in contract negotiations with the FAA. The union seeks to get the best contract terms in regard to pay, benefits, and working conditions.

ASIPs can also join professional associations, such as the Aircraft Owners and Pilots Association, to take advantage of networking opportunities and other professional resources and services.

Tips for Entry

1. Visit the Web page for the Flight Inspection Operations Division to learn more about what ASIPs do. You can access this Web page by going to the Web site for the FAA Office of Aviation System Standards. Go to http://avn.faa.gov, then click on the link for flight inspection.
2. To learn more about ASIPs on the Internet, enter the keywords *airspace system inspection pilots* into any search engine.

AVIATION MEDICAL EXAMINER (AME)

CAREER PROFILE

Duties: Conduct medical examinations of pilots and air traffic controllers for FAA medical certificates; process medical certificate applications; perform duties as required

Alternate Title(s): General Practitioner or other title that reflects a medical specialty

Salary Range: Not applicable

Employment Prospects: Not applicable

Advancement Prospects: Not applicable

Prerequisites:

Education or Training—Complete an Aviation Medical Examiner seminar

Experience—Be a practicing physician

Special Skills and Personality Traits—Communication and interpersonal skills; impartial, fair, ethical

Special Requirements—Be a practicing, licensed physician

CAREER LADDER

Senior Aviation Medical Examiner

Aviation Medical Examiner

Physician

Position Description

Aviation Medical Examiners (AMEs) play an important role in the safety and efficiency of air transportation. They determine whether pilots meet the medical standards established by federal aviation regulations to operate aircraft. All pilots—student, private, recreational, commercial, public service, and airline pilots—must possess a current Federal Aviation Administration (FAA) medical certificate. AMEs give medical examinations to pilots who are applying for initial or renewal medical certificates. If pilots pass their examinations, AMEs issue them FAA medical certificates, which certify that they are medically fit to perform flight duties.

AMEs are not FAA employees. They are private physicians who have been appointed by the FAA to perform pilot medical examinations in their local areas. These doctors are engaged in different specialties, such as family practice, internal medicine, general surgery, aviation medicine, ophthalmology, and psychiatry. The FAA medical examination is one of the services that they offer as part of their medical practice.

AMEs perform medical examinations for the issuance of three classes of medical certificates. Pilots must obtain the appropriate level of medical certification for the type of pilot certificate they are seeking or currently hold. AMEs are also authorized to issue a combined medical and student-pilot certificate to applicants meeting medical standards and student pilot requirements. Some AMEs are designated to perform medical examinations for air traffic controllers and other aviation professionals who must meet FAA medical standards to perform their jobs.

All FAA medical examinations involve obtaining an applicant's medical history, performing a physical examination, and completing laboratory tests. AMEs are expected to perform a thorough and careful examination to ensure that aircraft are under the control of medically fit pilots. They are also required to comply with appropriate FAA policies and procedures.

AMEs make one of three decisions upon completing a medical examination. They may approve a pilot's application and immediately issue a medical certificate to the pilot. They may deny an application if the applicant does not meet any of the medical standards required for the medical certificate he or she is seeking. (An applicant can appeal an AME's decision and request a special issuance of a medical certificate from the FAA.) Thirdly, AMEs may defer making a decision about an application because a further review of medical problems is needed, the medical examination is incomplete, or for other reasons.

AMEs are required to complete FAA forms for all medical examinations that they perform regardless of the final outcome—issuance of a medical certificate, denial of an application, or deferral of a decision. AMEs make sure that the forms are filled out accurately and that they are complete, dated, signed, and electronically forwarded to the FAA.

Many AMEs are assisted by members of their staff (such as a nurse, physician's assistant, or laboratory assistant) to perform pilot medical examinations. AMEs train and supervise staff members to do various tasks, such as performing laboratory tests and completing FAA forms. AMEs are always accountable for the quality and accuracy of everything done by their staff.

Most AMEs offer consultation to individuals who are unsure if their medical conditions may disqualify them from obtaining medical certification. Pilots may consult AMEs about newly developed or worsening medical conditions to determine whether they meet medical requirements for flying.

Many AMEs perform educator and consultant roles for the FAA. For example, they might:

- give lectures on medical topics or clinical demonstrations on examination techniques at AME seminars
- make presentations on aeromedical issues at FAA aviation safety seminars for pilots
- assist in investigations of aviation accidents
- offer advice on whether pilots should be granted a medical certificate if they have recently developed a health condition, experienced a major illness, or undergone surgery
- offer advice on whether patients can be safely transported on aircraft

Salaries

AMEs charge pilots a fee for their medical examinations. According to a survey in the winter 2001 issue of *Federal Air Surgeon's Medical Bulletin,* the average fees charged for medical examinations by responding AMEs ranged from $67 for third-class medical certification to $77 for first-class medical certification.

Employment Prospects

Aviation Medical Examiners may be solo practitioners, partners in group practices, or employees of health care networks. More than 5,000 AMEs perform medical examinations for air traffic controllers and pilots in the United States and in foreign countries. Some AMEs conduct examinations specifically for federal agencies such as the military and the National Aeronautics and Space Administration (NASA).

Generally, openings become available when physicians retire, move away from their area, or decide to stop offering pilot medical examinations. The FAA usually appoints new AMEs in locations where there is a strong demand for aeromedical certification services.

Advancement Prospects

There are no advancement opportunities for AMEs.

When physicians receive their initial designation as AMEs, they are only authorized to perform medical examinations for second-class and third-class medical certificates. After serving three years as an AME, physicians may apply for the senior AME designation, which allows them to perform first-class medical examinations.

Education and Training

Candidates must complete a basic Aviation Medical Examiner seminar, which lasts several days at the FAA Civil Aerospace Medical Institute in Oklahoma City. The seminar covers such topics as FAA policies, federal aviation regulations, the AME's responsibilities, the AME's role in aviation safety, aviation physiology, aviation medicine, airmen medical certification standards, the medical certification process, and clinical examination techniques. To maintain their designation, AMEs must complete an AME seminar every three years.

Special Requirements

To become an Aviation Medical Examiner, applicants must be practicing, licensed physicians in the states where they will be performing FAA medical examinations.

Experience, Skills, and Personality Traits

Applicants must be practicing physicians who have an office in the area where they wish to serve.

AMEs should have good communication and interpersonal skills, as they must meet and handle pilots from different backgrounds. Being impartial, fair, and ethical are some personality traits that successful AMEs share.

Unions and Associations

AMEs may join professional societies, such as the Aerospace Medical Association and the Civil Aviation Medical Association, that serve the interests of physicians involved in aviation medicine. These professional associations offer AMEs the opportunity to network with colleagues and to take advantage of various professional services and resources.

Tips for Entry

1. To obtain more information about becoming an AME, contact a regional FAA Flight Surgeon's Office.
2. When you apply for AME designation, you must provide three references from physicians within your area. If you prefer, you may attach an official statement from your state licensing board that describes your professional standing in the medical community.
3. To learn more about aviation medicine, check out the joint Web site for the Office of Aerospace Medicine and the Civil Aerospace Medical Institute at http://www.cami.jccbi.gov.

NTSB AIR SAFETY INVESTIGATOR

CAREER PROFILE

Duties: Conduct investigations of aviation accidents, incidents, or safety hazards for the purpose of improving aviation safety; gather, analyze, and interpret evidence to determine the cause of accidents; prepare reports and other paperwork; perform other duties as required

Alternate Title(s): Investigator-in-Charge

Salary Range: $24,000 to $114,000

Employment Prospects: Fair

Advancement Prospects: Fair

Prerequisites:

Education or Training—Bachelor's degree; complete NTSB training program

Experience—Qualifications vary for the entry-level, field, and specialist positions; candidates must meet minimum flight requirements

Special Skills and Personality Traits—Critical-thinking, problem-solving, organizational, technical writing, teamwork, leadership, communication, and interpersonal skills; impartial, ethical, tactful, resourceful, patient, persistent, detail-oriented, dedicated

Special Requirements—Possess at least a commercial pilot certificate and an FAA medical certificate; driver's license

CAREER LADDER

Senior Investigator or Technical Specialist

Air Safety Investigator

Air Safety Investigator Trainee

Position Description

The U.S. National Transportation Safety Board (NTSB) conducts investigations of accidents, incidents, and other safety hazards occurring in the national air, rail, marine, and highway systems for the sole purpose of improving transportation safety. The NTSB is an independent federal agency; it is not affiliated with the U.S. Department of Transportation nor any of its divisions, such as the Federal Aviation Administration (FAA).

Air Safety Investigators are the NTSB staff members who are responsible for conducting aviation investigations. They do not enforce aviation regulations nor do they prove who is at fault for causing an accident or incident. Their role is to examine the facts, conditions, and circumstances that led to an aircraft accident, incident, or other safety hazard. Then, upon determining the probable causes, they recommend corrective measures that may prevent similar accidents or incidents from occurring.

NTSB Air Safety Investigators are authorized to oversee investigations of all aviation accidents or incidents that occur in the United States and its territories, as well as in international waters. They also act as the U.S. representatives in accident investigations that take place in foreign countries involving U.S. carriers or aircraft manufactured by U.S. companies.

Investigators handle cases involving all types, makes, and models of aircraft—gliders, helicopters, single-engine airplanes, seaplanes, turboprop airplanes, jets, and so on. Their investigations involve accidents and incidents that happen in general aviation (including private, corporate, commercial, and public service flying), as well as ones that occur with air carrier operations (including major, national, regional, independent and international airlines).

Some of the different cases that investigators might handle include accidents involving pilot error, structural failure, equipment malfunction, or fire; midair collisions; partial disintegration or complete destruction of aircraft in flight; crashes resulting in total destruction of aircraft and loss of human lives; and accidents in which the wreckage cannot be located.

Air Safety Investigators look into the different aspects of the aviation industry to uncover the probable causes of an accident. For example, in an incident in which a corporate aircraft crashed upon landing, some of the areas that investigators might examine are federal aviation regulations, the company's aviation management policies, the aircraft's structure and wreckage, the aircraft's avionics systems, the aircraft maintenance history, the pilot's records, the company's training programs, the role of the air traffic control system, and the response of search and rescue teams.

Aviation investigations are conducted by a team composed of NTSB Air Safety Investigators. The team always includes a representative from the FAA as well as representatives from various organizations in the aviation industry who can provide expertise to the investigations. For example, a team investigating a scheduled air carrier accident might include representatives from the airline owning the aircraft; aircraft and aircraft parts manufacturing companies; pilot, aircraft mechanic and air traffic controller unions; and professional aviation groups. A senior NTSB Air Safety Investigator, known as the investigator-in-charge, is responsible for supervising and directing the investigation team.

When an accident (or incident) occurs, field investigations generally start by spending several days or a few weeks at an accident scene. NTSB Air Safety Investigators carefully walk and climb through the wreckage to search and gather evidence. They document the details of the crash by taking photographs, sketching diagrams, writing detailed notes, and so on.

After they complete their inspections, investigators may supervise the reconstruction of the wreckage to determine what factors may have contributed to the accident. Aircraft engines may also be disassembled and tested by manufacturers, under the investigators' supervision.

Field investigations also involve interviewing witnesses, crew members, air traffic controllers, dispatchers, and others. Additionally, Air Safety Investigators examine various documents such as aircraft maintenance records, pilot medical records and performance files, witness statements, and public hearing transcripts. They also review tape recordings of pilot conversations with air traffic controllers, computer data, radar data, instruction manuals, photographs, charts, and other materials.

Investigators are responsible for maintaining accurate written records of the facts, conditions, and circumstances that they uncover. After completing their investigations, they prepare a report of their findings and conclusions along with their safety recommendations to prevent future accidents.

NTSB Air Safety Investigators perform other duties, which may include:

- conducting or participating in meetings and conferences with civil organizations and government agencies, as representatives of the NTSB
- examining witnesses at public hearings for aviation accidents
- maintaining relationships with other federal agencies (such as the FBI, the FAA, or the U.S. Department of State), state or local aviation commissions, local law enforcement agencies, medical examiners, and so on
- providing status reports on investigations to an NTSB spokesperson or public affairs officer who provides factual updates to the media and the general public
- testifying before Congress on findings and issues related to aviation accidents

Depending on the complexity of a case, one or more NTSB technical specialists may be part of an investigative team. These are Air Safety Investigators who have expertise in a particular area, such as air carrier flight operations, aircraft structures, aircraft avionics systems, weather, or human performance. Specialists assist in field investigations, as well as conduct special studies or basic research to further develop the facts in a case. In major accidents, the investigation is divided into several groups representing specific areas of expertise with the technical experts in charge of the different groups.

Other technical specialists are experts in performing a specific aspect of investigations. For example, some Air Safety Investigators specialize in analysis, conducting public hearings, or preparing investigation reports.

Some Air Safety Investigators are part of the NTSB "Go Team," which is based at NTSB headquarters in Washington, D.C. They are technical specialists who are assigned to investigate major airline crashes anywhere in the world.

NTSB Air Safety Investigators are on call 24 hours a day and are frequently given assignments outside of regular work hours. They are ready to travel at any time to aviation crash sites throughout the world, which may be in such settings as swamps, mountains, jungles, deserts, shorelines, or urban areas. Because of the hazardous conditions that may be found at accidents, investigators wear protective clothing and equipment and follow strict safety procedures.

Salaries

Earnings for Air Safety Investigators vary, depending on such factors as their experience, job position, and geographical location. Their salaries are based on the federal pay schedule known as the general schedule (GS). Entry-level investigators start at the GS-5 or GS-7 level, while senior investigators may earn salaries up to the GS-15 level.

In 2004, the basic pay for GS-5 to GS-15 employees ranged from $24,075 to $113,674. Employees who live in areas with higher costs of living usually earn additional pay.

Employment Prospects

The NTSB is a small federal agency with more than 400 employees that handle safety investigations in all transportation areas. Air Safety Investigators may be based at NTSB headquarters in Washington, D.C., or at one of the regional offices.

Job openings become available as investigators retire, resign, or transfer to other positions. Additional positions are created from time to time to meet growing needs as long as funding is available.

Advancement Prospects

Trainees can advance through the ranks as field investigators, technical specialists, and investigators-in-charge. Investigators with management and administrative ambitions can pursue such positions with the NTSB. Those with entrepreneurial interests may become independent consultants in the private sector.

Education and Training

Entry-level Air Safety Investigators normally possess bachelor's degrees in aviation, engineering, physical science discipline, mathematics, or other related field.

New hires receive formal instruction and on-the-job training from senior investigators. NTSB Air Safety investigators receive recurrent training throughout their careers to maintain, sharpen, and update their skills.

Special Requirements

To be eligible for Air Safety Investigator positions, applicants must be U.S. citizens. They must also be able to read, write, speak, and understand English fluently. NTSB Air Safety Investigators must possess either a commercial pilot certificate with an instrument rating or an airline transport pilot (ATP) certificate, along with a current first-class or second-class FAA medical certificate. Furthermore, they must have a valid state driver's license.

Experience, Skills, and Personality Traits

Qualifications differ for the entry-level, field, and specialist positions. For example, entry-level (GS-5 or GS-7) candidates must have experience that demonstrates a broad knowledge of any of the following: aircraft design, manufacture and maintenance operations, operational requirements, facilities, practices, or procedures related to aviation activities. Their experience may have been gained through employment as a commercial or airline pilot, a certified aircraft mechanic, a certified flight instructor, an operations engineer with a military unit, or other acceptable occupations.

All candidates must have completed a minimum number of hours of flight time as a pilot, which vary for the different positions.

To perform their work effectively, Air Safety Investigators must have excellent critical-thinking, problem-solving, organizational, and technical writing skills. Having strong teamwork, leadership, communication, and interpersonal skills is also essential, as they must be able to work with many people from different professions and backgrounds.

Successful Air Safety Investigators have several personality traits in common, such as being impartial, ethical, tactful, resourceful, patient, persistent, detail-oriented, and dedicated.

Unions and Associations

NTSB Air Safety Investigators might join the International Society of Air Safety Investigators, a professional association that offers networking opportunities and other professional services and resources.

Tips for Entry

1. Many NTSB Air Safety Investigators began as NTSB student interns or trainees while they were in college. To learn more about the intern and student career experience program, talk with a college career counselor or contact an NTSB regional or field office.
2. To learn about current job vacancies at the NTSB, call the toll-free number (800) 573-0937. You can also read about NTSB openings at http://www.ntsb.gov/Vacancies/listing.htm.
3. You can make a good impression on your application by following instructions and filling it out completely and neatly. You might draft your answers on a sheet of paper (or get an extra application), then edit your answers so that they are brief, yet accurate and precise. Check that you have spelled all words and names correctly.
4. Learn more about NTSB Air Safety Investigators on the Internet. One place to start is at the aviation Web page at the NTSB Web site, http://www.ntsb.gov/aviation/aviation.htm.

AIRPORT FIREFIGHTER

CAREER PROFILE

Duties: Provide firefighting, rescue, fire protection, emergency medical services, and other duties; respond to all types of emergencies, such as fires, aircraft crashes, car accidents, bomb threats, and medical emergencies; perform duties as required

Alternate Title(s): Aircraft Rescuer/Firefighter; Airport Safety Officer

Salary Range: $19,000 to $59,000

Employment Prospects: Limited

Advancement Prospects: Good

Prerequisites:

Education or Training—High school diploma; complete an FAA-approved training program

Experience—Have previous firefighting experience

Special Skills and Personality Traits—Communication, interpersonal, teamwork, reading, writing, and self-management skills; calm, alert, dependable, honest, courteous, cooperative, courageous

Special Requirements—Driver's license; emergency medical service certification

CAREER LADDER

Lieutenant

Airport Firefighter

Airport Firefighter Trainee

Position Description

Airport Firefighters are responsible for protecting lives and property at municipal airports, international airports, and military air bases. They are trained to respond quickly and efficiently to all types of emergencies that may occur—structural fires, aircraft fires, aircraft crashes, car accidents, bomb threats, terrorism alerts, hazardous materials emergencies, medical emergencies, and so on. Airport Firefighters provide firefighting, rescue, fire protection, and emergency medical services 24 hours a day.

Airport Firefighters are especially trained to provide aircraft rescue and firefighting (ARFF) services, which involves the operation of special heavy-duty and complex aircraft rescue and firefighting vehicles and equipment. They follow strict Federal Aviation Administration (FAA) regulations, which govern ARFF response times, procedures, and training requirements.

Fire stations are strategically located near runways, as Airport Firefighters are required to reach aircraft emergencies and begin applying fire retardant within a few minutes of an alarm. As they cross runways to reach an emergency, they are alert to incoming and outgoing aircraft. In addition, they are in communication with the airport control tower, the local fire dispatcher, and, at some airports, with the National Guard.

The first priority of Airport Firefighters is to rescue the passengers and crew, who may need to be extricated from the aircraft. They must work quickly, as aviation fuels burn at very high temperatures, and the aircraft cabin can reach unbearable temperatures within minutes. They fight only that part of the fire that interferes with the rescue to allow more time for rescuing individuals. For example, Airport Firefighters spray the outside of the fuselage with overflowing streams of foam or water to draw off heat from the inside of the aircraft. Once a rescue is completed, they then redirect their energies to suppressing the fire.

In addition to firefighting, rescue, and emergency services responsibilities, many Airport Firefighters are involved in fire prevention duties. Many of them conduct routine fire and safety inspections of fuel farms, hangars, and other airport property to ensure that all fire protection regulations and codes are in compliance. They may also assist in presenting fire prevention training seminars to airline or airport employees.

Some Airport Firefighters play a dual role of performing firefighting and law enforcement duties. These firefighters are trained and certified as police officers. As police officers, they are responsible for providing law enforcement services and aviation security as required by the FAA.

All Airport Firefighters perform many additional tasks, which include:

- performing routine inspections and maintenance of all rescue and firefighting vehicles and equipment
- maintaining fire stations and grounds to ensure a clean, safe, and healthy working environment
- participating in routine drills and training sessions
- performing desk watch duty
- preparing required reports and paperwork

Airport Firefighters must be physically fit and have the stamina and endurance to handle intense, hard, and dangerous work. They are constantly exposed to high noise levels, extreme heat, toxic chemicals (such as nitrogen dioxide and carbon monoxide), and hazardous materials. Their duties involve climbing up and down ladders; running or walking in environments of extreme heat; crawling in confined spaces; and lifting and carrying persons, ladders, tools, and firefighting equipment. To minimize the risk of exposure to smoke, chemicals, and gases that may adversely affect their health, Airport Firefighters wear heavy protective clothing and equipment.

Airport Firefighters often work 50 hours or more each week. They are assigned to rotating shifts. Work schedules vary with the different agencies. For example, firefighters at one agency might work a 24-hour shift, followed by 48 hours off, whereas those at another agency might work 10-hour day shifts or 14-hour night shifts for three days, followed by three or four days off. While on duty, Airport Firefighters live and work at their fire stations.

Salaries

Earnings for Airport Firefighters vary, depending on such factors as their experience, employer, and geographical location. The estimated annual salary for most firefighters, including Airport Firefighters, ranged from $18,780 to $59,240, according to the May 2003 *Occupational Employment Statistics* survey, (by the U.S. Bureau of Labor Statistics).

Employment Prospects

In general, Airport Firefighters are employed by local or state fire departments. Some of them work for private firms that offer aircraft rescue and firefighting services.

Most job openings will become available as Airport Firefighters retire or transfer to other positions. The turnover rate for Airport Firefighter positions is low, and the competition for available positions is high. Employers may increase or reduce their workforce, depending on the needs of their airport units.

Advancement Prospects

Airport Firefighters can advance through the ranks, which usually progress from engineer to lieutenant, to captain, to battalion chief, to assistant chief, to deputy chief, and finally to chief. Promotions are based on job performance, competitive examinations, and seniority. Many fire departments require that applicants possess a bachelor's degree in fire science, public administration, or a related field for positions of battalion chief and higher.

Airport Firefighters can pursue other career paths by becoming a fire inspector, fire investigator, or fire protection engineer.

Education and Training

Minimally, Airport Firefighters must possess a high school diploma or a general equivalency diploma. Some employers require that firefighters also have an associate's degree or some college training, preferably in fire science or a related field. In addition, Airport Firefighters must have completed basic firefighting instruction at a fire academy or other institution.

Airport Firefighters complete FAA-approved training programs, which cover such areas as airport operations; aircraft construction and equipment; emergency aircraft evacuation; rescue and firefighting personnel safety; use of firefighting equipment and appliances; and basic emergency medical care.

Airport Firefighters fulfill mandatory training requirements to maintain and update firefighting skills and knowledge. Furthermore, they participate in at least one live fire drill each year. This drill includes a pit fire with an aircraft mock-up to simulate the type of aircraft fire that they may encounter.

Special Requirements

Applicants must meet specific age, residency, medical, and other requirements, which vary from one employer to the next. They are also required to possess a valid driver's license and a first-responder or emergency medical technician certification. Employers may hire candidates without the proper licensure and certifications on the condition that they obtain them within a specific time period. All required licensure and certifications must be maintained throughout their employment.

Firefighters may be required to obtain and maintain a security clearance.

Experience, Skills, and Personality Traits

Depending on the employer, applicants must have one to three years of firefighting experience, which may have been gained through paid or volunteer work. Some employers prefer to hire candidates who have previous aircraft rescue and firefighting experience.

Airport Firefighters must have excellent communication, interpersonal, and teamwork skills. In addition, they need good reading and writing skills. They also must have strong self-management skills, such as being able to handle stressful situations, organize and prioritize tasks, understand and follow directions, and work independently. Being calm, alert, dependable, honest, courteous, cooperative, and courageous are some personality traits that successful Airport Firefighters share.

Unions and Associations

Many Airport Firefighters belong to the International Association of Fire Fighters, which represents members in contractual negotiations.

Airport Firefighters might belong to professional associations that offer networking opportunities and other professional services and resources. Two national associations that serve the interests of Airport Firefighters are the Aircraft Rescue and Fire Fighting Working Group and the National Fire Protection Association.

Tips for Entry

1. Gain experience by volunteering at your local fire department.
2. Some fire departments have an apprenticeship program that includes both formal instruction and on-the-job training. Contact your local fire department to see if it may offer one and how you can apply for the program.
3. Many fire departments post listings of job vacancies, as well as information about recruitment on their Web sites. To find the Web site for a particular fire department, enter its name into a search engine.
4. Learn more about Airport Firefighters on the Internet. To get a list of relevant Web sites, enter the keywords *airport fire department, airport firefighters,* or *aircraft rescue and firefighting* into a search engine.

AVIATION SECURITY AND LAW

AIRPORT SECURITY SCREENER

CAREER PROFILE

Duties: Prevent lethal objects and hazardous materials from being carried on board aircraft; screen passengers, baggage, and cargo for forbidden items; operate various electronic and imaging machines; perform duties as required

Alternate Title(s): Transportation Security Screener; Airport Security Worker

Salary Range: $24,000 to $47,000

Employment Prospects: Fair

Advancement Prospects: Fair

Prerequisites:

Education or Training—High school diploma; complete security screener training program; obtain appropriate certification for operating screening equipment

Experience—One year's experience as an Airport Security Screener, a security officer, an X-ray technician, or in another related job

Special Skills and Personality Traits—Interpersonal, customer service, communication, and self-management skills; alert, courteous, honest, efficient, dependable

CAREER LADDER

Supervisory Screener

Lead Security Screener

Security Screener

Position Description

Airport Security Screeners play a vital role in the protection and security of people, aircraft, and airports. Their job is to prevent knives, swords, firearms, explosives, and other dangerous objects that can be used as weapons from being carried onto aircraft for criminal or terrorist purposes. Screeners also make sure that flammable liquids, solvents, poisons, and other hazardous materials that can cause fatal accidents are not being brought on board as well. Each day of the year, Airport Security Screeners check thousands of passengers as well as thousands of pieces of baggage and cargo for forbidden items.

In the United States, Airport Security Screeners are federal employees who work at more than 400 U.S. airports. They are hired and trained by the Transportation Security Administration (TSA), which is part of the U.S. Department of Homeland Security.

Airport Security Screeners are assigned to various stations in an airport to process passengers and baggage. Those screeners assigned at security checkpoints handle passengers before they reach their departure gates. They work efficiently and calmly as they screen passengers and their carry-on items. At all times, screeners try to keep lines flowing smoothly and in an orderly fashion. Local, state, or federal law enforcement officers may be also stationed at these checkpoints to provide additional security.

Screeners operate various types of electronic and imaging equipment to detect forbidden objects on passengers and in their carry-on items. Passengers walk through metal-detector machines that sense any metal objects. Screeners ask passengers to empty their pockets and remove any pieces of clothing that the screeners believe may be causing the machine to beep. They may also use metal-detector wands to scan closely over passengers' bodies. If Airport Security Screeners feel it is necessary, they may perform pat-down searches of passengers.

X-ray machines are used to inspect passengers' carry-on items. Passengers place their purses, backpacks, briefcases, luggage, and other objects on conveyor belts. As each object passes through the machine, X-rays penetrate through the object and project an image on a screen for Airport Security Screeners to examine. They look for certain clues that indicate suspicious metal, organic, or inorganic items. If they believe a closer inspection is needed, they may remove the bag and ask its owner to open the bag for them to search.

At some airports, screeners use special procedures to examine electronic devices—such as laptops—for trace residue of chemicals that may have been used to make explosives.

Airport Security Screeners are also assigned to stations where they examine cargo or passengers' check-in baggage. They use other types of X-ray machines to view the contents of luggage, packages, boxes, and so forth before they are loaded into the cargo section of an aircraft. Senior screeners may be assigned to operate equipment that detects explosives in baggage or cargo.

Most Airport Security Screeners are rotated to work at the different stations. They often stand for long periods of time and handle objects that weigh up to 40 or more pounds. Screeners are constantly aware of their surroundings and are alert for potentially threatening situations. They are expected to act in a calm and professional manner, particularly when dealing with frustrated, angry, or upset passengers.

Airport Security Screeners also perform other tasks. For example, they write incident reports and statements, make log entries into security records, and assist with inquiries or investigations into security issues at their airports. Screeners may be required to attend meetings to receive classified or security-sensitive information.

Lead security screeners are experienced staff members who are in charge of a team of screeners. Some of their duties include coordinating work activities, monitoring the progress of their crew's work, making work assignments, training team members, and preparing staff evaluations. Lead screeners may resolve staff complaints or refer them to their supervisor. Lead screeners also represent their teams in meetings with security supervisors and managers regarding work problems and issues.

Airport Security Screeners usually work a 40-hour weekly schedule, which may include working nights, weekends, and holidays. On occasion they are required to work overtime.

Salaries

Salaries vary, depending on such factors as education, experience, job rank, and geographical location. In 2003, the base annual salary for Airport Security Screeners ranged from $23,600 to $35,400 and for lead security screeners, from $31,100 to $46,700.

Employment Prospects

In response to the terrorist attacks that took place in the United States on September 11, 2001, the Aviation and Transportation Security Act of 2001 was enacted to federalize more than 400 U.S. airports. The federal government became responsible for all security, including screening personnel, at those airports.

Job opportunities are expected to become available as Security Screeners retire, resign, transfer to other positions, or leave the work force. The U.S. Congress may increase or decrease the total number of Airport Security Screener positions according to the changing needs of airport security. As of May 2004, TSA could employ up to 45,000 full-time Airport Security Screeners.

In order to be eligible for a Security Screener position, applicants must meet the following requirements:

- be a U.S. citizen
- be able to read, write, and understand English
- pass the selection process, which includes an aptitude test, English-language proficiency test, medical examination, physical abilities test, oral interview, drug screening, background investigation, and security check

A full background check requires three to six months to complete; therefore candidates are offered employment on a conditional basis. If recruits do not pass the background check, their employment is terminated.

Advancement Prospects

Airport Security Screeners can advance through the ranks to become lead screeners and supervisory screeners. Most screeners measure success by earning higher wages and receiving greater responsibilities.

Education and Training

Minimally, Airport Security Screeners must possess a high school diploma or a general equivalency diploma.

New hires receive both classroom training and on-the-job training. They receive instruction in such areas as stress management, conflict resolution, customer services skills, and the various screening procedures. They also receive certification on the screening equipment, such as the X-ray machine, that they would be operating.

Airport Security Screeners complete recurrent training and certification exams on a regular basis. They also receive training on new security equipment and job procedures.

Experience, Skills, and Personality Traits

Applicants for entry-level positions should have at least one year of work experience as an Airport Security Screener, security officer, X-ray technician, or other related job.

Airport Security Screeners must have excellent interpersonal, customer service, and communication skills. Their job also requires that they have strong self-management skills, which include the ability to work under highly stressful conditions, follow directions, and organize and prioritize tasks.

Being alert, courteous, honest, efficient, and dependable are some personality traits that successful Airport Security Screeners share.

Unions and Associations

In March 2003, Airport Security Screeners formed a local chapter of the American Federation of Government Employees. On behalf of all Airport Security Screeners, the union lobbies Congress, advances their rights in the courts, and represents them at grievance and discrimination hearings.

Tips for Entry

1. You must complete a separate job application for each location where you would like to work.
2. The TSA maintains for each airport a pool of eligible applicants who are available for hire when openings occur. Eligible applicants are kept on file for one year.
3. To learn about job openings, visit the TSA Web site. Go to http://www.tsa.gov, then click on the link for employment.

AIRPORT POLICE OFFICER

CAREER PROFILE

Duties: Provide law enforcement services and airport security; preserve the peace, protect life and property, and provide public service; enforce local, state, and federal laws and regulations; perform duties as required

Alternate Title(s): Law Enforcement Officer; Airport Public Safety Officer

Salary Range: $26,000 to $67,000

Employment Prospects: Good

Advancement Prospects: Excellent

Prerequisites:

Education or Training—High school diploma; college training or degree may be required, complete employer's airport security training program

Experience—Previous law enforcement experience generally required

Special Skills and Personality Traits—Problem-solving, observational, teamwork, communication, interpersonal, public relations, writing, computer, and self-management skills; cooperative, trustworthy, level-headed, quick-thinking, dependable, courteous

Special Requirements—Police officer certificate; driver's license

CAREER LADDER

Special Assignments, Detective, or Sergeant

Airport Police Officer

Police Officer or Recruit

Position Description

Airport Police Officers are responsible for providing law enforcement services and aviation security at airports to ensure a safe environment for travelers, tenants, employees, and the general public. Their responsibilities include preserving the peace, protecting life and property, and providing public service. They enforce local and state laws, regulations, and ordinances as well as federal laws and regulations relating to aviation security.

Airport Police Officers are stationed on airport grounds. At some airports, officers are members of a local police department, assigned to their department's special airport unit or division. At other airports, the police force is its own department under the independent and autonomous control of the airport authorities.

Airport Police Officers patrol airport terminals, security checkpoints, ramps, runways, parking lots, perimeters, and other airport property 24 hours a day, every day of the year. They cover their assigned routes on foot, in patrol vehicles, or on bicycles. Some officers are trained as canine handlers and conduct their duties with police dogs.

As sworn peace officers, Airport Police Officers are authorized to carry firearms and to apprehend and arrest individuals who are suspected of breaking the law. These officers perform their duties calmly and efficiently, while making decisions quickly to resolve situations. They respond to calls from security screeners, airport employees, airline personnel, air traffic controllers, airport tenants (such as restaurants, gift shops, and car rental companies), travelers, and others. They investigate various criminal activities such as vandalism, shoplifting, theft, drug dealing, assault, rape, murder, and bomb threats. They also look into such problems as lost items, public nuisances, and missing persons.

At federalized airports, Airport Police Officers routinely monitor security checkpoints in the airport terminals. They handle situations created by unruly passengers and investigate the discovery of weapons, drugs, and other illegal items. Airport Police Officers also investigate any security breaches and, if necessary, secure areas and evacuate people from the airport in the interest of public safety.

Airport Police Officers also enforce traffic codes at the airport and provide traffic control in and out of airports and on nearby highways during emergencies or special events. Additionally, they investigate traffic accidents that occur on airport grounds. (At some airports, the police departments hire civilian security officers to perform traffic duties.)

In addition, Airport Police Officers respond to emergency situations such as vehicle accidents, heart attacks, or childbirth. They provide first aid, CPR (cardiovascular pulmonary resuscitation), and other emergency medical care that they are certified to perform.

Furthermore, Airport Police Offices provide general information about airport facilities to travelers and the general public. They also coordinate police efforts for special events—such as the arrival of visiting dignitaries—that require heightened security.

Airport Police Officers are responsible for understanding and following standard police operating procedures for responding to dispatch calls, making arrests, interviewing suspects and witnesses, conducting searches, operating radios, using firearms, and so forth. They keep a daily field notebook about their activities and complete paperwork on incidents. All police logs and reports must be accurate and detailed as they become permanent public records that can be used as evidence in court trials.

Airport Police Officers become familiar with aviation terminology and airport operations. They also are knowledgeable about the protocols and procedures established by federal agencies for handling aviation security and responding to aircraft accidents and other emergencies. Some of them are also trained to assist with aviation safety; for example, they might conduct safety inspections or assist with removing snow or debris on runways.

Airport Police Officers work cooperatively with other law enforcement agencies that operate within the airport's jurisdiction. These include other local police departments as well as sheriff's offices and state police departments. They also assist various federal agencies with diverse activities involving aviation security, aviation safety, narcotics surveillance, contraband, and so on. Some of these agencies include the Transportation Security Administration (TSA), the Federal Aviation Administration (FAA), the U.S. Immigration and Customs Enforcement, the FBI, the Drug Enforcement Administration, and the U.S. Department of Agriculture.

Airport Police Officers are required to maintain the physical standards for which they were hired. They stand, walk, and climb stairs for long periods of time as they patrol their assigned areas inside or outside airport properties. They are expected to be ready to move quickly in response to dispatch calls, as well as to apprehend criminal suspects. In addition, they must have the strength to lift heavy objects and injured persons.

Airport Police Officers may be employed full time or part time. They work rotating shifts, which may include working nights, weekends, and holidays. On occasion, they are required to work overtime. Many officers are on call 24 hours a day to handle emergencies, as well as to fill in for absent officers.

Salaries

Annual salaries for Airport Police Officers vary, depending on such factors as education, their experience, rank, and geographical location. In addition to their salary, Police Officers receive overtime compensation. According to the May 2003 *Occupational Employment Statistics* survey (by the U.S. Bureau of Labor Statistics), the estimated annual salary for most Police Officers ranged between $26,000 and $67,470.

Employment Prospects

Most job openings are created to replace officers who retire, transfer to other positions, or leave law enforcement work.

Since the terrorist acts took place in the United States on September 11, 2001, the demand for stronger airport security has increased. Law enforcement agencies will create additional positions to meet security needs as long as funding is available.

Advancement Prospects

Airport Police Officers can follow various career paths, depending on their interests and ambitions. Those interested in administrative and managerial positions can rise through the ranks as sergeants, lieutenants, captains, and so forth. They must have additional experience and education as well as pass competitive exams and reviews.

Police officers can also choose to pursue a career in police investigations. They become eligible to take the competitive detective exam after completing two or three years of patrol duty. In larger airport police departments, officers can volunteer for special details, such as bike patrol, K-9 units, bomb squad, and SWAT teams, when they meet eligibility requirements.

Education and Training

Applicants must have a high school diploma or general equivalency diploma. Many departments also require applicants to have a minimum number of college credits with courses in police science or other related study. Some police departments require applicants to have either an associate's or bachelor's degree in criminal justice, law enforcement, criminology, or a related field.

New hires complete airport security training, which covers the use of firearms, procedures for aviation security activities, and law enforcement responsibilities in airport security. Airport Police Officers must complete recurrent training to maintain their certifications, as well as to update their skills and knowledge in law enforcement and aviation security.

Special Requirements

Airport Police Officers must hold a current POST (peace officer standard and training) certificate, which is earned upon completion of basic training at a police academy.

To become an Airport Police Officer, applicants must meet the following general requirements:

- be a U.S. citizen; some agencies may hire noncitizens as long as they will become naturalized citizens within a specific time period
- meet the minimum age qualification, which varies with each agency
- meet vision and hearing qualifications
- have no criminal record
- have no misdemeanor conviction of domestic violence, which disqualifies a person from obtaining a permit to carry weapons
- hold a valid driver's license
- pass a selection process that includes a written examination, oral interview, medical exam, physical ability test, drug and alcohol screening, psychological evaluation, polygraph examination, and background investigation

Some agencies require that applicants possess an emergency medical technician certification or be able to obtain the certification within a specific time period after being hired.

Experience, Skills, and Personality Traits

Police departments generally require that officers have one or more years of experience on the police force before they may apply for an assignment with their airport police unit. Airport police departments typically prefer to hire candidates who have previous law enforcement experience.

To perform their job effectively, Airport Police Officers must have excellent problem-solving, observational, and teamwork skills. They also need strong communication, interpersonal, and public relations skills, as they must be able to work well with the public, airport personnel, and other law enforcement officers. Having good writing and computer skills is essential, too. Furthermore, officers must have exceptional self-management skills, such as the ability to work independently, handle very stressful situations, prioritize tasks, and understand and follow directions.

Some personality traits that successful Airport Police Officers share are being cooperative, trustworthy, levelheaded, quick-thinking, dependable, and courteous.

Unions and Associations

Airport Police Officers are usually members of a union that represents them in contract negotiations with their employers. The union seeks to get the best contract terms in regard to pay, benefits, and working conditions. It also handles any grievances that officers may have against their employers.

Many Airport Police Officers join local, state, regional, national, or international associations to take advantage of networking opportunities, education programs, and other professional services and resources. Some professional societies that are available to Airport Police Officers are the International Association of Airport and Seaport Police, the Fraternal Order of Police, the American Federation of Police and Concerned Citizens, and the International Association of Women Police.

Tips for Entry

1. As a high school student, you might gain experience by joining the Police Explorers or the police reserves, or by doing volunteer work with a local law enforcement agency.
2. To help you prepare for the written police examination, review one of the general study guides that are available. You may be able to find a copy of a police examination study guide at your public library.
3. Your eligibility will be based on the information you provide on your application about your education and experience. Therefore, it is essential that you provide correct and accurate details.
4. If your police department has an airport police unit, let the unit's commander know of your interest, even if a position is not currently available.
5. Learn more about Airport Police Officers on the Internet. To get a list of relevant Web sites to read, enter the keywords *airport police officers, airport police department,* or *airport police unit* into a search engine.

FEDERAL AIR MARSHAL

CAREER PROFILE

Duties: Provide protection and security on board U.S. air carriers; prevent acts of terrorism; perform duties as required

Alternate Title(s): Special Agent

Salary Range: $35,000 to $81,000+

Employment Prospects: Poor

Advancement Prospects: Fair

Prerequisites:

Education or Training—Bachelor's degree (or three years of qualifying work experience); complete the air marshal training program

Experience—Previous law enforcement experience preferred

Special Skills and Personality Traits—Crisis management abilities; marksmanship skills; analytical, leadership, communication, self-management, writing, and computer skills; calm, observant, decisive, flexible, level-headed

CAREER LADDER

Senior Air Marshal

Air Marshal

Recruit

Position Description

Federal Air Marshals are law enforcement officers who perform their duties in the sky. As members of the Federal Air Marshal Service, they handle any terrorist acts that might occur aboard U.S. air carriers. These special agents—men and women—fly daily on domestic and international flights. Their main responsibility is to stop any individuals who may be on board a flight from committing terrorist acts. Federal Air Marshals may also respond to other criminal incidents or in-flight emergencies.

Federal Air Marshals are sometimes called sky marshals. In the early 1970s, the Federal Air Marshal Service was managed by the U.S. Marshals Service and known as the sky marshal program. It eventually became part of the Federal Aviation Administration (FAA), and the Air Marshals were mostly deployed on international routes.

In 2003, the Federal Air Marshal Service was transferred to the U.S. Department of Homeland Security and at the end of the year became a branch of the agency called the Immigration and Customs Enforcement (ICE). About 5,000 ICE agents are expected to be cross-trained in the duties of Federal Air Marshals so that they can provide additional support when needed. Existing Federal Air Marshals will also be trained to perform other duties in ICE.

Federal Air Marshals usually work in teams of two but, at times, may be required to perform their job alone. They are authorized to carry firearms and make arrests without warrants. They are highly skilled experts in marksmanship and explosives, and are trained to use their weapons on board aircraft with the least amount of force. These law enforcement officers perform their work undercover in the guise of everyday travelers. Only pilots and flight crew are aware of their presence on board flights.

The job of Federal Air Marshals involves extensive travel. They fly to different cities for several weeks at a time. Their international assignments often require them to travel to foreign countries that are politically or economically unstable. They may also stay in locations that present health hazards due to poor sanitation or unsafe water. While they are deployed on assignment, they have limited contact with their families.

Federal Air Marshals are responsible for maintaining the qualifications for which they were hired. For example, they complete regular training sessions in order to keep their marksmanship skills at top levels. They are also subject to random drug and alcohol screening and are required to pass annual physicals to meet and maintain medical standards. Furthermore, Federal Air Marshals are responsible for keeping up with new federal laws and regulations that govern civil aviation security.

Federal Air Marshals work irregular hours and shifts. They work long days, and are on call 24 hours a day.

Salaries

Annual earnings for Federal Air Marshals vary, depending on such factors as their experience, overtime hours, and geographical location. In 2003, the annual salaries for Federal Air Marshals ranged from $35,100 for least experienced officers to $80,800, for officers with the most experience. Agents who live in areas with a higher cost of living receive an adjustment to their wages.

Employment Prospects

After the terrorist attacks that took place in the United States on September 11, 2001, the Federal Air Marshal Service greatly expanded their numbers from less than a hundred to several thousand Federal Air Marshals. The service does not reveal the exact number of Federal Air Marshals for security reasons.

The competition for jobs is very high. When the recruitment period was closed in early 2002, the program received hundreds of thousands of applications. Those meeting qualifications were placed on an eligibility list from which managers draw when openings occur.

The Federal Air Marshal Service recruits for new applicants to meet their needs, as long as funding is available. New agents are hired to replace those who retire, resign, or transfer to other positions.

To be eligible for a Federal Air Marshal position, applicants must meet the following qualifications:

- be a U.S. citizen
- be under 40 years old upon appointment
- meet vision, hearing, and other medical standards
- be eligible for and maintain a top-secret security clearance
- pass all steps of the selection process, which includes an interview, firearms proficiency test, medical exam, physical fitness test, psychological screening, drug screening, security check, and background investigation

Advancement Prospects

Federal Air Marshals realize advancement by earning higher pay and by receiving assignments of their choice. They can advance to supervisory and managerial positions by becoming lead and supervisory special agents. Those with managerial ambitions might pursue higher management and administrative positions in the Federal Air Marshal Service as well as in other agencies of the Department of Homeland Security.

Federal Air Marshals are eligible to retire after 25 years of service. Some retired marshals pursue second careers in aviation security by becoming security consultants.

Education and Training

Minimally, Federal Air Marshals must possess bachelor's degrees for entry-level positions. Qualifying work experience may be substituted for some or all of the educational requirement for entry-level positions.

Federal Air Marshals are initially hired as recruits and must successfully complete an intensive training program, which covers such areas as marksmanship, tactical procedures, and physical fitness. In order to maintain their positions, they must complete recurrent training to maintain and update their skills.

Experience, Skills, and Personality Traits

Employers generally prefer that candidates have previous law enforcement experience, particularly in civil aviation security. Candidates should also be knowledgeable about federal laws and regulations that govern aviation security. In addition, they should be able to demonstrate the ability to work well in a crisis management environment and to exhibit superior marksmanship skills.

To be effective at their job, Federal Air Marshals must have excellent analytical, leadership, and communication skills. They must also have superior self-management skills, which include the ability to work independently, handle stressful situations, follow directions, and organize and set priorities. Having strong writing and computer skills is also important.

Some personality traits that successful Federal Air Marshals share are being calm, observant, decisive, flexible, and level-headed.

Unions and Associations

Federal Air Marshals might join the Federal Law Enforcement Officers Association, a professional association that offers networking opportunities as well as professional services and resources.

Tips for Entry

1. When applying for a position, be prepared to provide proof of citizenship, date of birth, education, training, and all other information requested on your application. You will also need to provide at least three references who are knowledgeable about your professional or educational accomplishments or about your work experience and skills.

2. Persons who have been convicted of committing acts of domestic violence are ineligible to possess or receive firearms and therefore cannot be employed as Federal Air Marshals.
3. To learn more about the Federal Air Marshal Service and the U.S. Immigration and Customs Enforcement (ICE), visit the ICE Web site at http://www.ice.gov.

AVIATION LAWYER

CAREER PROFILE

Duties: Provide legal advice to clients; perform various legal services such as handling legal transactions or representing clients in courts; perform duties as required

Alternate Title(s): Associate; Partner; Staff Attorney; Corporate Counsel; FAA Attorney

Salary Range: $45,000 to $146,000+

Employment Prospects: Good

Advancement Prospects: Good

Prerequisites:

Education or Training—Bachelor's degree and a law (J.D.) degree; complete employer's training programs

Experience—Entry-level positions generally require previous experience as law clerks; government agencies usually require one or more years' experience as a practicing lawyer

Special Skills and Personality Traits—Research, writing, communication, interpersonal, and self-management skills; cooperative, creative, flexible, analytical, persistent, conscientious, dedicated

Special Requirements—Attorney's license; must be registered with a federal court in order to practice before it

CAREER LADDER

Partner or Solo Practitioner

Senior Associate or Solo Practitioner

Junior Associate

Law Student

Position Description

Aviation Lawyers specialize in the practice of aviation law, which governs the manufacture, ownership, operation, and maintenance of aircraft, as well as the maintenance of airports and other aviation facilities. These attorneys are knowledgeable about the aeronautical sciences. Many have technical expertise in such fields as aeronautical engineering, avionics, air traffic control, meteorology, and accident reconstruction. Many of them are also experienced pilots, although this is not a requirement for becoming an Aviation Lawyer.

Aviation Lawyers represent the varied interests of diverse clients in the aviation and aerospace industries. Clients may be private pilots, aircraft mechanics, families of air crash victims, charter operations, airline companies, fixed base operators, airports, aviation insurers, aircraft manufacturers, regulatory agencies, governments, or others. Some Aviation Lawyers also provide legal assistance to clients in foreign countries.

Aviation Lawyers advise their clients of their legal rights and obligations, as well as suggest legal plans of action. They establish a special relationship with each client and are obligated to put each client's interests above their own.

The practice of aviation law covers a wide range of legal services, and lawyers typically specialize in offering services in which they are most interested. Many Aviation Lawyers specialize in transactional work. They advise clients with legal transactions such as aircraft leases, business contracts, financing, insurance claims, acquisitions of aircraft or aviation businesses, company mergers, or joint ventures with other companies. They also assist clients with completing applications for licensure, certifications, registrations, loans, insurance, and so forth.

Some Aviation Lawyers specialize in trial practice (or litigation) before state and federal courts. They represent clients in lawsuits that arise out of aircraft accidents or business disputes. As litigation specialists, Aviation Lawyers are responsible for preparing cases for trial, developing legal strategies, handling negotiations and settlements, and, if necessary, appealing court decisions.

Another area in which Aviation Lawyers specialize is providing legal assistance to clients who have received citations from local, state, or federal government agencies for violating aviation regulations. Aviation Lawyers assist clients with their defense. These lawyers prepare written statements, represent clients at administrative hearings, and make appeals on their clients' behalf if they are unsatisfied with the results of their hearings.

Some other services that Aviation Lawyers might offer to clients are:

- provide mediation, arbitration, or other alternative dispute resolution services to help opposing parties reach a solution to their problems (such as contractual disputes) without going through court trials or administrative hearings
- advise clients about current regulatory, industry, and aeropolitical issues
- lobby members of the U.S. Congress or state legislatures on behalf of their clients about aviation issues that affect them
- testify before Congressional or state legislature committees regarding proposed aviation legislation
- assist clients to develop internal compliance programs
- provide advice on acquisitions, organizational restructuring, investments, and other business matters

Aviation Lawyers work in a variety of settings. Many of them work in private law firms as associates or partners. Some are solo practitioners. Private Aviation Lawyers might practice in one or more substantive areas besides aviation law—such as maritime law, employment law, real estate law, corporate law, or bankruptcy.

Some Aviation Lawyers work as staff attorneys for the federal and state government agencies that administer and enforce aviation regulations. These lawyers provide legal counsel and advocacy in the public interest.

Other Aviation Lawyers work as in-house counsels, or corporate counsels, for airlines, airport authorities, aircraft manufacturers, and other companies in the aviation and aerospace industries. As employees of private companies, Aviation Lawyers represent only their employers. They serve the legal interests of the corporations and not the people who run the companies. Their work generally involves taking care of transactional matters and providing business advice. At all times, Aviation Lawyers must make sure that their legal and business advice do not mix.

Aviation Lawyers perform a wide range of tasks to complete their jobs. They conduct legal research to learn what laws apply to the cases of their clients. They review and analyze legal documents. They write legal correspondence and draft legal documents, such as contracts and court briefs. They keep up with the aviation laws and regulations relating to their areas of practice. They also supervise legal secretaries, paralegals, and other legal support staff that assist them with their work.

On occasion, many Aviation Lawyers provide pro bono (free) legal services to economically disadvantaged individuals.

In addition to practicing law, many Aviation Lawyers are involved in teaching and writing about aviation law. Some of them teach one or more courses at law schools, colleges, or universities. Many make presentations or conduct seminars at professional meetings and conferences. Many Aviation Lawyers contribute articles, write columns, or act as editors for law journals, law publications, and law-related Web sites.

Aviation Lawyers often work more than 40 hours in order to complete various tasks, such as meeting with clients, conducting legal research, reading legal documents, and writing legal correspondence.

Salaries

Salaries for Aviation Lawyers vary, depending on such factors as their experience, type of employer, and geographical location. Typically, lawyers with large firms in large cities (such as New York, Boston, and Los Angeles) earn the highest salaries. The U.S. Bureau of Labor Statistics, in its May 2003 *Occupational Employment Statistics* survey, reports that the estimated annual salary for most lawyers ranged between $45,380 and $145,600.

According to a 2002 salary survey by the National Association of Law Placement, the median base salaries for associates in firms with two to 25 lawyers ranged from $53,500 for first-year associates to $92,250 for eighth-year associates. The range for associates in large firms with 501 or more lawyers was between $118,000 for first-year associates and $180,000 for eighth-year associates.

Employment Prospects

Employment in aviation law is fairly steady, but the competition is strong. With perseverance, Aviation Lawyers can eventually find the type of employment that they seek. Opportunities are available in small, midsize, and large law firms that practice aviation law. The Federal Aviation Administration (FAA), the National Transportation Safety Board, and state transportation agencies also employ Aviation Lawyers. In addition, commercial airlines and other companies in the aviation and aerospace industries employ lawyers with expertise in aviation law.

Advancement Prospects

In law firms, Aviation Lawyers can rise through the ranks from junior associate to senior associate to partner. As partners in a firm, lawyers earn a share in the profits of their law firm. Obtaining positions with higher pay, more prestige, or more complex responsibilities may require seeking employment with other law firms.

Government lawyers can advance to supervisory and administrative positions, based on their abilities as well as job availability.

Aviation Lawyers with entrepreneurial ambitions can work towards establishing successful law firms.

Other career paths are also open to Aviation Lawyers. They can become judges, law professors, lobbyists, politicians, FBI special agents, and corporate executives.

Education and Training

Aviation Lawyers hold a juris doctor (J.D.) degree, which they usually earn after three years of study at a law school. Most employers require that attorneys have graduated from a law school accredited by the American Bar Association.

Two general requirements for admission into any law school are the possession of a bachelor's degree (in any field) and the submission of scores from the Law School Admission Test (LSAT). All other entry requirements vary with the different schools.

In general, the first year of law school covers basic courses in contracts, torts, civil procedures, constitutional law, legal research, legal writing, and so forth. Students take elective courses in different areas of law during the last two years of school. They also participate in legal clinics, moot courts, and practice trials to gain practical experience.

Law firms typically provide their associates with in-house training and education programs. Many firms have mentor programs that team new associates with senior members.

Aviation Lawyers enroll in training and education programs throughout their careers to strengthen and build their legal skills and knowledge of aviation law.

Special Requirements

To practice law in any of the 50 states, the District of Columbia, or a U.S. territory, Aviation Lawyers must possess valid licensure. This requires passing the state (or D.C. or territory) bar examination where they plan to practice. Attorneys must complete continuing education units in order to renew their license.

Licensed attorneys may represent clients in other states without obtaining a license as long as they are working in association with licensed attorneys in those states.

To practice law in the federal courts, Aviation Lawyers must first register for admission in each federal court in which they plan to practice.

Experience, Skills, and Personality Traits

Requirements vary with the different employers. Law firms generally prefer to recruit newly graduated attorneys who have completed law clerkships in law firms, court systems, government agencies, corporate legal departments, or other organizations. Government agencies usually require their candidates to have one or more years of work experience as practicing lawyers.

Candidates should be knowledgeable about state and federal aviation laws and regulations and have technical expertise in aeronautics and the aviation industry. Having work experience in the aviation industry is highly desirable. For example, a candidate may have several years of prior experience working as a commercial pilot, an aeronautical engineer, or an FAA safety inspector.

Like all other lawyers, Aviation Lawyers should have excellent research, writing, and communication skills. Additionally, excellent interpersonal skills are essential, as they must be able to work effectively with colleagues, clients, law staff, court systems, and others. Aviation Lawyers also need strong self-management skills, including the ability to work independently, handle stressful situations, meet deadlines, and organize and prioritize tasks.

Being cooperative, creative, flexible, analytical, persistent, conscientious, and dedicated are some personality traits that successful Aviation Lawyers share.

Unions and Associations

Aviation Lawyers join various professional associations to take advantage of networking opportunities, education programs, and other professional resources and services. Most Aviation Lawyers are members of local and state bar associations. In some states, membership in the state bar association is mandatory. Many attorneys are also members of a national professional association such as the National Lawyers Association or the American Bar Association. In addition, many Aviation Lawyers belong to one or more of the following professional associations:

- Lawyer-Pilots Bar Association
- Aviation Section, Association of Trial Lawyers of America
- Aviation and Space Law Committee (part of the American Bar Association's Tort Trial and Insurance Practice Section)
- Forum on Air and Space Law (part of the American Bar Association)
- Aviation Litigation Committee (part of the American Bar Association)

Attorneys that practice before the U.S. National Transportation Safety Board, FAA, or U.S. Department of Transportation may join the National Transportation Safety Board Bar Association.

Tips for Entry

1. For general information about becoming an attorney, visit the Web site for National Association for Law Placement, http://www.nalp.org.
2. To gain experience, obtain an internship with a law firm that has a practice area in aviation law.
3. Join a professional association and participate in its activities to build up your network of contacts. Some associations offer student memberships.

4. To find out about attorney openings with the federal government, inquire directly at the field office for the FAA or other government agency where you are interested in working. Also check out the agency's Web site for employment information.
5. Learn more about aviation law and Aviation Lawyers on the Internet. To get a list of relevant Web sites, enter the keywords *aviation law, aviation law firm,* or *aviation lawyers* into a search engine.

AVIATION MANAGEMENT

AVIATION MANAGER

CAREER PROFILE

Duties: Oversee an aviation or aerospace program, department, division, or organization; perform duties as required of position

Alternate Title(s): A title that reflects a particular position such as Airport Director; Airline Station Manager; or Vice President of Flight Operations

Salary Range: $29,000 to $146,000

Employment Prospects: Good

Advancement Prospects: Good

Prerequisites:

Education or Training—Bachelor's degree usually required

Experience—Knowledgeable about the industry and the particular area in which one would be working; experienced or knowledgeable in accounting, finances, human relations, and other business areas; several years of work experience in one's field

Special Skills and Personality Traits—Leadership, teamwork, communication, interpersonal, organizational, analytical, negotiation, and writing skills; detail-oriented, flexible, decisive, determined, confident, self-motivated

Special Requirements—An FAA pilot certificate or FAA mechanic certificate with appropriate ratings may be required

CAREER LADDER

Senior Manager or General Manager

Midlevel Manager

Supervisor or Specialist

Position Description

Aviation Managers are responsible for overseeing aviation and aerospace programs, departments, divisions, and organizations. They are in charge of flight operations, ground operations, aviation maintenance departments, repair shops, airline departments, aviation service firms, aerospace companies, aviation education programs, regulatory divisions, and so on. Their job is to ensure that the daily operations under their direction are running smoothly and efficiently in addition to being cost effective for their organizations.

Some Aviation Managers are administrative services managers. They plan, direct, and coordinate support services that an organization needs to run efficiently. Examples of those support services include human resources, personnel training, finance, marketing, public relations, business services, information systems, and security.

Aviation Managers may be first-line supervisors, midlevel managers, or senior managers. First-line supervisors direct the work units that perform the jobs in an organization. Midlevel managers direct one or more departments, consisting of several work units, within an organization. Senior managers are usually executive officers; they are in charge of major departments or divisions in an organization. General managers, or operations managers, oversee the operations of an organization (such as an airport). In many organizations, the highest management position is the chief executive officer.

The layers of management vary from one organization to the next. Generally, the larger an organization, the more levels of management it has to ensure that the specific missions, goals, and objectives of the organization are being met.

Aviation Managers are employed in all areas of the aviation and aerospace industries such as:

- civilian airports—general aviation and commercial service airports
- commercial air carriers—including regional, national, and international airlines
- flight departments that are part of companies, nonprofit organizations, educational institutions, and other organizations that own and use aircraft for business transportation
- general aviation operators, such as air taxi (or air charter) services, fixed base operators (FBOs), aircraft management programs, air tour outfits, flight schools, air ambulance services, and so on
- businesses and companies that offer aviation supplies and services to pilots and operators—such as aircraft maintenance and repairs, avionics systems, ground handling services, fueling services, aviation insurance, and aviation management consulting services
- aerospace companies that are engaged in the development and manufacture of aircraft, aircraft engines, aircraft parts and accessories, missiles, space vehicle systems, and related goods
- aviation-related firms that supply products and services, such as paints, aircraft interiors, computer software, avionics systems, and consulting services to aerospace manufacturers

Aviation Managers also work in local, state, and federal government settings. Many work for agencies that perform various activities related to aviation or aerospace, such as enforcing aviation laws and regulations, providing aviation security, investigating aircraft accidents and incidents, conducting aviation research, or promoting aerospace education programs. Some federal agencies that employ Aviation Managers are: the Federal Aviation Administration (FAA), the National Transportation Safety Board, the Transportation Security Administration, the National Aeronautics and Space Administration, and the Office of Aeronautical Charting and Cartography.

Aviation Managers are also employed by state aviation departments that regulate and promote aviation at the state level. Locally, Aviation Managers are hired as airport managers to oversee the operation, maintenance, and administration of airports owned by municipalities or counties.

Some Aviation Managers direct flight operations run by government agencies for specific purposes, such as for firefighting or for law enforcement. For example, the Office of Aircraft Services in the U.S. Department of the Interior oversees flight operations that are part of firefighting divisions.

Many Aviation Managers work for nonprofit and nongovernmental organizations that serve the interests of various aviation professionals and groups. These include professional societies, trade associations, unions, public-interest organizations, community service organizations, and so on.

Regardless of their positions or work settings, Aviation Managers have several duties in common. They are responsible for fulfilling the missions, goals, and objectives of their employers. They plan, direct, and coordinate all activities of their programs, departments, divisions, or organizations. In addition, they enforce employers' policies as well as ensure that employers are in compliance with applicable laws and regulations pertaining to aviation, workplace, environment, and other areas.

Aviation Managers typically supervise and coordinate the work activities of staff members, who may be junior managers, professionals, technicians, administrative support workers, or others. Aviation Managers are involved in the hiring and firing process of personnel, and participate in the planning and coordinating of personnel training programs.

Aviation Managers perform a wide variety of administrative duties. For example, they might assist with or direct any of the following tasks:

- the preparation and administration of budgets
- the purchase of supplies, equipment, materials, and so on
- the development of short-range and long-range program goals
- the preparation and negotiation of contractual agreements with vendors, consultants, subcontractors, and others
- the preparation of correspondence, reports, records, and other required paperwork

In addition, Aviation Managers perform tasks appropriate to their specific role. For instance, aviation program managers with government agencies may be responsible for developing aviation education programs for school-age audiences, producing aviation safety materials, monitoring scheduled air service, and directing such activities as hazard removal from airports.

In some organizations, Aviation Managers perform pilot duties. For example, an Aviation Manager of a state department aviation program may be responsible for transporting executive officials to meetings in various locations.

Junior managers are typically supervised by midlevel managers who, in turn, are directed by senior managers. General managers and chief executive officers usually report to owners or boards of directors.

Aviation Managers generally work more than 40 hours a week. Many of them work long hours to complete tasks, meet deadlines, attend meetings, resolve problems, and so on. Senior managers and top executives usually have flexible schedules. Some managers, particularly first-line supervisors, work shifts. Some Aviation Managers are required to be on call 24 hours a day to handle emergencies.

Aviation Managers may be required to travel to other cities, states, or countries to complete work assignments, meet with customers, attend conferences, or perform other business duties.

Salaries

Salaries for Aviation Managers vary, depending on their qualifications, positions, responsibilities, type and size of their employers, geographical locations, and other factors.

The U.S. Bureau of Labor Statistics, in its May 2003 *Occupational Employment Statistics* survey, reports these estimated salary ranges for most managers (in all industries):

- administrative services managers, $28,690 to $107,490
- transportation managers, $36,940 to $109,330
- industrial production managers, $41,270 to $120,080
- general and operations managers, $34,850 to $112,730
- chief executives, $55,720 to $145,600

Employment Prospects

The number of opportunities for Aviation Managers fluctuate with the health of the economy. For example, when the national economy is in a downturn, job openings are typically fewer in the aviation and aerospace industry. However, experienced and well-qualified managers can usually find positions, as their role is essential to the success of organizations.

Most job openings become available as Aviation Managers become promoted to higher positions, transfer to other jobs, retire, or resign. Employers, particularly in large airports and airlines, sometimes create new managerial positions to meet their growing needs.

Advancement Prospects

Aviation Managers can advance through the ranks from first-line supervisors to midlevel managers to senior managers. Most advancement opportunities become available as managers retire, resign, or transfer to other positions.

Advancement prospects are generally better in large organizations that utilize several management layers. Managers in small or midsize organizations often move to other organizations to accept higher management-level positions or similar positions where they may earn higher salaries and hold greater responsibilities or challenges. Obtaining advanced degrees in aviation management, business administration, or related fields may enhance an individual's prospects for advancement to higher positions.

Aviation Managers with entrepreneurial interests might start their own management consulting businesses after years of experience.

Education and Training

Formal educational requirements vary with the different types of management positions. Many employers require that managers possess a bachelor's degree in a field related to the position for which they are applying. For instance, applicants for an airport director position might be required to hold a bachelor's degree in airport management, business administration, public administration, civil engineering, accounting, or another related field. Some employers prefer to hire candidates with advanced degrees for top-level management positions. Many employers allow qualifying work experience or a combination of education and work experience to be substituted for the educational requirement.

Special Requirements

Aviation Managers must hold the proper pilot certificate and ratings—which are granted by the Federal Aviation Administration (FAA)—if they will be performing any flight duties. They must possess the proper FAA mechanic certificate and ratings, if they will be performing any aircraft maintenance duties.

Some employers require that job candidates first successfully pass a drug test and a security background check before they can be hired.

Experience, Special Skills, and Personality Traits

Work experience requirements vary by job position as well as by employer. In general, Aviation Managers are knowledgeable about the aviation industry and, in particular, about the area (such as airports, airlines, or state aviation) in which they are working. They are also familiar with the appropriate federal aviation regulations, aviation safety laws, and other aviation issues pertinent to their work settings. They also have experience with or are knowledgeable of such business areas as accounting, finances, human relations, and marketing, and how they apply specifically to aviation or aerospace settings. Further, Aviation Managers possess several years of extensive work experience in their particular fields. Aviation Managers have typically worked up through the ranks, starting at staff positions and eventually progressing to supervisory and managerial positions.

To be effective at their job, Aviation Managers must have excellent leadership and teamwork skills. They should also have strong communication and interpersonal skills, as they must be able to establish effective working relationships with staff members, higher level managers, customers or clients, regulatory personnel, and others. Aviation Managers must also have superior organizational, analytical, negotiation, and writing skills.

Being detail-oriented, flexible, decisive, determined, confident, and self-motivated are some personality traits that successful Aviation Managers share.

Unions and Associations

Many Aviation Managers join professional associations to take advantage of networking opportunities, education workshops, professional certification, and other professional services and resources. They can join professional associations that serve their particular area of aviation management. For example, airport managers might belong to the American Association of Airport Executives, business aviation managers might belong to the National Business Aviation Association, and aviation maintenance managers might belong to the Professional Aviation Maintenance Association.

Aviation Managers are also eligible to join professional societies that serve their field; for instance, public relations managers may belong to the Public Relations Society of America, whereas training managers may belong to the American Society for Training and Development. In addition, Aviation Managers might join associations that serve the interests of all professional managers, such as the American Management Association.

Tips for Entry

1. High school students can begin to prepare for an aviation management career by taking courses in science and business. Additionally, they should take courses in English, reading, public speaking, and mathematics to start building a strong foundation in writing, reading, communication, and math skills.
2. To enhance their advancement prospects, individuals have enrolled in business courses at local colleges.
3. Carefully read the job description for the position in which you are interested. Make sure you meet the educational and experience requirements. Tailor your résumé and job application to show how you are the best candidate for the job.
4. Suppose a particular job interests you, but you do not meet the experience or education requirements for a job. Try for the job anyway. Many employers will allow for combinations of experience and education to substitute for minimum qualifications. You must be ready and able to demonstrate how you meet the minimum requirements.
5. Use the Internet to learn about private companies, government agencies, or other organizations where you would like to work. Many organizations post job listings and their job application process on their Web sites. To see if a particular organization has a Web site, enter its name into a search engine.

AIRPORT MANAGER

CAREER PROFILE

Duties: Oversee the administration, operation, and maintenance of airports; handle budgets, airport planning, community relations, and other activities; perform duties as required

Alternate Title(s): Airport Director; Airport Operations Officer; Aviation Manager

Salary Range: $35,000 to $113,000

Employment Prospects: Fair

Advancement Prospects: Fair

Prerequisites:

Education or Training—Bachelor's or advanced degree

Experience—Several years of supervisory and managerial experience in airport settings

Special Skills and Personality Traits—Writing, communication, computer, interpersonal, customer service, marketing, negotiation, problem-solving, and self-management skills; tactful, diplomatic, patient, self-motivated, enthusiastic, resourceful

CAREER LADDER

Airport Director (larger airport)

Airport Manager

Assistant Airport Manager or an Airport Department Manager

Position Description

Every year, millions of travelers and many tons of cargo are transported by small and large aircraft throughout the world. All flights—whether flown by private, commercial, corporate, or airline pilots—start and end their journeys at airports. These airports range from single grass airstrips to airports the size of small cities. It is the job of Airport Managers to ensure that airport operations—from air traffic to ground traffic—flow safely and smoothly from day to day.

Many of the airports in the United States are privately owned by individuals or businesses. Some are publicly owned by local and state governments. Airport Managers enforce the missions and objectives of their employers. They develop and implement goals, policies, and programs that are in compliance with airport master plans and business plans as well as with government laws and regulations.

In the United States, civilian airports are categorized as either general aviation or commercial service airports. Airport Managers in general aviation usually oversee small and midsized airports that serve one or more communities. General aviation airports are primarily used by private pilots and corporate flight departments as well as by commercial pilots and operators who offer aviation services for hire (such as crop dusting, flight instruction, air charter services, air ambulance services, and aerial surveys).

Managers of commercial service airports are usually in charge of large facilities that provide for scheduled flights on a regional, nationwide, or international basis. These airports, also known as air carrier airports or hub airports, are mostly used by airlines which operate large jet aircraft to transport hundreds of passengers and thousands of pounds of baggage and cargo each day.

Airport Managers are in charge of directing and coordinating all airport operations, such as passenger terminal operations, ground handling operations, baggage handling operations, cargo operations, airport security, and protective services. These managers plan and supervise airport emergency plans and safety programs. They coordinate regular inspections of buildings, grounds, runways, roads, equipment, and so on to check for proper maintenance and needed improvements or repairs. In addition, they respond to emergencies (such as bad weather or an airport security breach) and take appropriate action immediately.

Further, their job requires Airport Managers to continually analyze, research, and solve various problems as they occur. Airport Managers also make sure that airports are in compliance with all local, state, and federal laws and regulations regarding airport operations and aviation safety. Additionally, they enforce all applicable government laws concerning the environment, the workplace, construction, and other aspects that relate to their operations. For example, airports that handle international flights must comply with customs, agricultural, and immigration laws.

Along with overseeing daily operations, Airport Managers are responsible for supervising various other activities. One activity is the coordination of capital improvement projects, such as the renovation of a terminal building or the upgrade of approach lighting systems on airport runways. Another activity is the management of leases of airport tenants (such as airlines, fixed base operators, air charter services, restaurants, retail shops, and car rental agencies) who rent space for offices, check-in counters, baggage areas, aircraft storage, and so on.

Budgets and financial management are other essential activities. Airport Managers prepare and administer annual operating budgets as well as budgets for construction projects. They also monitor expenses and track revenues. Further, they handle or supervise the preparation, negotiation, and administration of contractual agreements with airport tenants, vendors, subcontractors, consultants, advertisers, and others.

Still another activity is airport planning. Managers oversee the planning for future needs for their airport and its facilities. They determine what types of airport development are needed to keep up with future airport use. They coordinate research studies that lead to answers to such questions as: Does the airport need more hangars? Should new runways be built? How can terminal buildings be improved to meet the needs of passengers? Are there sufficient access roads to the airport? Should parking areas be expanded? Is a permanent fire station needed on airport grounds? Airport Managers work with airport engineers, airport planners, and others to develop and implement plans. Managers may also be involved in preparing applications and proposals for grants and loans to fund capital improvement projects.

Maintaining positive relations with airport users, civic groups, and surrounding communities is another important part of an Airport Manager's job. Airport Managers respond to questions from the media and the public about the airport, as well as about air transportation matters such as airport security, noise issues, flight delays, or the impact on the environment by proposed capital improvement projects. Additionally, Airport Managers coordinate efforts to promote the use of airport facilities through such activities as preparing press releases and making presentations to civic groups. Further, Airport Managers keep up to date with proposed projects (such as road construction) or regulations (such as zoning changes) by local communities that may affect aviation safety or the use of the airport.

An Airport Manager's job requires a variety of administrative duties. For example, tasks might include writing correspondence, preparing required reports, supervising the maintenance of business management records, and conducting staff meetings. Airport Managers also act as liaisons between the airport and government agencies, including local law enforcement departments, state aviation department, and such federal agencies as the Federal Aviation Administration (FAA), the Transportation Security Association, the National Transportation Safety Board, the U.S. Immigration and Customs Enforcement and the U.S. Department of Agriculture.

Airport Managers of municipal airports are usually required to participate in local government meetings and community projects relating to aviation matters. They are also required to provide regular reports to local government bodies (such as the city council or airport commission) on the progress of airport activities, development proposals, budgets, and other aviation or airport-related subjects.

Another area of responsibility is providing direction and guidance to all airport personnel, including assistant managers, professionals, office support workers, maintenance staff, and so on. At large facilities, Airport Managers typically direct a management team that supervises the various airport departments. Airport Managers are responsible for developing personnel policies and procedures as well as employee training programs. At some airports, Airport Managers participate in the negotiation of collective bargaining agreements.

At small general aviation airports, the Airport Manager may be the owner or manager of a fixed base operator (FBO). This is an airport-based firm that sells such services as fueling services, flight instruction, ground handling services, air charter services, and aircraft repairs. The Airport Manager might provide flying lessons, perform aircraft maintenance, sell aircraft, or perform other tasks.

Airport Managers are expected to keep up with current trends in airport development, aviation industry, aviation regulations, and so on. They read various industry publications in print and online, network with colleagues, attend trade and professional conventions, enroll in seminars, and so on.

Most Airport Managers work a 40-hour week and often put in additional hours to complete tasks, meet deadlines, attend meetings, and handle emergencies.

Salaries

Salaries vary, depending on such factors as education, experience, airport size, and geographical location. The U.S. Bureau of Labor Statistics, in its May 2003 *Occupational Employment Statistics* survey, reports that the estimated annual salary for most general and operations managers ranged between $34,850 and $112,730.

Employment Prospects

More than 18,000 airports are located throughout the United States, with about 30 percent of them owned by local or state governments. The remaining airports are privately owned. More than 500 airports are commercial service airports that provide facilities for domestic and international air carriers, whereas the thousands of others, are general aviation airports.

Although employment opportunities in the aviation industry fluctuate with the economy, employment with airports tends to be stable through economic downturns.

Opportunities become available as Airport Managers are promoted, accept a position with another employer, or retire. The competition for positions is strong and fierce.

Advancement Prospects

Airport Managers of small airports usually advance by seeking management positions at midsize and large airports. Some Airport Managers measure their success by earning higher salaries and gaining a reputation for professional excellence.

Airport Managers might also pursue senior aviation management positions with state aviation agencies or with such federal agencies as the FAA or the National Transportation Safety Board. Experienced individuals with entrepreneurial ambitions might become airport management consultants.

Education and Training

Employers usually require that Airport Managers possess at least a bachelor's degree in airport administration, aviation management, public administration, business administration, aeronautical engineering, or another related field. At smaller facilities, employers may hire candidates with an associate's degree or high school diploma if they have qualifying work experience.

Experience, Skills, and Personality Traits

Qualifications for Airport Manager positions vary with the different employers. For example, candidates for large metropolitan airports typically must meet more demanding requirements than those for smaller airports.

Employers generally seek candidates who have several years of work experience performing management and supervisory duties in airport settings. Preferred candidates are highly familiar with the various aspects of airport operations, such as airport maintenance, airport planning. airport security, airport safety, legal contracts, public relations, marketing, and human resources. Additionally, candidates are knowledgeable about local, state, and federal laws and regulations applicable to airport use, management, and safety. Further, candidates demonstrate the ability to effectively lead a staff of employees performing diverse functions.

To perform their work well, Airport Managers must have excellent writing and communication skills as well as strong computer skills. They need effective interpersonal skills as they must be able to form and maintain relationships with public officials, government agencies, airport tenants, the media, the general public, and others. Having strong customer service, marketing, negotiation, and problem-solving skills is also essential for their job. In addition, Airport Managers need excellent self-management skills, such as the ability to handle several projects at a time, prioritize tasks, meet deadlines, and handle stressful situations.

Some personality traits that successful Airport Managers share include being tactful, diplomatic, patient, self-motivated, enthusiastic, and resourceful.

Unions and Associations

Many Airport Managers belong to state or regional associations that serve the professional interests of managers in their area. Airport Managers may also join a national professional society known as the American Association of Airport Executives. By joining professional associations, Airport Managers can take advantage of networking opportunities, along with education programs, certification programs, and other professional services and resources.

Tips for Entry

1. Various academic institutions throughout the United States offer degree or certificate programs in airport administration that specifically train students for entry into the field of airport management. These programs may offer internships or other types of work experience at airports.
2. Many employers allow applicants to substitute education for experience. For example, an employer may allow for a master's degree in airport or aviation management to be substituted for one or two years of work experience.
3. To enhance their employability, Airport Managers may apply for the Accredited Airport Executive (AAE) credential, issued by the American Association of Airport Executives, when they meet its program's requirements. For more information, write to: American Association of Airport Executives, 601 Madison Street, Alexandria, VA 22314. You can also learn more at its Web site, http://www.airportnet.org.
4. Use the Internet to learn more about the airports where you might like to work. Many airports have Web sites that provide a description of their operations, airport tenants, employment opportunities, and so forth. To learn if a particular airport is on the Web, enter its name into any search engine.

AIRLINE STATION MANAGER

CAREER PROFILE

Duties: Oversee an airline's station operations at a particular airport; manage, direct, and coordinate all flight and ground operations; perform duties as required

Alternate Title(s): District Operations Manager

Salary Range: $37,000 to $109,000

Employment Prospects: Fair

Advancement Prospects: Fair

Prerequisites:

Education or Training—Bachelor's degree; complete management training provided by employer

Experience—Be highly experienced in airline station operations; supervisory and management experience

Special Skills and Personality Traits—Leadership, teamwork, interpersonal, customer service, communication, organizational, time management, and computer skills; goal-oriented, analytical, open-minded, caring, persistent, decisive

CAREER LADDER

Division Manager of Station Operations

Station Manager

Assistant Station Manager or Manager of a Specific Operation (such as ramp services)

Position Description

Commercial airlines offer scheduled flights for passengers and cargo to small and large cities throughout the United States and around the world. The different airlines establish station operations at those airports where they provide flight service. Airline personnel known as Station Managers are responsible for the oversight of airport operations. They direct, coordinate, and manage all areas of airport operations, including flight operations, passenger services, ramp services, aviation maintenance, and system operations.

Airline Station Managers make sure that all flight and ground operations work smoothly and efficiently each and every day. These middle managers ensure that flights are running safely and on time; pilots and flight crew are assigned to every flight scheduled out of their station; passengers are being served in a satisfactory manner; cargo and luggage are being loaded and unloaded properly; aircraft are being fueled, serviced, and turned around efficiently; and so on.

Airline Station Managers are responsible for enforcing the mission and objectives of their employers. They assist in the development of new policies and procedures to meet specific goals and objectives for their particular stations. Those managers also monitor the performance of staff workers to ensure job quality, as well as to seek ways to improve operations, such as passenger services or ramp services. In addition, Airline Station Managers participate in creating plans to increase ticket sales and freight service.

The profitable success of an airline station is also dependent upon the Airline Station Manager's effectiveness as a leader. Station managers are in charge of all airline personnel assigned to their stations—pilots, flight attendants, aircraft dispatchers, ramp agents, cargo agents, aviation maintenance technicians, passenger service representatives, gate agents, administrative staff, and others.

Depending on the size of the airport operations, station managers may be overseeing a handful of staff members or as many as several hundred. Managers at large, complex stations may be directing a personnel staff of 1,000 or more. At some stations, some or all ground handling services are contracted to outside companies. Airline Station Managers are responsible for ensuring that the contractors provide an acceptable quality of service. Whether supervising staff members directly or through a team of department managers, Airline Station Managers are responsible for making sure that the communication and coordination between the different areas of operation are flowing smoothly.

Airline Station Managers handle various administrative duties, which vary from day to day. Some of their tasks include:

- determining functions and work priorities for the different areas of airport operations
- administering the station budget
- helping prepare the annual budget
- making sure that the station operations are in compliance with all applicable local, state, and federal laws and regulations
- serving as the airline's representative with governmental agencies such as their state aviation agency, the Federal Aviation Administration (FAA), and the Transportation Security Administration (TSA)
- attending meetings with airport authorities to discuss problems or issues
- planning and coordinating employee training programs
- handling employee issues
- preparing correspondence, technical reports, legal forms, and other required material

Every day, Airline Station Managers make decisions about a variety of events that occur in a day. Each day also offers Airline Station Managers new and different challenges. They troubleshoot various types of problems as they arise, such as passengers' complaints, security breeches, employee problems, flight delays, aircraft mechanical failures, and bad weather.

At small airports, Airline Station Managers may be required to assist with any number of ground crew duties. For example, they might sell tickets, check in passengers, handle passenger problems, load or unload baggage, or marshal aircraft in and out of position.

Airline Station Managers are assigned to airports in the United States or in other countries. They mostly work in offices at airports. They have a 40-hour work schedule but sometimes work long hours to attend meetings and complete tasks.

Salaries

Salaries vary, depending on such factors as experience, job responsibilities, employer, and geographical location. Formal salary information for Airline Station Managers is unavailable. However, according to the May 2003 *Occupational Employment Statistics* survey (by the U.S. Bureau of Labor), the estimated salary for most transportation managers ranged between $36,940 to $109,330.

Employment Prospects

Airline Station Managers are mostly employed by the various air carriers—regional, national, and international airlines. Some are employed by companies that offer operations services on a contractual basis to airlines.

In general, job openings become available to replace Airline Station Managers who are transferring to other stations, being promoted to higher positions, or retiring. As employers grow, they will create additional positions to meet their needs.

Advancement Prospects

Many Airline Station Managers have risen through the ranks, starting as ramp agent, ticket agent, reservation agent, passenger service agent, and so on. Airline Station Managers can advance in any number of ways. They can earn higher salaries, be assigned to larger stations, or establish new stations.

From Airline Station Manager, they may be promoted to the position of director or vice-president who oversees all stations. Depending on their background, ambitions, and interests, Airline Station Managers can also pursue management positions in other divisions, such as marketing or training.

Education and Training

Most employers prefer that Airline Station Managers possess a bachelor's degree in business administration or a related field. Many employers allow candidates to substitute equivalent experience, or a combination of education and experience, for a bachelor's degree.

Employers typically provide new Airline Station Managers with training, including classroom work and on-the-job training.

Experience, Special Skills, and Personality Traits

Employers typically seek Airline Station Managers who are highly experienced in airline station operations and have a work history of increasing supervisory and management responsibilities. Preferred candidates demonstrate a working knowledge of the different areas of station operations and of the airline industry in general. They are also knowledgeable about business, economics, and airline management. In addition, they are familiar with applicable local, state, and federal laws and regulations to station operations.

Airline Station Managers need excellent leadership and teamwork skills, along with effective interpersonal, customer service, and communication skills. Additionally, their job requires that they have strong organizational and time management skills. Having proficient computer skills is also important, as they must be able to work with word processing, spreadsheets, accounting, multimedia, and other types of software applications to complete their various tasks.

Being goal-oriented, analytical, open-minded, caring, persistent, and decisive are some personality traits that successful Airline Station Managers share.

Unions and Associations

Airline Station Managers are eligible to join professional associations, such as the American Management Association, that serve the interests of management professionals in general. By joining such societies, they can take advantage of training programs, management resources, and other professional services and resources.

Tips for Entry

1. Preparing for a career in airline management starts in middle school and high school. Many of the essential skills that managers need to succeed—such as critical-thinking, comprehension, report writing, public speaking, and computational skills—are built upon skills learned in English, mathematics, social studies, and science classes.
2. Learn as much about the different aspects of business as you can—accounting, human relations, finance, time management, and so on. Many colleges and universities offer academic and continuing education programs at night and on weekends to meet the needs of full-time workers.
3. Be willing to relocate to an airline station in another city or state.
4. As a staff member, let your supervisor know of your interest in becoming an Airline Station Manager. Ask them for suggestions on the experiences, skills, and training that you can start obtaining to prepare yourself for a management career.
5. Use the Internet to learn about the different airlines for which you would like to work. To find an airline's Web site, enter its name into any search engine.

FIXED BASE OPERATOR (FBO) MANAGER

CAREER PROFILE

Duties: Direct, coordinate, and manage a retail firm that offers aviation services and products to general aviation pilots and operators; perform administrative and management duties as required; may provide flight instruction, sell aircraft, or perform other services provided by their FBO

Alternate Title(s): FBO General Manager; FBO Owner

Salary Range: $35,000 to $113,000

Employment Prospects: Fair

Advancement Prospects: Poor

Prerequisites:

Education or Training—Educational requirements vary with the different employers

Experience—Have experience working with FBOs in different capacities; administrative and management experience

Special Skills and Personality Traits—Leadership, customer service, communication, interpersonal, teamwork, and self-management skills; energetic, enthusiastic, analytical, self-confident, decisive, flexible, determined

Special Requirements—FAA pilot certificate or FAA mechanic certificate with appropriate ratings may be required

CAREER LADDER

FBO Owner or FBO Manager of a Larger Business

FBO Manager

FBO Assistant Manager or an FBO Department Manager

Position Description

Fixed base operators (or FBOs) are retail establishments that sell aviation services and products primarily to general aviation pilots and operators, such as recreational pilots, commercial pilots, air charter operators, corporate flight departments, and air ambulance operators. (Some FBOs also offer their services to commercial airlines, government aviation operations, and the military.) FBO Managers are responsible for overseeing these operations and making sure they are running smoothly and efficiently every business day.

FBOs are located at general aviation airports as well as at commercial service airports. Historically, FBOs began as fuel stations for pilots. Today, they continue to offer fueling services, with many FBOs providing such services on a 24-hour basis. In addition, FBOs offer various aviation services and products to their customers, such as:

- ground handling services—such as aircraft marshaling, towing, deicing, aircraft cleaning, and lavatory services
- aircraft parking and storage, including aircraft tiedown and/or hangar storage
- passenger and crew services, such as baggage handling and catering
- aircraft sales, as well as sales of aircraft parts, pilot books, and other pilot accessories
- aircraft rentals or leasing to pilots for recreational, business, or training purposes
- flying lessons, including ground and flight instruction
- air taxi or air charter services
- technical services, such as aircraft maintenance, the installation and repair of avionics, or repair and overhaul services on propellers
- aircraft management services in which aircraft owners contract FBOs to operate and manage their aircraft

Many FBOs have crew lounges for pilots to use while waiting or planning for trips. Some FBOs also offer courtesy services to pilots, air crew, and passengers. For example, an FBO might make arrangements for local tours, hotel accommodations, or car rentals for pilots.

As general managers, FBO Managers direct, manage, and coordinate the various aspects of their operations. They make sure that FBOs are in compliance with all appropriate local, state, and federal laws and regulations. Their job also involves executing the policies, objectives, and vision of their employers. In addition, FBO Managers develop short-range and long-range plans to enhance operations and improve customer service, as well as to ensure the profitable growth of the FBOs.

FBO Managers are responsible for the supervision and guidance of all personnel. Depending on the size of the FBO and the activities they offer, the staff may consist of linepersons (also known as ramp service persons), aircraft mechanics, pilots, flight instructors, salespeople, customer service representatives, and administrative personnel. In large organizations, FBO Managers rely on junior managers to oversee their particular departments.

In addition, FBO Managers are responsible for many administrative aspects of the business. For example, they oversee such activities as budgeting, purchasing, human resources, personnel training, and marketing. Their administrative and management duties vary from day to day. Some of their tasks include:

- monitoring expenses
- tracking revenues
- negotiating leases and contractual agreements
- meeting with airport authorities to discuss operational issues
- hiring employees
- planning employee training programs
- making sure quality standards of services are being met
- coordinating the marketing of the services and products that their FBO offers
- establishing and maintaining good relations with customers
- preparing correspondence, reports, business management records, inventories, government documentation, and other materials

Depending on the size of the FBO, Managers may be involved in performing some or all of the services offered by their firms. For example, FBO Managers might give flight lessons, repair electrical equipment, sell aircraft, pilot charter flights, or load baggage onto aircraft.

Most FBO Managers work full time. They usually have flexible work schedules and often work evenings and weekends to complete tasks, attend meetings, or to provide services to customers. Many FBO Managers are on call after work hours to respond to emergencies.

Salaries

Salaries for FBO Managers vary, depending on such factors as experience, job duties, size of operations, and geographical location. Current salary surveys for FBO Managers are unavailable. However, an idea of their earnings may be gained by looking at the salary information for general managers that is reported by the U.S. Bureau of Labor Statistics. According to its May 2003 *Occupational Employment Statistics* survey, the estimated annual salary for most general managers ranged between $34,850 and $112,730.

Employment Prospects

More than 3,000 FBOs are located throughout the United States. More than 50 percent are family-owned FBOs. Others are independently owned businesses or part of a network of FBOs. Some facilities are Million Air FBO franchises.

Job openings typically become available as individuals retire, resign, or transfer to other positions. Additional positions are created when new FBOs are established. Opportunities are generally better for highly experienced FBO Managers with a proven record of profitability and achievement than for novice managers.

Advancement Prospects

The FBO Manager occupies the top managerial position within independent organizations. Individuals might realize advancement by pursuing positions with other FBOs that would offer them higher salaries or greater challenges. Managers at large FBOs may advance to such higher managerial positions as district operations manager and vice president of operations.

Depending on their experience, ambitions, and interests, FBO Managers can follow other career paths in aviation, by seeking managerial positions with airports, airlines, and professional associations. Individuals with entrepreneurial ambitions may choose to start their own FBO establishment.

Education and Training

Educational requirements vary with different employers. Some FBOs require that candidates have some college training or possess bachelor's degrees, preferably in aviation management, business administration, or another related field. Qualifying experience is readily substituted for college degrees.

Special Requirements

FBO Managers must hold the proper FAA pilot certificate and ratings if they will be performing any flight duties. They must possess the proper FAA mechanic certificate and ratings, if they will be performing any aircraft maintenance duties.

Experience, Special Skills, and Personality Traits

Most FBO Managers worked their way up through the ranks by starting as linepersons and, through the years, gaining experience in the different areas of FBO operations. Many of them also trained to become pilots and/or aircraft mechanics while working mostly in general aviation.

Employers typically select candidates who have work histories with increasing supervisory and managerial responsibilities while working in the FBO industry. They demonstrate the ability to handle the business aspects of FBO operations, including accounting, finances, human resources, community relations, and customer service. In addition, preferred candidates must be familiar with the various services (such as aircraft maintenance, sales, or flight instruction) that their prospective employers offer.

To perform their work effectively, FBO Managers must possess excellent leadership and customer service skills. They also need superior communication, interpersonal, and teamwork skills. In addition, they have highly developed self-management skills, such as the ability to handle stressful situations, work independently, and organize and prioritize tasks.

Being energetic, enthusiastic, analytical, self-confident, decisive, flexible, and determined are some personality traits that successful FBO Managers share.

Unions and Associations

No professional associations specifically serve the interests of FBO Managers. They are eligible, however, to join such professional societies as the National Business Aviation Association or the Aircraft of Owners and Pilots Association to take advantage of networking opportunities and other resources.

Tips for Entry

1. Young people might start gaining experience by volunteering or obtaining part-time work as a lineperson at an FBO in their area.
2. To enhance their employability, individuals stay current with the latest developments in aviation management techniques. They might enroll in workshops, seminars, or programs offered by academic institutions or aviation trade and professional associations such as the American Association of Airport Executives.
3. Use the Internet to learn about different FBOs and the various services they provide. To get a list of relevant Web sites to read, enter the keywords *fixed base operator* or *fixed base operators* into any search engine.

FLIGHT MANAGER (CORPORATE FLIGHT DEPARTMENTS)

CAREER PROFILE

Duties: Oversee flight operations that are part of private businesses and companies; direct and coordinate activities, such as crew scheduling and aircraft maintenance; supervise staff; perform administrative responsibilities; perform duties as required

Alternate Title(s): Aviation Department Manager; Director of Flight Operations; Vice President of Transportation

Salary Range: $50,000 to $200,000

Employment Prospects: Good

Advancement Prospects: Fair

Prerequisites:

Education or Training—Bachelor's degree in aviation management or related field generally preferred

Experience—Extensive experience in aircraft operations; be familiar with business issues related to aviation departments

Special Skills and Personality Traits—Leadership, communication, interpersonal, teamwork, and self-management skills; flexible, determined, decisive, analytical, detail-oriented, loyal

Special Requirements—FAA pilot certificate with appropriate ratings may be required

CAREER LADDER

Manager of Larger Flight Department

Flight Department Manager

Chief Pilot or Aircraft Maintenance Director

Position Description

Flight Managers of corporate flight departments oversee flight operations for businesses and companies. Many private corporations own and use aircraft to provide flexible, efficient, reliable, and safe transportation for business purposes.

For example, business aircraft are used for:

- flying executives and managers to business meetings and conferences
- carrying staff members to job assignments at customer sites or different company facilities
- delivering mail, packages, equipment, and other freight to company facilities or other locations
- transporting customers, press, or other interest groups to company facilities for tours
- performing acts of charity, such as transporting patients to hospitals

The use of business aircraft is known as business aviation, which is a segment of general aviation. Business aircraft include airplanes, seaplanes, helicopters, and jets. The size and complexity of flight operations vary from one company to the next. For example, a Flight Manager at a large company might oversee 50 different aircraft, whereas a Flight Manager at a midsize company might manage two aircraft.

Corporate flight operations generally provide on-demand services. Flight Managers are expected to have aircraft and crew ready to fly to any location at any hour of the day. Corporate aircraft may travel to nearby communities or to other regions, states, or countries. They can be flown to thousands more cities than those served by the airlines. At some companies, flight operations include flying company shuttles between facilities on a regular schedule.

Flight Managers direct and coordinate all activities of flight and ground operations—crew scheduling, aircraft dispatching, flight planning, catering, customer service, ground handling, cargo loading, aircraft maintenance, and so on. Additionally, managers constantly find ways to improve and enhance aircraft operations. For example, a Flight Manager might plan new aircraft purchases for his or her company. Furthermore, some Flight Managers also perform the role of corporate pilot or aviation maintenance technician.

Flight Managers are responsible for the direction and guidance of both flight and nonflight personnel. The staff size differs from company to company. For example, one Flight Manager might supervise a pilot and one office staff member, whereas another Flight Manager might oversee a large staff of pilots, aviation maintenance technicians, aircraft dispatchers, flight attendants, and office personnel.

Flight Managers have various administrative duties as well. They plan and implement policies, procedures, and programs to ensure the safety, efficiency, and cost effectiveness of the flight department. For example, Flight Managers create safety programs, accident tracking systems, quality programs, emergency preparedness plans, and security programs. Flight Managers also ensure that flight operations are in compliance with all local, state, and federal laws and regulations relevant to aviation operations, air safety, and aviation security.

The job of Flight Managers also involves the oversight of budgeting and financing tasks. For example, they plan and administer the departmental budget, monitor operating costs, control inventory, and negotiate fuel rates. Additionally, they oversee contractual agreements with vendors and consultants that provide aircraft maintenance, fueling, ground handling, flight attendant, air charter, or other services.

Flight Managers handle human resources responsibilities as well. They develop job descriptions. They are involved in the hiring and firing of flight department personnel, evaluating job performance of staff members, and planning and coordinating staff training programs. In addition, managers ensure that laws and regulations governing the workplace are being followed.

Flight Managers are expected to stay up to date with trends in business aviation and in the aviation industry. In addition, they keep up with community issues that may affect their flight operations.

The organizational structure of a corporate flight department varies from company to company. In some companies, Flight Managers report to a higher department such as the transportation or sales department. In others, Flight Managers report directly to a vice president or other member of the senior management team.

Salaries

Salaries vary, depending on various factors such as employer, flight operations, job responsibilities, and geographical location. Annual salaries for corporate Flight Managers can range from $50,000 to $80,000 or more. Managers in large companies overseeing large flight departments may earn up to $100,000 or $200,000 per year.

Employment Prospects

Corporate Flight Managers are employed by companies and other organizations that operate aircraft under Part 91 of the federal aviation regulations. As Part 91 operators, these organizations own and operate aircraft only for business purposes.

Employment is also available as business aviation managers with companies that operate under Part 135 of the federal aviation regulations. Part 135 operators rent, lease, or sell business aircraft as well as offer aircraft management services for a fee. Part 135 operators include air charter services, fixed base operators (FBOs), aircraft management firms, and aviation companies that offer fractional ownership programs.

Business aviation has been steadily growing since the early 1990s and is expected to continue as more companies realize the economic benefits of owning business aircraft. In recent years, fractional ownership programs have experienced substantial growth.

The turnover rate among Flight Managers with Part 91 operators is generally lower than with Part 135 operators. Most opportunities become available as Managers retire or transfer to other positions.

Advancement Prospects

Advancement opportunities are typically better with large organizations that have extensive aviation needs. In large organizations, Flight Managers may advance to executive positions such as vice president of transportation or director of flight operations. Most Flight Managers in small organizations advance by accepting positions with other employers. Those who have a broad background in business may be qualified to pursue other managerial positions within an organization.

Experienced Flight Managers with entrepreneurial ambitions and interests can become consultants or business owners who offer their services to develop new flight departments or to improve current flight departments.

Education and Training

Employers prefer that Flight Managers possess a bachelor's degree in aviation management or another field of management. Many employers allow a combination of education and experience to be substituted for the educational requirement.

Some employers offer management development programs to flight department personnel to train them for future leadership positions in the department as well as in the company.

Special Requirements

Corporate Flight Managers who perform pilot duties must hold a valid commercial pilot's certificate with instrument and multiengine ratings, which are granted by the Federal Aviation Administration (FAA). Some organizations require that pilots have an air transport pilot (ATP) certificate. In addition, pilots must hold ratings in the category, class, and type of aircraft which they operate. Further, they are required to hold a first-class or second-class FAA medical certificate.

Experience, Special Skills, and Personality Traits

Employers seek Flight Managers who have years of experience in aircraft operations and, in particular, in business aviation. Many Flight Managers have extensive experience as pilots or aviation maintenance technicians in business settings. They have risen through the ranks, while gaining increasing responsibilities including supervisory and management duties. In addition, they are familiar with business issues related to running aviation departments.

Employers hire candidates who have proven leadership skills. Candidates also demonstrate effective communication, interpersonal, and teamwork skills, as they must be able to work well with various people from different backgrounds. Further, they must possess strong self-management skills—such as the ability to organize and prioritize tasks, meet deadlines, resolve problems quickly, and handle stressful situations.

Being flexible, determined, decisive, analytical, detail-oriented, and loyal are some personality traits that successful Flight Managers have in common.

Unions and Associations

The National Business Aviation Association serves the particular interests of business aviation. Flight Managers are eligible to join this trade association, in which they would be able to take advantage of professional services such as education programs, professional certification, and networking opportunities.

Tips for Entry

1. According to the National Business Aviation Association, an increasing number of business aviation managers have master's or other advanced degrees and are experienced in accounting, financial, and business administrative practices.
2. The National Business Aviation Association and the University Aviation Association have developed a program called the Professional Development Program (PDP) to train future flight department leaders. This program is offered by certain colleges, universities, and private aviation companies. To learn more, check out the following Web page at the National Business Aviation Association Web site, http://www.nbaa.org/pdp.
3. Use the Internet to learn more about business aviation and flight departments. You might start by visiting the National Business Aviation Association Web site at http://www.nbaa.org.

AIRPORT ENGINEERING, PLANNING, AND MAINTENANCE

AIRPORT ENGINEER

CAREER PROFILE

Duties: Participate in the planning, design, construction, and maintenance of airports; perform administrative and supervisory responsibilities; perform duties as required

Alternate Title(s): Airport Facilities Engineer; Airport Design Engineer; Airport Planner, or other title that reflects a particular area

Salary Range: $41,000 to $100,000+

Employment Prospects: Fair

Advancement Prospects: Fair

Prerequisites:

Education or Training—Bachelor's degree in civil engineering or a related field

Experience—Qualifications vary; entry-level engineers should have two or more years of airport, transportation, or civil engineering experience; aviation experience is desirable

Special Skills and Personality Traits—Communication, interpersonal, teamwork, leadership, project management, writing, and computer skills; creative, curious, analytical, organized, detail-oriented

Special Requirements—Professional Engineer (P.E.) license may be required

CAREER LADDER

Lead or Project Supervisor

Airport Engineer

Civil Engineer or Airport Engineer Intern

Position Description

Airport engineering is a subdiscipline of civil engineering. Airport Engineers apply their skills and experience to the planning, design, construction, operation, and maintenance of airport facilities. For example, they might help prepare airport master plans, design noise-abatement systems, oversee the renovation of terminal buildings, or coordinate work activities of repair maintenance projects. Many Airport Engineers work in several or all of these airport engineering areas throughout their careers.

In general, Airport Engineers perform an administrative and supervisory role. Their job requires them to make independent judgments and complex technical decisions. They are responsible for overseeing projects, programs, and departments. They direct and coordinate the work activities of professionals (such as airport planners), technicians, and administrative staff. They may also supervise consultants who are performing airport engineering services.

Airport Engineers are responsible for ensuring that engineering activities conform with airport policies and procedures as well as with engineering practices and standards. They also make sure that all activities under their supervision are in compliance with local, state, and federal laws and regulations regarding airports, aviation safety, environment, zoning codes, and so on.

Some Airport Engineers specialize in a particular aspect of airport engineering, such as airport design engineering, airport planning, or environmental engineering. Their job titles may reflect their specialty.

Airport Engineers work in different settings—airports, airport engineering consulting firms, and governmental aviation agencies. Their particular duties vary, depending on their job responsibilities, skill levels, and work settings.

Many Airport Engineers are airport employees. They are involved in all areas of airport engineering. As airport planners, they might oversee or participate in the preparation of airport master plans and capital improvement projects to expand or improve airport facilities. As airport designers, Airport Engineers create designs for runways, taxiways, noise-abatement systems, terminal buildings, parking areas, baggage-handling systems, airport security systems, and various other types of airport systems and facilities. By using computers, they come up with several alternative designs to determine the most efficient design that is also the most cost effective.

In the area of construction, Airport Engineers perform project management responsibilities. They oversee various improvement, renovation, and remodeling projects—such as repaving the airfield aprons, constructing a new terminal building, or expanding the public parking lots. They are responsible for the correct and accurate completion of construction projects. Some of their duties include supervising the work activities of construction projects to ensure that they conform with design specifications.

In addition, many Airport Engineers are responsible for directing and coordinating maintenance and repair services of runways, taxiways, terminal buildings, and all other airport facilities. Some of their duties include overseeing maintenance supervisors, making sure that building codes are being followed, and providing technical advice to maintenance workers.

Airport staff engineers also perform a variety of administrative duties. For example, they might:

- prepare applications for government grants for construction projects
- participate in the selection of consulting engineering firms for planning, design, or construction oversight services
- negotiate contracts with consultants
- help establish engineering standards and construction policies
- meet with government officials or local communities to discuss airport issues or problems
- prepare reports and other required paperwork
- maintain accurate records

Many other Airport Engineers are consulting engineers. They work for engineering, architectural, or construction firms that offer airport engineering services. These Airport Engineers work on airport development projects, usually as part of a project team. They may be involved in the area of planning, design, or construction. They typically work closely with their clients' project managers.

Many consulting Airport Engineers are involved in business development. They continually seek out new clients, as well as maintain relationships with existing clients for repeat business.

Still other Airport Engineers are employed by the Federal Aviation Administration (FAA) and state government aviation agencies. They mainly coordinate funding programs for airport improvement or expansion projects. They might perform such tasks as determining the eligibility of applicants, reviewing construction plans, approving the funding of projects, and conducting airport inspections.

Many state Airport Engineers also provide technical services to airports and airport engineering consulting firms. They offer technical assistance in preparing airport master plans, performing environmental assessments, and designing facilities. They also respond to questions regarding airport engineering and construction.

Airport Engineers generally work in office settings. They may be required to work outdoors from time to time, to inspect construction projects or airport facilities. They occasionally work long hours to complete tasks, attend meetings, or meet pressing deadlines. Some Airport Engineers are on call 24 hours a day to respond to emergencies.

Salaries

Salaries vary, depending on such factors as experience, job responsibilities, type of employer, and geographical location. Highly experienced Airport Engineers can earn salaries up to $100,000, according to some experts in the field. The U.S. Bureau of Labor Statistics, in its May 2003 *Occupational Employment Statistics* survey, reports that the estimated earnings for most civil engineers (which includes Airport Engineers) ranged between $40,860 and $92,010.

Employment Prospects

The job market in airport engineering is generally stable, since airports continually need to make airport modifications and upgrades. Job prospects are particularly good for Airport Engineers with senior-level experience. Most opportunities become available as Airport Engineers retire, advance to higher positions, or transfer to other jobs or careers.

Advancement Prospects

As Airport Engineers gain experience, they can become technical specialists and project managers. In addition, they can pursue higher management positions within their work setting. Those with entrepreneurial ambitions can become independent consultants or owners of consulting firms. Engineers who are interested in teaching and conducting research can pursue academic careers, which may require obtaining advanced degrees.

Education and Training

Most Airport Engineers possess a bachelor's degree in civil engineering or another engineering field such as environmental engineering, mechanical engineering, or electrical engineering. Some engineers hold a bachelor's degree in such related fields as planning, natural or physical science, or computer science. Some employers may require that Airport Engineers have a master's degree.

Throughout their careers, many Airport Engineers enroll in continuing education and training programs to update their skills and keep up with advancements in their field. They might complete courses, seminars, or workshops that are offered by employers, academic institutions, vendors, and professional engineering societies.

Special Requirements

Many employers require or strongly prefer that engineers possess Professional Engineer (P.E.) licensure. Employers may hire individuals who are licensed Engineers-in-Training (EIT) if they are able to obtain P.E. licensure within a specific time period.

The P.E. licensing process consists of two stages. Engineers who successfully pass the first examination become licensed as Engineers-in-Training. After working several years under the supervision of licensed engineers, they become eligible to take the second examination for the Professional Engineer licensure.

Requirements for P.E. licensure vary with each state, territory, and Washington, D.C. For specific information, contact the state board of engineering examiners for the area in which you wish to practice.

Experience, Special Skills, and Personality Traits

Qualifications for Airport Engineers vary, depending on their job responsibilities, work setting, and other factors. To enter this field, candidates are generally required to have two or more years of experience working on airport, transportation, or other related civil engineering projects. Candidates seeking senior positions are typically required to have several years of airport engineering experience. Candidates who have aviation experience, such as pilot or airport management experience, are desired by many employers. The best candidates would be proficient in more than one engineering discipline—civil, structural, electrical, and/or mechanical engineering. Furthermore, they would be familiar with civil and airport engineering principles and practices.

To perform their work effectively, Airport Engineers need excellent communication, interpersonal, teamwork, leadership, and project management skills. In addition, Airport Engineers must have strong writing skills and computer skills, with proficiency using the Computer-Aided Drafting and Design (CADD) program and other engineering software programs.

Being creative, curious, analytical, organized, and detail-oriented are some personality traits that successful Airport Engineers have in common.

Unions and Associations

By joining professional associations, Airport Engineers can take advantage of professional services such as continuing education programs, professional certification, and networking opportunities. Many Airport Engineers are members of one or more of the following societies: the American Society of Civil Engineers, the American Association of Airport Executives, or the Institute of Transportation Engineers. Airport Engineers who work in state agencies might join the National Association of State Aviation Officials. Professional engineers might join the National Society of Professional Engineers.

Tips for Entry

1. As a college student, join a student chapter of a professional association, such as the American Society of Civil Engineers. Take advantage of the support programs that the organization offers. For example, some engineering societies offer scholarships, student competitions, discussion forums, and job listings.
2. To learn about available job opportunities at a particular organization, contact the manager of the airport engineering department or a human resources officer.
3. Job candidates at commercial service airports are usually required to pass an extensive security screening before they can be hired. Furthermore, they must meet security requirements as a continuing condition of employment.
4. Use the Internet to learn more about airport engineering. One Web page you might visit is the airport engineering page at the iCivilEngineer Web site, http://www.icivilengineer.com/Transportation_Engineering/Airport_Engineering. To get a list of other relevant Web sites, enter the keywords *airport engineers* or *airport engineering* into a search engine.

AIRPORT PLANNER

CAREER PROFILE

Duties: Assist in planning the growth and development of airports; prepare various airport plans; perform duties as required

Alternate Title(s): Aviation Planner; Transportation Planner; a title that reflects a particular role such as Project Planner or Environmental Planner

Salary Range: $32,000 to $79,000

Employment Prospects: Fair

Advancement Prospects: Fair

Prerequisites:

Education or Training—Bachelor's degree, preferably in civil engineering, architecture, aviation planning, or a related field

Experience—Previous planning experience in airport settings; aviation experience desirable

Special Skills and Personality Traits—Analytical, communication, writing, research, presentation, interpersonal, and teamwork skills; flexible, energetic, creative, pragmatic, innovative

Special Requirements—Professional Engineer (P.E.) licensure may be required

CAREER LADDER

Senior Airport Planner

Airport Planner

Airport Planner (entry-level)

Position Description

Airport Planners are involved in planning the growth and development of airports—from small, private helipads to midsize community airports to international airports the size of small cities. They perform analyses and formulate plans that help airport owners and managers determine how they should improve airports to meet the needs of airport operators and users.

Airport Planners are involved in developing various types of airport plans. They assist in creating plans to construct new airports. They prepare, review, or update airport master plans, which explain the current uses of airport facilities, as well as describe how facilities should be developed to meet future needs. (The airport master plan is used for obtaining state or federal grants to fund capital improvement projects.) In addition, Airport Planners prepare plans for proposed capital improvement projects for airport facilities, such as the construction of additional parking lots, the renovation of a terminal building, or the expansion of runways.

The planning process for a master plan, a capital improvement project, or other airport plan is generally long and complicated. It involves conducting research, analyzing information, identifying needs and requirements, evaluating alternative programs, preparing financial plans, submitting plans, and so forth. Airport Planners also perform environmental studies to determine how proposed airport construction might impact the environment—including land, air, water, and wildlife.

The approval of airport plans is based on the ability to meet the needs of not only the airport users and operators but also the needs of the communities that the airports serve. Therefore Airport Planners work closely with local government officials and the general public. They keep communities informed of proposed plans as well as encourage their feedback. Some Airport Planners make presentations before city councils, airport commissions, civic groups, and other community organizations.

Airport Planners generally work together on planning projects. They may function in one or more specific roles, such as researcher, technical analyst, designer, environmental planner, or project manager. They perform a wide range of duties, which vary according to their skill levels and experience. Some of their duties may include:

- ensuring that airport plans are in compliance with airport policies, as well as with all applicable local, state, and federal laws and regulations
- directing and coordinating the work of junior planners and support staff members
- assist in the supervision and training of subordinate personnel
- participate in the selection of consultants and negotiation of contracts
- coordinate the work of consultants
- preparing correspondence, position statements, or technical reports about airport planning policies
- representing the planning department at meetings with regulatory agencies, community organizations, airport tenants, and others
- keeping up to date with new and proposed legislation regarding zoning codes, building codes, environmental regulations, airport security regulations, and so on

Computers are an important tool for Airport Planners. They use various software applications to help them gather and analyze information, make forecasts, write reports, and prepare multimedia presentations. Many of them also use computer databases such as Geographic Information Systems (GIS) to produce maps that show alternative plans for airport development.

Airport Planners work a 40-hour week but frequently work evenings and on weekends to complete tasks, meet deadlines, or to attend meetings or public hearings. They may spend some time in the field to inspect and document land conditions.

Salaries

Salaries vary, depending on such factors as education, experience, employer, and geographical location. According to the May 2003 *Occupational Employment Statistics* survey (by the U.S. Bureau of Labor Statistics), the estimated salary range for most urban and regional planners ranged between $32,360 and $78,720.

Employment Prospects

Some Airport Planners work for airports and airport authorities such as the Metropolitan Washington Airports Authority. Other Airport Planners are hired by engineering and construction firms that offer airport planning services. Airport Planners are also employed by the Federal Aviation Administration (FAA) and state government aviation agencies.

Job prospects in general are fair for Airport Planners, since airports continually seek ways to increase the capacity of airports or to make airport modifications and upgrades. The terrorist attacks in the United States on September 11, 2001, and the enactment of the Transportation Security Act have stimulated the development of various new capital improvement projects to expand, rebuild, or improve U.S. airports.

Advancement Prospects

Opportunities for advancement vary according to the ambitions and interests of individuals. At an airport, Airport Planners can advance through the departmental ranks as lead planners, supervisors, and managers. With contracting firms, Airport Planners may advance to assume responsibilities in business development and project management. Those with entrepreneurial ambitions can become independent consultants or owners of businesses that provide airport planning services.

Education and Training

Minimally, Airport Planners hold bachelor's degrees, preferably in civil engineering, planning, aviation management, or a related field. Some employers require advanced degrees for senior positions. They may choose candidates without advanced degrees if they have qualifying experience.

Special Requirements

Airport Planners who are also engineers may be required to be licensed as Professional Engineers (P.E.) in the areas where they practice. Requirements for P.E. licensure vary among states, territories, and Washington, D.C. For specific information, contact the state board of engineering examiners where you wish to practice.

Experience, Special Skills, and Personality Traits

Employers typically prefer that entry-level candidates have some planning experience working in airport settings. Their experience may have been acquired through internships, summer employment, or work-study programs. Having aviation experience, such as flying experience, is desirable but not necessary.

To perform their work effectively, Airport Planners need strong analytical, communication, writing, research, and presentation skills. Having excellent interpersonal and teamwork skills is also important, as they must be able to work well with people from diverse backgrounds.

Some personality traits that successful Airport Planners share are being flexible, energetic, creative, pragmatic, and innovative. They are also visionaries.

Unions and Associations

Many Airport Planners join local, regional, and national professional associations to take advantage of networking opportunities, training programs, and other professional services and resources. Two professional societies that are available to Airport Planners are the American Planning Association and the Institute of Transportation Engineers.

Tips for Entry

1. Attend local government planning meetings to gain exposure to the field of planning.
2. Some Airport Planners recommend that individuals become proficient with such software as the Computer-Aided Design and Drafting (CADD) program and Geographic Information Systems (GIS).
3. Talk to different Airport Planners to learn about courses, computer programs, skills, and experience that may help prepare you for a career in airport planning.
4. As a college student, develop a portfolio and bring it to job interviews and job fairs. Place samples of your best school and work projects in the portfolio.
5. Use the Internet to learn more about the field of airport planning, as well as about planning in general. Two Web sites you might visit are the American Planning Association, http://www.planning.org, and Planetizen: The Planning and Development Network, http://www.planetizen.com. To get a list of Web sites pertaining to airport planning, enter the keywords *airport planning* or *airport planners* into a search engine.

FAA ELECTRONICS TECHNICIAN

CAREER PROFILE

Duties: Install and maintain electronic equipment and systems that are used for air traffic control, aerial navigation, surveillance, and communications in the National Airspace System; may assist in the development, design, and evaluation of new electronics equipment and systems; perform duties as required

Alternate Title(s): None

Salary Range: $31,000 to $69,000

Employment Prospects: Poor

Advancement Prospects: Fair

Prerequisites:

Education or Training—Associate's degree in electronics technology; completion of FAA training programs

Experience—Previous experience as electronics technician, computer specialist, avionics technician, or another related occupation generally required

Special Skills and Personality Traits—Math, computer, communication, writing, interpersonal, teamwork, and self-management skills; problem-solver, respectful, detail-oriented, logical, physically fit, manual dexterity

CAREER LADDER

Airway Transportation System Specialist

Electronics Technician

Electronics Technician (entry-level)

Position Description

The Federal Aviation Administration (FAA) is responsible for operating the National Airspace System (NAS), the network of equipment, services, and facilities that control the flow of thousands of flights each day throughout U.S. airspace. The FAA Airway Facilities Service has the oversight of ensuring that the NAS is performing safely, smoothly, and efficiently at all times. Within this organization, Electronics Technicians are responsible for installing and maintaining electronic equipment and systems that are used for air traffic control, aerial navigation, surveillance, and communications between aircraft and ground services.

Electronics Technicians work on various complex systems such as radar, radio, computer, communication, weather, automation, and air navigational systems. The different systems are located at or near airports, as well as in air traffic control facilities (including control towers, air route traffic control centers, and automated flight service stations) throughout the United States and its territories. Electronics Technicians may travel to remote locations such as open fields and mountaintops to perform their duties.

Electronics Technicians' duties include installing electronic equipment and lighting aids according to specifications. They also perform maintenance of the equipment and systems to which they are assigned. On a regular basis they do preventative maintenance to ensure that equipment and systems are working and operating correctly and accurately. They inspect and test equipment, making any necessary adjustments and replacing defective parts. Technicians also do corrective maintenance on equipment and systems that are malfunctioning or not working. They perform troubleshooting procedures to resolve problems, and repair or replace equipment accordingly. Their work is reviewed by senior technicians or electronics engineers.

Sometimes Electronics Technicians are involved in research projects, working under the direction and supervision of researchers or administrative officials. They help scientists and engineers to design, develop, and evaluate new types of electronics equipment for the NAS. For example, their work assignments might involve conducting laboratory or field tests, modifying electronic equipment for specific uses, or building a unit or device for a piece of electronic equipment based on a researcher's ideas. Additionally, technicians might be asked to maintain a daily work log, prepare informal reports, and prepare schematic or circuit diagrams.

Entry-level Electronics Technicians generally serve as assistants to experienced technicians and perform routine tasks such as wiring circuits and replacing components. As Electronics Technicians gain experience, they receive greater responsibilities and less technical supervision.

Electronics Technicians often refer to instructional documents prepared by manufacturers, especially when working with unfamiliar equipment. To help them complete their tasks, they read operating instructions, study schematic diagrams, review troubleshooting procedures, refer to technical literature, and so on. They might also consult other Electronics Technicians, engineers, or representatives of manufacturers for technical advice. With some equipment, Electronics Technicians may complete a factory training class or workshop.

The job of Electronics Technicians involves some physical activity. They might climb ladders; stoop, crouch, squat, and kneel; lift and carry objects weighing 20 to 50 pounds or more; and so on. Those working outdoors deal with varying weather and environmental conditions.

Electronics Technicians work a standard 40-hour week. Many of them are assigned to rotating shifts that include working evenings and weekends. Some Electronics Technicians travel throughout their region to complete their assignments, which may include going to remote locations such as mountaintops.

Salaries

Salaries vary, depending on such factors as experience, pay band, and geographical location. FAA Electronics Technicians earn salaries within the F, G, and H pay bands of the FAA core compensation plan. In 2002–03, the annual salaries for F–H pay bands ranged from $31,100 to $68,800. FAA employees who live in metropolitan areas receive a locality pay to compensate for the higher cost of living.

Employment Prospects

As of 2003, the FAA has been subject to a hiring freeze for Electronics Technicians and was expected to abide by the freeze for an indefinite time. Entry-level technicians are hired each year, but they must be graduates of the FAA College Training Initiative–Electronics Technician (CTI–ET) program.

Opportunities in the future should become better due to the fact that many Electronics Technicians will be eligible to retire within the next few years.

Advancement Prospects

Journeyman Electronics Technicians can advance to specialist or to quality assurance positions. Those interested in management can rise through the ranks to such positions as system specialist supervisor, NAS area specialist, and NAS operations manager.

Education and Training

Electronics Technicians should possess at least a high school diploma or a general equivalency diploma. Additionally, an associate degree in electronics technology is generally required.

In recent years, novice technicians are required to be graduates of the FAA Collegiate Training Initiative–Electronics Technician (CTI–ET) program. This program is offered at a few two-year colleges, four-year colleges, and universities throughout the United States. Students receive academic training and on-the-job work experience, which prepares them for entry-level positions. Upon graduation with an associate's degree in electronics technology, they receive a permanent position as an FAA Electronics Technician.

The FAA provides Electronics Technicians with continued training and certification programs throughout their career to update and learn new skills. Training comes in various forms, including self-directed study, computer-based training, FAA academy training, and on-the-job training.

Experience, Special Skills, and Personality Traits

For non-entry-level positions, the FAA hires employees who have previous civilian or military experience as Electronics Technicians, computer specialists, avionics technicians, or other related occupations. (Remember: Currently, only graduates of CTI–ET programs can qualify for entry-level positions.)

Electronics Technicians need adequate math skills and computer skills; they also need strong communication and writing skills, as they must be able to provide both oral and written reports. Interpersonal and teamwork skills are also essential for their job. Further, they must have solid self-management skills, which include the ability to understand and follow directions, work independently, prioritize tasks, and handle stressful situations.

Being a problem solver, respectful, detail oriented, and logical are some personality traits that successful Electronics Technicians share. They are also physically fit and have manual dexterity.

Unions and Associations

FAA Electronics Technicians are members of the Professional Airways Systems Specialists, a union that conducts contract negotiations for them. It seeks to get the best contractual terms relating to pay, job benefits, and working conditions.

Tips for Entry

1. In high school, take courses in mathematics, science (particularly physical science), English, and reading to build a foundation of skills and knowledge, that will come in handy on your job.
2. The FAA has several special programs under which employees are hired. To find out if you might qualify under a special program, contact an FAA district office. You can also find information at the FAA Career Opportunities Web page, http://jobs.faa.gov.
3. Be ready to verify all information that you provide on your job application. For example, you may be asked to supply the FAA with copies of college transcripts or proof of military service.
4. To learn more about the FAA Airway Facilities Service, check out its Web page on the Internet. Go to http://www.faa.gov/ats/aaf.

AIRPORT MAINTENANCE WORKER

CAREER PROFILE

Duties: Perform maintenance and repair work on buildings, airfields, equipment, and machinery; may be assigned a variety of tasks that involve general carpentry, electrical work, plumbing, locksmithing, janitorial service, or other trade or craft; perform duties as required

Alternate Title(s): Airport Maintenance Technician; Airport Maintenance Mechanic

Salary Range: $17,000 to $48,000

Employment Prospects: Fair

Advancement Prospects: Fair

Prerequisites:

Education or Training—High school diploma

Experience—One or more years of skilled maintenance and repair work in one or more trades, preferably in airport settings

Special Skills and Personality Traits—Reading, writing, math, communication, teamwork, interpersonal, and self-management skills; have physical strength, agility, and manual dexterity; resourceful, self-motivated, capable, friendly, versatile

Special Requirements—Driver's license

CAREER LADDER

Lead Airport Maintenance Worker

Airport Maintenance Worker

Airport Maintenance Worker (entry-level)

Position Description

Airport Maintenance Workers provide maintenance and repair work to buildings and grounds at civil airports (commercial service and general aviation airports). Their ability to perform their jobs quickly and properly contributes to the efficiency, safety, and smoothness of airport operations every day of the year.

Airport Maintenance Workers are skilled in the manual trades or crafts—such as carpentry, roofing, masonry, plumbing, electrical work, heating and air conditioning, painting, locksmithing, and janitorial services. Many Airport Maintenance Workers are cross-trained in several trades and are thus able to perform a variety of tasks; for example, an Airport Maintenance Worker would be able to complete assignments that require general plumbing, carpentry, roofing, or painting tasks. Other Airport Maintenance Workers specialize in particular trades, doing the jobs of carpenters, electricians, locksmiths, heating and air conditioning technicians, and so on.

To ensure that airport operations are in continuous working order, Aircraft Maintenance Workers perform preventative maintenance. They make regularly scheduled inspections of equipment, systems, facilities, and grounds to locate and correct any problems before breakdowns can occur. They also perform corrective maintenance by making repairs after breakdowns occur. For example, if the air conditioning system in a terminal building is not working properly, Aircraft Maintenance Workers determine what is wrong and make the necessary repairs.

Airport Maintenance Workers are involved in a wide range of building and grounds services. Workers who are assigned to the maintenance of airport buildings may perform such activities as:

- repairing faucets, drain lines, or service lines
- installing or replacing doors, windows, wall partitions, or ceilings
- repairing furniture such as desks, cabinets, or counters

- replacing or repairing lights, electrical outlets, fixtures, switches, circuit breakers, electric motors, and so on
- servicing electrical equipment such as heating and air conditioning units
- performing janitorial services, which include vacuuming, mopping, cleaning restrooms, and emptying trash cans

Airport Maintenance Workers also take care of the airfields. Their duties include inspecting, maintaining, and repairing runways, taxiways, roads, and parking areas according to the rules and regulations of the Federal Aviation Administration (FAA). Some of them also maintain and repair sensitive air navigational systems, such as beacons, runway lights, taxiway lights, path indicators, and other various airport electronics and electrical equipment. They may also repair and replace signs, paint stripes on ground surfaces, maintain and repair airport security fencing, and monitor runways for wildlife hazards.

In addition, Airport Maintenance Workers perform groundskeeping duties. These tasks include mowing the grassed areas of the airfield, planting flowers and ornamental plants, removing weeds, trimming hedges and trees, applying pesticides, picking up litter, and so on. In locations with snowy conditions, Airport Maintenance Workers are involved in routine snow removal, using sand, deicing chemicals, and special vehicles.

Many Airport Maintenance Workers participate in the inspection, maintenance, and repair of various machinery used throughout the airport. This includes elevators, escalators, moving sidewalks, passenger loading bridges, baggage handling systems, groundskeeping equipment, incinerators, and service vehicles.

On occasion, Airport Maintenance Workers may become involved in special projects. For example, a team of workers might be assigned to remodel a stairwell in a terminal building, construct new curbs, build wall units for administrative offices, or redo landscaping.

Some Airport Maintenance Workers have been trained to be part of the aircraft rescue and firefighting units. They assist with structural fires, aircraft fires, aircraft crashes, car accidents, bomb threats, terrorism alerts, hazardous materials emergencies, medical emergencies, and so on.

Airport Maintenance Workers work under the supervision and direction of crew leaders or maintenance supervisors. Maintenance crew members receive their assignments verbally or in the form of written instructions, diagrams, or sketches. Their work is usually reviewed by a supervisor to ensure that repairs or maintenance have been completed correctly and accurately. All Airport Maintenance Workers are expected to follow all safety regulations, rules, and practices.

Being able to communicate is essential, thus Airport Maintenance Workers carry and use two-way radios to communicate with supervisors, colleagues, airport operators, and others. Their job also requires that Airport Maintenance Workers handle various precision-measuring devices, hand tools, power equipment, and testing instruments. Many of their tasks require them to operate light to heavy equipment such as mowers, pickup trucks, forklifts, aerial lifts, backhoes, snowplows, and dump trucks.

Airport Maintenance Workers are exposed to such hazards as chemicals, gas fumes, and high-voltage equipment as well as to vibrating machinery and high levels of noise from aircraft, equipment, and power tools. Many Airport Maintenance Workers must handle extensive hours working in varying temperatures and weather conditions.

Their work often involves strenuous physical activity. For example, they might stand, stoop, squat, or kneel for long periods of time to complete various tasks; they might climb ladders or crouch in confined spaces; and they might lift, carry, or move heavy objects.

Airport Maintenance Workers work full time or part time. Many of them are assigned to rotating shifts, which can include working nights, weekends, and holidays. Working overtime is sometimes required.

Salaries

Salaries vary, depending on such factors as experience, job duties, employer, and geographical location. Formal salary data pertaining specifically to Airport Maintenance Workers is unavailable. According to the May 2003 *Occupational Employment Statistics* survey (by the U.S. Bureau of Labor Statistics), the estimated annual salary for most general maintenance and repair workers ranged from $17,180 to $47,760.

Employment Prospects

Job prospects are generally better at large airports in metropolitan areas. Most opportunities become available to replace Airport Maintenance Workers who retire, become promoted, or transfer to other occupations.

Advancement Prospects

Airport Maintenance Workers can advance to become crewleaders and supervisors. Those with managerial ambitions can pursue careers as airport maintenance managers, which usually requires further education and training in airport maintenance management. Individuals who gain a broad background in airport operations might follow a career path in airport management.

Education and Training

Minimally, employers require that Airport Maintenance Workers possess at least a high school diploma or a general equivalency diploma.

Many Airport Maintenance Workers learned their trades through vocational training programs, apprenticeships, or on-the-job training.

Employers typically provide Airport Maintenance Workers with on-the-job training in airport maintenance, operations, and safety.

Special Requirements

Airport Maintenance Workers are required to hold a valid state driver's license.

Job candidates may be required to pass an extensive security screening and a drug test in order to qualify for employment.

Experience, Special Skills, and Personality Traits

Work experience requirements vary with the different airports. Many employers require that candidates have one or more years of work experience in the maintenance and repair of airport facilities. Employers also hire candidates who have a few years of skilled maintenance and repair work in one or more of the standard trades, such as carpentry, electrical work, plumbing, or air-conditioning.

To perform their jobs effectively, Airport Maintenance Workers need basic reading skills, including the ability to understand diagrams, schematics, sketches, and other visual aids. Having good writing, math, and communication skills is also essential. In addition, they must have good teamwork and interpersonal skills, as well as excellent self-management skills, such as being able to work independently, organize and prioritize tasks, complete tasks on time, and understand and follow instructions.

Their jobs require that they have physical strength, agility, and manual dexterity. Being resourceful, self-motivated, capable, friendly, and versatile are some personality traits that successful Airport Maintenance Workers share.

Unions and Associations

Many Airport Maintenance Workers belong to a union, such as the Service Employees International Union. A union represents members in negotiations with their employers for contractual terms relating to pay, benefits, and working conditions.

Tips for Entry

1. Vocational and apprenticeship programs in carpentry, electronics, plumbing, and other trades and crafts may be available in your area. If you are in high school or community college, talk with a guidance counselor for information. Job counselors at state employment offices can also provide information about these programs.
2. Contact airport personnel departments directly to learn about job openings.
3. Many airports have Web sites on the Internet. Along with providing general information about airport operations, airports post job listings and other information on their Web sites. To see if a particular airport has a Web site, enter its name in a search engine.
4. Use the Internet to learn more about airport maintenance. To get a list of relevant Web sites to visit, enter the keywords *airport maintenance department* or *airport maintenance workers* into any search engine.

AVIATION TRAINING, EDUCATION, AND COMMUNICATIONS

FLIGHT INSTRUCTOR

CAREER PROFILE

Duties: Provide beginning and advanced flying lessons; perform duties as required

Alternate Title(s): Certified Flight Instructor (CFI)

Salary Range: $12,000 to $41,000

Employment Prospects: Good

Advancement Prospects: Good

Prerequisites:

Education or Training—High school diploma

Experience—Be an experienced pilot; teaching experience may be preferred

Special Skills and Personality Traits—Communication, interpersonal, motivational, leadership, and self-management skills; freelancers need business, public relations, organizational, and management skills; enthusiastic, patient, calm, respectful, responsible, dedicated, flexible, creative

Special Requirements—Hold appropriate FAA flight instructor certification and ratings

CAREER LADDER

Assistant Chief Flight Instructor

Flight Instructor

Novice Flight Instructor

Position Description

Certified Flight Instructors have earned the proper authorization from the Federal Aviation Administration (FAA) to give flying lessons to individuals who wish to fly aircraft for pleasure or for pilot careers. Different instructors offer lessons in the operation of airplanes, seaplanes, jet planes, helicopters, power-lift aircraft, gliders, or gyroscopes. They provide the necessary flight instruction that students must successfully complete to obtain pilot certificates and ratings granted by the FAA.

Flight Instructors work in different settings throughout the United States. Many of them are employed by private flight schools. Some of these schools are independent institutions, whereas others are affiliated with fixed base operators (FBOs), which sell general aviation services and products. Some Flight Instructors are employed by colleges and universities, serving as staff members of aviation degree programs. Others are freelance (or independent) Flight Instructors, usually working out of general aviation airports.

Flight Instructors play a valuable role in aviation because they provide the first flying lessons to future private, commercial, public service, and airline pilots. They teach essential concepts and skills that individuals must know and master in order to become safe and competent pilots. They cover such topics as aerodynamics, aircraft construction, airport operations, navigation, weather, cockpit management, safety, and federal aviation regulations.

In addition, they teach students specific procedures and maneuvers such as taxiing, takeoffs, landings, turns, instrument maneuvers, navigating by landmarks, and preflight and postflight procedures. Flight Instructors also create simulated emergency situations (such as becoming lost, tail-spinning, or equipment malfunctioning) so students can recognize problems and know what emergency procedures to perform. Furthermore, Flight Instructors determine when students are ready to perform solo flights and to take their examinations for pilot certifications and ratings.

Many Flight Instructors teach students who are seeking advanced certificates—commercial pilot, air transport pilot, or flight instructor certificate—or advanced ratings, such as instrument or multiengine ratings. They also assist students who are going for additional pilot ratings in a category (such as airplane), class (such as multiengine), or type (a specific make and model of aircraft such as a Boeing 737).

Staff instructors follow the curriculum designed by their flight school or collegiate aviation program, whereas independent instructors develop their own course outlines. All lessons must adhere to strict guidelines and requirements set by the FAA. Certified Flight Instructors may perform ground instruction and simulator instruction in addition to giving flight lessons.

Like any teacher, Flight Instructors prepare lesson plans, instructional activities, and study materials. They provide instruction at a pace that fits the individual abilities and learning styles of their students. They also use a variety of teaching methods to reinforce their students' learning. In addition, Flight Instructors administer oral, written, and performance tests to evaluate their students' comprehension and skills.

Flight Instructors also perform various administrative tasks. For example, they prepare flight schedules for students, maintain student training records and logbooks, and complete required paperwork. In addition, they are responsible for ensuring that their students are meeting all course objectives, standards, and training requirements. Furthermore, these instructors monitor the maintenance of training aircraft and report any problems to aircraft maintenance technicians.

Along with their teaching duties, self-employed Flight Instructors must handle tasks involved in running a business. They are responsible for collecting student fees, doing bookkeeping, paying bills and taxes, overseeing the maintenance of training aircraft, and so on. They also set aside time to promote their business and to interview prospective students.

Flight Instructors work part time or full time. Many part-time instructors continue working in their primary occupations as airline pilots, air charter pilots, agricultural pilots, aerial photographers, and so forth. Some part-time instructors own aircraft repair shops, fixed base operators, or other aviation businesses.

Flight Instructors generally work irregular hours and hold flight lessons at times that are convenient for their students. In addition, their hours are dependent on the weather. They generally work more hours during the summer months and on any weekend when the weather is clear and calm for flying.

Salaries

Earnings for Flight Instructors vary, depending on such factors as experience, whether employed part time or full time, employer, and geographical location. Most Flight Instructors are paid on an hourly basis, which ranges widely from $10 to $75. The Airline Employment Assistance Corps reports that Flight Instructors earn between $12,300 and $40,530 per year.

Employment Prospects

There is generally a steady need for new Flight Instructors, as instructors are able to accumulate sufficient flight time and experience while teaching to qualify them for entry-level pilot positions with airlines, air charter services, and corporate flight departments. In the next few years, the airlines should be experiencing an increased demand for qualified pilots because half their workforce will reach the mandatory retirement age. As more Flight Instructors become airline pilots, the demand for experienced Flight Instructors should increase as well.

Advancement Prospects

For many Flight Instructors, the ultimate goal is to become airline, corporate, commercial, or public service pilots. Thus, they provide flying lessons as one way to accumulate the required flying hours for entry-level pilot positions.

Career Flight Instructors can advance according to their interests and ambitions. Those with management and administrative ambitions can pursue such positions as chief flight instructors, flight school managers, or managers of airline training departments. With additional education and experience, they can teach academic courses in aviation degree programs. Flight Instructors with entrepreneurial ambitions can become independent instructors or start their own flight schools.

Education and Training

Minimally, Flight Instructors must possess a high school diploma or general equivalency diploma. Many Flight Instructors possess a bachelor's or advanced degree in their fields of interest. (A college degree is usually required to be hired for airline pilot positions and many commercial pilot jobs.)

In order to become a Certified Flight Instructor, individuals must successfully complete flight instructor training required by the FAA. They learn the fundamentals of teaching, which includes such topics as the learning process, student evaluation and testing, course development, and lesson planning.

Flight Instructors are responsible for their own professional development. They read books and magazines about flight instruction, network with colleagues, enroll in continuing education courses, participate in training workshops, and so on.

Special Requirements

Flight Instructors must possess the FAA flight instructor certificate, which is an advanced pilot certificate. They must also hold the appropriate flight instructor rating for each type of instruction—such as instrument, multiengine, glider, or helicopter—that they wish to offer. Additionally, they must possess a third-class (or higher) FAA medical certificate.

The minimum qualifications for becoming a Certified Flight Instructor (CFI) are:

- be at least 18 years old
- be able to read, write, speak, and understand the English language

- possess either a commercial pilot certificate with an instrument rating or an air transport pilot certificate
- receive logbook endorsements from authorized instructors for having completed all required flight instructor training
- pass all required knowledge and practical tests

Flight Instructors must obtain additional flight instructor ratings if they plan to offer instrument instruction (CFII) and multiengine instruction (MEI).

Experience, Special Skills, and Personality Traits

Flight Instructors are experienced pilots, with the appropriate knowledge and skills proficiency in the category, class, and type of aircraft that they teach. Some employers prefer to hire candidates who have previous flight instructing experience.

To work well with students, Flight Instructors need excellent communication, interpersonal, motivational, and leadership skills. In addition, they must have solid self-management skills—the ability to work well under pressure, make sound judgments, follow directions, and so on. To be successful freelancers, they need adequate business, management, and marketing skills.

Being enthusiastic, patient, calm, respectful, responsible, dedicated, flexible, and creative are some personality traits that successful Flight Instructors have in common. They also share a passion for both flying and teaching others how to fly.

Unions and Associations

Flight Instructors can join national, state, and local professional organizations to take advantage of networking opportunities, training programs, and other professional services. Many instructors belong to the National Association of Flight Instructors, which is the professional society devoted to Flight Instructors of all kinds—airplane, helicopter, glider, hot-air balloon, etc.

Flight Instructors also join other professional associations that serve their particular interests such as the Aircraft Owners and Pilots Association, the Soaring Society of America (SSA), the Professional Helicopter Pilots Association, and the Ninety-Nines, Inc.

Tips for Entry

1. Some flight schools and academic programs offer teaching jobs to successful graduates of their flight programs.
2. To enhance their employability (as well as professional credibility), Flight Instructors obtain the master CFI designation that is granted by the National Association of Flight Instructors. To learn more, visit its Web site at http://www.nafinet.org.
3. For more information about flight instruction certification, visit the FAA Web site at http://www.faa.gov. There, click on the link "Licenses and Certificates."
4. Use the Internet to learn more about the field of flight instruction. One Web site you might visit is for the National Association of Flight Instructors, http://www.nafinet.org. To get general information about learning to fly, check out the articles Web page at the Student Pilot Network Web site: http://www.ufly.com/articles. For those interested in becoming glider instructors, visit the SSA Instructor Page (at Soaring Safety Foundation): http://www.soaringsafety.org/ip.asp.

AVIATION TRAINING DEVELOPER

CAREER PROFILE

Duties: Plan, develop, design, deliver, and assess employee training programs; create print and technology-based instructional materials; perform duties as required of position

Alternate Title(s): Training and Development Specialist; Instructional Designer

Salary Range: $26,000 to $75,000

Employment Prospects: Fair

Advancement Prospects: Fair

Prerequisites:

Education or Training—Bachelor's degree in instructional technology, education, or another related field

Experience—Previous experience developing training programs and materials for adult learners in the aviation or aerospace industry

Special Skills and Personality Traits—Communication, interpersonal, teamwork, organizational, management, writing, presentation, and computer skills; patient, tactful, energetic, enthusiastic, creative, flexible, self-motivated

CAREER LADDER

Training Department Manager

Training Developer

Trainer or Training and Development Intern

Position Description

Aviation Training Developers are involved in the creation of effective employee training programs for airports, airlines, government aviation agencies, aerospace companies, aviation manufacturers, and other private and public organizations in the aviation and aerospace industries. Training and professional development programs contribute significantly to helping organizations to successfully achieve their missions and goals. Various programs are implemented to improve the morale and productivity of employees, to hone employees' skills or to teach new skills, and to maintain a safe and satisfactory work environment.

The following are some of the different programs that Aviation Training Developers may be assigned to handle:

- new employee orientation training
- technical training (such as aircraft maintenance workshops or simulator training for pilots)
- professional skills training for specific departments (such as the customer service department) or specific employee positions (such as supervisors, division managers, or sales representatives)
- employee safety training
- informational workshops on work-related topics, such as diversity or sexual harassment in the workplace
- basic skills training (remediation of literacy and math skills)

Training Developers may work alone or as part of a team when working on a new training project. They may be assigned to be involved with the planning, development, instructional design, delivery, or assessment of a training program. Senior specialists are assigned as project managers and are responsible for the direction and management of training projects. They make sure that projects are completed on schedule and within a given budget. Additionally, they ensure that training programs adhere to appropriate policies and standards as well as local, state, and federal laws and regulations.

Aviation Training Developers work closely with subject matter experts (department managers, supervisors, technicians, professionals, or other personnel) as they design specific instructional programs. The subject matter experts help the specialists determine the content of the program—the topics to teach, learning objectives, sequence of teaching, types of practice exercises, and so on. They also discuss evaluation strategies for measuring employee performance upon completion of training.

Aviation Training Developers determine the most effective way to deliver the instruction. Training programs may be implemented in such forms as classroom instruction, workshops, seminars, individual coaching, on-the-job training, interactive video training, computer-based training, or intranet instruction. Training Developers also produce print, visual, and/or technology-based instructional materials that include both trainer and participant guides. In designing programs and materials, Aviation Training Developers integrate adult learning principles and take into account the different abilities and learning styles of a program's participants.

Aviation Training Developers also perform other duties, which vary from one specialist to the next. Some of them are responsible for maintaining training programs. On a regular basis, they review and evaluate the effectiveness of current programs. When necessary, they update courses and instructional materials. Other Training Developers are responsible for managing the development of all training programs within their organization. This includes coordinating and administering contracts with outside vendors who provide specific training programs.

Additional responsibilities might include:

- conducting employee training classes or courses
- training the instructors, department supervisors, or other personnel who will be training staff members
- developing training programs, training materials, or user documents for their employers' customers or clients
- assisting with the development of marketing and sales materials

Aviation Training Developers typically work 40 hours a week. On occasion, they work evenings and weekends to complete assignments and meet deadlines.

Salaries

Salaries vary and depend on factors such as education, experience, job responsibilities, and the size and type of employer. Training Developers in large organizations can expect to earn higher wages. According to the May 2003 *Occupational Employment Statistics* survey (by the U.S. Bureau of Labor Statistics), the estimated annual salary for most training and development specialists ranged from $25,550 to $74,670.

Employment Prospects

Most Aviation Training Developers work in the training departments of companies, government agencies, and other organizations. Some specialists are independent consultants, whereas others are employed by training and development firms that offer their services to organizations on a contractual basis.

The demand for Aviation Training Developers is constant, as employers continually need to train and retrain employees. Most job opportunities become available as developers retire, advance to higher positions, or transfer to other organizations. Aviation organizations will create additional positions to fit their growing needs.

Advancement Prospects

Aviation Training Developers can advance to supervisory and management positions, which may require transferring to other organizations. Those with entrepreneurial ambitions can become independent consultants or owners of businesses that offer training and development services.

Education and Training

Minimally, Aviation Training Developers need a bachelor's degree, preferably in instructional technology, education, or another related field. Some employers require that candidates have a master's degree but will waive the requirement if candidates have qualifying work experience.

Aviation Training Developers are expected to update and improve their skills, as well as keep up with current training and development research. They network with colleagues, enroll in training workshops and continuing education courses, read professional books and journals, participate in professional conferences, and so on.

Experience, Special Skills, and Personality Traits

In general, employers seek candidates who have several years of experience in developing training programs. Aviation Training Developers are also knowledgeable about adult learning principles and methodologies. Many employers desire candidates who have experience with creating computer-based or technology-based learning materials. Further, candidates must have experience working in the aviation or aerospace industry.

Aviation Training Developers need superior communication, interpersonal, and teamwork skills, as they must be able to work effectively with different people from diverse backgrounds. They also need strong organizational, management, writing, and presentation skills. In addition, they have the appropriate computer skills, including the ability to use word processing, desktop publishing, and other software.

Successful Aviation Training Developers share several personality traits, such as being patient, tactful, energetic, enthusiastic, creative, flexible, and self-motivated.

Unions and Associations

Many Aviation Training Developers join local, state, and national professional associations to take advantage of continuing education programs, networking opportunities, and other professional services. One organization they might join is the American Society for Training and Development.

Tips for Entry

1. Get experience teaching adult learners. You might tutor adult students in college settings or volunteer to teach adults in adult literacy programs. Or you might teach adult classes in continuing education programs sponsored by community centers, community colleges, and other organizations.
2. In college, seek out internship opportunities with an airport, airline, aerospace company, government aviation agency, or another organization in the aviation or aerospace industry.
3. Keep up with advances in technology and update your skills as needed.
4. Use the Internet to learn more about the field of training and development. You might start by visiting the American Society for Training and Development Web site at http://www.astd.org. To learn about the aviation training field, check out the following two Web sites: Neil Krey's Flight Deck, http://s92270093.onlinehome.us/fltdeck, and Aviation Industry CBT (Computer-Based Training) Committee, http://www.aicc.org.

AVIATION PROFESSOR

CAREER PROFILE

Duties: Provide instruction in flight operations, aviation maintenance technology, aviation management, and other areas at colleges and universities; perform duties as required of position

Alternate Title(s): Instructor; Assistant Professor; Associate Professor; Professor

Salary Range: $52,000 to $74,000

Employment Prospects: Fair

Advancement Prospects: Fair

Prerequisites:

Education or Training—Educational requirements vary with different institutions

Experience—Be a highly experienced aviation professional; have previous experience teaching adults

Special Skills and Personality Traits—Communication, presentation, human relations, organizational, and management skills; independent, curious, flexible, dedicated, creative

Special Requirements—A proper FAA pilot certificate with appropriate ratings required for flight instructors; a proper FAA mechanic certificate with an airframe and powerplant (A&P) rating required for aviation maintenance professors

CAREER LADDER

Professor

Associate Professor

Assistant Professor

Instructor

Position Description

Collegiate aviation refers to degree programs in aviation or aerospace technology that are offered at colleges and universities. The programs generally concentrate in three areas: flight operations (also known as the professional pilot program), aviation maintenance technology, and aviation management. Some institutions also offer such specialized programs as aviation computer science, flight education, or space studies.

Aviation Professors are responsible for preparing students for a wide range of careers in the aviation, aerospace, and aviation-related industries. Most professors are current or former professionals with extensive experience as airline pilots, air-taxi operators, airport managers, business aviation managers, air traffic controllers, avionics technicians, aviation maintenance managers, airport engineers, aviation security specialists, researchers, software developers, public relations specialists, entrepreneurs, and so on.

Some Aviation Professors teach in two-year colleges, which are also known as community colleges, junior colleges, or technical colleges. These colleges serve the educational needs of the local communities as well as provide training for the local professions, businesses, industries, and government agencies. Students may earn associate degrees in various aviation fields. (General education courses in community colleges usually fulfill lower undergraduate requirements in four-year colleges and universities.)

Other Aviation Professors teach undergraduate and graduate students in four-year colleges and universities. Most of these institutions offer aviation programs leading to bachelor's degrees; some universities offer aviation programs that lead to master's or doctoral degrees.

Aviation Professors teach a wide range of courses, such as aerodynamics, flight physiology, crew resource management, airline flight operations, aviation maintenance inspection, airport management, aviation law, aviation safety, airport management, and international aviation.

For each of their courses, Aviation Professors develop a course syllabus that outlines the sequence of topics to be taught as well as bibliographies for required reading assignments. They are also responsible for preparing lectures and laboratory experiments. Depending on the course, Professors lecture to large groups of students, lead small seminar discussions, or supervise students in laboratories. Some Professors teach online courses or conduct courses on cable or closed-circuit television. Their various tasks include reading student reports, administering exams, providing students with feedback on their work, and evaluating students' performances. Furthermore, most Aviation Professors have the duty of advising students on academic and career matters.

Aviation Professors in four-year colleges and universities usually conduct research in topics that interest them (such as flight simulation, human factors, or aviation safety). Some Aviation Professors are involved in basic research to extend knowledge about aviation or aerospace technology. Others conduct applied research to develop new or improved products, systems, techniques, or procedures in flight operations, aviation management, airport security, and so on. Sometimes Aviation Professors are involved in research projects with colleagues from other disciplines. For example, an Aviation Professor conducting research on pilot behavior might collaborate with professors from the psychology department.

Professors are responsible for obtaining funds for their projects. The money pays for equipment and supplies, travel, overhead costs, financial support for themselves and research assistants, and so on. Thus, their tasks include seeking appropriate funding sources (such as the federal government) and preparing grant proposals. Aviation Professors are expected to share the results of their research work through scientific papers or presentations at professional conferences.

Aviation Professors are required to participate in faculty meetings where they discuss and handle departmental matters, curriculum, hiring, and so on. They also serve on academic and administrative advisory committees that deal with institutional policies. Additionally, Aviation Professors are usually required to perform community service. For example, Aviation Professors might serve on committees, panels, or commissions established by government agencies.

On most campuses, Aviation Professors hold four academic ranks—instructor, assistant professor, associate professor, or (full) professor. Professors may be hired on either a tenure or nontenure track. Tenured professors are assured of a job at an institution until they retire or resign. They cannot be fired without just cause and due process. Tenure-track positions start at either the instructor or assistant professor level with tenure usually being attained at the associate professor rank.

Some faculty members in aviation departments are employed as adjunct instructors. They work part time and are usually assigned to teach one to three courses a semester (or quarter). They might also teach courses in continuing education programs. Adjunct instructors have limited administrative and student advising duties.

Aviation Professors have flexible hours, which may include teaching classes at night or on weekends. Full-time faculty generally teach between 12 to 15 hours per week; graduate faculty usually teach fewer hours. The total number of hours they actually work can add up to 40 to 50 or more hours per week. This includes time spent teaching courses, holding office hours, preparing for classes, grading papers and exams, conducting research, participating in staff and committee meetings, and so on.

Salaries

Salaries vary and depend on such factors as experience, education, academic institution, and geographic location. A 2002–03 survey by the American Association of University Professors reports the following average annual salaries for faculty (of all ranks) at different institutions:

- $51,619 at two-year colleges
- $54,051 at institutions that award only bachelor's degrees
- $58,769 at institutions where the highest degree awarded is the master's degree
- $73,997 at institutions where the highest degree awarded is the doctorate

Employment Prospects

Collegiate aviation is a small field, which has been gradually expanding in the last decade. Generally, opportunities are created as college professors retire or transfer to other workplaces or occupations. Institutions may create additional positions as enrollment grows, if funding is available.

Fewer tenure-track positions have become available each year. Due to tight budgets, institutions have been hiring more adjunct faculty and have been offering prospective full-time faculty limited contracts of one to five years, which may be renewed. The competition is high for both tenure and nontenure track positions.

Job prospects should improve in the coming years as college and university enrollment in aviation programs is expected to increase considerably. The downsizing of the military has caused civilian training programs to become the major source of trained aviation professionals. Furthermore, a large segment of the workforce in the aviation industry (including pilots, air traffic control specialists, aviation maintenance technicians, aviation managers, and so on) will be reaching retirement age within the next few years. This should result in the creation of additional job openings to teach the future workforce.

Advancement Prospects

College Professors earn appointment rankings. They start at the instructor level and advance to assistant professor, then associate professor, and finally full professor. Those interested in managerial positions can become department chairs and advance up the administrative ladder as academic deans, administrative directors, provosts, and, eventually, presidents.

Education and Training

Because collegiate aviation is relatively new compared to other academic programs, the education requirements for aviation instructors and professors are still less strict. At two-year colleges, faculty may be hired with associate's, bachelor's, or master's degrees. Four-year colleges and universities require that applicants possess at least master's degrees. Having a doctoral degree in an aviation-related field is preferable—and usually required—in research universities. College degrees may be in an aviation field or in another discipline.

Most aviation instructors and professors have earned their degrees in such fields as aviation management, business administration, civil engineering, aerospace engineering, atmospheric science, psychology, and education. Many of them pursue advanced degrees in aviation or other aviation-related disciplines while they are teaching.

Professors are responsible for keeping up with developments in their fields through independent study, networking with colleagues, and participating in professional conferences and workshops.

Special Requirements

Professors who provide flight instruction must hold either the commercial pilot or air transport pilot (ATP) certificate, along with instrument and multiengine ratings—which are granted by the Federal Aviation Administration (FAA). Additionally, they must possess an FAA flight instructor certificate.

Aviation maintenance instructors and professors must hold a valid FAA mechanic certificate with an airframe and powerplant (A&P) rating.

Experience, Special Skills, and Personality Traits

Employers typically seek candidates who are highly experienced in their profession, such as aviation managers or commercial pilots. They also require that candidates have previous experience teaching adults, which may have been gained through work as flight instructors, supervisors, airline training instructors, college lecturers, and so on.

To be effective educators, Aviation Professors should have excellent communication and presentation skills. They also require strong human relations skills, as they must be able to work well with students, colleagues, administrators, community leaders, and the general public. Furthermore, strong organizational and management skills are needed to complete their various duties each day.

Successful Aviation Professors share several personality traits, such as being independent, curious, flexible, dedicated, and creative.

Unions and Associations

Aviation Professors belong to different professional societies to take advantage of networking opportunities, professional development, and other professional resources and services. Many of them are members of the University Aviation Association, which serves the specific interests of aviation educators in academic institutions.

Aviation Professors also join associations that serve the interests of academic faculty, such as the American Association for Higher Education, the National Association of Scholars, or the American Association of University Professors. Community college faculty might join the American Association for Adult and Continuing Education. College instructors in public institutions are eligible to join the higher education divisions of either of these teacher unions: the National Education Association or the American Federation of Teachers.

Furthermore, many Aviation Professors belong to societies that serve their particular interests in aviation, such as the Aircraft Owners and Pilots Association; the Women in Aviation, International; the National Association of Flight Instructors; the Professional Aviation Maintenance Association; the American Association of Airport Executives; or the National Business Aviation Association.

Tips for Entry

1. To gain work experience, contact institutions about temporary or adjunct positions. Many colleges and universities maintain a list of qualified candidates whom they contact when new instructors are needed. It is common for colleges to hire new instructors at the last minute for part-time instructors who have suddenly left for full-time positions.
2. The *Collegiate Aviation Guide* (compiled by the University Aviation Association) is a good resource to use while performing a job hunt. This book offers information about academic institutions in the United States and other countries that offer aviation degree programs.
3. The Internet is a valuable tool for keeping up to date with issues and trends in collegiate aviation, higher education in general, networking with colleagues around the world, doing a job search, and so on. Some Web sites that may provide you with helpful information are University Aviation Association, http://uaa.auburn.edu; American Association for Higher Education, http://www.aahe.org; American Association of Community Colleges, http://www.aacc.nche.edu; and the *Chronicle of Higher Education,* http://chronicle.com.

AVIATION EDUCATION SPECIALIST (NONSCHOOL SETTINGS)

CAREER PROFILE

Duties: Plan, develop, manage, and promote aviation and space education programs in informal settings; develop curriculum and educational materials; perform other duties as required

Alternate Title(s): Aviation Educator

Salary Range: $13,000 to $60,000

Employment Prospects: Poor

Advancement Prospects: Poor

Prerequisites:

Education or Training—Bachelor's degree or advanced degree, depending on the employer

Experience—Strong background in aviation; experience working in aviation or space education programs

Special Skills and Personality Traits—Interpersonal, teamwork, communication, writing, computer, and self-management skills; self-motivated, creative, enthusiastic, flexible, organized

CAREER LADDER

Senior Education Specialist or Program Coordinator

Aviation Education Specialist

Assistant Aviation Educator

Position Description

Aviation Education Specialists are responsible for planning, developing, managing, and promoting informal education programs that provide a broader understanding of civil aviation and of space missions among the general public. They also create programs that expose young people to the wide range of careers in the aviation and aerospace industries.

These educators are employed in nonschool settings. They may work in educational programs that are run by the Federal Aviation Administration (FAA), National Aeronautics and Space Administration (NASA), state government agencies, aviation museums, science centers, universities and colleges, aviation trade and professional associations, or nonprofit organizations.

They develop a variety of programs to attract the interests of different audiences—schoolchildren, teachers, or the general public. Their main objective is to create programs that entertain audiences, as well as to teach them informally about aviation or space. Aviation educators plan and coordinate a wide array of activities. For example, they might sponsor air shows, aviation camps, or lecture series; set up exhibits at museums or libraries; give presentations, workshops, and seminars; produce videotapes, software, and publications; and develop online learning programs.

Aviation Education Specialists are also involved in designing and delivering educational outreach programs. They travel to schools, youth centers, community centers, and other organizations to give workshops and presentations. They use films, slideshows, and other multimedia tools to bring aviation alive with their lectures. They might also bring model planes, rockets, and other objects to involve audiences in the learning experience.

Many Aviation Education Specialists develop curriculum programs and lesson plans for elementary, middle school, and high school levels. Some specialists conduct workshops to instruct school teachers on how they might teach certain topics in their classrooms. For example, they might present teaching and student materials, offer teaching strategies, and demonstrate how to perform enrichment activities. Some Aviation Education Specialists also offer technical advice and support to informal education programs sponsored by science centers, museums, planetariums, and other institutions.

Some Aviation Education Specialists in state aviation agencies are involved in developing safety education programs for pilots, aviation maintenance technicians, flight instructors, and other aviation professionals. These programs promote safe practices and procedures for flight operations, aircraft maintenance and repairs, and so on. Specialists might also be responsible for conducting seminars, clinics, workshops, or other activities for aviation professionals throughout their state.

All Aviation Education Specialists perform a variety of other duties. For example, they may be responsible for:

- coordinating schedules and logistics for events, presentations, or workshops
- setting up and maintaining displays or exhibits, which may include writing interpretive materials
- writing grant proposals for future or current programs
- training and supervising junior staff, interns, and volunteers
- developing marketing and public relations materials such as newsletters, informational brochures, and Web pages
- writing correspondence, preparing reports, completing required paperwork, and maintaining accurate records
- attending staff meetings and professional conferences

Furthermore, Aviation Education Specialists are expected to stay current with educational issues, curriculum frameworks, and educational standards. Additionally, they keep up to date with the latest developments in aviation and space.

Aviation Education Specialists work part time or full time. They may be required to work evenings, weekends, and holidays.

Salaries

Salaries vary, and depend on such factors as education, experience, job responsibilities, and type of employer. Salary information is unavailable for Aviation Education Specialists, but an idea of their earnings can be obtained by looking at similar occupations. For example, education coordinators of public programs and school programs for science centers generally earned between $13,000 to $66,000 in 2000, according to the "Science Center Workforce 2001" (a report by the Association of Science-Technology Centers).

Employment Prospects

Most opportunities become available as Aviation Education Specialists transfer to other positions. Many jobs are based on the funding of grant proposals and so may last only for a specific period of time.

The availability of government funding fluctuates with the health of the economy. During economic downturns, aviation and space education programs usually expect to find fewer grant opportunities.

Advancement Prospects

Advancement opportunities are limited to supervisory and program management positions. Many Aviation Education Specialists measure their success by receiving greater responsibilities, earning higher salaries, and gaining professional recognition for their work.

Education and Training

Educational requirements vary with different employers. Some employers require that applicants have at least a bachelor's degree, while others require a master's degree. Some employers prefer candidates with a doctoral degree. Degrees may be earned in the fields of education, aviation, science, engineering, or a related area.

Most Aviation Education Specialists continue their professional growth through self-study, training workshops, continuing education programs, networking with colleagues, and so on.

Experience, Special Skills, and Personality Traits

Aviation Education Specialists usually have a strong background in aviation. Some of them are pilots. Many of them have also been employed in general aviation, commercial airlines, or aviation agency settings. They typically have previous experience working with aviation or space education programs in school, academic, or informal settings.

To perform their work effectively, Aviation Education Specialists need excellent interpersonal, teamwork, and communication skills. They must also have strong writing and computer skills. In addition, they have good self-management skills, including the ability to handle multiple tasks, prioritize tasks, work independently, meet deadlines, and handle stressful situations.

Being self-motivated, creative, enthusiastic, flexible, and organized are some personality traits that successful Aviation Education Specialists share.

Unions and Associations

Aviation Education Specialists can join professional societies (at the local, state, and national levels) that serve their interests in aviation. These organizations offer professional services and resources such as training programs, networking opportunities, publications, and information about current developments. For example, aviation educators might belong to such aviation associations as the Aircraft Owners and Pilots Association, the Ninety-Nines, Inc., or the National Business Aviation Association.

Tips for Entry

1. As a high school student, you can start gaining knowledge and skills that will be valuable for an aviation

career. For example, you might get involved in the Aviation Explorers, the Civil Air Patrol Cadet program, or another youth group that emphasizes aviation interests. Also take advantage of aviation education programs offered in your area.

2. Gain valuable experience by volunteering in education or outreach programs at an aviation museum or aviation education program. If none are located in your area, then volunteer at a local science museum, technology center, zoo, or other institution.

3. Learn more about aviation and space education programs on the Internet. Some Web sites you might visit include National Coalition for Aviation Education, http://www.aviationeducation.org; FAA Aviation Education Program, http://www.faa.gov/education/index.cfm; and NASA Education Enterprise, http://education.nasa.gov/index.html. You might also check out the resources available at the Civil Air Patrol Web site. Go to http://level2.cap.gov, click on the *Programs* link and then the *Aerospace Education* link.

AVIATION CURATOR

CAREER PROFILE

Duties: Oversee the care and presentation of aircraft collections; manage aircraft restoration projects; perform management duties; perform other duties as required

Alternate Title(s): Collection Manager

Salary Range: $20,000 to $66,000

Employment Prospects: Poor

Advancement Prospects: Poor

Prerequisites:

Education or Training—Master's or doctoral degree

Experience—Be knowledgeable about aircraft and aircraft restoration and have aircraft maintenance expertise; aviation experience is mandatory

Special Skills and Personality Traits—Management, business, research, communication, writing, computer, interpersonal, teamwork, and self-management skills; energetic, self-motivated, creative, intuitive, curious, flexible

CAREER LADDER

Chief Curator (at larger museums) or Museum Director

Curator

Assistant or Associate Curator

Position Description

Aviation Curators are dedicated to preserving aviation history as well as to educating the general public about the evolution of aviation and aerospace technology. They are in charge of the collections of aircraft, aviation artifacts, and aviation-related items that are displayed at aviation museums. Aircraft collections include original and restored civil, military, and experimental aircraft. Many collections also exhibit reproductions of historically significant aircraft such as the airplane flown by Orville and Wilbur Wright at Kitty Hawk. In addition, some aviation museums present collections of space technology, including such items as rockets, missiles, satellites, and lunar modules.

Curators work for aviation museums that are owned by local, state, or federal government agencies, by nonprofit organizations (such as aviation historical associations), or by private individuals or enterprises. Some aviation museums are part of a larger museum. For example, the National Air and Space Museum is a division of the Smithsonian Museum.

Aviation Curators manage collections that belong to their institutions as well as those that are lent to them by donors or other institutions. They are responsible for the care and presentation of all aircraft, objects, and materials that are in their collections. For example, they coordinate activities involved in the preservation of aircraft to keep them from deteriorating while they are on display. In small museums, Aviation Curators are in charge of all collections, while curators at larger museums may be assigned to manage one or more collections. At very large institutions, Aviation Curators may be assigned to perform only research or administrative duties.

Aviation Curators are involved in various activities, working closely with other staff members—such as directors, archivists, technicians, and educators—and volunteers. For example, Aviation Curators' activities might include:

- organizing, describing, and classifying items in the collections
- removing items from display and making sure that they are safely and securely stored away
- overseeing the acquisition of military, civil, and experimental aircraft through donations and purchases
- directing aircraft restoration projects, which are projects that carefully restore airplanes to their original conditions
- developing and designing displays

- conducting historical research on aircraft aviators, events, and other topics of interest
- making presentations about their collections at professional conferences as well as at meetings and functions of civic groups
- answering questions about museum collections from the media, authors, other museums, or the general public

Aircraft Curators are also responsible for developing museum exhibits that bring concepts of aviation history and technology to life. They work with other staff members to plan, design, and prepare entertaining exhibits that communicate ideas clearly.

In addition, Aviation Curators perform various administrative tasks. For example, they administer museum policies; manage budgets; maintain collection records; evaluate exhibits and collections programs; train and supervise staff, interns, and volunteers; write grant proposals; and assist in fund-raising. Many curators assist with public relations and perform tasks to help promote museum programs, events, and activities. They might write press releases or develop informational brochures for patrons, for example. Some Aviation Curators participate in the development of educational and public outreach programs for their institutions.

The curators at small aviation museums are responsible for the day-to-day management of museum operations in addition to their curator duties. They oversee the administration of the museum and the management of all museum activities and programs. They also are responsible for maintaining museum facilities; in other words, making sure that the electricity, plumbing, heating, air conditioning, and other systems are in working order and that buildings and grounds are properly maintained.

Some Aviation Curators are lecturers or adjunct (part-time) instructors at colleges and universities, teaching undergraduate, graduate, or continuing education programs. They might teach courses in museum science, aviation history, or another aviation field. Many Aviation Curators write articles, monographs, books, and other material about aviation history, aircraft restoration, and other aviation topics.

Aviation Curators often work long hours to complete their various tasks, meet deadlines, coordinate events, attend conferences, and so on.

Salaries

Salaries vary, depending on such factors as education, experience, type and size of employer, and geographical location. Aviation Curators usually earn higher salaries in government museums than in civilian markets. The U.S. Bureau of Labor Statistics, in its May 2003 *Occupational Employment Statistics* survey, reports that the estimated annual salary for most curators (in all fields) ranged between $20,250 and $66,460.

Employment Prospects

Opportunities for Aviation Curators are generally poor since there are few aviation museums and most of them are nonprofit institutions with limited budgets. Job openings typically become available as Aviation Curators retire or transfer to other positions. The turnover rate for Curators, however, is low and the competition is very high.

The job prospects are generally better with government and military museums.

Advancement Prospects

Advancement opportunities are limited to museum director positions, which usually means that curators seek such employment at other museums. Most Aviation Curators measure their success through job satisfaction, by earning higher wages, and by gaining professional recognition.

Education and Training

Employers generally require that Aviation Curators possess a master's or doctoral degree in history, aeronautical engineering, or a related field. Many employers, however, hire candidates who have a bachelor's degree if they possess technical expertise in aircraft maintenance and aviation history.

Many colleges and universities have graduate programs or certificate-based programs in museum studies with a focus in curatorship.

Experience, Skills, and Personality Traits

Aviation Curators must be knowledgeable about aircraft and aircraft restoration, and possess technical expertise in aircraft maintenance. Having aviation experience is mandatory, preferably as a pilot or an aircraft mechanic. In fact, many of today's Aviation Curators are retired military pilots and/or aircraft maintenance officers.

In order to handle the different aspects of their jobs, Aviation Curators need management and business skills, especially if they are overseeing small museums. They also need effective research, communication, and writing skills, along with good computer skills. In addition, Aviation Curators have strong interpersonal and teamwork skills. Further, they should have excellent self-management skills, such as the ability to work independently, meet deadlines, and organize and prioritize tasks.

Being energetic, self-motivated, creative, intuitive, curious, and flexible are some personality traits that successful Aviation Curators share.

Unions and Associations

Many Aviation Curators join professional associations to take advantage of education programs, networking opportunities, professional resources, and other professional services.

Many belong to the American Association of Museums as well as regional and state museum associations.

Tips for Entry

1. If you are a middle school or high school student, start learning about aviation history and aircraft restoration. Read books and magazines and visit aviation museums. You can also start developing skills by making airplane models.
2. Volunteer at an aviation museum to gain experience. Get involved in the different areas of operations—aircraft restoration, business, education, exhibition development, publications, and so on.
3. On your résumé, be sure to present clearly and precisely your qualifications as they relate to aviation, aircraft maintenance, curatorship, museum management, and so forth.
4. Learn more about aviation museums on the Internet. Some Web sites you might visit are Smithsonian National Air and Space Museum, http://www.nasm.si.edu; U.S. Marine Corps Flying Leatherneck Aviation Museum, http://flyingleatherneck.netfirms.com; College Park Aviation Museum, http://www.collegeparkavationmuseum.com; and Cradle of Aviation Museum, http:///www.cradleofaviation.org.

AVIATION WRITER

CAREER PROFILE

Duties: Develop and write objective and accurate news reports, feature articles, books, documentation, manuals, public relations, or other written materials for general public and professional audiences; perform duties as required of position

Alternate Title(s): Aviation Journalist; Technical Writer; Public Relations Officer; Aerospace Communicator, or other title that reflects a specific occupation or specialty

Salary Range: $18,000 to $87,000

Employment Prospects: Fair

Advancement Prospects: Fair

Prerequisites:

Education or Training—Bachelor's degree generally required

Experience—Have writing experience, relevant to position desired

Special Skills and Personality Traits—Organizational, research, self-management, communication, interpersonal, and computer skills; accurate, ethical, patient persistent, resourceful, flexible, self-motivated, disciplined

CAREER LADDER

Editor, Project Leader, or Freelance Writer

Aviation Writer (journeyman level)

Aviation Writer (entry level)

Position Description

The field of aviation writing consists of many specialties—journalism, nonfiction writing, technical writing, public relations, copywriting, script writing, Web development, and so on. Most Aviation Writers work in various specialized areas throughout their careers. They might compose news or feature articles, produce instruction manuals or documentation for technical devices, write books about aviation history or aviation issues, prepare grant proposals or marketing materials, and so on. Regardless of their specialty, Aviation Writers have a common objective: to present information about the aviation and aerospace industries that is clearly understood by readers. They describe and explain complicated concepts and technical terminology in simple, yet accurate, language.

The responsibilities and duties of Aviation Writers vary, according to their specialty. Aviation journalists report on newsworthy events, people, companies, and activities that are happening in the aviation and aerospace industries. They also present information about current issues (such as aviation security), aviation legislation, and governmental aviation policies and regulations.

Aviation journalists are also known as reporters, newswriters, and correspondents. They are employed by newspapers, news magazines, radio, television, and online news services. Some aviation journalists work for the general media, such as daily newspapers. Along with covering the aviation beat, they are usually assigned to write news or feature articles in other general areas. Other aviation journalists work for trade media devoted to aviation and aerospace audiences. Some aviation journalists are also book authors, producing in-depth reporting on science and technical topics that interest them.

Many Aviation Writers work as public relations specialists for airlines, airports, aviation businesses, aerospace companies, governmental aviation agencies, aviation museums, aviation trade associations, and other organizations. They are involved in promoting their employers' products and services to their target audiences. Public relations specialists are also known as information officers or press writers. They write press releases, speeches, scripts for television spots, and other publicity material. Many of them perform other duties such as producing in-house newsletters and writing promotional materials.

Aviation technical writers are also Aviation Writers. They develop and prepare a variety of technical materials for aerospace companies, government agencies, aviation software companies, book publishers, and manufacturers of aviation or aviation-related products. They create such materials as pilot training handbooks, assembly instructions, maintenance manuals, catalogs, and project proposals. Their duties include planning projects, writing and editing materials, and overseeing the preparation of illustrations, graphics, and photographs. Technical Writers typically work closely with engineers and other subject matter experts.

Other Aviation Writers are involved in such areas as:

- creating educational materials for informal educational settings such as science museums, nature centers, and science programs
- writing scripts for documentaries, educational films, and multimedia projects
- preparing advertising copy to publicize special events (such as air shows) or to promote the sale of goods and services
- producing information newsletters for companies or organizations, which will be distributed to customers or the general public
- developing and writing content for Web sites

A large part of their work involves conducting research for their projects whether they are writing news articles, press releases, brochures, nonfiction books, or technical manuals. Aviation Writers seek appropriate subject matter experts and may sometimes travel to other cities or states to conduct interviews with them. They might also talk with interviewees over the telephone and through e-mail. Aviation Writers also spend time conducting research in the library, on computer databases, and on the Internet to find pertinent information for their projects.

Many Aviation Writers are usually juggling several writing projects at the same time, each at different stages. They are constantly under pressure to meet their deadlines. Thus, they gather details efficiently, yet thoroughly. Unless they are writing personal commentary, Aviation Writers must present the information objectively. They cannot inject their own opinions or biases into their writings. They also make sure that their stories are accurate and correct, therefore they check and recheck their facts. They revise and edit their writing so the language is clear and their products adhere to standard writing formats and guidelines.

Some Aviation Writers perform the editor role in addition to their writing duties. As editors, they are responsible for the overall content of the publication (such as a magazine or newsletter) or a writing project (such as technical handbook or company brochure). Their editorial duties include planning the contents of a publication or project, reviewing and editing the work of other writers, preparing written materials for production, and coordinating the production of publications.

Many Aviation Writers are self-employed. They complete assignments or projects on a contractual basis for different publishers, companies, and organizations. As freelance Aviation Writers, they handle various tasks related to running a small business. They pay bills and taxes, collect fees from clients, do bookkeeping, maintain office equipment, and so on. In addition, they set aside time in their schedule just for seeking out future work.

Aviation Writers are involved in their own professional development. They keep up with current developments in aviation or aerospace industries, as well as continue to improve their writing craft. They also continually learn new skills such as using graphics software or developing Web sites.

Aviation Writers—whether they are staff members or self-employed—typically work long and irregular hours in order to follow up on story ideas and to meet deadlines.

Salaries

Salaries vary, depending on such factors as specialty, employer, education, experience, geographical location, and other factors. The U.S. Bureau of Labor Statistics, in its May 2003 *Occupational Employment Statistics* survey, reports the following estimated annual salaries were earned by most professional writers:

- writers and authors: $22,090 to $87,390
- reporters and correspondents: $17,900 to $71,520
- technical writers: $30,600 to $83,360
- public relations specialists: $25,050 to $77,830

Employment Prospects

Staff positions typically become available as Aviation Writers retire or transfer to other positions or careers. Organizations will create additional positions to meet their growing needs.

Advancement Prospects

Aviation Writers generally realize advancement by earning higher incomes, by receiving more complicated assignments, and by being recognized for the high quality of their work.

Depending on their ambitions and interests, experienced Aviation Writers may pursue such careers as columnists, special correspondents, book authors, editors, news bureau directors, publishers, or communication consultants. Technical writers and public relations specialists might pursue management and administrative positions, by rising through the ranks as supervisors, department managers, senior managers, and executive officers.

Education and Training

Educational requirements vary with the different employers. Most Aviation Writers possess bachelor's or master's degrees in various fields, including journalism, aviation, science, engineering, English, liberal arts, and business.

In general, individuals typically earn a bachelor's degree in journalism if they plan to have a career in newspapers or magazines. Those preferring a nonjournalism path might major in English, communications, aviation, public relations, or another area that interests them.

Embry-Riddle Aeronautical University offers a bachelor's of science degree program in communication, which trains students to be knowledgeable about both aviation and communications through academic courses and cooperative education internships.

Experience, Skills, and Personality Traits

Qualifications vary for the different occupations, depending on the type of position and employer. In general, employers require that Aviation Writers have writing experience (such as newswriting, reporting, feature writing, public relations, or technical writing) relevant to the position for which they are applying. Additionally, Aviation Writers must be knowledgeable about the subject matter that they would be writing, as well as about the audiences for whom they would be writing. Having experience in aviation is highly desirable.

Many Aviation Writers have years of experience in the aviation industry as pilots, flight attendants, aviation maintenance technicians, aerospace engineers, aviation managers, aviation attorneys, aviation safety investigators, aviation business owners, and so forth.

To perform their work well, Aviation Writers must have excellent organizational, research, and self-management skills, such as the ability to meet deadlines, work independently, take initiative, and prioritize tasks. Their job also requires that they have superior communication and interpersonal skills, as they must be able to talk and listen to people from diverse backgrounds. Furthermore, Aviation Writers need adequate computer skills to perform various tasks such as word processing and searching electronic databases.

Being accurate, ethical, patient, persistent, resourceful, flexible, self-motivated, and disciplined are some personality traits that successful Aviation Writers have in common. They also share a passion for both writing and aviation.

Unions and Associations

Aviation Writers can join various types of professional societies to take advantage of networking opportunities, job banks, and other professional services and resources.

Aviation Writers might join general professional writing associations such as the Authors Guild, the National Writers Union, or the American Society of Journalists and Authors. Technical writers might join the Society of Aerospace Communicators and the Society for Technical Communication, whereas public relations specialists might join the Public Relations Society of America.

In addition, Aviation Writers are eligible to join aviation organizations that serve their areas of interest. The following are a few of the various associations that are available: the Aircraft Owners and Pilots Association, the Soaring Society of America, the American Helicopter Society International, the Association for Women in Aviation Maintenance, the Experimental Aircraft Association, the National Business Aviation Association, the Ninety-Nines, Inc., and the American Aviation Historical Society.

Tips for Entry

1. In high school or college, you can start gaining practical experience by working on school (or college) newspapers, literary magazines, or radio and television stations.
2. As a college student, obtain an internship or part-time job with a newspaper, magazine, publisher, public relations agency, or another organization that can give you exposure to and experience with writing in a professional setting.
3. Contact employers directly about employment. Express your interest in a permanent or freelance position. Be ready to describe both your publishing experience and aviation experience.
4. Use the Internet to check out various online aviation magazine and news services. Two Web sites you might visit are AVweb.com, http://www.avweb.com; and Landings, http://www.landings.com; You can also find a listing of aviation magazines and periodicals at the Thirty Thousand Feet Aviation Directory by going to http://www.thirtythousandfeet.com/magazine.htm.

AVIATION PUBLIC RELATIONS (PR) SPECIALIST

CAREER PROFILE

Duties: Inform and educate target audiences about organizations' policies, activities, and accomplishments; perform various functions, such as maintaining positive relationships with the media, developing publicity programs, and preparing in-house communications; perform duties as required

Alternate Title(s): Public Relations Officer; Information Officer; Communications Specialist; Press Officer

Salary Range: $25,000 to $78,000

Employment Prospects: Good

Advancement Prospects: Fair

Prerequisites:

Education or Training—Bachelor's degree in journalism, communication, or related field

Experience—Previous public relations experience; a foundation in the business or area of prospective employers; aviation background is desirable

Special Skills and Personality Traits—Writing, communication, interpersonal, teamwork, problem-solving, decision-making, time management, computer, desktop publishing, and online researching skills; creative, imaginative, outgoing, credible, diplomatic, self-motivated, organized, flexible, resilient

CAREER LADDER

Senior Public Relations Specialist

Public Relations Specialist

Assistant Public Relations Specialist

Position Description

Aviation Public Relations (PR) Specialists are responsible for building and maintaining a favorable image of their organizations in the minds of their target audiences—such as customers (or clients or patrons), employees, investors, local communities, and the general public. Because the success of their organizations are based on the support of their audiences, PR Specialists strive to maintain positive relationships with them.

Aviation PR Specialists work for airports, airlines, air charter services, air ambulance services, flight schools, aircraft management services, government aviation agencies, aerospace companies, manufacturers of aviation and aviation-related products, aviation museums, aviation trade associations, nonprofit groups, and other organizations. They are employees of public relations or communications departments of such organizations. Some of them are employed by consulting firms that specialize in offering public relations services.

Their primary job is to inform and educate target audiences and the general public about the policies, accomplishments, and activities of their organizations. For example, airline PR specialists would inform potential customers about flight services to new destinations. Aviation PR Specialists also handle issues that are unique to the aviation and aerospace industries (such as aviation safety and airport security). Additionally, they are responsible for managing damage control of their organization's public image during crises. For example, in such situations as aircraft crashes, financial losses, or employee strikes, airline PR specialists would provide information to the media, investors, and the general public that would instill continued confidence in their companies.

In order to perform their work effectively, Aviation PR Specialists become familiar with the overall operations of their organizations. They also conduct research to learn about their targeted audiences and how they can be influenced. Some are responsible for advising the management of their organizations about the attitudes, behaviors, and concerns of their audiences.

Aviation PR Specialists are involved with many other functions. Building and maintaining relationships with the media is probably the most familiar one. Aviation PR Specialists develop relationships of mutual respect and cooperation with media that reach local, regional, and national audiences as well as with outlets that are devoted to the aviation and aerospace industries. Aviation PR Specialists write and distribute press releases to the media along with providing them with general information and handouts about their organizations. They also conduct follow-ups with the media to ensure that their organizations are being covered favorably.

Many Aviation PR Specialists are involved in developing and implementing publicity programs that may stimulate interest and acceptance of their organizations. They might arrange speaking engagements for themselves (or for representatives from their organizations) at schools, community events, civic groups, trade shows, and other functions. Specialists might also create and produce promotional materials (such as brochures, booklets, and Web sites) about their organizations and their products and services. Furthermore, Aviation PR Specialists might plan and coordinate special events such as news conferences, open houses, charity functions, and contests.

In corporations, some Aviation PR Specialists focus on financial relations. These specialists are responsible for building and maintaining positive relationships with corporate investors. They make sure that the financial community is informed of their company's current activities and future plans.

Other Aviation PR Specialists are involved in influencing public policy regarding the needs of their employers. They are responsible for maintaining close relations with local, state, and federal legislators as well as with regulatory agencies such as the Federal Aviation Administration (FAA), the Transportation Security Administration (TSA), or state aviation agencies. Their job is to make sure that legislators and regulatory agencies are fully aware of their organizations' positions on aviation issues, proposed aviation legislation, and impending regulations.

Many Aviation PR Specialists are responsible for creating in-house communications. For example, they might prepare annual reports, write project proposals, produce newsletters, draft speeches for officials, and respond to information requests by customers or the media.

The duties of Aviation PR Specialists vary, depending on their position, responsibilities, the size of their department, and other factors. Entry-level professionals perform routine tasks such as maintaining files, scanning and clipping newspaper and magazine articles about their employers; maintaining publicity files; assembling information for speeches, press releases, and promotional materials; answering questions from the public; and escorting visitors. As they gain experience, they are assigned to more complex tasks, such as writing press releases, designing Web sites, and coordinating public relations programs.

In large public relations departments, Aviation PR Specialists may focus on one or more areas. Those working in small departments or for small organizations are involved in all aspects of public relations. They may also be involved with advertising and marketing activities.

Aviation PR Specialists generally work a standard 40-hour week. They sometimes work additional hours, including evenings and weekends, to meet deadlines, travel to assignments, make presentations, and attend meetings, community events, or social functions. When crisis situations occur, they are expected to be on call or to stay on the job until their work is no longer required.

Salaries

Salaries vary, depending on such factors as experience, education, job responsibilities, employer, and geographical location. Aviation PR Specialists in corporations generally earn more that those in nonprofit organizations. Those with management responsibilities also make higher wages. According to the May 2003 *Occupational Employment Statistics* survey (by the U.S. Bureau of Labor Statistics), the estimated annual salary for most Public Relations Specialists (in all settings) ranged between $25,050 and $77,830.

Employment Prospects

The U.S. Bureau of Labor Statistics reports that the employment of public relations specialists in general should grow 36 percent or more through 2010. Keep in mind that the aviation industry is influenced by the health of the economy. For example, during economic downturns, employers generally hire fewer employees and often lay off personnel. Well-trained, highly experienced Aviation PR Specialists with a strong background in aviation, however, should be able to find opportunities at any time. In general, opportunities are created to replace specialists who have retired or transferred to other positions.

Advancement Prospects

Supervisory and management opportunities are typically better in large companies and organizations that have several layers of management. Aviation PR Specialists can advance to such executive-level positions as manager, director, or vice president, depending on the organization.

Many Aviation PR Specialists measure their success by earning higher salaries, receiving greater responsibilities, and gaining professional recognition for their work.

Experienced specialists with entrepreneurial ambitions can start their own consulting firms.

Education and Training

Many Aviation PR Specialists have earned a bachelor's degree in journalism, communication, marketing, or public relations or a related field. Some hold a master's degree in communication or journalism, whereas others possess a master's degree in business administration.

Embry-Riddle Aeronautical University offers a bachelor's of science degree program in communication, which trains students to be knowledgeable about both aviation and communication through academic courses and cooperative education internships.

Aviation PR Specialists are expected to continue their professional development throughout their careers. Many enroll in training programs and continuing education programs to update and learn new skills.

Experience, Special Skills, and Personality Traits

Entry-level candidates should have some experience in all areas of public relations—writing, researching, media interaction, and marketing. They may have gained experience through internships, part-time employment, or in other related jobs, such as news reporting or marketing. In addition, entry-level candidates should have a foundation in the business of their prospective employers. Having a background, or strong interest, in aviation is desirable. Journey-level candidates are expected to have experience working in the aviation or aerospace industry.

Aviation PR Specialists must have excellent writing and communication skills. They must be able to organize information in content and context, as well as be able to translate technical terms into everyday language. In addition, they should have strong interpersonal, teamwork, problem-solving, decision-making, and time-management skills. Furthermore, they need adequate computer, desktop publishing, and online researching skills.

Being creative, imaginative, outgoing, credible, diplomatic, self-motivated, organized, flexible, and resilient are some personality traits that successful Aviation Public Relations Specialists have in common.

Unions and Associations

Many Aviation Public Relations Specialists are members of professional associations to take advantage of professional services such as continuing education programs, publications, job listings, and networking opportunities. Two national professional associations that they might join are the Public Relations Society of America and the International Association of Business Communicators.

Tips for Entry

1. Develop a career plan for yourself that includes job search strategies. Contact a counselor at a college career center or a state employment office for assistance in building job search skills.
2. Maintain a portfolio of your best work—newspaper articles, press releases, television scripts, multimedia presentations, and so forth. Be ready to show your portfolio at job interviews and job fairs.
3. Many airports and other employers in the aviation and aerospace industries have small communications departments. To start gaining experience in either industry, consider taking any job in the communications/public affairs department and working your way up to a public relations position.
4. Use the Internet to learn more about public relations. You might start by visiting the Public Relations Society of America Web site, http://www.prsa.org.

AVIATION CONSULTING AND SALES

AVIATION CONSULTANT

CAREER PROFILE

Duties: Offer consulting services to individuals, businesses, agencies, and other organizations; provide solutions to various aviation issues and problems; perform duties as required

Alternate Title(s): A title that reflects a specialty such as Aviation Management Consultant; Aerospace Engineering Consultant; or Aviation Safety Consultant

Salary Range: Varies with the different consultants

Employment Prospects: Good

Advancement Prospects: Fair

Prerequisites:

Education or Training—Many consultants have college degrees

Experience—Extensive experience working in a particular field

Special Skills and Personality Traits—Leadership, teamwork, interpersonal, communication, analytical, problem-solving, time management, writing, presentation, and computer skills; business owners also need organizational and marketing skills; creative, self-motivated, disciplined, assertive, flexible, patient, detail-oriented

Special Requirements—Professional licensure or certification may be required; independent contractors and business owners need proper business licenses

CAREER LADDER

Senior Consultant

Consultant

Executive, Manager, Specialist, or Professional

Position Description

Aviation Consultants provide their clients with professional expertise—the knowledge and skills they acquired through training and experience. They offer themselves as resources to handle projects for which clients need technical, business, or management advice that is unavailable from within their clients' organizations. They are able to help clients improve their organizations' efficiency, structure, or profits. And because they are not part of their clients' workforce, the consultants are able to stay objective and not be influenced by company politics.

Aviation Consultants may be independent contractors or salaried employees of aviation consulting firms. They typically concentrate on serving specific markets, such as commercial pilots, aviation businesses, corporate flight departments, airports, air carriers, airlines, flight schools, general aviation operators, aerospace companies, aviation-related manufacturers, or governmental aviation agencies.

Aviation Consultants provide technical services in almost every aspect of the aviation and aerospace industries. Consultants are available to offer assistance in the areas of pilot career counseling, flight operations, air traffic control, aviation safety, airport security, aviation maintenance, avionics technology, aircraft appraisal, aeronautical engineering, airport planning, aviation public relations, employee training programs, and so on.

Many Aviation Consultants are involved in aviation management consulting services. They provide business advice to aviation businesses, companies, governmental agencies, and other organizations. Management consultants are hired to analyze and evaluate specific business problems and to recommend practical solutions to managers. Consultants may also be contracted to implement the solutions. Aviation management consultants might work on such projects as:

- reorganizing corporate structures
- improving some aspects of their clients' operations such as production, marketing, human resources, and information systems
- developing strategies for their clients to enter new marketplaces or remain competitive within existing markets
- advising clients about merging, buying, and selling companies

Experienced management consultants usually perform supervisory, project management, and client relations duties. Many of them participate in business development, which involves generating new work or clients for their firms. Tasks include making presentations to potential clients and promoting their firms at professional conferences and trade shows. Many management consultants prepare proposals for prospective clients, which describe how their consulting firms plan to handle projects (Companies usually solicit proposals from several firms for projects and choose the proposal that best suits their needs.)

Some Aviation Consultants offer litigation or expert witness services to attorneys who are preparing criminal or civil cases that involve aviation or aerospace matters. For example, an attorney handling a lawsuit that involves a plane accident might require several Aviation Consultants to help with such matters as pilot procedures, aircraft design, and crash reconstruction.

Aviation Consultants who offer litigation consulting services help attorneys prepare their cases. They perform pretrial services, such as reviewing cases to help lawyers identify the issues and facts; educating lawyers about the subject matter; helping attorneys draw up strategies; gathering and preparing physical evidence; interviewing eyewitnesses; conducting tests to approve or disprove certain facts or issues; and preparing reports that lawyers would use with motions, proceedings, or settlement negotiations.

Aviation Consultants who offer expert witness services are hired by attorneys to testify at arbitrations, depositions, or trials. They may be asked to provide sworn testimony, which must be impartial and unbiased, for one of two purposes. One purpose is to provide technical information so that judges and juries can understand specific issues of a case. The other purpose is to provide an expert opinion about a particular issue or fact in a case.

Aviation Consultants often work on several projects at a time; and depending on a project, they may work alone or with other consultants. Although consultants are in different fields, they perform several of the same general tasks, such as preparing reports for their clients, completing required paperwork, and keeping accurate records of their work activities.

As small business owners, independent Aviation Consultants perform certain duties to ensure the success of their operations. They establish consulting fees, develop standard client contracts, and make sure all necessary professional and business licenses are current. They perform a variety of administrative tasks, such as billing clients, paying bills and taxes, keeping accurate records, ordering office supplies, maintaining office space, and promoting their business. Independent Aviation Consultants also set aside time to seek out additional business.

Aviation Consultants may work part time or full time. Some independent consultants continue working full time at their primary occupation as airline pilots, aviation safety inspectors, college professors, aviation maintenance technicians, and so on.

Consultants often work long hours to complete tasks and meet deadlines. Many Aviation Consultants travel frequently to their clients' worksites to meet with them and to work on projects. On occasion, consultants take on projects that require living away from home for several days, weeks, or months.

Salaries

Annual incomes for Aviation Consultants depend on various factors, such as their education, experience, job position, specialty, fees, and geographical location. In many consulting firms, employees also receive additional compensation in the form of performance-based bonuses, profit sharing, or stock ownership.

Gross earnings for independent Aviation Consultants vary from year to year, depending on the amount of business they have generated. Independent consultants might charge their clients hourly rates or a flat fee for projects.

Salary information for the different types of Aviation Consultants is unavailable, but an estimate of their income can be obtained by looking at earnings for consultants in general. One example is for litigation consultants. They charge hourly fees that generally range between $100 to $2,000 per hour. Another example is for management consultants. According to *WetFeet.com's Industry Insider Guide,* salaries for management consultants range between $30,000 to $130,000 or more.

Employment Prospects

Aviation Consultants are found throughout the United States. Many professionals (such as aviation managers, engineers, aviation safety specialists, aviation training specialists, and airline pilots) become independent Aviation Consultants after many years in their fields. Some offer consulting services on a part-time basis while continuing to work in their fields.

In general, the competition for obtaining consulting work is strong; however, opportunities for highly experienced Aviation Consultants are readily available. Many individuals, businesses, and organizations in the aviation and aerospace industries continually seek various aviation experts to help them accomplish their mission and objectives.

Job openings with aviation consulting firms typically become available as consultants retire or transfer to other positions. A consulting firm will create additional positions as it grows and expands.

Advancement Prospects

Staff consultants may rise through the ranks as senior consultants, project managers, and partners. Consultants might seek positions with other firms to receive greater responsibilities, earn higher wages, or be promoted to higher positions.

Many Aviation Consultants measure their success by earning a higher income or by gaining professional recognition.

Education and Training

Many Aviation Consultants possess a bachelor's and an advanced degree, usually in fields that relate to their specialty. For example, many airport consultants have college degrees in civil engineering, planning, airport management, aviation management, or another related field.

Consulting firms typically provide new consultants with training, which may consist of formal training and/or on-the-job training.

Special Requirements

Depending on their specialty, Aviation Consultants may be required to maintain current professional licensure; for example, Aviation Consultants offering airport engineering services may be required to hold a Professional Engineer (P.E.) license. Those Aviation Consultants involved in flight training or aircraft inspections must hold appropriate pilot or aircraft mechanic certificates and ratings which are granted by the Federal Aviation Administration (FAA).

Independent Aviation Consultants and business owners must obtain appropriate local and state business licenses. For specific information about business licenses, contact the local (city or county) government administrative office in the city where you plan to operate a business.

Experience, Special Skills, and Personality Traits

Aviation Consultants typically have extensive experience in their specialty, such as aviation safety, airport planning, aviation management, public relations, aircraft appraisals, flight operations, air traffic control, or aerospace engineering. Many became Aviation Consultants after having served several decades in their professions as pilots, managers, engineers, trainers, technicians, and so forth.

To perform their work well, Aviation Consultants must have excellent leadership, teamwork, interpersonal, and communication skills. They also need superior analytical, problem-solving, and time management skills. Having strong writing, presentation, and computer skills is also essential.

Self-employed consultants and consulting firm owners must also have good organizational and marketing skills in order to succeed in business.

Successful Aviation Consultants share several personality traits, such as being creative, self-motivated, disciplined, assertive, flexible, patient, and detail oriented.

Unions and Associations

Many Aviation Consultants are members of professional and trade associations so they can take advantage of networking opportunities, training programs, and various other professional resources and services. For example, aviation management consultants are eligible to join the Institute of Management Consultants USA, Inc.

In addition, Aviation Consultants join aviation associations that serve their particular fields or interests. The following are a few associations to which different Aviation Consultants belong:

- National Business Aviation Association
- Airport Consultants Council
- National Association of Flight Instructors
- Professional Aviation Maintenance Association
- International Society of Air Safety Investigators
- American Association of Airport Executives

Tips for Entry

1. Although a career as an independent consultant may be years away, you can start preparing now. Read business books and publications such as The *Wall Street Journal* and *Business Week* to learn about the business world. Also enroll in business courses that can help you become a skilled business owner. Talk with school counselors and Aviation Consultants to learn about courses you might take.
2. Obtain a college internship with a consulting firm in your field to gain valuable experience.
3. Contact the consulting firms where you would like to work and ask about job openings. Also, talk with your networking contacts to learn about current and upcoming vacancies. In addition, check with college career counseling centers for leads.
4. Use the Internet to learn more about Aviation Consultants. To get a list of relevant Web sites, enter the keywords *aviation consultants* or *aviation consulting* into a search engine. You may also find Web sites for particular specialties such as airport consulting or aviation litigation consulting by entering the name of the specialty in a search engine.

AVIATION SALES REPRESENTATIVE

CAREER PROFILE

Duties: Promote and sell products directly to customers in the field; build and maintain a customer base; perform duties as required

Alternate Title(s): Sales Engineer; Manufacturer's Agent; a title that reflects a particular field, such as Avionics Sales Representative; Air Charter Sales Representative; or Aircraft Sales Representative

Salary Range: $30,000 to $111,000

Employment Prospects: Fair

Advancement Prospects: Good

Prerequisites:

Education or Training—High school diploma; many employers require a bachelor's degree

Experience—Several years of technical and sales experience preferred

Special Skills and Personality Traits—Leadership, customer service, communication, presentation, teamwork, organizational, time management, problem-solving, math, writing, and computer skills; outgoing, enthusiastic, diplomatic, trustworthy, persuasive, persistent, flexible, self-motivated, self-reliant, quick learner, thick-skinned

CAREER LADDER

Sales Manager

Senior Aviation Sales Representative

Junior Aviation Sales Representative

Position Description

Aviation Sales Representatives are responsible for promoting the products or services that their employers offer for sale. Their job is to contact prospective customers and make sales presentations that demonstrate how their company's products or services can fulfill the customers' particular needs.

Aviation Sales Representatives are employed throughout the aviation and aerospace industries. They work for manufacturers as well as for wholesale distributors and firms that resell products. Some of them work for companies that offer specific types of aviation services.

Aviation Sales Representatives promote products or services to target markets that may be manufacturers, wholesale distributors, retail establishments, repair shops, governmental aviation agencies, airports, air carriers, pilots, and so on. Some of the various employers for whom Sales Representatives work include:

- aerospace companies, which manufacture aircraft, spacecraft, missiles, aircraft engines, aircraft parts and accessories, and related goods
- aviation-related manufacturers that produce various products, such as computer software, avionics systems, paints, aircraft interiors, and aircraft polishing products, which are then sold to aerospace companies
- aviation companies that offer various aviation products and services—such as aviation weather products, flight charts, aviation fuel, electronic security systems, aircraft management services, and ground handling services—to pilots, general aviation operators, commercial airlines, airports, and others
- air charter companies and commercial airlines, which offer business travel services to corporations

Aviation Sales Representatives are experts about the products and services they sell. Many of them, in fact, have extensive aviation or aerospace backgrounds. Thus, they are comfortable using the technical language of their customers and discussing aviation or aerospace issues that concern them.

Aviation Sales Representatives are assigned to cover geographical regions, or territories, which may consist of several cities, counties, states, and even foreign countries. They are responsible for building and maintaining a customer (or client) base within their territories, and are usually expected to meet with a certain number of customers each day. To find new customers, Sales Representatives follow up on leads they obtain from existing customers, their employers, professional and trade associations, or other sources.

Many Sales Representatives are "outside sales" workers. They travel throughout their assigned territories to meet with customers. They do research about potential customers before contacting them, so they can discuss how their products may meet the customers' needs. They make initial contacts through phone calls or e-mails, and introduce themselves and their products or services. They also schedule appointments to meet with prospective clients. Meetings with customers are usually brief. Sales Representatives demonstrate how their products or services can be useful to customers' businesses.

Some Aviation Sales Representatives are called sales engineers. They have engineering or other technical backgrounds, and use their expertise to sell electronic, electrical, or mechanical products. They may be involved in training customers how to operate and maintain products. They also provide follow-up visits to make sure products are operating properly.

Some Aviation Sales Representatives are hired as "inside sales" representatives. They make telephone sales calls to prospective customers to generate sales leads for other sales staff members. They are usually required to make a minimum number of calls; for example, an inside sales representative for an aircraft parts manufacturer may be expected to make at least 25 calls each day on behalf of his employer's sales staff.

The goal for many Aviation Sales Representatives is to establish trusting, long-term relationships with customers to encourage their repeat business. They become familiar with their clients' needs and provide them with valuable information that may be useful for developing their businesses. Many Sales Representatives take customers out to lunch or dinner and sometimes entertain them at sports events or other entertainment venues.

Aviation Sales Representatives' jobs involve performing a variety of duties. For example, they may:

- schedule appointments with potential customers
- take sales orders from customers
- negotiate sales contracts
- help customers with problems regarding products or services
- conduct training programs for customers
- prepare sales reports, expense account forms, and other required paperwork
- attend company sales meetings to review sales performance and discuss sales goals
- attend trade shows, professional conferences, and conventions to promote products and make new contacts

Aviation Sales Representatives perform other duties besides their sales responsibilities. For example, they may be involved in the development of new products, marketing strategies, or promotional packages. In addition, Aviation Sales Representatives are expected to stay abreast of issues and trends in their fields. Furthermore, they keep up with the competition by monitoring the cost of competing products or services and by studying literature about new products or services developed by their competitors.

Some Aviation Sales Representatives work on a contractual basis as independent sales agents. They are hired either by manufacturers' agents firms or directly by the manufacturers themselves. Independent sales agents often sell different, but complementary, product lines for two or more manufacturers within the industry.

Most Aviation Sales Representatives work a standard 40-hour week.

Outside Aviation Sales Representatives have flexible hours, which may include working evenings and on weekends. They arrange their schedules to meet with customers at their convenience. They travel by automobile or airplane to cover their assigned territory; their work sometimes requires them to stay away from home for several days or weeks at a time.

Salaries

Aviation Sales Representatives receive income based on salary, commission, or a combination of both salary and commission. Many companies reward outstanding job performances with monetary bonuses and/or gifts such as free vacation trips. Outside sales workers may be reimbursed for such expenses as meals, lodging, transportation, and home office costs. Many employers provide outside sales representatives with company cars and frequent flyer mileage.

Annual earnings for Aviation Sales Representatives vary, depending on various factors. These include an individual's qualifications and ambitions, the type of employer and industry, the products or services being sold, and the general well-being of the economy. Their earnings also vary from year to year. The U.S. Bureau of Labor Statistics, in its May 2003 *Occupational Employment Statistics* survey, reports that the estimated annual earnings for most sales representatives of technical and scientific products ranged between $29,760 and $111,080.

Employment Prospects

Job opportunities in aviation sales are generally dependent on market demands, the health of the economy, and issues and legislation that affect the aviation and aerospace industries. In addition, opportunities vary among the different areas of the aviation and aerospace industries. Prospects are generally better for Aviation Sales Representatives with technical expertise and demonstrated success in sales.

Most job openings become available to replace professionals who retire or transfer to other positions. Employers will create new positions as they expand their sales force.

Advancement Prospects

Aviation Sales Representatives can rise through the ranks as trainers, supervisors, branch managers, district managers, and executive administrators. They may have to find employment with other organizations to obtain higher positions. Some Aviation Sales Representatives use their experience as stepping stones into other areas such as marketing, advertising, or consulting.

Many Aviation Sales Representatives measure their success by earning higher incomes, meeting or exceeding sales targets, receiving sales accounts or territories of their choice, and becoming top sales representatives for their firms.

Education and Training

Educational requirements vary with the different employers. Minimally, Aviation Sales Representatives need a high school diploma or general equivalency diploma. Some employers require, or strongly prefer, that candidates hold a bachelor's degree in an appropriate field. For example, aerospace companies may require that sales representatives hold an appropriate engineering degree. However, many employers are willing to hire candidates who have no college degree if they have qualifying sales experience.

Employers usually provide formal training programs as well as on-the-job training for sales representatives. New outside sales representatives typically work under the supervision of senior sales representatives for several months before being allowed to go solo.

Experience, Special Skills, and Personality Traits

Employers generally prefer to hire Aviation Sales Representatives who have several years of experience in the aviation or aerospace industry, particularly in the areas in which they would be working. Prospective candidates should also have previous sales experience. Some employers are willing to hire aviation professionals or technicians without sales experience if they show enthusiasm and a strong desire to succeed.

To perform their work effectively, Aviation Sales Representatives must have superior leadership, customer service, communication, and presentation skills. They also need strong teamwork, organizational, time management, and problem-solving skills. They should have adequate math, writing, and computer skills.

Being outgoing, enthusiastic, diplomatic, trustworthy, persuasive, persistent, flexible, self-motivated, and self-reliant are some personality traits that successful Aviation Sales Representatives have in common. They are also quick learners. In addition, they are thick-skinned, as they must be able to handle rejections that come with the job.

Unions and Associations

Aviation Sales Representatives are eligible to join professional societies such as the National Association of Sales Professionals, which serves the general interests of sales representatives in all industries. These organizations offer continuing education programs, professional publications, and other professional services and resources.

Aviation Sales Representatives are also eligible to join aviation trade and professional associations that serve the interests of the target markets they serve. By joining such organizations, they can take advantage of networking opportunities, keep up to date with current issues, and utilize other resources.

Tips for Entry

1. As a student, obtain a part-time or summer job working in sales to see if it is a field that interests you.
2. Learn as much as you can about the aviation or aerospace field in which you are interested in working. Read books and trade magazines, talk with professionals in the field, join professional organizations, and so on. Also gain practical experience working in the field.
3. To obtain jobs at many firms, applicants must be able to pass a selection process that includes a drug screening and an extensive background check.
4. A willingness to relocate may enhance your chances of obtaining the position you desire.
5. Take advantage of the Internet in your job search for an Aviation Sales Representative position. You can find job listings as well as information about the companies where you would like to work. To learn if a company has a Web site, enter its name into a search engine.

AIRCRAFT BROKER

CAREER PROFILE

Duties: Sell used aircraft; develop marketing plans; may buy aircraft for others, appraise the value of aircraft, or perform other major duties; perform duties as required

Alternate Title(s): None

Salary Range: Salary information unavailable

Employment Prospects: Fair

Advancement Prospects: Poor

Prerequisites:

Education or Training—No standard educational requirements

Experience—Have extensive experience as pilot and in other areas, such as aircraft sales, aviation management, or aircraft maintenance

Special Skills and Personality Traits—Communication, interpersonal, customer service, negotiation, and marketing skills; ethical, reputable, trustful, creative, persistent, dedicated, tactful, outgoing

Special Requirements—FAA pilot certificate and/or mechanic certificate may be required

CAREER LADDER

Owner of Aircraft Brokerage Firm

Aircraft Broker

Aircraft Sales Professional

Position Description

Aircraft Brokers are experts in selling used aircraft. They offer aircraft sales and marketing services to clients who wish to sell their airplanes, helicopters, jets, or other aircraft. Their clients may be private pilots, corporate flight departments, air charter services, fixed base operators (FBOs), aircraft management services, government agencies, or others.

The aircraft sales process entails several stages, from preparation of aircraft for sale to the delivery of aircraft. Aircraft Brokers may be in the business of offering full services or only certain services, such as marketing and making sales presentations to potential buyers. Clients decide which services they would want Aircraft Brokers to provide on their behalf.

There are several steps that must be taken before an aircraft is listed for sale. Aircraft Brokers may be involved in some or all of them. These steps include:

- performing an inspection of an aircraft to determine its condition, as well as to identify any maintenance or repairs it may need before selling it
- appraising the aircraft for its current value
- conducting research (such as analyzing market trends and the competition) to establish a fair and marketable sales price for an aircraft
- cleaning and detailing the exterior and interior of the aircraft
- gathering and reviewing maintenance records and other important documents pertaining to the aircraft

All Aircraft Brokers are responsible for developing a marketing plan for their clients to reach as broad a clientele as possible. They also create or coordinate the development of advertisements, detailed spec sheets, brochures, and other promotional pieces that communicate the best features of their clients' aircraft.

Brokers place advertisements in various general newspapers as well as trade publications at the local, state, national, and worldwide levels. Many Aircraft Brokers also take advantage of the Internet by placing ads or listings at electronic aviation news services and other appropriate Web sites. Some Aircraft Brokers have Web sites that include a listing of used aircraft that are for sale. Aircraft Brokers might also develop individual Web pages to showcase their clients' aircraft. In addition, Aircraft Brokers contact aircraft dealers and other parties whom they think may be interested in buying their clients' aircraft.

Most Aircraft Brokers handle all contact with prospective buyers. They respond to phone calls and e-mails from interested parties, which sometimes require further research for information about an aircraft. Aircraft Brokers meet with prospective buyers to make sales presentations, which may include a demonstration of the aircraft. A sales meeting may require Aircraft Brokers to fly an aircraft to another city or state to meet with potential buyers.

Many Aircraft Brokers are also involved in the negotiation process. On behalf of their clients, they negotiate selling prices and the terms of sale with aircraft buyers. Upon reaching a sales agreement, full-service brokers prepare all the necessary paperwork required by local and state authorities, as well as the Federal Aviation Administration (FAA) regarding aircraft sales transactions. Some Aircraft Brokers have the capacity to help buyers obtain financing for the purchase of an aircraft. Brokers also handle any questions or problems that may arise before the closing of the sale, which entails getting assistance from attorneys, tax accountants, or other professionals when needed.

Aircraft Brokers and aircraft owners enter into contractual agreements, which describe the broker and client relationship. Brokers and clients agree on such matters as an owner's requirements (such as the minimum asking price and the time frame given to sell the aircraft), the types of services that an Aircraft Broker would perform, and the broker's commission fee. Throughout the sales process, Aircraft Brokers are expected to provide their clients with status reports on a regular basis. For example, an Aircraft Broker might provide clients with biweekly updates on the number of sales inquiries they received about their aircraft.

Aircraft Brokers may perform other types of work in addition to their brokerage work. They might also sell new aircraft, appraise aircraft, or perform aircraft maintenance. Some Aircraft Brokers also offer aircraft acquisition services to parties who wish to purchase aircraft. In this role, they are known as either acquisition agents or buyer's agents. As acquisition agents, they comb the market for available aircraft that fit the particular needs of their clients. They provide their clients with pertinent information about various aircraft to help them decide which aircraft is the best to purchase. They also help clients with prepurchase inspections, negotiations, and the completion of all necessary paperwork.

Aircraft Brokers work long and irregular hours. They often work evenings and on weekends to meet with clients or potential buyers.

Salaries

Aircraft Brokers' incomes are based on the total amount of commissions they earn in a year. A search on the Internet found that some Aircraft Brokers charge between a 3 and 10 percent commission rate. For example, if Aircraft Brokers charge a 4 percent commission rate, then they would earn $8,000 when they sell an aircraft for $200,000. There are several types of commission arrangements upon which brokers and clients may agree. For example, Aircraft Brokers might receive a flat fee, a percentage of the sales price, or a minimum brokerage fee plus a percentage of the sales price.

Annual earnings vary, depending on such factors as an individual's ambition, the market, the type of aircraft being sold, the total amount of sales, and commission rates. Earnings also vary from year to year.

Formal salary information for Aircraft Brokers is unavailable.

Employment Prospects

Aircraft Brokers are either self-employed or employed by aircraft brokerage firms or aircraft dealers. Many brokers specialize in selling certain types of aircraft.

Opportunities for independent brokers depend on the demand for their services as well as on the number of Aviation Brokers with whom they would be competing for the same clientele. Staff positions generally become available as businesses seek additional Aviation Brokers to meet their growing needs or to replace employees who have retired or resigned.

Advancement Prospects

Many Aircraft Brokers measure their success by earning higher incomes and through gaining recognition for their sales talents and skills. Those with entrepreneurial ambitions can pursue self-employment or establish their own aircraft brokerage firms.

Education and Training

There are no standard educational requirements to become an Aircraft Broker. Many Aircraft Brokers hold a bachelor's degree and an advanced degree in fields that interest them.

Individuals entering the brokerage field usually learn on the job under the supervision of experienced Aircraft Brokers.

Special Requirements

Aircraft Brokers who fly aircraft to buyers must possess current FAA pilot certificates with appropriate flight ratings. Brokers who perform aircraft maintenance work must hold the proper FAA aircraft mechanic certificate and ratings.

Experience, Special Skills, and Personality Traits

Aircraft Brokers typically have extensive experience as private, commercial, or airline pilots. Many of them also have vast experience in such areas as aircraft sales, aircraft maintenance, aviation management, and aircraft management services. Prospective clients typically seek out Aircraft Brokers who have demonstrated experience and success in making aircraft sales and purchases.

Because they must be able to handle various people from diverse backgrounds, Aircraft Brokers need superior communication and interpersonal skills. In addition, they must have excellent customer service, negotiation, and marketing skills. Being ethical, reputable, trustful, creative, persistent, dedicated, tactful, and outgoing are some personality traits that successful Aircraft Broker have in common.

Unions and Associations

Aircraft Brokers belong to local, state, or national professional associations that serve their particular interests in the aviation industry. For example, they might join such organizations as the National Aircraft Resale Association, the Aircraft Owners and Pilots Association, or the National Business Aviation Association. By joining professional associations, Aircraft Brokers can take advantage of networking opportunities, continuing education programs, and other professional services and resources.

Tips for Entry

1. As a high school or college student, obtain part-time or summer jobs as salespersons to gain valuable experience. If possible, try to find sales jobs in an aviation setting, such as an FBO or aviation museum gift shop.
2. Be sure to take advantage of your network of contacts when you conduct your job search. Jobs are often found through word of mouth.
3. If you are interested in eventually becoming a self-employed Aircraft Broker or owning a brokerage firm, learn how to start a business. Also find out what kind of business skills you should obtain. On the Internet, you can learn more at the U.S. Small Business Administration (SBA) Web site, http://www.sba.gov.
4. Learn more about the field of aircraft brokerage on the Internet. To find relevant Web sites, enter either the keywords *aircraft brokerage* or *aircraft brokers* into a search engine.

AVIATION INSURANCE AGENT

CAREER PROFILE

Duties: Sell insurance policies to individuals, businesses, and organizations in the aviation or aerospace industry; build and maintain a clientele; perform duties as required

Alternate Title(s): Aviation Insurance Broker

Salary Range: $22,000 to $105,000

Employment Prospects: Fair

Advancement Prospects: Fair

Prerequisites:

Education or Training—High school diploma

Experience—Strong background in aviation with sales or business experience

Special Skills and Personality Traits—Communication, interpersonal, customer service, problem-solving, time management, writing, and computer skills; enthusiastic, outgoing, confident, flexible, disciplined, self-motivated; not be easily discouraged

Special Requirements—Must possess professional state licensure to sell insurance

CAREER LADDER

Agency Manager or Agency Owner

Aviation Insurance Agent

Trainee

Position Description

Aviation Insurance Agents sell insurance to private pilots, commercial pilots, air carriers, airports, corporate flight departments, fixed base operators (FBOs), repair shops, aircraft management firms, government aviation agencies, air ambulance services, aerospace companies, aircraft parts manufacturers, hot-air balloon outfits, and others in the aviation and aerospace industries. These specialized insurance agents are familiar with the types of events (such as flight delays, aircraft crashes, or product failure) that could be risks for their clients. Therefore, they are able to advise individuals, businesses, and organizations about insurance products that would give them the financial protection they need for bodily injuries, property damages, and other losses that could happen in the future.

Although Aviation Insurance Agents sell insurance policies for aviation insurance companies, they are not employees. They are either employees of insurance agencies or are self-employed and head their own agencies.

Most Aviation Insurance Agents are independent agents who are licensed by several aviation insurance companies to sell their insurance products. Those agents who sell insurance for only one insurance company are known as captive agents. Some Aviation Insurance Agents are brokers. Like independent agents, aviation insurance brokers sell policies from several aviation insurance companies.

Aviation Insurance Agents handle different lines of insurance. Most of them sell property and casualty insurance policies, which cover the risk of loss or damage to policy owners' property (such as aircraft, facilities, machinery, equipment, and vehicles). They also sell liability policies, which cover the risk of bodily injury or property damage caused by other people while on their property or as other people use their property. Aviation Insurance Agents may also handle life insurance, health insurance, or disability insurance products.

Many Aviation Insurance Agents concentrate on serving specific areas of concern, such as airlines, airports, corporate flight departments, aerospace companies, helicopter operators, or general aviation pilots and operators. Some agents who serve commercial clients (such as airlines) might also sell workers' compensation insurance, health insurance, life insurance, auto insurance, or other types of insurance that address the non-aviation needs of their clients.

Independent Aviation Insurance Agents (and brokers) represent the insured, or the insurance buyers, rather than the insurers. They help the insured obtain the best insurance coverage that offers the most value for their premiums. They interview clients to learn about their clients' needs as well as about the condition of the properties or individuals for which or whom they wish coverage. Agents determine what risks are involved, and advise clients on what types of insurance they need and how much coverage they should buy. They also describe the different insurance programs that are available.

Once clients choose insurance plans that interest them, Aviation Insurance Agents prepare applications for their clients in order to obtain quotes for the cost of the insurance coverage their clients desire. Agents provide accurate information about their clients, the types of activities for which they want coverage, previous losses their clients suffered, and so on. The agents then submit the applications to the insurance companies, where underwriters review applications and determine whether to grant coverage to the applicants and how much the premiums would be for insurance policies.

If clients are interested in an insurance policy, but do not like certain terms, then Aviation Insurance Agents negotiate with the underwriter to obtain better terms. When clients agree with the coverage, then underwriters issue them insurance policies.

Aviation Insurance Agents also provide follow-up services for their clients. They maintain regular contact to ensure that the clients are satisfied with their current coverage and to learn of any changes in their insurance needs. Agents also handle policy renewals and offer advice about what clients can do to lower the price of their premiums. In addition, Aviation Insurance Agents help their clients settle insurance claims.

Generating new business is another important aspect of the Aviation Insurance Agent's job. Some sales leads are developed through contacts provided by clients. Agents also join civic, social, and professional organizations to build their network of contacts. In addition, Aviation Insurance Agents place advertisements in general, professional, and trade publications to reach their target clientele. They may also promote their insurance programs through direct mailings. Some Aviation Insurance Agents establish Web sites on the Internet to market their insurance products.

Aviation Insurance Agents are expected to keep up to date with issues that concern their clients in order to stay competitive, because their clients can choose to do business with other agents. Aviation Insurance Agents keep up with changes in tax laws, as well as with aviation legislation and regulations. Furthermore, they meet with company representatives to learn about new insurance products and services.

As business owners, independent Aviation Insurance Agents are responsible for the daily administration of their operations. They must therefore handle various duties such as developing office policies, paying bills and taxes, keeping accurate financial records, renewing professional and business licenses, and maintaining offices. If they employ staff, agents are responsible for training, supervising, and coordinating the work activities of their employees.

Aviation Insurance Agents often travel to offices, homes, or other locations to meet with their clients. Their hours are flexible, as they usually schedule meetings at times that are convenient for their clients. Agents generally work a 40-hour week and occasionally put in additional hours to complete paperwork or prepare for sales presentations. It is not uncommon for them to work evenings and on weekends.

Salaries

Aviation Insurance Agents' income is based on the commission fees they earn from selling insurance. Agency employees may earn salaries as well.

Annual earnings for Aviation Insurance Agents vary, depending on such factors as their employer, their qualifications, the total amount of insurance policies they sold, and their geographical location. According to the May 2003 *Occupational Employment Statistics* survey (by the U.S. Bureau of Labor Statistics), the estimated annual salary for most insurance agents, in all industries, ranged between $21,940 and $104,920.

Employment Prospects

Aviation Insurance Agents are found throughout the United States and the world. Many of them work for large aviation insurance agencies.

Job openings at aviation insurance agencies generally become available as agents retire, transfer to other positions, or leave to open their own agencies. Additional positions are created within an agency as it grows and expands. Opportunities for self-employed Aviation Insurance Agents depend on the demand for their services and the number of agents with whom they would be competing for the same clientele.

Advancement Prospects

Many Aviation Insurance Agents measure their success by building and maintaining a strong client base, earning higher incomes, and gaining professional recognition among their peers.

Staff members at aviation insurance agencies can pursue managerial positions, which may require seeking positions at other agencies. Their best prospects are with large agencies that have several layers of management. Aviation Insurance Agents with entrepreneurial ambitions typically aim to establish their own agencies.

Education and Training

Minimally, Aviation Insurance Agents must possess a high school diploma or a general equivalency diploma. Some employers prefer to hire agents with a bachelor's degree, which may be in any field.

Insurance agencies typically provide employees with training programs.

Special Requirements

Aviation Insurance Agents must obtain professional licensure in the states where they plan to sell insurance. Agents may need to fulfill continuing education requirements to renew their licenses. In some states, Aviation Insurance Agents may be required to hold separate licenses for selling different types of insurance (such as life insurance or property and casualty insurance). Requirements for professional licensure varies with each state. For specific information, contact the state department of insurance where you wish to practice.

Experience, Special Skills, and Personality Traits

Employers seek applicants who have previous sales or business experience with a strong background in aviation. Many Aviation Insurance Agents gained experience in the aviation insurance field by working as underwriters for aviation insurance companies. Most Aviation Insurance Agents have extensive experience in aviation, having had previous careers as commercial pilots, aircraft maintenance technicians, aviation managers, and so on. Many Aviation Insurance Agents are private pilots.

Some skills that Aviation Insurance Agents need to perform their work effectively are communication, interpersonal, customer service, problem-solving, and time-management skills. In addition, they need adequate writing and computer skills.

Some personality traits that successful Aviation Insurance Agents have in common are being enthusiastic, outgoing, confident, flexible, disciplined, and self-motivated. Furthermore, they do not easily become discouraged.

Unions and Associations

Many Aviation Insurance Agents belong to professional associations to take advantage of networking opportunities, as well as other professional services and resources. For example, many agents are members of the Aviation Insurance Association, which serves the particular interests of the aviation insurance industry. Independent Aviation Insurance Agents might join the Independent Insurance Agents and Brokers of America.

Tips for Entry

1. In high school, you might develop your communication and presentation skills, as well as your self-confidence, by participating in acting classes, school plays, public speaking activities, debates, and so on.
2. To further enhance their employability and professional credibility, Aviation Insurance Agents might obtain the Certified Aviation Insurance Professional (CAIP) designation, granted by the Aviation Insurance Association.
3. Many aviation insurance firms have Web sites on the Internet. You can learn about the company, its policies, services, and people from an agency's Web site. You may also find job listings. Some agencies also post articles about current aviation issues.
4. Learn more about the aviation insurance industry on the Internet. One place to start is at the Aviation Insurance Association Web site, http://www.aiaweb.org. To find other relevant Web sites, enter the keywords *aviation insurance* into any search engine.

AVIATION RECREATION, SPORTS, AND ENTERTAINMENT

AEROBATIC PILOT

CAREER PROFILE

Duties: Entertain spectators at air shows with routines made up of rolls, loops, spins, falls, and so on; may offer flight instruction and/or rides, perform stunts in the motion picture industry, or conduct other related activities; perform duties as required

Alternate Title(s): Air Show Performer; Stunt Pilot

Salary Range: $16,000 to $102,000+

Employment Prospects: Fair

Advancement Prospects: Poor

Prerequisites:

Education or Training—Intensive aerobatics and emergency maneuver training

Experience—May have previously gained experienced through aerobatic competitions

Special Skills and Personality Traits—Exceptional flying skills; an understanding of the physics of flight and the performance characteristics of his or her aircraft; disciplined, persistent, sensible, creative, self-sufficient, organized, reserved, critical

Special Requirements—FAA commercial pilot certificate with instrument rating and appropriate aircraft category, type, and model ratings; FAA aerobatic competency card may be required

CAREER LADDER

Air Show Performer—Headliner

Air Show Performer

Novice Air Show Performer

Position Description

Most, if not all, professional Aerobatic Pilots are air show performers. They entertain millions of spectators each year by maneuvering their aircraft into gravity-defying rolls, loops, figure-eights, spins, turns, stalls, and falls. From below, aircraft look like they are out of control as they loop-to-loop through the sky or spiral downward at speeds of 100 miles per hour or more. But at the exactly right moment, Aerobatic Pilots level their aircraft, and the sound of a gasping audience turns instantly to the joyous noise of applause.

Air shows are held throughout the United States and the world, mostly for the purpose of generating interest in aviation. New, historical, and experimental aircraft are often on display, and various air sports—skydiving, hot air ballooning, hang gliding, and aerobatic flying—are showcased to exhibit the fantastic skills of pilots and parachutists. Most air shows are commercial ventures or charity events for the general public. Some are private air shows, contracted by corporations and other organizations to entertain employees and their families, clients or customers, and other important people.

Aerobatic Pilots perform their routines at low altitudes within invisible boundaries, known as "the box," above the spectators. Aerobatic Pilots may be solo performers or members of a team act who fly synchronized routines. Some Aerobatic Pilots are known for performing comedy acts or novelty acts. To add to the entertainment value of their routines, many air show performers paint their aircraft in bright, vibrant colors. Some Aerobatic Pilots set their performances to music or discharge smoky trails to emphasize the patterns they are flying.

Aerobatic Pilots generally fly small sturdy airplanes with lots of horsepower. In the United States, only aircraft that have been certified by the Federal Aviation Administration (FAA) as being appropriate for aerobatic flight can be flown. Many Aerobatic Pilots use trainers, or training airplanes, that are used to teach beginning pilots. Others fly custom-built aircraft, which are categorized as experimental aircraft.

All performances are carefully planned by Aerobatic Pilots. They create routines that are within their personal abilities, as well as within the physical capacities and limitations of their aircraft. They then spend many hours practicing until they feel they have gained precise control of the combinations of rolls, loops, and spins. In other words, Aerobatic Pilots feel that they can execute the sequence of maneuvers consistently, accurately, and safely above hundreds or thousands of people.

Safety is an important aspect of all air shows. Before an air show begins, Aerobatic Pilots (or their representatives) attend a briefing with the air show operators. They are introduced to air show officials who are air traffic controllers, air bosses, FAA monitors, and air show directors. They also receive such information as weather conditions, emergency procedures, radio frequencies for communication, air show boundaries, taxi procedures, obstacles, flight restrictions, event schedules, and so on. If pilots do not attend a preshow briefing, they are usually not allowed to perform.

Air show performers may receive sponsorships from one or more companies to promote their products or services. This may involve wearing the company logo on their performance uniforms and painting the company name or logo on their aircraft. Air show performers might also make public endorsements of their sponsors' products. Sponsors may be aircraft manufacturers, aviation insurance companies, and aviation or aviation-related firms, as well as non-aviation corporations such as oil companies or computer manufacturers.

In addition to performing at air shows, Aerobatic Pilots engage in related activities. Many of them are independent instructors or heads of their own flight schools. They teach beginning and advanced aerobatic lessons to private, commercial, and airline pilots. Their students include those who wish to perform aerobatics for fun, as well as those whose goal is to become air show performers. Many students take aerobatic lessons to enhance their flying skills.

Some Aerobatic Pilots offer adventure rides for a fee. They take customers up in their planes and perform a succession of maneuvers to give them the opportunity to experience the thrilling sport of aerobatic flying.

Performing aerial stunts in the film industry is another activity in which some Aerobatic Pilots are involved. They perform complex and dangerous, but carefully planned, stunts for commercials and scenes in television programs and motion pictures.

Many Aerobatic Pilots participate in professional aerobatic competitions, nationally and worldwide. In competitions, Aerobatic Pilots are judged on their precision in flying a specific set of sequenced maneuvers.

Many experienced pilots become involved in coaching and mentoring novice air show performers. In addition, they might serve as judges at aerobatic competitions. Some Aerobatic Pilots also serve on committees that work with the FAA to address safety issues, regulatory procedures, and training programs in the air show industry.

Professional Aerobatic Pilots usually conduct their performance, teaching, and other aerobatic flight activities as independent contractors or small business owners. This involves attending to a variety of business duties, such as paying taxes, collecting performance fees, and negotiating performance contracts. They also devote time to completing marketing and public relations tasks in order to promote themselves and to generate new business.

Most Aerobatic Pilots continue to hold full-time or part-time jobs in aviation and non-aviation occupations to supplement their incomes.

Aerobatic Pilots travel frequently throughout the United States and to foreign countries to perform at air shows or participate in aerobatic competitions.

Salaries

Aerobatic Pilots' incomes are earned from one or more sources, such as air show performances, sponsorships, and teaching. Compensation for an air show performance may be in the form of money, fuel and oil, or expenses for attending the air show. Compensation terms for sponsorship contracts vary widely; for example, different sponsors might provide pilots with a salary, free equipment, or a special deal on purchasing a new aircraft.

Formal information about Aerobatics Pilots' wages is unavailable. According to an expert in the field, annual earnings for air show performers can range from a few thousand dollars to seven figures for a few of the top performers.

The U.S. Bureau of Labor Statistics, in its May 2003 *Occupational Employment Statistics* survey, reports that most commercial pilots earned an estimated annual salary that ranged between $26,470 and $101,890, and for most entertainment and sports occupations, between $16,000 and $75,200.

Employment Prospects

Pilots willing to dedicate themselves to learning and practicing the craft and art of aerobatic flying, as well as to making a livelihood in this field, can become professional Aerobatic Pilots. However, breaking into the air show business is difficult, and it has become increasingly more competitive in recent years, according to some experts in the field. This is due to such factors as fewer air shows, the rising cost of aerobatic airplanes, and stricter regulations for entering the field. Aerobatic Pilots who offer the most precise and entertaining performances have better chances of consistently getting air show engagements.

Advancement Prospects

Aerobatic Pilots generally realize success by gaining professional recognition among peers, becoming highly popular air show performers, and earning higher incomes. Highly successful Aerobatic Pilots are sought out by top air shows around the world.

Education and Training

Aerobatic Pilots complete intensive aerobatic and emergency maneuver training with experienced pilots. As they begin their air show careers, Pilots receive professional coaching and mentoring.

Aerobatic Pilots continue training throughout their careers to hone their skills and learn new maneuvers or fly new aircraft.

Special Requirements

Professional Aerobatic Pilots must possess either the commercial pilot certificate or the air transport pilot (ATP) certificate, which are granted by the FAA. They must also hold appropriate FAA ratings for the category, type, and model aircraft that they are flying. Additionally, they must have either the first-class or second-class FAA medical certificate. Pilots who are teaching flight lessons must hold an FAA flight instructor certificate.

In order to perform at FAA authorized air shows, Aerobatic Pilots must possess the FAA air show competency card.

Experience, Special Skills, and Personality Traits

Many air show performers gain experience by participating in aerobatic competitions. By progressing through the competition ranks in an orderly manner, Aerobatic Pilots develop essential airmanship skills and safe flying habits.

Aerobatic Pilots have exceptional flying skills. They also have a thorough understanding of the physics of flight as well as the performance characteristics of their aircraft.

Some personality traits that successful Aerobatic Pilots have in common are being disciplined, persistent, sensible, creative, self-sufficient, organized, reserved, and critical.

Unions and Associations

Aerobatic Pilots can join professional organizations to take advantage of professional services such as education programs, networking opportunities, and professional resources. Two organizations that are available are the International Council of Air Shows and the International Aerobatic Club. Aerobatic Pilots who work for the motion picture industry are eligible to join the Motion Picture Pilot Association.

Tips for Entry

1. Volunteer to work at air shows to get a practical idea of how they operate.
2. Choose an aerobatics flight instructor whom you can trust and, if possible, whose professionalism is one you wish to achieve. To find qualified flight instructors, contact aerobatics organizations or your local Flight Standards District Office.
3. Build up your experience and popularity as an air show performer.
4. Learn more about air shows and aerobatic flying on the Internet. You might start by visiting these Web sites: Aerobatics Server, http://acro.harvard.edu/ACRO; FAA National Airshow Program, http://www.faa.gov/avr/afs/airshow; and International Council of Air Shows, http://www.airshows.org.

COMMERCIAL HOT-AIR BALLOON PILOT

CAREER PROFILE

Duties: Offer balloon rides for a fee; perform preflight, flight, and postflight duties; may conduct related hot-air balloon activities; as operation owner, perform business duties; perform duties as required

Alternate Title(s): Balloonist; Corporate Balloon Pilot

Salary Range: $26,000 to $102,000

Employment Prospects: Fair

Advancement Prospects: Poor

Prerequisites:

Education or Training—Three to six months of flight training

Experience—Experience working with hot-air balloon outfits, preferable; experience working with people; knowledgeable about local geography

Special Skills and Personality Traits—Communication, interpersonal, customer service, and self-management skills; accounting, finance, marketing, and other business skills for business owner; friendly, cooperative, calm, level-headed, flexible, focused, self-reliant

Special Requirements—Commercial pilot certificate with a hot-air balloon rating

CAREER LADDER

Chief Balloon Pilot and/or Balloon Operation Owner

Commercial Hot-Air Balloon Pilot

Private Hot-Air Balloon Pilot

Position Description

It is just around sunrise or sunset that Hot-Air Balloon Pilots launch their aircraft into the sky. Around this time of the day, balloons can usually float with the gentle speed of the wind as their pilots guide them toward desired landing sites. The balloons are completely nonmotorized; rather, they are powered by warm air. Pilots use their knowledge of air currents to steer balloons and, to ensure they stay airborne, pilots occasionally turn up a burner to heat that air inside their balloons.

Many Hot-Air Balloon Pilots are commercial pilots. Most of them operate or are employed by outfits that offer balloon rides to individuals, groups, businesses, and others for a fee. Although the ride itself is usually an hour long, the adventure for passengers may last about three hours. Passengers watch, and sometimes participate in, the process of setting up the hot air balloon for the launch and taking the balloon apart and storing it after the landing.

Hot air balloons vary in size, and some are as tall as 100 feet high. They are composed of three main parts. The part that becomes filled with air is known as the envelope. It is attached to a basket by strong cables. Depending on the size of the balloon, the basket might carry between two and 10 passengers. The last major part is the burner and fuel system, which can produce a very hot and long flame quickly to heat the air inside the envelope whenever the pilot wants. Pilots use propane for fuel and carry several tanks to last for several hours of flight if necessary.

Hot-Air Balloon Pilots schedule their flights during the times of the day when the winds are the most stable and calm. Thus, passengers are taken up within two or three hours of sunrise or sunset.

Hot-Air Balloon Pilots work with ground crews, which may consist of one or more crew members. The crews help the pilots transport the equipment and passengers to the launch sites, as well as to inflate and launch the balloons.

While the pilots are guiding their balloons through the sky, the crews follow below in their vehicles. Hot-Air Balloon Pilots maintain contact with the ground crews by two-way radios. The crews let the pilots know about any changing weather conditions, obstacles, and hazards that may affect their flights. The pilots, in turn, keep the crews informed about the direction of their flights and where they intend to land.

Hot-Air Balloon Pilots seek landing sites in open fields, which may require obtaining permission from landowners. Pilots might contact landowners prior to launching or have their crews obtain permission once the pilots know where they want to land. The crews are usually at the landing site waiting for the balloons. Once the passengers have safely disembarked from the baskets, the crews and pilots deflate the balloons and pack them away.

Most Hot-Air Balloon Pilots hold small ceremonies for their passengers to celebrate the end of their adventure, offering them snacks and beverages.

As pilots-in-command, Hot-Air Balloon Pilots are responsible for performing various preflight, flight, and postflight duties. For example, they:

- prepare flight plans, which outline their routes and estimated times of arrivals
- obtain weather briefings for the area where they will fly
- monitor weather conditions during flights
- perform preflight and postflight checks to ensure that the balloons and all their parts are in proper working order
- complete flight reports, pilot logbooks, and other required paperwork
- comply with all federal aviation regulations as well as their companies' policies and protocols
- maintain regular airworthiness checks of their aircraft, by having them inspected and certified by authorized maintenance personnel

Many Hot-Air Balloon Pilots are involved in other ballooning activities to supplement their incomes. They might offer flight instruction to individuals seeking private or commercial pilot certificates with a hot-air balloon rating. Some Hot-Air Balloon Pilots offer repair services for hot-air balloon equipment. Some participate as performers at air shows, professional sports events, and other special events. Hot-Air Balloon Pilots might also be contracted to fly balloons as part of marketing programs to promote products, services, or charity events for local businesses, national corporations, nonprofit organizations, and so on.

Business owners are responsible for the day-to-day operations. Depending on the size of their companies, they oversee or conduct various business administrative functions, such as accounting, finances, marketing, public relations, and human resources. They also make sure that balloon equipment, as well as vehicles, trailers, radios, tools, and other equipment, are maintained and repaired properly. In addition, they follow the appropriate federal aviation regulations that govern their operations. Furthermore, they continually find ways to generate more business.

Hot-Air Balloon Pilots work irregular hours and schedules.

Salaries

Annual earnings for commercial Hot-Air Balloon Pilots vary, depending on whether they are employees or business owners, the total number of balloon rides that were sold, their fees, their geographical location, and other factors. The U.S. Bureau of Labor Statistics, in its May 2003 *Occupational Employment Statistics* survey, reports that most commercial pilots earned an estimated annual salary that ranged between $26,470 and $101,890.

Employment Prospects

Hot-Air Balloon Pilots are either employees or owners of hot-air balloon operations, which are found throughout the United States. Job opportunities become available as pilots transfer to other positions or occupations, or business operations expand and additional pilots are needed.

Advancement Prospects

Hot-Air Balloon Pilots generally realize success by gaining professional recognition among peers and earning higher incomes. In large operations, pilots can usually advance to such managerial positions as chief pilot and operations manager. Entrepreneurial pilots follow a path toward opening their own hot-air balloon operations.

Education and Training

In order to become commercial Hot-Air Balloon Pilots, individuals must complete flight instruction, which covers such topics as launches, landings, performance maneuvers, navigation, emergency operations, preflight and postflight procedures, and fundamentals of instructing. Flight training usually takes between three to six months to complete.

Hot-Air Balloon Pilots continue training throughout their careers to hone their skills, as well as to learn to fly new aircraft.

Special Requirements

Hot-Air Balloon Pilots must possess a commercial pilot certificate with a hot-air balloon rating—which are granted by the Federal Aviation Administration (FAA)—in order to operate balloons for hire and to offer flying lessons for hot-air balloons. To qualify for this certification, individuals must meet the following requirements:

- be at least 18 years old
- be able to read, speak, write, and understand the English language

- hold a private pilot certificate with a hot-air balloon rating
- complete required number of hours of flight instruction
- complete required solo flights
- receive a logbook endorsement by an authorized instructor
- pass the FAA's knowledge and practical tests

Commercial pilots must undergo and pass regular flight reviews each year to maintain their certification.

Experience, Special Skills, and Personality Traits

Employers typically seek Hot-Air Balloon Pilots who have experience working well with people. Having work experience with hot-air balloon companies is preferable. In addition, pilots should be knowledgeable about the geography of the area where they would work.

Hot-Air Balloon Pilots need effective communication, interpersonal, and customer service skills, as they must be able to handle people from diverse backgrounds. In addition, they must have excellent self-management skills, such as being able to work independently, handle pressure, and organize and prioritize tasks.

To run their businesses effectively, owners should have basic accounting, finance, marketing, and other business skills.

Being friendly, cooperative, calm, level-headed, flexible, focused, and self-reliant are some personality traits that successful Hot-Air Balloon Pilots share.

Unions and Associations

Hot-Air Balloon Pilots can join the Balloon Federation of America or their local or state balloonist association to take advantage of professional resources and services such as networking opportunities, education programs, and reference publications.

Tips for Entry

1. Attend a hot-air balloon festival to get an idea of the hot-air balloon industry.
2. The minimum age is 14 years old for an FAA student pilot certificate for hot-air ballooning. However, you must be 16 years old in order to take the FAA exam for a private pilot certificate.
3. Volunteer to be a crew member to gain experience working around hot-air balloons.
4. Some pilots cannot afford to pay wages to their crew members. In exchange, they offer members free balloon rides or flight lessons.
5. Use the Internet to learn more about hot-air ballooning. You might start by visiting these two Web sites: Balloon Federation of America, http://www.bfa.net; and Hot Air Ballooning (by The Sky's the Limit), http://launch.net. You may also find other pertinent Web sites by entering the keywords *hot air balloon pilots* or *hot air ballooning* into a search engine.

HANG GLIDING INSTRUCTOR

CAREER PROFILE

Duties: Teach beginning and advanced lessons in hang gliding; perform administrative and other functions; occasionally engage in other hang gliding activities, such as exhibition jumping; perform duties as required

Alternate Title(s): Basic Instructor; Advanced Instructor; Tandem Instructor

Salary Range: About $25,000 per year for full-time instructors

Employment Prospects: Good

Advancement Prospects: Poor

Prerequisites:

Education or Training—Complete a USHGA instructor certification program

Experience—Be an experienced hang glider pilot; have prior hang gliding teaching experience

Special Skills and Personality Traits—Leadership, motivational, interpersonal, communication, and self-management skills; be physically fit and mentally alert; enthusiastic, outgoing, patient, encouraging, professional, flexible, focused

Special Requirements—USHGA instructor certification; first aid and CPR certification

CAREER LADDER

Chief Instructor and/or Operations Owner

Hang Gliding Instructor

Novice Instructor

Position Description

Hang Gliding Instructors offer lessons in the sport of hang gliding, which is considered by many to be the simplest form of human flight. Hang glider pilots soar through the sky supported only by a nonpowered, wing-shaped frame covered with light material. They are hooked into a harness that is suspended from their hang glider and, by shifting their weight, they control their aircraft—turning it to the left or right, or going up or down in the sky. With their knowledge of micrometeorology, these pilots can fly for several hours and go cross-country for many miles, or even climb in altitude up to 15,000 feet or more.

In the United States, the sport of hang gliding is partly regulated by the Federal Aviation Administration (FAA). However, hang gliding operations and training are governed voluntarily through the U.S. Hang Gliding Association (USHGA), a nonprofit organization that represents the hang gliding community. The USHGA has established safety policies and procedures that are followed by its members as well as by nonmembers.

Most, if not all, Hang Gliding Instructors in the United States are certified by the USHGA. They offer both beginning and advanced hang gliding lessons. Along with teaching proper techniques for launching, controlling, and landing hang gliders, Hang Gliding Instructors cover topics about preflight briefings, postlanding procedures, and wind conditions such as thermals and ridge lifts.

Hang Gliding Instructors offer lessons in two methods of launching; students can choose to learn one or both methods. One method is the traditional foot launch, in which pilots run down a hillside into the wind and, upon reaching the right speed, the wind lifts up the hang glider. The other method is called the tow launch. A hang glider is attached by a static line to a stationary winch, a truck, or an ultralight aircraft (called an aerotug). Once the hang glider is in flight, it is released.

Some Hang Gliding Instructors offer training in tandem flight, in which two pilots may fly together from the same hang glider. The pilots are hooked into separate harnesses and hang side by side from a hang glider, which is specially built with wheels for landing gear to allow launchings and landings on level ground. The hang glider is towed up into the sky by an aerotug and released at a desired altitude. Tandem instructors teach students how to control the tandem glider while it is in flight and when it is being towed, as well as how to set up an approach for landing and how to land the tandem glider.

Hang Gliding Instructors provide students with individual attention as they practice their techniques. Instructors impart to students the importance of practicing safety and good judgment at all times. They teach students proper hang gliding habits, or behavior, so they can respond appropriately to all types of flying conditions and situations.

Hang Gliding Instructors teach students skills that help them earn pilot ratings granted by the USHGA. Most hang gliding sites in the United States require evidence from pilots of their skill level before they may be allowed to fly. Pilots can meet this requirement by presenting proof of their USHGA pilot rating. The USHGA established a system of ratings that identify five pilot proficiency levels—beginner, novice, intermediate, advanced, and master. Pilots with beginner and novice ratings are generally required to fly under the supervision of Hang Gliding Instructors.

Along with providing instruction, Hang Gliding Instructors help novice and experienced pilots select hang gliders that match their skill levels and interests. They are also available to answer questions about the sport and to advise pilots on how they can improve their techniques.

Hang Gliding Instructors are also involved in the issuance of pilot ratings. They administer knowledge examinations and observe pilots as they perform skills for their desired rating level. When pilots pass, Hang Gliding Instructors then recommend to the USHGA that the pilots satisfactorily meet the proficiency level for specific pilot ratings.

Hang Gliding Instructors have other duties as well. They perform such administrative tasks as providing general information about their schools, registering students, collecting liability forms, and completing formal reports such as accident reports. They also handle the training equipment that are used for lessons. Their tasks include setting up training equipment for lessons, performing preflight checks on the equipment, making test flights, and safely breaking down and storing away equipment. Many Hang Gliding Instructors fulfill other functions for their employers. For example, they might perform receptionist tasks, book lessons, make routine repairs on equipment, sell equipment, or assist in developing marketing and public relations activities.

Some Hang Gliding Instructors are owners of hang gliding schools or shops. As business owners, they are responsible for overseeing their operations on a daily basis, which includes paying bills and taxes, renewing business licenses, maintaining business records and files, supervising and training employees, and so on.

Hang Gliding Instructors mostly work outdoors and, depending on their environment, might work in humid, hot, or cold weather. Their work is often physically demanding and requires running, walking, standing, climbing, crouching, kneeling, stooping, and reaching.

Hang Gliding Instructors work part or full time. In the northern states, many instructors are employed from April or May until the weather becomes too cold or snowy for hang gliding.

Salaries

Annual earnings depend on such factors as work status (part or full time), size of employer, lesson fees, and geographical location.

Formal salary information for Hang Gliding Instructors is unavailable. According to an expert in the field, full-time instructors generally earn about $25,000 a year.

Employment Prospects

Hang Gliding Instructors are employed by hang gliding shops and schools throughout the United States. According to the Hang Gliding Instructor's Forum (http://www.angelfire.com/ct/instructor), as of February 2003, 248 instructors were working in 33 states. The six states with the largest employment in this field included California, Florida, Georgia, New York, Washington, and Texas.

Positions generally become available when Hang Gliding Instructors resign or transfer to other positions or occupations. School owners will create additional positions to meet growing demands.

Some experts in the field say that finding and keeping talented Hang Gliding Instructors is difficult due to the hard work and low pay that comes with this job.

Advancement Prospects

Advancement opportunities are limited to becoming either chief instructors or managers of school operations. Those with entrepreneurial ambitions can pursue a path toward becoming school owners.

Education and Training

Certified Hang Gliding Instructors must successfully complete a formal instructor certification program, established by the USHGA. The short but comprehensive program includes teacher training as well as an apprenticeship.

Hang Gliding Instructors are expected to continually improve and update both their teaching skills and flying skills.

Special Requirements

To become a certified Hang Gliding Instructor, hang glider pilots must be members of the USHGA and possess an intermediate pilot rating. Additionally, pilots must hold first aid and CPR certification.

Instructors must obtain instructor ratings for the types of lessons (such as tandem or tow-launch instruction) they wish to teach.

Experience, Special Skills, and Personality Traits

Hang Gliding Instructors are experienced hang glider pilots and have been active in the sport for a few years. Novice instructors typically have gained teaching experience through the USHGA instructor certification program.

To work well with students, Hang Gliding Instructors should have strong leadership, motivational, interpersonal, and communication skills. Additionally, they need solid self-management skills—such as the ability to work independently, make sound judgments, and organize and prioritize tasks. In addition, Hang Gliding Instructors need to be physically fit and mentally alert.

Being enthusiastic, outgoing, patient, encouraging, professional, flexible, and focused are some personality traits that Hang Gliding Instructors have in common.

Unions and Associations

Certified Hang Gliding Instructors are members of the United States Hang Gliding Association (USHGA). Many are also members of local or regional hang gliding associations or hang gliding clubs. By being members of such organizations, they can take advantage of networking opportunities, training programs, and other professional services and resources.

Tips for Entry

1. To find a USHGA-certified school near you, contact USHGA by calling (719) 632-8300 or (800) 616-8300. You can also find a list of schools by visiting its Web site at http://.ushga.org.
2. Contact hang gliding schools, shops, and clubs where you would like to work about their part-time or full-time opportunities.
3. Learn more about the sport of hang gliding on the Internet. To find pertinent Web sites, enter the keywords *hang gliding, hang gliding instruction,* or *hang gliding school* into a search engine.

SKYDIVING INSTRUCTOR

CAREER PROFILE

Duties: Teach beginning skydiving lessons; may perform other roles at skydiving school; may conduct related skydiving activities such as exhibition jumping; perform duties as required

Alternate Title(s): Coach; Tandem Instructor

Salary Range: $20,000 to $45,000

Employment Prospects: Good

Advancement Prospects: Poor

Prerequisites:

Education or Training—Complete a USPA instructor training course; to become a tandem instructor, complete a tandem equipment course

Experience—Be an experienced skydiver; serve previously as a skydiving coach

Special Skills and Personality Traits—Leadership, motivational, interpersonal, communication, and self-management skills; dedicated, self-reliant, patient, calm, enthusiastic, alert, flexible

Special Requirements—USPA instructor certification; may be required to hold certification or licensure to perform related activities such as competition judging or parachute rigging

CAREER LADDER

Chief Instructor and/or School Owner

Skydiving Instructor

Coach

Position Description

Skydiving Instructors teach beginning lessons in the sport of skydiving, which is the closest thing to flying under their own power that humans can do. This extreme sport requires participants to jump out of aircraft while in flight, then to freefall at speeds of 100 to 200 miles per hour before deploying (opening) their parachutes for a slower descent to Earth. While freefalling, which is often described as floating in the air, skydivers can perform precise and controlled maneuvers, such as going up or down, moving forward or backward, and diving or tumbling.

In the United States, skydiving is partly regulated by the Federal Aviation Association (FAA). However, skydiving operations, training, and licensure are self-regulated by the skydiving community under the guidance of the United States Parachute Association (USPA). The USPA establishes programs and safety requirements, which are adhered to by its individual members as well as by its group members, which are the skydiving centers that offer skydiving training and jumping events.

Most, if not all, Skydiving Instructors in the United States are certified by the USPA. They teach basic skydiving lessons that include ground instruction and a series of parachute jumps completed under their supervision. Instructors cover such topics as exiting the aircraft, deploying the parachute, flight control, landing, and emergencies. They also teach students how their equipment works as well as how to pack their parachutes. Additionally, students learn about parachute riggers, pilots, and aircraft mechanics and their roles in conducting safe jumps.

Skydiving Instructors usually teach students how to jump by using one of the following methods (students determine which training method they wish to use):

- The static-line method: A line is attached from the aircraft to a student's parachute via a static attachment. As the student falls away from the aircraft, the parachute is deployed immediately.

- The instructor-assisted deployment (IAD) method: This method is similar to the static-line method. However, the instructor is responsible for deploying a student's parachute as the student exits the airplane.
- The harness hold, or accelerated free fall (AFF), method: The student exits the aircraft together with two instructors who hold on to the student's parachute harness. They execute the freefall together, with the instructors providing in-air instruction and guidance. Once the student deploys his or her parachute, the instructors let go of the student's harness.

Instructors strongly emphasize the importance of safety in skydiving. They teach students about pre-jump safety checks and briefings. They also coach students on developing skills to respond quickly to emergency situations. To help reinforce learning, Skydiving Instructors provide students with handouts and use videotapes and other teaching aids. At a few skydiving schools, vertical wind tunnels are available as tools for freefall instruction. Large fans produce air currents strong enough to support one or more students so that instructors can teach them basic freefall control and maneuvering skills.

Many Skydiving Instructors follow the suggested training outline developed by the USPA to ensure that their schools meet all safety requirements for student training. The beginning lessons are carefully structured, providing students with the skills and knowledge required to obtain the class A license, granted by the USPA.

The USPA license is used by skydivers as proof of their skill level, which skydiving centers require before they allow jumpers to take advantage of their services. USPA licensure is divided into four classes—A (the lowest level), B, C, and D (the highest level). Each class indicates the skill level and jumping privileges of the license holder. For example, with a class A license, skydivers may jump without instructor supervision, pack their own main parachute, engage in basic group jumps, and perform water jumps. USPA licenses are recognized by most skydiving centers throughout the world.

Many Skydiving Instructors offer tandem lessons to introduce individuals to the sport of skydiving. Ground instruction is generally an hour long and provides students with a general background of the sport and with procedures to prepare them for their jump. The student and Skydiving Instructor wear a special parachute system in which the student is attached to the instructor. The instructor has complete control of the jump, from exiting the airplane to deploying the parachute to landing on the ground.

Skydiving Instructors also provide direct supervision to students or skydivers who must undergo refresher training. In addition, instructors conduct training for any changes in deployment or emergency procedures.

USPA Skydiving Instructors may administer examinations and verify that jumpers meet skills and knowledge requirements for A, B, and C licensure. To verify skydivers for a C license, Skydiving Instructors must hold one of the following positions: USPA instructor-examiner, safety and training adviser, or member of the USPA board of directors.

Many Skydiving Instructors become involved in various USPA activities. They might serve as judges for competitions. They might be appointed as USPA safety and training advisers for their skydiving centers, in which they would perform such duties as providing safety information to parachutists and acting as liaisons between the skydiving centers and USPA. Senior Skydiving Instructors become instructor examiners (I/E) who train and certify coaches and instructors. Skydiving Instructors might also serve on USPA committees that address various skydiving issues, including safety, training, and federal aviation regulations.

Many Skydiving Instructors also participate in other skydiving activities. Some of them offer their services as exhibition jumpers to various private and public organizations. Skydivers are often part of entertainment acts at such special events as air shows, professional football games, car races, county fairs, charity functions, corporate parties, and grand openings. Exhibition jumpers are sometimes hired by businesses to promote their products or services at special events by carrying banners or wearing company logos. In addition, skydivers may be contracted to execute jumps for print and media publicity campaigns or for scenes in television shows and movies.

Most Skydiving Instructors work part time, usually on weekends. Full-time instructors are typically employed at one or more related jobs to supplement their income. Many Skydiving Instructors perform a parachute rigger's job, in which they pack reserve parachutes and complete equipment maintenance. Some Skydiving Instructors offer photography and videotaping services to parachutists who want still photos or videos of their jumps. Instructors who are licensed pilots and aircraft mechanics may take on the additional duties of flying and maintaining planes for their employers.

Salaries

Skydiving Instructors generally earn incomes based on the fees they receive for lessons and jumps. Therefore, their annual earnings vary, depending on their fees, the number of students they teach, the demand for their skydiving center's services, their geographical location, and other factors. Most Skydiving Instructors generally earn between $20,000 to $30,000 per year. Tandem instructors are usually the best-paid Skydiving Instructors, and some of them earn wages in the $40,000 range.

Many Skydiving Instructors supplement their income by engaging in related activities such as packing parachute rigs, becoming instructor-examiners, or performing exhibition jumps.

Employment Prospects

According to *Skydiving Magazine,* there are about 400 skydiving centers in the United States; most centers are located at small general aviation airports. Some centers are open through the week, whereas others operate only on weekends.

Opportunities are generally better for part-time positions than full-time ones. According to an expert in the field, most operations are short-staffed and could use additional Skydiving Instructors.

Advancement Prospects

Management opportunities are limited to the positions of managers and business owners of skydiving centers.

Many Skydiving Instructors realize success by being able to make a livelihood in skydiving on a full-time basis. Instructors might measure their advancement by obtaining higher USPA instructor ratings, earning higher incomes, and gaining professional recognition for their work.

Education and Training

To become certified Skydiving Instructors, skydivers must successfully complete instructor training courses that are registered with the USPA. They receive instruction from Skydiving Instructors in their area who hold the USPA instructor-examiner rating.

In order to become tandem trainers, Skydiving Instructors must first complete an FAA-approved course of instruction on the equipment they would be using. The tandem course is usually provided by the appropriate tandem equipment manufacturer.

Special Requirements

In order to become USPA-certified Skydiving Instructors, skydivers must be USPA members and possess at least the USPA class C license. They must also hold either the coach or instructor rating. To conduct the tandem method, harness-hold method, or other training method, Skydiving Instructors must possess the USPA instructor rating.

Skydiving Instructors may also be required to hold other certification or licensure, depending on other related activities they perform. Those Skydiving Instructors who engage in exhibition jumping or competition judging must possess appropriate USPA ratings to conduct such activities. In addition, Skydiving Instructors who do such jobs as parachute rigging, aircraft mechanics, or flying must possess appropriate certification from the FAA.

Experience, Special Skills, and Personality Traits

Skydiving Instructors are highly experienced skydivers. Minimally, they must have performed at least 200 jumps before they can qualify for the USPA instructor rating. They typically gain experience by first working as skydiving coaches who provide assistance to instructors.

Like other flight instructors, Skydiving Instructors should have strong leadership, motivational, interpersonal, and communication skills to work well with students. Additionally, they need solid self-management skills—such as the ability to work well under pressure, make sound judgments, work independently, and organize and prioritize tasks.

Being dedicated, self-reliant, patient, calm, enthusiastic, alert, and flexible are some personality traits that successful Skydiving Instructors have in common.

Unions and Associations

Certified Skydiving Instructors are members of the United States Parachute Association. Their membership entitles them to networking opportunities, training programs, professional licensure, and other professional services and resources.

Tips for Entry

1. You must be at least 18 years old to start skydiving. In some states, some skydiving centers allow 16-year-olds to skydive as long as they have written permission from their parents.
2. To find skydiving operations in your area, look in your telephone directory under *parachute jumping instruction* or *skydiving and skydiving instruction.*
3. Learn more about skydiving by reading the *Skydiver's Information Manual* by the USPA. You can obtain a copy from the organization by writing to USPA, 1440 Duke Street, Alexandria, VA, 22314. You can also call (703) 836-3495. You can also browse the online version of the manual at the USPA Web site, http://www.uspa.org.
4. Being able to teach more than one instructional method, perform parachute rigging, do videotaping, and perform other jobs can enhance your employability with most skydiving centers.
5. Use the Internet to learn more about skydiving and Skydiving Instructors. You might start by visiting the USPA Web site at http://www.uspa.org. To get a list of other relevant Web sites, enter the keywords *skydiving, skydiving instruction,* or *skydiving center* into a search engine.

MILITARY AVIATION

MILITARY PILOT

CAREER PROFILE

Duties: Fly aircraft on military missions; perform preflight, flight, and postflight duties; perform tasks specific to a mission; perform duties as required

Alternate Title(s): A title that reflects a specialty such as Helicopter Pilot; Fighter Pilot; or Airlift Pilot

Salary Range: $26,000 to $143,000

Employment Prospects: Good

Advancement Prospects: Good

Prerequisites:

Education or Training—Complete officer training and military flight training programs

Experience—No previous flying experience required

Special Skills and Personality Traits—Leadership, interpersonal, communication, motor and self-management skills; calm, self-confident, determined, alert, enthusiastic, courageous, flexible

CAREER LADDER

Flight Leader

Senior Pilot

Pilot

Position Description

Military Pilots are responsible for the safe and efficient operation of aircraft during aerial missions for their military service. They fly highly complex airplanes and helicopters, such as jet fighters, bomber planes, tankers, and twin-powered helicopters. The aircraft they have been trained to fly are generally used for specific types of missions.

Men and women Military Pilots are involved in a wide range of military missions, such as:

- air attack and bombing operations
- reconnaissance
- surveillance
- airlifts of military personnel and cargo to military bases or airfields
- airdrops of paratroopers or supplies to locations where aircraft cannot land
- search-and-rescue operations
- transportation for the wounded to medical facilities
- fueling of aircraft in mid-air
- administrative or liaison missions, such as transporting senior officers and dignitaries to important meetings or delivering mail to military personnel
- special operations

Military Pilots also perform goodwill and humanitarian missions throughout the world. For example, Military Pilots might take part in fighting forest fires. For another example, pilots might deliver food, medical supplies, and other needed items to regions that are suffering from violence or natural disasters (such as hurricanes and earthquakes).

Military Pilots are responsible for the safety of their crew and their aircraft. Pilots-in-command are in charge of the flight as well as the mission. They supervise and direct the activities of aircrew members, who may be junior pilots, navigators, flight engineers, and loadmasters. They perform a variety of preflight, flight, and postflight duties, some of which include:

- preparing a flight plan that outlines their flight route, departure and arrival times, and alternate locations for landings
- reviewing weather forecasts, advisories, and other weather reports for the route and the areas where they plan to fly; also monitoring weather conditions during their flights
- performing (or directing) the preflight and postflight inspection of both the inside and outside of their aircraft to ensure that all parts and systems are working properly

- briefing other crew members about the mission, weather conditions, route, emergency procedures, and other important information
- obtaining instructions from air traffic controllers
- controlling engines, flight controls, and other aircraft systems
- responding to emergencies as they occur
- completing pilot logs and other required paperwork

In addition, Military Pilots perform duties related to their particular missions. For example, combat pilots might shoot weapons or release bombs during combat, and reconnaissance pilots might take photographs of enemy positions and activities.

Military Pilots in the U.S. Armed Forces are commissioned officers. They are committed to the primary mission of defending the United States domestically and worldwide. As military officers, their first duty is to serve as leaders, directing and managing all details of their units.

Furthermore, Military Pilots perform air operations that support the overall mission of their particular service. The U.S. Army oversees all land combat operations, whereas the U.S. Navy is in charge of sea defense and the U.S. Air Force manages the national airspace defense. The U.S. Marine Corps provides short-term amphibious tactics, which involve both land and water maneuvers. The U.S. Coast Guard provides law enforcement, environmental protection, search and rescue operations, and maritime navigation safeguards along U.S. shores; they also participate in conflict situations when needed. The U.S. National Guard acts as an armed force in each of the U.S. states and territories during domestic conflicts or natural disasters; they also give assistance on a national level during times of war or national emergencies.

New U.S. Military Pilots are commissioned as second lieutenants in the U.S. Army, U.S. Air Force, and U.S. Marines. In the U.S. Navy and U.S. Coast Guard, new pilots are commissioned as ensigns. Initially, commissioned officers serve a minimum number of years, which vary with the different services. For example, U.S. Air Force pilots are committed to 10 years of service after completing their pilot training.

U.S. Military Pilots are stationed at military bases in the United States or in other parts of the world. Some of them are stationed aboard air carriers and other military ships, where flights take off and land on the decks of those ships. Military Pilots receive new tours of duty (or assignments) every few years. Officers typically serve one or more assignments overseas.

Salaries

The annual earnings for Military Pilots in the U.S. military are based on the combination of basic pay and additional pay for performing aviation and other special duties. In addition, they receive a variety of benefits, such as vacation leave, a housing allowance, free medical and dental care, and tuition assistance for obtaining advanced degrees.

Basic pay for Military Pilots is based on the basic pay schedule for commissioned officers, which is the same for all military branches. The rate of basic pay for officers is based on their rank, pay grade, and number of years of service. The basic pay scale for U.S. commissioned officers in 2003 ranged from about $26,000 to about $143,000.

Employment Prospects

Competition for Military Pilot positions is high. However, opportunities are available each year to replace officers who have transferred to other duties, retired, or completed their service obligation. A military service also creates additional pilot slots to meet the demands of the field.

All U.S. military services, except for the Coast Guard, accept pilot applications from civilians. To apply for a pilot position with the Coast Guard, a civilian applicant must have previously served as a Military Pilot in another service. Pilot opportunities in the Coast Guard are available to graduates of its Officer Candidate School or the U.S. Coast Guard Academy.

Military Pilots can find various job opportunities as commercial pilots after completing or retiring from military service. For example, they may find employment with passenger or cargo air carriers, air charter companies, corporate flight departments, government agencies, law enforcement agencies, emergency medical services, crop dusting firms, flight schools, and so on. Furthermore, former Military Pilots can seek careers in aviation management, aviation education, air traffic control, space flight, and other aviation and aerospace fields.

Advancement Prospects

Military Pilots have access to various options to develop a military career that meets their interests and satisfaction. As career Military Pilots, they can pursue a variety of positions, by becoming test pilots, airlift pilots, special operations pilots, pilot instructors, air traffic controllers, or astronauts. As they gain additional experience and leadership training, they can rise through the ranks to hold command or senior management positions,

Furthermore, after completing a minimum number of tours, Military Pilots may pursue other occupations such as recruiters or public affairs officers. Those officers interested in such professional careers as engineers, lawyers, or physicians can take advantage of continuing education programs to obtain the required advanced degrees.

Education and Training

U.S. Military Pilots must possess a bachelor's degree, which may be in any field.

Military Pilot candidates first complete an officer training program and then a pilot training program.

Pilot candidates usually complete their officer training through one of three routes:

- Qualified high school graduates enter a service academy—the U.S. Military Academy (army), the U.S. Naval Academy (navy and marines), the U.S. Air Force Academy, or the U.S. Coast Guard Academy. Along with satisfying the officer training requirement, students earn a bachelor's degree in a field of their choice.
- College students participate in a Reserve Officers' Training Corps (ROTC) program for the army, navy, air force, or marines. Along with their regular coursework for their bachelor's degree, ROTC cadets enroll in military training courses and perform weekly drills. They also participate in training exercises during the summer.
- College graduates complete Officer Candidate School (OCS) or Officer Training School (OTS) for the service they wish to serve. They complete a three to four month program that consists of academic studies and physical training. They also learn about the service's rules, regulations, responsibilities, and lifestyle.

Each service offers other types of officer training programs for undergraduate or graduate students. In addition, programs are available for enlisted personnel to earn commissions as officers. For more information, contact a recruiter in the service that interests you.

Once officer training is complete, Military Pilot candidates begin their flight instruction, which generally takes between one to two years to complete. Candidates first receive ground instruction in such topics as aerodynamics, weather, flight rules, and federal aviation regulations. Next, they complete primary flight instruction, which entails the use of flight simulators as well as actual flying. Upon successfully completing basic flight training, pilots proceed to advanced training in the types of aircraft that they will be assigned to fly.

Throughout their careers, officers have opportunities to receive leadership training in order to gain the knowledge and skills needed to advance to senior positions. In addition, pilots may participate in education programs to earn advanced degrees in technical, scientific, engineering, or managerial fields that are particularly in demand by their military service.

Experience, Special Skills, and Personality Traits

Flying experience is not necessary for an individual to become a Military Pilot. In general, the military seeks officer candidates who have well-rounded backgrounds, along with the willingness to serve their country in both peaceful and dangerous times.

Military Pilots need excellent leadership, interpersonal, and communication skills, as they must be able to work well with others. In addition, they must have superior self-management skills, including the ability to handle stressful situations, work independently, and understand and follow directions.

Some personality traits that successful Military Pilots have in common are being calm, self-confident, determined, alert, enthusiastic, courageous, and flexible.

Unions and Associations

Military Pilots might join professional associations such as the Order of Daedalians, the Women Military Aviators, Inc., or the American Helicopter Society International. By joining such associations, they can take advantage of networking opportunities, as well as other professional resources and services.

Tips for Entry

1. Keep your grades up in school.
2. To become a commissioned officer in the U.S. military, you must meet age, physical, and medical requirements; have high moral standards; and be a U.S. citizen or a U.S. permanent resident. Additionally, you must score high on aptitude tests. You may be able to receive an exemption or waiver to requirements you do not meet.
3. Research the various military branches. Be sure you understand what their missions are, what types of aircraft they fly, and the types of flying opportunities that are available. Think about your career plans for after you leave the military. Ask yourself which service would best prepare you for your career as a commercial pilot.
4. Competition for Military Pilot positions is stiff. To enhance your chances, you might consider obtaining a private pilot certificate.
5. To learn more about the different service academies, check out their Web sites on the Internet. They are the U.S. Military Academy at West Point, http://www.usma.edu; U.S. Air Force Academy, http://www.usafa.af.mil; U.S. Naval Academy, http://www.usna.edu; and U.S. Coast Guard Academy, http://www.cga.edu.

AIRPLANE NAVIGATOR

CAREER PROFILE

Duties: Maintain aircraft's flight course throughout a mission; prepare flight plans; perform tasks specific to a mission; perform duties as required

Alternate Title(s): A title that reflects a specialty, such as Bomber Navigator or Tanker Navigator; Naval Flight Officer

Salary Range: $26,000 to $143,000

Employment Prospects: Good

Advancement Prospects: Good

Prerequisites:

Education or Training—Bachelor's degree; complete an officer training program and a navigator training program

Experience—No previous experience required

Special Skills and Personality Traits—Map and chart reading skills, concentration, teamwork, interpersonal, and communication skills; accurate, detail-oriented, mature, self-motivated

CAREER LADDER

Flight Operations Director

Senior Navigator

Navigator

Position Description

Airplane Navigators are aircrew members aboard military aircraft. Their job is to make sure their aircraft are traveling on the right course toward their destinations. While using navigation, computer, communications, and radar systems, Airplane Navigators determine an aircraft's position, direction of travel, and other pertinent information while in flight. Navigators also utilize their knowledge of air navigation, meteorology, flight theory, aircraft operating procedures, flying directives, and mission tactics.

Airplane Navigators specialize in particular types of aircraft that are operated for specific missions. For example, Airplane Navigators on jet fighters and bombers fly combat missions, whereas those on cargo planes complete airdrop and airlift missions.

Regardless of the aircraft they serve, Airplane Navigators perform many duties that are similar. While working with pilots, Navigators prepare flight plans for their missions. They review mission tasks, weather reports, and other vital information to determine their flight routes, destinations, and alternative airfields or air bases for landings. In addition, Navigators perform other duties, such as:

- inspecting and testing navigation systems before flights
- filing flight plans
- conducting briefings with crew members regarding mission plans and assignments
- ensuring that preflight inspections have been made and that aircraft are properly loaded, equipped, and manned
- monitoring navigational systems
- providing pilots with instrument readings and other flight information while in flight
- operating radios and communication equipment to send and receive messages
- maintaining flight logs

Navigators may also perform duties that are specific to their missions. For example, tanker navigators might assist with guiding tankers and other airplanes during in-flight refueling operations; reconnaissance navigators might use radar equipment to locate and track ships, submarines, or other aircraft; and bomber navigators might operate weapons systems.

In the U.S. Armed Forces, Airplane Navigators are men and women officers. They are committed to the primary mission of defending the United States domestically and worldwide. Their first duty is to serve as leaders. Their responsibilities involve directing and managing all details of their units, including the supervision of enlisted personnel and subordinate officers.

Initially, commissioned officers serve a minimum number of years, which vary with the different services. For example, U.S. Air Force navigators are committed to six years of service after completing their job training.

Airplane Navigators in the U.S. military are given new tours of duty (or assignments) every few years. They may be stationed at military bases in the United States or in foreign countries. Some of them are stationed aboard air carriers and other military ships that transport aircraft. Officers typically serve one or more assignments overseas.

Salaries

The annual earnings for Airplane Navigators in the U.S. military is based on the combination of basic pay and additional pay for performing aviation and other special duties. In addition, they receive a variety of benefits, such as vacation leave, a housing allowance, free medical and dental care, and tuition assistance for obtaining advanced degrees.

Basic pay for military Airplane Navigators is based on the basic pay schedule for commissioned officers, which is the same for all military branches. The rate of basic pay for officers is based on their rank, pay grade, and number of years of service. The basic pay scale for U.S. commissioned officers in 2003 ranged from about $26,000 to about $143,000.

Employment Prospects

About 6,000 Airplane Navigators serve in the U.S. military services. Opportunities are available in all five branches of the U.S. Armed Forces. New Navigators are needed each year to replace officers who have transferred to other duties, retired, or completed their service obligation. A military service will create additional slots to meet the demands of the field.

Advancement Prospects

Within their field, Airplane Navigators can become senior navigators, flight operations directors, and squadron commanders. They can also advance in rank. Officers are promoted according to their job performance as well as their ability to perform the duties of the next rank.

Each U.S. military branch has its own ranking system upon which officers can become eligible for the next rank. For example, in the U.S. Navy, officers begin their careers as ensigns. After two years, they become eligible for promotion to the rank of lieutenant junior grade. After two more years, they may be promoted to the rank of lieutenant. To become a lieutenant commander, one needs nine to 11 years of experience; a commander, 15 to 17 years; and a captain, 21 to 23 years.

Education and Training

Airplane Navigators in the U.S. military must possess a bachelor's degree, which may be in any field.

Candidates for the Airplane Navigator field must first complete officer training programs. Most U.S. military officers complete training through one of these routes:

- Qualified high school graduates enter a service academy—the U.S. Naval Academy (navy and marines), the U.S. Air Force Academy, or the U.S. Coast Guard Academy. Along with satisfying the officer training requirement, students earn a bachelor's degree in their choice of fields.
- College students participate in Reserve Officers' Training Corps (ROTC) program for the navy, air force, or marines. Along with completing their coursework for their bachelor's degree, ROTC cadets enroll in military training courses and perform weekly drills. They also participate in training exercises during the summer.
- College graduates complete Officer Candidate School (OCS) or Officer Training School (OTS), which are three to four month programs that consist of academic studies and physical training. They also learn about the rules, regulations, responsibilities, and lifestyle of the military service in which they have chosen to serve.

Upon completion of officer training programs, Airplane Navigator candidates earn commissions as officers. They are commissioned as ensigns, if they are in the navy or Coast Guard, or as second lieutenants, if they are in the air force or marines. Next, the candidates complete job training in their specialties. Initial training includes six to 12 months of classroom instruction, which covers such topics as principles and methods of navigation; operation communication, radar, and other systems; inspection of navigation equipment and systems; and combat navigation procedures. In addition, trainees receive practical experience that includes training in aircraft simulators and actual flying.

Throughout their careers, Airplane Navigators receive advanced training to update and enhance their knowledge and skills.

Airplane Navigators also receive training in military education to gain the necessary skills and knowledge to advance to senior management and command positions. Furthermore, they can take advantage of education programs to earn advanced degrees in technical, scientific, engineering, or managerial fields that are in particular demand by their military service.

Experience, Special Skills, and Personality Traits

Prior experience is not necessary for individuals to become Airplane Navigators. In general, the military seeks candidates who have a strong interest in flying.

Airplane Navigators must have excellent skills in reading maps and charts. They also have strong concentration skills. In addition, they should have good teamwork, interpersonal, and communication skills. Being accurate, detail-oriented, mature, and self-motivated are some personality traits that successful Airplane Navigators share.

Unions and Associations

Military Airplane Navigators might join organizations composed of current and former air crew members who have worked on specific aircraft or served in particular aviation units. These organizations offer networking and social opportunities to their members as well as other services and resources. For example, U.S. Air Force navigators might join the Air Force Navigator Observer Association.

Tips for Entry

1. Experts in the field suggest that students interested in the field of airplane navigation should take courses in cartography, geography, and surveying.
2. While in school, participate in sports, student government, and other extracurricular activities to establish a well-rounded background as well as to develop leadership skills and physical fitness.
3. All U.S. military branches require that commissioned officers be U.S. citizens, be physically fit, and be of high moral character. There are also age requirements, which vary with the different branches.
4. Some navigation specialties are open only to men. For further information, talk with a recruiter for the service in which you wish to serve.
5. Learn more about ROTC programs for the different services on the Internet. The Web sites are the U.S. Army ROTC, http://www.armyrotc.com; U.S. Air Force ROTC, http://www.afrotc.com; and U.S. Navy ROTC, http://www.nrotc.navy.mil.

FLIGHT ENGINEER

CAREER PROFILE

Duties: Provide technical expertise about aircraft and aircraft systems; perform various preflight, flight, and postflight duties; perform duties as required

Alternate Title(s): Aviation Maintenance Technician (U.S. Coast Guard)

Salary Range: $13,000 to $55,000

Employment Prospects: Fair

Advancement Prospects: Good

Prerequisites:

Education or Training—High school diploma; complete basic training for recruits; complete a job training program

Experience—Several years of military experience required; have experience working with military aircraft

Special Skills and Personality Traits—Mechanical aptitude; reading, math, problem-solving, teamwork, interpersonal, and communication skills, independent, confident, decisive, level-headed

CAREER LADDER

Senior Flight Engineer

Journeyman Flight Engineer

Apprentice Flight Engineer

Position Description

Flight Engineers serve as crew members aboard military aircraft—helicopters as well as airplanes. They sit in the cockpit alongside the pilots and navigators and work together with them to complete safe and efficient missions. The Flight Engineer's role is to provide technical expertise about an aircraft, as he or she has been highly trained in how the various complex parts of the aircraft work and function.

As members of the U.S. Armed Forces, Flight Engineers are dedicated to the role of protecting and defending the United States. They are involved in various types of missions, depending on the aircraft on which they serve. For example, Flight Engineers are assigned to the various types of aircraft that specifically perform airlifts, refuel aircraft in the sky, do reconnaissance, or engage in combat. Before every flight, Flight Engineers and other aircrew members meet to be briefed on their mission, emergency procedures, and other vital information.

Flight Engineers are responsible for completing various duties before a flight takes off. One major duty is performing a careful preflight inspection of both the inside and outside of the aircraft. Their visual evaluation requires checking an aircraft's many parts and systems while looking for leaks, malfunctions, and other defects. In addition, they review mechanics' reports of maintenance or repair work that was recently done on the aircraft.

Another major preflight responsibility for Flight Engineers is estimating the aircraft's performance and fuel requirements to ensure that missions can be completed. They gather and calculate data for the length of runways used for takeoff and landing, the mileage of their route, the cruising altitude, estimated airspeed, weather conditions, engine fuel consumption, and so on. Flight Engineers use data tables and charts as well as computers or electronic calculators to help them with their computations.

Flight Engineers are also responsible for calculating the weight and balance of their aircraft to make sure that it has not exceeded the amount of weight that it can safely carry. In addition, Flight Engineers monitor the loading of cargo, fuel, and passengers and verify that the load is distributed evenly in the aircraft.

While in flight, Flight Engineers assist pilots with the operation of an aircraft by following their orders and instructions. They assist pilots with starting and shutting down aircraft engines, and throughout the flight, Flight Engineers operate engine controls to maintain an efficient flow of fuel to the engines.

Flight Engineers are also responsible for monitoring, controlling, and regulating the various aircraft systems—such as navigation, communication, hydraulic, electric, ventilation, air conditioning, and lubrication systems. Should any malfunctions occur while in flight, Flight Engineers determine the cause of the problems and make the necessary replacements, adjustments, or repairs, if possible.

Upon completion of their missions, Flight Engineers perform postflight inspections. If any mechanical problems occur, they report them to aircraft mechanic chiefs. Flight Engineers also maintain complete and accurate aircraft forms, records, and logs about their flights.

In the U.S. Armed Forces, Flight Engineers are enlisted men and women. (They hold one of the highest rated occupations for enlisted personnel.) Their initial service obligation ranges from three to six years, depending on the military branch in which they serve. They are given new tours of duty (or assignments) every few years. They may be stationed at a military base in the United States or in a foreign country. Some of them are assigned to units stationed aboard air carriers and other military ships that transport aircraft.

Salaries

Flight Engineers in the U.S. military earn basic pay, which is based on their rank, pay grade, and number of years of service. In 2003, the basic pay scale for military enlisted personnel ranged from about $13,000 to $55,000. Flight Engineers also receive additional pay for performing aviation duty and other special assignments.

All military personnel receive various benefits, such as a housing allowance, free medical and dental care, and tuition assistance for academic or technical programs.

Employment Prospects

Opportunities for Flight Engineers in the U.S. military are found with the U.S. Air Force, the U.S. Navy, and the U.S. Marine Corps. In the U.S. Coast Guard, the role of Flight Engineer is fulfilled by aviation maintenance technicians.

New Flight Engineers are needed each year to replace personnel who leave the service or transfer to other positions or occupations. The number of positions varies, depending on the demands of the field.

Opportunities for civilian Flight Engineers are available with commercial air carriers, but the demand is decreasing with the advancement of technology. As more aircraft become computerized, the need for a third crew member diminishes.

Advancement Prospects

Flight Engineers can advance in rank and pay grade, as well as by receiving greater responsibilities, such as performing supervisory or training duties. Within their field, they can advance to such managerial positions as flight engineer chiefs or air crew chiefs. They also can rise through the ranks in their particular service; for example, enlisted personnel in the U.S. Marine Corps can be promoted to the rank of sergeant major.

Each military branch provides opportunities for enlisted personnel to pursue further technical training and college degrees. The military also offers programs that allow enlisted personnel to become commissioned officers.

Education and Training

Minimally, Flight Engineers in the U.S. military must possess a high school diploma. (A general equivalency diploma may be acceptable. For information, ask a recruiter about specific qualifications for Flight Engineers.)

Initially, Flight Engineers complete four to six months of intensive job training at their service's flight engineer school. They complete formal classroom instruction and gain hands-on experience in flight theory, the operation of aircraft systems, aircraft inspection, flight planning, emergency procedures, and other areas. Their training sessions take place on actual flights and in flight simulators. Upon graduation, they are given their first assignment where they receive on-the-job training.

Flight Engineers continue to receive advanced training throughout their careers in the military.

Experience, Special Skills, and Personality Traits

Enlisted personnel must have several years of military experience before they can apply for the Flight Engineer specialty. They must also have experience working with military aircraft. Many Flight Engineers have a background in aircraft maintenance.

To perform their work well, Flight Engineers must have a mechanical aptitude. They must also have strong reading skills, particularly the ability to read and understand technical diagrams, schematics, charts, and manuals. In addition, they need strong math and problem-solving skills. Furthermore, Flight Engineers must have effective teamwork, interpersonal, and communication skills. Being independent, confident, decisive, and level-headed are some personality traits that successful Flight Engineers have in common.

Unions and Associations

Flight Engineers might join an organization composed of current and former air crew members who have worked on specific aircraft or served in particular aviation units. These organizations offer networking and social opportunities, as well as other services and resources to their members.

Tips for Entry

1. In high school, take courses in general mathematics and shop mechanics to help you prepare for a career as a military Flight Engineer.
2. To enlist in the U.S. military services, you must meet certain age limits, which vary with the different services. You must also be a U.S. citizen or a permanent resident with proper immigration documents. In addition, you must be of high moral character and meet specific physical conditions. Further, you must earn the minimum qualifying score on the aptitude tests for the Flight Engineer occupation.
3. Before joining the military, be sure you understand what your commitment to service would involve. Talk with current and former enlisted personnel and officers about their military experiences, especially those who served in the military branch that interests you. Also read books and brochures about that military branch, as well as check out the information provided at its Web site.
4. You can use the Internet to learn more about the various military services that need Flight Engineers. Go to U.S. Air Force, http://www.af.mil; U.S. Navy, http://www.navy.mil; U.S. Marine Corps, http://www.usmc.mil; and U.S. Coast Guard, http://www.uscg.mil.

AIRCRAFT LOADMASTER

CAREER PROFILE

Duties: Direct the loading and unloading of cargo on and off military planes; compute the weight and balance of an aircraft; perform preflight, inflight, and postflight duties; perform duties as required

Alternate Title(s): None

Salary Range: $13,000 to $55,000

Employment Prospects: Good

Advancement Prospects: Good

Prerequisites:

Education or Training—High school diploma; complete basic training for recruits; complete a job training program

Experience—No previous experience required

Special Skills and Personality Traits—Math, reading, teamwork, interpersonal, and communication skills, adventurous, outgoing, independent, aggressive, professional, compassionate, decisive

CAREER LADDER

Chief Loadmaster

Loadmaster

Apprentice Loadmaster

Position Description

In the U.S. Armed Forces, Aircraft Loadmasters play a valuable role in the delivery of military personnel and cargo to air bases and airfields throughout the world. Aircraft Loadmasters are aircrew members who serve aboard cargo or transport aircraft that are flown in airlift operations. Military airlift missions involve the transportation of military personnel and cargo between military bases throughout the world. During times of war or armed conflict, some Aircraft Loadmasters are assigned to airlift units that fly cargo and personnel directly to the front lines.

Aircraft Loadmasters are in charge of directing the proper loading and unloading of cargo—which may include such items as mail, baggage, food, medical supplies, office equipment, weapons, vehicles, tanks, helicopters, and ships. Loadmasters are responsible for fitting all cargo in an aircraft while making sure the weight of the cargo is evenly distributed throughout the aircraft. They also ensure all cargo items are tightly secured in place before takeoff.

On occasion, Aircraft Loadmasters participate in special missions. For example, they may be involved in transporting special vehicles and helicopters to foreign countries where the U.S. president will travel. Many Aircraft Loadmasters participate in humanitarian airlifts, by delivering food, medical supplies, and assistance to regions throughout the world that have gone through hurricanes, earthquakes, and other natural disasters. During peacetime, Aircraft Loadmasters often participate in goodwill missions to U.S. communities, such as by airlifting snow-blowing machines to snowbound airports.

During some missions, cargo planes are unable to land, and therefore airdrops are required. Cargo, and sometimes personnel, must exit moving planes and descend to the earth's surface by parachute. Cargo and the platforms on which they are strapped are attached to parachutes. The parachutes in turn are connected to systems that Aircraft Loadmasters use to deploy the parachutes after the cargo is a safe distance from the aircraft. Loadmasters are also responsible for supervising military parachutists as they exit from their aircraft.

In large cargo planes, Aircraft Loadmasters usually work in teams of two or three. Each team member is responsible for a particular section of the cargo bay in the aircraft. He or she directs various activities, such as the use of forklifts, winches, and other cargo-loading equipment and the proper application of straps, chains, nets, and other restraint devices to keep cargo from shifting.

Aircraft Loadmasters are also responsible for computing the weight and balance of an aircraft, which includes calculating the quantity of cargo and personnel. Loadmasters must make sure that the aircraft does not exceed the amount of weight it can carry. In addition, they determine how much weight can be placed in the different sections of the cargo bay to avoid structural damage. Furthermore, Aircraft Loadmasters decide if hazardous cargo is safe to be shipped and if it is compatible with other cargo.

Aircraft Loadmasters also have duties that are specific to their role as aircrew members. They perform preflight and postflight checks of aircraft and aircraft systems, such as airdrop equipment, in accordance with flight manuals. They are in charge of formal documents such as cargo manifests and customs forms. In addition, they are responsible for the security of mail, baggage, and cargo during flights.

Aircraft Loadmasters are responsible for fulfilling the flight attendant role on missions by providing for the safety and comfort of all military and nonmilitary passengers. They brief passengers at takeoff about the use of seat belts, emergency procedures, the location of bathroom facilities, and other important information. They assist passengers as needed; for example, they might provide passengers with blankets or first aid. Loadmasters also pass out refreshments and meals to passengers.

Not all Aircraft Loadmasters are assigned to aircrew duty. Some of them are assigned to units at airfields in remote locations where no airlift command and control exists. These Loadmasters provide and manage the oversight of cargo preparation as well as the loading and unloading of all cargo that is moved into and out of the area.

Aircraft Loadmasters are enlisted men and women. As members of the U.S. Armed Forces, they are dedicated to the role of protecting and defending the United States. Their initial service obligation ranges from three to six years, depending on the military branch in which they serve. They are given new tours of duty (or assignments) every few years. They may be stationed at a base or airfield in the United States or in a foreign country.

Salaries

Aircraft Loadmasters in the U.S. military earn basic pay, which is based on their rank, pay grade, and number of years of service. In 2003, the basic pay scale for military enlisted personnel ranged from about $13,000 to $55,000. Military loadmasters also receive additional pay for performing aviation duty and other special duty assignments.

All military personnel receive various benefits such as a housing allowance, free medical and dental care, and tuition assistance for academic or technical programs.

Employment Prospects

Opportunities for Aircraft Loadmasters in the U.S. military are available with the U.S. Air Force, the U.S. Navy, and the U.S. Marines. Each year, new Loadmasters are needed to replace personnel who have transferred to other duties or occupations, or have completed their service obligation. A service will create additional positions to meet demands in the field.

After leaving military service, Aircraft Loadmasters may find opportunities as cargo specialists with passenger and cargo air carriers.

Advancement Prospects

Within their field, Aircraft Loadmasters can become team leaders, supervisors, instructor loadmasters, and field examiner loadmasters. They can also rise through the ranks in their particular service; for example, enlisted personnel in the U.S. Air Force can be promoted to the rank of chief master sergeant.

Each military branch provides opportunities for enlisted personnel to pursue further technical training and college degrees. The military also offers programs that allow enlisted personnel to become commissioned officers.

Education and Training

Aircraft Loadmasters in the U.S. military must be high school graduates. (Some services may accept general equivalency diplomas. For specific information, ask a recruiter from the service that interests you.)

Recruits first complete several weeks of recruit training (also known as basic training) in which they learn about their military branch, its history, mission, and customs. They are also trained in basic discipline and teamwork. U.S. Marine Corps recruits participate in combat skills training after completing their basic training.

Upon completion of basic training, recruits then undergo initial training for becoming Aircraft Loadmasters. This involves both formal classroom instruction and on-the-job training. They are taught basic skills such as computing aircraft weight and balance, restraining cargo on the aircraft, the transportation of hazardous materials, the principles of airdrop, and the operation of cargo-loading equipment (such as power winches and forklifts). After completing basic instruction, loadmaster candidates are assigned to specific aircraft where they apply and practice their skills. In addition, they receive instruction in becoming an aircrew member, as well as to learn basic survival techniques for emergencies and other situations. The on-the-job training phase generally lasts nine to 10 months and includes supervised flying missions. Those who successfully complete their job training become certified Aircraft Loadmasters.

Throughout their careers, Aircraft Loadmasters receive training to update their skills and knowledge.

Experience, Special Skills, and Personality Traits

No prior experience is needed for individuals to become Aircraft Loadmasters in the U.S. military. Applicants should have an interest in flying, as well as prefer to do physical work.

Some skills essential to an Aircraft Loadmaster's job are math skills and reading skills, including the ability to read and understand diagrams and charts. Aircraft Loadmasters should also have strong teamwork, interpersonal, and communication skills. Being adventurous, outgoing, independent, aggressive, professional, compassionate, and decisive are some personality traits that Aircraft Loadmasters have in common.

Unions and Associations

Many Aircraft Loadmasters are members of the Professional Loadmaster Association, which is a nonprofit organization made up of current and former military and civilian Aircraft Loadmasters. The organization offers many professional services and resources, including opportunities to network with peers.

Tips for Entry

1. Take courses in mathematics and general science while you are in high school to prepare you for this field.
2. To enlist in the U.S. military, individuals must meet certain age limits, which vary with the different services. They must also be U.S. citizens or permanent residents with proper immigration documents. In addition, they must be of high moral character and meet specific physical conditions. Further, they must earn the minimum qualifying score on the aptitude tests for the Aircraft Loadmaster occupation.
3. To learn more about military life, check out this Web site on the Internet: "Today's Military" by the Department of Defense. The URL is http://www.todaysmilitary.com.
4. Lean more about the Aircraft Loadmaster specialty on the Internet. You might start by visiting the Professional Loadmaster Association's Web site at http://www.loadmasters.com.

AIRCRAFT LAUNCH AND RECOVERY SPECIALIST

CAREER PROFILE

Duties: Operate and maintain equipment and systems that help aircraft take off and land safely aboard ships at sea; perform duties as required

Alternate Title(s): Aircraft Launch and Recovery Technician

Salary Range: $13,000 to $55,000

Employment Prospects: Fair

Advancement Prospects: Good

Prerequisites:

Education or Training—High school diploma; complete basic training for recruits; complete a job training program

Experience—No previous experience required

Special Skills and Personality Traits—Proficient in using hand tools and test equipment; communication, teamwork, and interpersonal skills; accurate, disciplined, self-confident

CAREER LADDER

Crew Supervisor

Launch and Recovery Specialist

Apprentice Launch and Recovery Specialist

Position Description

Aircraft Launch and Recovery Specialists are responsible for helping pilots safely take off and land on military ships. Their job is to operate the equipment and systems that have been designed to launch and recover aircraft aboard ships' decks while at sea. These operations may take place during the day or night.

In the U.S. Armed Forces, Aircraft Launch and Recovery Specialists serve as crew members aboard a fleet of warships, which carry various types of fixed-wing and rotary-wing aircraft. The ships' decks have been especially designed as flight decks, in which short runways have been constructed along the length of the decks. Several dozen aircraft—such as jet fighter planes, bombers, tankers, and helicopters—are safely tied down on a ship's flight deck or stored on the hangar deck below. When the need arises, pilots depart in their aircraft from these military ships to engage in battle, transport troops and supplies, perform search-and-rescue missions, go on reconnaissance, and complete various other missions. Pilots return to their ships upon completion of their missions.

Many Aircraft Launch and Recovery Specialists work aboard the U.S. Navy's largest warships, known as aircraft carriers. The carriers are often described as being small cities at sea, as they are independently able to support the 5,000 or more crew members who work and live aboard these ships for several months at a time.

Aircraft Launch and Recovery Specialists are also found aboard other naval ships, such as U.S. Marine amphibious warships and Coast Guard cutters, which are generally smaller than the aircraft carriers. Unlike aircraft carriers, these ships mostly carry different types of helicopters.

Participating in launch and recovery operations is one of the major responsibilities of Aircraft Launch and Recovery Specialists. Some of their tasks include:

- operating elevators to transfer aircraft between flight decks and hangar decks
- directing launch or recovery operations by using hand or light signals
- inspecting equipment before and after they use them to ensure they are properly working
- handling emergency situations, such as aircraft fires

Aircraft Launch and Recovery Specialists use a variety of procedures for assisting the various aircraft. Helicopters are generally guided through takeoff and landing operations with the aid of hand or light signals. Because of short runways, fixed-wing aircraft cannot perform normal takeoffs and landings. Therefore, they require the help of mechanical systems that are controlled by Aircraft Launch and Recovery Specialists.

Airplane takeoffs are assisted by steam-powered catapult systems. An airplane, such as a jet fighter, is attached to a catapult. Once the catapult has developed sufficient energy, it can then thrust the aircraft from the ship's flight deck at speeds up to 165 miles per hour. Airplane landings are assisted by strong arresting cables, barricades, and other equipment. All ship-based airplanes are attached with tailhooks, which catch the arresting cables that are stretched across the flight deck. The cables are able to bring an aircraft traveling at over 100 miles per hour to a complete stop.

Aircraft Launch and Recovery Specialists are also responsible for the maintenance of the launch and recovery equipment. They perform preventative maintenance as well as make complex repairs. Their tasks require the use of hand tools as well as electrical and mechanical test equipment to calibrate, adjust, and test the launch and recovery equipment.

Aircraft Launch and Recovery Specialists also perform various administrative duties. For example, they might maintain an inventory of supplies, equipment, and spare parts; prepare maintenance schedules; maintain logs of airplane launches and recoveries; and keep equipment maintenance records up to date.

Some Specialists are assigned to work in airfields that are set up near training sites and combat zones. They essentially perform the same duties as they would at sea. Specific duties they complete on land include installing crash barriers and barricades on the airfields and installing and maintaining visual landing aids (such as runway lighting systems).

Novice Aircraft Launch and Recovery Specialists typically perform routine tasks under the supervision of senior Specialists. As they become more adept at their jobs, they receive greater responsibilities. For example, they might perform more difficult equipment repairs and supervise novice crew members.

Specialists work on flight decks, where they are exposed to aircraft noise and fumes. They wear life jackets, heavy-duty helmets, and other protective clothing.

Aircraft Launch and Recovery Specialists in the U.S. military are enlisted personnel. Their initial service obligation ranges from three to six years, depending on the military service in which they serve. They are given new tours of duty (or assignments) every few years.

Salaries

Aircraft Launch and Recovery Specialists in the U.S. military earn basic pay, which is based on their rank, pay grade, and number of years of service. In 2003, the basic pay scale for military enlisted personnel ranged from about $13,000 to $55,000. Depending on their service, Aircraft Launch and Recovery Specialists may receive additional pay for serving on an aviation team or performing dangerous or other special duties.

All military personnel receive various benefits, such as a housing allowance, free medical and dental care, and tuition assistance for academic or technical programs.

Employment Prospects

Opportunities for Aircraft Launch and Recovery Specialists are found in the U.S. Navy, U.S. Marines, and U.S. Coast Guard. There are about 2,500 of these specialists in the U.S. Armed Forces. New specialists are needed each year to replace those who have retired or transferred to other positions. Additional positions are created to meet the demands of the field.

Advancement Prospects

Within the field, Aircraft Launch and Recovery Specialists can advance to management positions by becoming crew supervisors and, ultimately, flight deck supervisors. They also can rise through the ranks in their particular service; for example, naval enlisted personnel can advance to the rank of master chief petty officer.

Each military branch provides opportunities for enlisted personnel to pursue further technical training and college degrees. The military also offers programs that allow enlisted personnel to become commissioned officers.

Education and Training

Minimally, to become a U.S. Navy, U.S. Marine Corp, or U.S. Coast Guard recruit, one must possess a high school diploma or a general equivalency diploma.

Recruits first complete several weeks of recruit training (also known as basic training), in which they learn about their military branch, its history, mission, and customs. They also are trained in basic discipline and teamwork. U.S. Marine Corps recruits participate in combat skills training after completing their basic training.

Apprentice Aircraft Launch and Recovery Specialists receive their initial job training, which involves several weeks of formal study, in the basic elements of aviation, including how planes take off and land. They also receive instruction and gain practice in the operation and maintenance of equipment.

Throughout their careers, Aircraft Launch and Recovery Specialists receive training to update their skills and knowledge about their job.

Experience, Special Skills, and Personality Traits

No prior experience is required for this job. An interest in aircraft flight operations and working on hydraulic and mechanical equipment is desirable.

Applicants should have the ability to use hand tools and test equipment. In addition, they must have strong communication, teamwork, and interpersonal skills, as they must be able to work well with others. Being accurate, disciplined, and self-confident are a few personality traits that successful Aircraft Launch and Recovery Specialists share.

Unions and Associations

Aircraft Launch and Recovery Specialists might join organizations composed of current and former aircrew members who have worked on specific aircraft or served in particular aviation units. These organizations offer networking and social opportunities, as well as other services and resources to their members.

Tips for Entry

1. Taking shop mechanics in high school may enhance your chances of being chosen for military catapult operations.
2. To join the U.S. Armed Forces, individuals must meet certain age limits, which vary with the different services. They must also be U.S. citizens or permanent residents with proper immigration documents. In addition, they must be of high moral character and meet specific physical conditions. Further, they must earn the minimum qualifying score on the aptitude tests for the Aircraft Launch and Recovery Specialist occupation.
3. The U.S. Navy, U.S. Marine Corps, and U.S. Coast Guard each have a Delayed Enlistment Program (DEP), which allows recruits to postpone their initial active-duty training for up to a full year.
4. You can use the Internet to learn more about the various services that employ Aircraft Launch and Recovery Specialists. The Web sites are U.S. Navy, http://www.navy.mil; U.S. Marine Corps, http://www.usmc.mil; and U.S. Coast Guard, http://www.uscg.mil.

FLIGHT SURGEON

CAREER PROFILE

Duties: Provide medical care and treatment to aviation personnel; perform clinical and administrative duties; perform duties as required

Alternate Title(s): None

Salary Range: $60,000 to $70,000 (entry-level pay)

Employment Prospects: Fair

Advancement Prospects: Good

Prerequisites:

Education or Training—M.D. or D.O. degree; complete the flight surgeon and officer training programs

Experience—Previous work experience in aerospace medicine not required

Special Skills and Personality Traits—Leadership, teamwork, communication, and interpersonal skills; honest, trustful, dedicated, detail-oriented, self-motivated

Special Requirements—Physician licensure

CAREER LADDER

Senior Flight Surgeon

Junior Flight Surgeon

Student Flight Surgeon

Position Description

Flight Surgeons are military physicians. They have been trained to understand the flight environment along with the physical and physiological effects it has on military aircrews. They specialize in providing medical care to pilots, navigators, flight engineers, air traffic controllers, aircraft loadmasters, and other aviation personnel. They are also responsible for determining whether aircrew members are physically and mentally fit to fly, particularly in times of war and other conflict situations.

In the U.S. Armed Forces, Flight Surgeons serve in all the military services—the U.S. Army, the U.S. Navy, the U.S. Air Force, the U.S. Marine Corps, and the U.S. Coast Guard. (The navy provides Flight Surgeons for the marines.) Flight Surgeons also serve in the U.S. National Guard. Flight Surgeons in all services, except the Coast Guard, may be on active duty or reserve duty.

Most Flight Surgeons are assigned to aviation squadrons. They are usually assisted by one or more medical care technicians to provide medical support to the squadrons. Aviation squadrons may be stationed at military bases, on aircraft carriers, or on other military ships. While stationed at a military base or aboard a ship, Flight Surgeons and their assistants become part of the staff at the base's or ship's medical treatment facility. When squadrons are deployed to conflict situations, Flight Surgeons accompany them.

Flight Surgeons are responsible for the care and treatment of all members of their squadrons. (Some Flight Surgeons provide medical care to family members of their squadrons as well.) Flight Surgeons are expected to become familiar with the types of missions their squadrons perform. They also maintain a close relationship with their squadrons and strive to develop a rapport and trust that encourages squadron members to freely approach them with early signs of health problems.

Flight Surgeons perform annual physical examinations and routine medical checkups to monitor and maintain the health of their squadrons. They evaluate illnesses and injuries as well as minor health conditions—such as colds—in the interest of flight safety and their ability to complete flight missions. If aircrew members have medical problems or are receiving treatment that may affect their job performance, Flight Surgeons may ground them temporarily until they are well.

Flight Surgeons also practice preventative medicine. They provide patients with personal protective measures to ensure continued good health. For example, they give aircrew members necessary immunizations, prescribe smoking cessation or weight control programs, and distribute information about good hygiene practices.

In addition to their clinical duties, Flight Surgeons handle various administrative responsibilities. One major duty is acting as aeromedical adviser to aviation unit commanders, which involves counseling them on matters that affect the health of the squadron. Flight Surgeons also participate in officer meetings, safety inspections, and squadron presentations, as well as drills and exercises. In addition, Flight Surgeons are involved in their unit's safety program, in which they assist with various education and training programs on such topics as life-support equipment, flight safety, ground safety, and weapons safety.

Another responsibility is assisting with flight mishaps. Flight Surgeons respond to aircraft crashes that occur on base as well as off base, including remote areas. They make sure that all survivors are treated and transported from the scene. They act as the liaison between the medical treatment facility and the crash scene. They also keep the medical command post up to date with information about the mishap.

Flight Surgeons also become part of the team that investigates aircraft mishaps. They provide their expertise in emotional and physiological responses to flight (such as disorientation, decision-making, or human error) that may have contributed to the crash.

Flight Surgeons are expected to participate in flying activities in order to become familiar with the types of stresses that aircrews experience. Some Flight Surgeons are trained military pilots and are qualified to fly with their units.

All Flight Surgeons in the U.S. military are commissioned officers. The primary duty of these men and women is to act as leaders in the defense of the United States. Newly commissioned Flight Surgeons in the U.S. Navy are lieutenants, whereas new Flight Surgeons in the U.S. Army and U.S. Air Force are commissioned as captains. U.S. Coast Guard Flight Surgeons are medical officers detailed from the U.S. Public Health Service (PHS). Newly commissioned PHS medical officers are lieutenants.

Salaries

The annual earnings for Flight Surgeons in the U.S. military are based on the combination of basic pay and additional pay for performing aviation duties and other special duties. In addition, they receive a variety of benefits, such as vacation leave and a housing allowance. According to an expert in the field, new Flight Surgeons generally earn between $60,000 and $70,000 per year.

Employment Prospects

New opportunities for Flight Surgeons in the U.S. Armed Forces are available each year. Many of these new positions are filled by medical students who have previously committed to military service prior to entering the Uniformed Services University of the Health Sciences or other medical schools.

Upon completion of military service, Flight Surgeons may find continued employment in aerospace medicine. They might find employment with the National Aeronautics and Space Administration (NASA), the Federal Aviation Administration (FAA), airlines, or aerospace manufacturers. They might maintain a private practice and specialize in aerospace medicine. In addition, they may become involved with medical research or teaching at research universities. Furthermore, they may find opportunities in preventative medicine, occupational medicine, or public health.

Advancement Prospects

Flight Surgeons can advance to senior management or command positions.

By completing a master's program in public health and medical residency training, Flight Surgeons can become aerospace medicine specialists. As specialists, they can pursue various types of military assignments, including teaching, research, administration, preventative medicine, and occupational medicine positions.

Education and Training

Candidates for Flight Surgeon positions must possess a doctor of medicine (M.D.) or doctor of osteopathy (D.O.) degrees. They must also have completed medical internships or one year of graduate medical education.

Candidates must successfully complete the intensive flight surgeon training program for their service. Candidates for Coast Guard Flight Surgeon positions complete their initial training with either the air force or army. The length of the flight surgeon training program varies with each service. The U.S. Army's program is six weeks long, while the U.S. Air Force's program is seven weeks long. The U.S. Navy's program is six months long, which includes instruction on aviation and other military medical assignments, as well as water survival, preflight training, and flight instruction.

In addition, Flight Surgeon candidates must complete an officer training program. They attend either an Officer Candidate School (OCS) or an Officer Training School (OTS), which is a three to four month program that consists of academic studies and physical training. They also learn about the rules, regulations, responsibilities, and lifestyle of the military branch in which they have chosen to serve.

Special Requirements

Flight Surgeons in the U.S. Armed Forces must be licensed to practice medicine in the United States, its territories, or the District of Columbia.

Experience, Special Skills, and Personality Traits

Prior experience working in aerospace medicine is not required.

To perform well on their jobs, Flight Surgeons need excellent leadership, teamwork, communication, and interpersonal skills. Being honest, trustful, dedicated, detail-oriented, and self-motivated are some personality traits that successful Flight Surgeons share.

Unions and Associations

Flight Surgeons can join various professional associations to take advantage of networking opportunities and other professional services and resources. Some of these organizations are:

- Aerospace Medical Association
- International Association of Military Flight Surgeon Pilots
- Society of U.S. Air Force Flight Surgeons
- Society of U.S. Naval Flight Surgeons
- Commissioned Officers Association of the U.S. Public Health Service, Inc.

Tips for Entry

1. As a high school or college student, experience first-hand what it might be like to be a doctor. Talk with doctors about their jobs and what they like about their work.
2. Gain experience working in the health care field by volunteering or working at a hospital or nursing home.
3. Some military services grant officer commissions to civilians while they are still in medical school or completing their internships or residencies. Ask a recruiter for information about these programs.
4. Learn more about Flight Surgeons on the Internet. One Web site you might visit is for the Society of U.S. Naval Flight Surgeons. Its URL is http://www.aerospacemed.org. To find other relevant Web sites, enter the keywords *flight surgeons* into a search engine.

AEROSPACE MANUFACTURING INDUSTRY

AEROSPACE ENGINEER

CAREER PROFILE

Duties: Vary, depending on function one performs in a company, such as research, design, or technical service; perform duties as required of position

Alternate Title(s): Aeronautical Engineer; Astronautical Engineer; a job title that reflects a function, such as Design Engineer or Field Service Engineer

Salary Range: $50,000 to $108,000

Employment Prospects: Fair

Advancement Prospects: Good

Prerequisites:

Education or Training—Bachelor's degree in aerospace engineering, mechanical engineering, or a related field

Experience—Previous work experience generally required; work experience in aerospace industry preferred

Special Skills and Personality Traits—Communication, writing, problem-solving, teamwork, interpersonal skills; creative, curious, detail-oriented, analytical, flexible, independent, logical

Special Requirements—Professional Engineer (P.E.) license may be required

CAREER LADDER

Senior Aerospace Engineer

Aerospace Engineer

Junior Aerospace Engineer

Position Description

Gliders. Airplanes. Helicopters. Commercial Airliners. Military bombers and jet fighters. Communication satellites. Missiles. Rockets. Space vehicles for human flight. Unmanned space probes that explore outer space. These are just a few of the many fantastic vehicles that Aerospace Engineers help to create.

Aerospace Engineers are among the many types of engineering specialists that work for aerospace manufacturing firms. They have been specifically trained to apply science, mathematics, and engineering principles to the design, development, and maintenance of aerospace vehicles, engines, systems, components, and parts. They may be involved in developing new products or finding ways to improve existing products for their companies.

Because the natural laws and theories for aircraft differ from those under which spacecraft operate, Aerospace Engineers specialize in either aeronautics or astronautics. Aeronautics is concerned with aircraft, and engineers in this field are known as aeronautical engineers. Astronautics deals with spacecraft, and the engineers in this field are called astronautical engineers.

Aerospace Engineers also specialize in several other ways. Many of them work on a particular type of aerospace product. Aeronautics engineers might focus on helicopters, single-engine airplanes, commercial transport planes, military fighter jets, and so on. Astronautics engineers might concentrate on such products as satellites, unmanned space probes, missiles, or rockets.

As they become experienced, Aerospace Engineers typically focus their expertise in a particular area of aerospace engineering. Some of these areas include aerodynamics, propulsion, fluid mechanics, structural design, celestial mechanics, navigational systems, flight tests, instrumentation, and guidance and control systems.

In addition, Aerospace Engineers specialize in performing specific engineering functions in the different phases of development and production of products. The following are just a few of the various types of positions that Aerospace Engineers might fill at a company.

- Research engineers apply basic principles and knowledge of science, mathematics, and engineering to the development of new (or improved) commercial products or manufacturing processes.
- Development engineers apply research findings to develop new or improved products or manufacturing processes.
- Analytical engineers conduct in-depth assessments of proposed products and evaluate whether the design of each product meets customer requirements.
- Design engineers take the concept or working model of a product and create a design that meets customer requirements and industry standards, and that can be manufactured economically.
- Test engineers design and oversee the performance testing of products in wind tunnels, as well as in actual flight.
- Project engineers plan, direct, and coordinate activities of company projects.
- Sales engineers contact customers and make sales presentations to demonstrate how products or services can fulfill their particular needs.
- Field service engineers examine performance reports on products and make recommendations to solve problems.

Aerospace Engineers collaborate on projects with engineers and scientists from various fields. For example, Aerospace Engineers would work closely with electrical engineers in the development of navigation, guidance, and control instruments.

Aerospace Engineers perform various duties, many of which are specific to their positions as research engineer, design engineer, and so on. Other duties are commonly performed by engineers in general. Examples of such tasks are:

- developing plans, procedures, or systems
- reviewing and evaluating data, plans, designs, documentation, specifications, or procedures
- troubleshooting problems
- providing estimates of cost, time, quantities, materials, and so on
- writing technical papers, instructions, and other materials
- preparing correspondence, reports, proposals, and other documents
- preparing blueprints and mathematical calculations for plans or designs
- attending project and departmental meetings
- providing advice and consultation to others
- supervising technicians and other staff members

Aerospace Engineers work in offices and laboratories as well as in machine shops and manufacturing plants. They usually work a 40-hour week but put in additional hours to complete tasks or to meet deadlines. Engineers sometimes travel to attend training sessions or professional conferences.

Salaries

Salaries for Aerospace Engineers vary, depending on their field, education, experience, employer, geographical location, and other factors. Typically, Aerospace Engineers with a master's or doctoral degree earn more than those with only a bachelor's degree. The U.S. Bureau of Labor Statistics, in its May 2003 *Occupational Employment Statistics* survey, reports that the estimated annual salary for most Aerospace Engineers ranged from $50,380 to $107,840.

Employment Prospects

The aerospace manufacturing industry is composed of companies that build aircraft, spacecraft, and other products for commercial aviation, defense, space exploration, and the telecommunications industry. The aerospace manufacturing industry also includes companies that make and sell the raw materials, parts, components, systems, and subsystems that go into building aerospace vehicles.

In addition to working for aerospace manufacturing firms, Aerospace Engineers are employed by such federal government agencies as the U.S. Department of Defense, the Federal Aviation Administration (FAA), and the National Aeronautics and Space Administration (NASA). They also work for engineering companies as well as research and testing firms that specialize in aircraft and spacecraft.

According to the U.S. Bureau of Labor Statistics, the job outlook for Aerospace Engineers is expected to increase by 10 to 20 percent between 2000 and 2010. In general, most job openings will be created to replace Aerospace Engineers who are retiring or transferring to other occupations. Job growth will depend on such factors as the state of the economy, the demand for products by the military, the federal government, and civilian consumers (such as airlines, corporations, and private pilots).

Aerospace Engineers can also use their skills and background to work in other fields such as bioengineering, mass transportation, communications, and environmental engineering.

Advancement Prospects

As they gain experience, Aerospace Engineers are promoted to senior positions in which they are given greater responsibilities. Those with management and administrative interests and talents can rise through the ranks as supervising engineers, managing engineers, and chief engineers. They can also advance to executive officer positions within their companies. Usually, advancement opportunities are better in large companies.

Those with entrepreneurial ambitions can become independent consultants or owners of engineering consulting firms.

Education and Training

Minimally, Aerospace Engineers must possess a bachelor's degree in aerospace engineering, mechanical engineering, or a related field. Employers usually require a master's or doctoral degree for research, consulting, and management positions. Aerospace Engineers who eventually wish to teach in academic settings must obtain a doctorate.

Aerospace Engineers enroll in education and training programs throughout their careers to update their knowledge and skills.

Special Requirements

Aerospace Engineers must be licensed as Professional Engineers (P.E.) if they offer engineering services directly to the public or perform work that affects the life, health, or property of the public. Requirements for P.E. licensure vary among the states, territories, and Washington, D.C. For specific information, contact the state board of engineering examiners where you wish to practice.

Experience, Special Skills, and Personality Traits

Entry-level candidates should have work experience related to the position for which they are applying. They may have gained their experience through internships, student research projects, summer employment, or other means. Having work experience in the aerospace industry is desirable.

To do their work effectively, Aerospace Engineers must have excellent communication, writing, problem-solving, teamwork, and interpersonal skills. Being creative, curious, detail-oriented, analytical, flexible, independent, and logical are some personality traits that successful Aerospace Engineers share.

Unions and Associations

Many Aerospace Engineers join professional associations to take advantage of professional services and resources such as continuing education programs, professional certification, and networking opportunities. Some national organizations that serve the diverse interests of these engineers are:

- American Helicopter Society International—The Vertical Flight Society
- American Institute of Aeronautics and Astronautics
- ASME International—Aerospace Division
- International Society of Allied Weight Engineers
- Society of Flight Test Engineers

Professional Engineers are eligible to join the National Society of Professional Engineers.

At some aerospace plants, Aerospace Engineers belong to a labor union, such as the International Federation of Professional and Technical Engineers, which represents them in negotiations for contractual terms relating to pay, benefits, and working conditions.

Tips for Entry

1. While in college, try to obtain internships or part-time jobs with aerospace companies during your summer breaks to gain experience in the industry.
2. Some aerospace companies recruit on college campuses for entry-level jobs.
3. Join student chapters of professional associations such as the American Institute of Aeronautics and Astronautics. Take advantage of activities that allow you to build up your network of contacts.
4. Learn more about aerospace engineering, as well as the aerospace industry, on the Internet. Some Web sites you might visit are American Institute of Aeronautics and Astronautics, http://www.aiaa.org; Aerospace Industries Association, http://www.aia-aerospace.org; Aerospace Technology, http://www.aerospace-technology.com; and Aerospaceweb.org, http://www.aerospaceweb.org.

ENGINEER

CAREER PROFILE

Duties: Be involved in the development of commercial products or manufacturing processes; perform a particular function, such as research, development, design, testing, production, or customer support; perform duties as required

Alternate Title(s): A title that reflects a specialty such as Materials Engineer; a title that reflects a function such as Design Engineer

Salary Range: $31,000 to $92,000

Employment Prospects: Good

Advancement Prospects: Excellent

Prerequisites:

Education or Training—Bachelor's degree in an engineering discipline; a master's or doctoral degree may be preferred for some positions

Experience—Previous work experience generally required; work experience in aerospace industry preferred

Special Skills and Personality Traits—Problem-solving, communication, interpersonal, teamwork, and self-management skills; curious, creative, innovative, persistent, determined, flexible, confident

Special Requirements—Professional Engineer (P.E.) license may be required

CAREER LADDER

Senior Engineer

Engineer

Junior or Assistant Engineer

Position Description

Engineers apply the principles of science and mathematics, as well as their engineering knowledge and skills, to create products and systems of all kinds that are useful for humanity.

In the aerospace manufacturing industry, Engineers are involved in the creation of safe and reliable products for commercial purposes. These products include aircraft, space vehicles, rockets, missiles, and satellites, as well as the many parts and systems that make up these complex machines. Engineers are also concerned in designing the tools, machinery, processes, and facilities needed for producing the products efficiently and economically for aerospace companies.

Aerospace companies typically employ Engineers from several engineering backgrounds. The following are just a few of the various engineering specialists who work in the aerospace industry.

- Aerospace engineers specialize in creating new or improved technologies for aircraft, spacecraft, missiles, and related parts.
- Electrical and electronic engineers are concerned with electrical and electronic devices and systems, as well as the use of electrical energy. They work on the various electrical components and systems that run aircraft, spacecraft, missiles, and rockets.
- Computer engineers are involved in developing the different types of computer hardware, software, and systems needed for aerospace vehicles. For example, they might work on avionics, robots, flight control systems, or communications systems.
- Mechanical engineers specialize in the creation of devices, machines, and mechanical systems for aerospace vehicles—such as engines, control devices, air-conditioning

systems, and hydraulic systems. They also design robots for use in manufacturing processes and create tools for other engineers to use.
- Materials engineers specialize in working with metals, ceramics, plastics (or polymers), and composites (which are made of two or more materials). They help manufacturers determine the best materials to use for their products, as well as develop new or improved materials for specific uses. For example, many materials engineers are involved in developing materials for aircraft that are lightweight, yet strong, and can handle very high temperatures.
- Chemical engineers deal with industrial chemical processes that change raw materials into products. They are involved with the use and production of chemicals as well as with the design of equipment for processing and treating chemicals.
- Environmental engineers address environmental issues that their companies must handle. They seek solutions that serve to prevent, control, and fix problems related to air quality, water quality, hazardous waste management, noise pollution, and other environmental concerns.
- Manufacturing engineers are involved in creating and maintaining efficient and reliable manufacturing systems for producing products. For example, manufacturing engineers develop ways to make products that are less expensive for their companies.
- Industrial engineers help companies use their resources—employees, machinery, information, materials, and so on—most effectively and economically. These specialists apply engineering analysis and techniques to solve problems in the production process, such as those involving high costs for supplies, low productivity by employees, or poor product quality.

The various Engineers work closely together on projects, each bringing their particular engineering expertise to a project. For example, aerospace engineers might work with electrical engineers to design navigation instruments, or with mechanical engineers to develop engines.

In addition to being hired for their particular engineering backgrounds, Engineers are employed to perform specific functions. They may be involved in any aspect of research, development, design, testing, production, or customer support. The following are some of the duties that certain Engineers perform in aerospace manufacturing companies. (Many Engineers work in more than one function throughout their careers.)

- Research engineers seek ways to apply basic principles and knowledge of science, mathematics, and engineering to creating new (or improved) commercial products or manufacturing processes.
- Development engineers apply research findings toward developing new or improved products or manufacturing processes.
- Analytical engineers conduct in-depth assessments of proposed products and evaluate whether the design of each product meets customer requirements.
- Design engineers take ideas or working models of products and create designs that can be manufactured economically, as well as meet customer requirements and industry standards.
- Test engineers design and perform a range of tests to determine whether products meet specifications
- Systems engineers are responsible for ensuring that all system components of a product design are interfacing correctly.
- Manufacturing production engineers oversee the daily operation of specific manufacturing processes, making sure that products are being made according to specifications.
- Process design engineers are involved in the development of new or improved manufacturing processes.
- Sales engineers contact customers and make sales presentations to demonstrate how products or services can fulfill their particular needs.
- Technical service engineers provide maintenance service and technical assistance to customers after products have been delivered to them.

Besides their fellow Engineers, they work with scientists, technicians, craftsmen, and production staff members in the different phases of development and production. Some Engineers also confer or collaborate with staff from other departments, such as marketing.

Engineers work in offices, laboratories, and production sites. They have a 40-hour work schedule, but put in additional hours as needed to complete tasks and to meet deadlines. In some companies, Engineers work shifts. Some Engineers are required to travel to meet with government officials, suppliers, or customers.

Salaries

Salaries for Engineers vary, depending on their field, education, experience, employer, geographical location, and other factors. According to the May 2003 *Occupational Employment Statistics* survey (by the U.S. Bureau of Labor Statistics), the estimated annual salary for most Engineers ranged between $30,870 and $92,040.

Employment Prospects

Engineers are employed by major aerospace firms, such as Boeing, Lockheed Martin, and Raytheon as well as by many smaller firms that produce specific parts and systems for the larger companies. Other engineering opportunities in the fields of aviation and aerospace may be found in the federal government, particularly with the U.S. Department of Defense, the Federal Aviation Administration (FAA), and the National Aeronautics and Space Administration (NASA).

In general, job prospects for well-prepared individuals in engineering are strong. Engineering is the second largest profession in the United States, and some experts are projecting a shortage of experienced Engineers in the future due to the lower number of students earning engineering degrees.

The U.S. Bureau of Labor Statistics reports that the demand for Engineers in the aerospace industry is projected to grow by 10 percent over the 2000–10 period. Replacements for a large number of Engineers are expected, as many of them will be reaching retirement age within this period. Electrical and computer engineers are predicted to be most in demand by employers.

Advancement Prospects

Depending on their interests and ambitions, Engineers can advance their careers in various ways. For example, they can seek positions in areas that interest them, such as design, process, technical support, or research. As they gain experience, Engineers become team leaders and project managers. Those with administrative and management ambitions can rise through the ranks to executive officer positions. Entrepreneurial Engineers can become independent consultants or owners of engineering consulting firms.

With their backgrounds, Engineers can obtain further education to pursue professional careers in such fields as medicine, law, politics, education, and business.

Education and Training

Minimally, Engineers must possess a bachelor's degree in the engineering discipline of their choice. Employers may require that Engineers have a master's or doctoral degree for some positions. For example, an aerospace manufacturing firm might prefer to hire Engineers with advanced degrees for research positions.

Engineers who eventually wish to teach in academic settings must obtain a doctorate.

Engineers enroll in education and training programs throughout their careers to update their knowledge and skills.

Special Requirements

Engineers must be licensed as Professional Engineers (P.E.) if they offer engineering services directly to the public or perform work that affects the life, health, or property of the public. Requirements for P.E. licensure vary among the states, territories, and Washington, D.C. For specific information, contact the state board of engineering examiners where you wish to practice.

Experience, Special Skills, and Personality Traits

Entry-level candidates should have work experience related to the position for which they are applying. They may have gained their experience through internships, student research projects, summer employment, or other means. Having work experience in the aerospace industry is desirable.

To work effectively at their jobs, Engineers must have excellent problem-solving, communication, interpersonal, and teamwork skills. They should also have strong self-management skills, such as the ability to meet deadlines, handle stressful situations, work independently, and organize and prioritize tasks.

Being curious, creative, innovative, persistent, determined, flexible, and confident are some personality traits that successful Engineers share.

Unions and Associations

Many Engineers belong to professional associations to take advantage of networking opportunities, training programs, professional certification, publications, job listings, and other professional services and resources. Some of the various societies that serve the diverse interests of Engineers include:

- American Institute for Chemical Engineers
- American Institute of Aeronautics and Astronautics
- American Society for Quality
- ASM International—The Materials Information Society
- ASME International (American Society of Mechanical Engineers)
- Association for Computing Machinery
- Institute of Electrical and Electronics Engineers
- Institute of Industrial Engineers
- Society of Women Engineers

Professional Engineers are eligible to join the National Society of Professional Engineers.

At some aerospace plants, Engineers belong to a labor union, such as the International Federation of Professional and Technical Engineers, which represents them in negotiations for contractual terms relating to pay, benefits, and working conditions.

Tips for Entry

1. In high school, you can prepare for a career in engineering by taking mathematics courses—algebra, geometry, trigonometry, and calculus—as well as such science courses as chemistry, physics, and biology. Courses in foreign languages, social studies, economics, composition, speech, and computer programming are also helpful.
2. Get an idea of the requirements needed for the types of engineering positions you wish to obtain. You could talk with engineers, request an information interview with employers, scan job ads, and read books about engineering.
3. When you are conducting a job search, take advantage of your college career center as well as professional societies that serve your field. In addition to offering job listings, these groups can help you learn effective job search skills and formulate a career plan.

4. Use the Internet to learn more about the field of engineering. Some Web sites that can provide you with information are Graduating Engineer and Computer Careers Online, http://www.graduatingengineer.com; Discover Engineering Online, http://www.discoverengineering.org; Junior Engineering Technical Society, http://www.jets.org; The Pre-Engineering Portal, http://www.engineerinyou.com; and National Academy of Engineering, http://www.nae.edu.

AEROSPACE ENGINEERING TECHNICIAN

CAREER PROFILE

Duties: Assist engineers and scientists in the development or production of aerospace products; perform duties as required of position

Alternate Title(s): Aerospace Technician; Aerospace Technologist

Salary Range: $36,000 to $74,000

Employment Prospects: Fair

Advancement Prospects: Fair

Prerequisites:

Education or Training—Associate or bachelor's degree in aerospace technology, engineering technology, or another related field

Experience—Related work experience generally required

Special Skills and Personality Traits—Communication, teamwork, interpersonal, computer, writing, math, and problem-solving skills; practical, resourceful, detail-oriented, curious, logical, creative

CAREER LADDER

Senior Aerospace Engineering Technician

Aerospace Engineering Technician

Trainee

Position Description

Aerospace Engineering Technicians are responsible for constructing, installing, testing, operating, and maintaining technologies that are designed to improve air travel and space exploration. They are involved in the creation of various types of aircraft, space vehicles, satellites, missiles, and rockets. They also are engaged in the development of engines, control devices, propulsion systems, navigation systems, launching and tracking systems, or any of the many thousands of parts and systems that go into building an aerospace vehicle.

In aerospace companies, they work on engineering teams composed of engineers, scientists, craftspeople, and others. Their role is to assist engineers and scientists with solving technical problems in the various phases of product development and manufacturing. These technicians also are responsible for carrying out the technical plans of the engineers and scientists. For example, Aerospace Engineering Technicians might prepare engineering drawings based on specifications; build prototypes or models of newly designed products; conduct tests on parts or systems under simulated operational conditions; construct facilities for testing vehicle parts or systems; monitor and inspect products to ensure that they meet quality standards; or identify ways to improve manufacturing processes.

As they become experienced, many Aerospace Engineering Technicians specialize in working in a particular segment of the aerospace industry, such as general aviation, commercial aviation, military aviation, or space exploration. Some technicians also specialize in a particular subject matter (such as aerodynamics, propulsion, or avionics) or a specific function (such as flight-test evaluation or quality control). In some companies, Aerospace Engineering Technicians hold job titles that reflect their specialty. For example, avionics technicians test, troubleshoot, repair, and operate electronic systems, while quality control technicians examine products to ensure that they meet approved standards.

Their duties vary, depending on the work they perform. For example, Aerospace Engineering Technicians who work in research and development assist with solving technical problems in a wide range of areas, such as fuel efficiency or air resistance. Their duties might include building test equipment, preparing experiments, operating wind tunnels, collecting and analyzing data, and assembling prototypes or models.

Aerospace Engineering Technicians also perform many tasks that are similar, regardless of their positions. Some of these general activities include:

- collecting and analyzing data
- making calculations
- evaluating information against standards
- discussing data requirements and results with engineers or other personnel
- setting up and testing prototypes or products
- constructing, operating, maintaining, and repairing test instruments
- determining the causes of equipment malfunctions
- preparing drawings, diagrams, blueprints and scale models, according to engineering specifications
- making or assembling prototypes while following engineering specifications
- preparing technical reports, specifications, estimates, and other materials
- setting up, operating, monitoring, and maintaining computer systems and devices to perform various tasks
- keeping all equipment and laboratories in working order

Entry-level Aerospace Engineering Technicians usually start their careers by performing routine tasks under the supervision of experienced technicians, engineers, or scientists. As they gain experience, they are assigned increasingly greater responsibilities. Senior technicians may also be responsible for supervising production workers or other employees.

Aerospace Engineering Technicians are expected to stay abreast of new developments and technologies. They read technical journals and books, network with colleagues, enroll in training and education programs, attend professional conferences, and so on.

Aerospace Engineering Technicians work in offices, in laboratories, or at production sites. They may be required to wear protective equipment to decrease the risk of exposure to chemicals, toxic materials, or other hazards. They generally work 40 hours a week and put in additional hours when required. In some companies, they work shifts.

Salaries

Salaries for Aerospace Engineering Technicians vary, depending on such factors as their education, experience, job responsibilities, employer, and geographical location. According to the May 2003 *Occupational Employment Statistics* survey (by the U.S. Bureau of Labor Statistics), the estimated annual salary for most Aerospace Engineering Technicians ranged between $36,120 and $73,690.

Employment Prospects

In addition to aerospace manufacturing firms, Aerospace Engineering Technicians are employed by the federal government, in particular the U.S. Department of Defense and the National Aeronautics and Space Administration (NASA).

According to the U.S. Bureau of Labor Statistics, the job prospects for engineering technicians are projected to grow by 10 to 20 percent in the United States through the year 2010. However, job growth for Aerospace Engineering Technicians is expected to increase more slowly—nine percent or less—during this same period.

Advancement Prospects

Many Aerospace Engineering Technicians realize advancement by earning higher salaries and receiving more difficult assignments. Technicians with leadership talents and skills can advance to lead and supervisory positions.

With additional education, Aerospace Engineering Technicians can become engineers.

Education and Training

Minimally, most employers require that Aerospace Engineering Technicians possess an associate degree in aerospace technology, engineering technology, or another related field. For technologist positions, employers generally require that applicants possess a bachelor's degree in engineering technology or a related field.

Most Technicians prepare for this field through formal training programs. They may acquire their training through aerospace technology or engineering technology programs at two-year and four-year colleges, technical institutes, vocational schools, or college extension programs. Some Aerospace Engineering Technicians receive training while serving in the U.S. Armed Forces.

Employers provide new employees with on-the-job training programs. Throughout their careers, Aerospace Engineering Technicians enroll in training and continuing education programs to update their technical skills and knowledge.

Experience, Special Skills, and Personality Traits

Requirements vary with the different employers, as well as with the type of position for which candidates apply. In general, employers seek candidates who have previous work experience related to the available position. Entry-level candidates may have gained experience through internships, work-study programs, summer employment, or similar means.

Having communication, teamwork, and interpersonal skills is essential for Aerospace Engineering Technicians, as they must be able to work well with engineers, scientists, and others. In addition, they must have adequate computer, writing, and math skills, as well as strong problem-solving skills.

Being practical, resourceful, detail-oriented, curious, logical, and creative are some personality traits that successful Aerospace Engineering Technicians have in common.

Unions and Associations

Many Aerospace Engineering Technicians belong to a labor union, such as the International Association of Machinists and Aerospace Workers. A union represents members in negotiations with their employers for contractual terms relating to pay, benefits, and working conditions.

Tips for Entry

1. While in high school, check out engineering technology programs at colleges you might like to attend. Find out which courses you can take in high school to prepare for those programs. Ask your school counselor or career guidance counselor for help.
2. Be aware that engineering technology programs vary in type and quality among public and private institutions. Carefully research programs before enrolling in them. Make sure they provide a balance of academic and hands-on learning that would give you the appropriate skills and experience to obtain jobs.
3. Companies often interchange the job titles *technician* and *technologist.* These two positions usually have the same responsibilities, but technologist positions generally require a bachelor's degree. Therefore, read job announcements carefully to make sure that you meet requirements and have qualifying experience for the job.
4. Use the Internet to learn more about aerospace engineering technicians. To get a list of relevant Web sites, enter the keywords *aerospace engineering technician* into any search engine.

RESEARCH SCIENTIST

CAREER PROFILE

Duties: Apply scientific principles to the development of new products and manufacturing processes or the improvement of existing ones; plan and conduct experiments; perform duties as required

Alternate Title(s): Research and Development (R&D) Scientist, a title that reflects a specialty such as Chemist; Physicist; or Materials Scientist

Salary Range: $31,000 to $132,000

Employment Prospects: Fair

Advancement Prospects: Good

Prerequisites:

Education or Training—Master's or doctoral degree in a science or mathematics discipline

Experience—Work and research experience related to the desired position is required

Special Skills and Personality Traits—Leadership, teamwork, interpersonal, writing, communication, presentation, and self-management skills; analytical, flexible, creative, curious, enthusiastic, dedicated

CAREER LADDER

Senior Research Scientist or Principal Investigator

Research Scientist

Research Associate

Position Description

In the aerospace manufacturing industry, Research Scientists have backgrounds in the various disciplines of physical science, life science, earth science (or geoscience), mathematics, computer science, and social science. They are chemists, physicists, material scientists, mathematicians, statisticians, operation research analysts, computer scientists, atmospheric scientists, environmental scientists, aerospace medicine specialists, and so forth.

These Research Scientists are engaged in the creation of a wide range of aerospace products, including general aviation aircraft, commercial airliners, military aircraft, missiles, rockets, satellites, engines, propulsion units, radar systems, computer systems, and navigation systems. They are also involved in the development and design of manufacturing processes that are more efficient and cost-effective for aerospace companies.

Unlike their colleagues in academic, governmental, or private research laboratories, industrial Research Scientists conduct applied research for commercial purposes. They apply principles and knowledge of their disciplines (such as chemistry) to create new products and manufacturing processes or to improve existing ones for their employers. On occasion, industrial Research Scientists conduct basic research in order to gain new knowledge or understanding about theories or concepts that would help them with their applied research.

Research Scientists are concerned with studying aircraft or space vehicles, the performance of aerospace vehicles, and pilots in flight. They may be involved in such investigations as:

- finding the most efficient shape for an aircraft so it offers least resistance in flight
- developing propulsion systems that allow vehicles to fly longer without refueling
- seeking new materials for airplanes that are stronger or that can handle higher temperatures while in flight
- developing new techniques for building aircraft that are more efficient

- solving the operating problems that occur when flying at higher speeds
- understanding human reactions to flight

Industrial Research Scientists typically work on projects in multidisciplinary teams, which are composed of scientists and engineers from different disciplines. Technicians, project managers, and others also are part of research projects. Some projects may involve collaboration with scientists from academic, government, or private research laboratories.

Regardless of their discipline, industrial Research Scientists perform many of the same duties in their work. For example, they:

- design and conduct experiments
- analyze and interpret data
- read scientific journals and other research literature
- plan and organize their work schedules
- make sure that governmental regulations as well as industry and company standards are being met
- meet with colleagues to discuss projects
- provide written or oral updates of studies at project meetings
- prepare written reports
- operate scientific instrumentation
- supervise research assistants and technicians, who provide administrative and research support

Research Scientists are required to follow standard company procedures and industry protocols. Furthermore, they are required to write detailed notes about the work they perform. Usually, their notes are submitted with applications for licenses, permits, patents, regulatory approval, as well as for other business and legal documentation.

Research Scientists are expected to stay up to date with developments and technologies in their scientific disciplines. This involves various activities, such as reading professional journals and books, attending professional conferences, enrolling in education or training programs, and networking with colleagues.

Research Scientists work mostly indoors in offices and laboratories. They generally work 40 hours a week but put in additional hours whenever necessary to complete various tasks.

Salaries

Salaries vary, depending on education, experience, discipline, industry, geographical location, and other factors. According to the May 2003 *Occupational Employment Statistics* survey (by the U.S. Bureau of Labor Statistics), most of the following scientists earned an estimated annual salary between these ranges:

- chemists, $31,220 to $93,100
- computer scientists, $45,070 to $128,200
- materials scientists, $37,520 to $110,340
- physicists, $49,880 to $131,570

Employment Prospects

Research Scientists are employed by small start-up companies as well as established corporations in the aerospace manufacturing industry. Most job openings are created to replace individuals who retire, transfer to other positions, or resign.

In addition to working in the private sector, aerospace scientists can pursue research opportunities at private and government research laboratories. They can also seek teaching positions at colleges and universities where they can also conduct research.

Advancement Prospects

Research Scientists can rise through the ranks of supervisory, managerial, and executive positions. For example, they can be promoted to higher positions and become principal investigators, program managers, laboratory directors, department managers, and executive officers. A Ph.D. may be required to obtain top management positions.

Education and Training

Holding a master's or doctoral degree is often the minimum requirement for a job as Research Scientist in the private sector. Research Scientists typically have earned advanced degrees in a physical science, biological science, geoscience, computer science, or mathematics discipline.

To obtain advanced degrees, students must first graduate from four-year colleges or universities with bachelor's degrees. Those students seeking a master's degree complete one or two years of study in their field. Earning a doctoral degree involves an additional five to eight years, which requires completing a dissertation based on original research.

Experience, Special Skills, and Personality Traits

Employers usually hire candidates who have work and research experience related to the positions for which they are applying. Experience may have been gained through past employment, student research projects, internships, fellowships, part-time employment, and so on. Ph.D. candidates for research scientist positions may be required to have several years of postdoctoral experience.

Research Scientists must have excellent leadership, teamwork, and interpersonal skills, as they must be able to work well with people from various backgrounds. They also need strong writing, communication, and presentation skills. In addition, they should have strong self-management skills, such as the ability to work independently, meet deadlines, and organize and prioritize tasks.

Successful Research Scientists share such personality traits as being analytical, flexible, creative, curious, enthusiastic, and dedicated.

Unions and Associations

Many Research Scientists belong to professional associations to take advantage of networking opportunities, continuing education programs, professional certification, publications, job listings, and other professional services and resources. They might join societies such as the American Institute of Aeronautics and Astronautics or Women in Aerospace, which serve the particular interests of scientists and others in aerospace technology. Research Scientists might also join scientific societies that represent scientists in general or their particular fields. Some of these professional associations include:

- American Association for the Advancement of Science
- Association for Computing Machinery
- American Chemical Society
- American Institute of Physics
- American Mathematical Society
- Society for Industrial and Applied Mathematics
- American Association for Artificial Intelligence

Tips for Entry

1. In high school, take courses in science, advanced mathematics, and English to begin preparing for a career in science.
2. Gain research experience during your undergraduate years by obtaining a research assistantship or by volunteering to work on a professor's research project.
3. Attend career fairs sponsored by colleges or community organizations. In addition to learning about job openings, take advantage of learning more about companies from their representatives.
4. Learn as much as you can about a company before you go to a job interview. One source for information is the Internet. Enter the name of the company into a search engine. You may find a Web site for the company as well as news articles about it.

COMPUTER SPECIALIST

CAREER PROFILE

Duties: Depending on the occupation, may conduct research, develop computer hardware, design software, analyze computer systems, oversee computer systems, provide computer technical support, or perform other primary responsibilities; perform duties as required of position

Alternate Title(s): A title that reflects a specific occupation such as Computer Hardware Engineer or Technical Support Specialist

Salary Range: $23,000 to $128,000

Employment Prospects: Good

Advancement Prospects: Good

Prerequisites:

Education or Training—Bachelor's degree, preferably in a computer science field

Experience—One or more years of work experience for entry-level positions; specialized experience for higher positions

Special Skills and Personality Traits—Analytical, problem-solving, communication, interpersonal, teamwork, and self-management skills; focused, detail-oriented, logical, patient, persistent, ingenious, imaginative

Special Requirements—Professional Engineer (P.E.) license may be required

CAREER LADDER

Senior Computer Specialist

Computer Specialist

Computer Specialist (entry-level)

Position Description

Various types of Computer Specialists are employed by aerospace manufacturing companies. Some of them are engaged in the development, design, production, or technical support of their firms' products. For example, Computer Specialists at a general aviation aircraft company might be part of a research and development team seeking to improve a control system for a single-engine airplane. Other Computer Specialists are involved in the planning, management, installation, and maintenance of their employers' computer-based information systems.

Among the Computer Specialists employed as industrial researchers are computer scientists. In aerospace manufacturing companies, they mostly conduct applied research to create new or improved products for commercial purposes. On occasion, they perform basic research to gain new knowledge and understanding about computers and computational processes in order to develop products. Research computer scientists study such diverse areas as computer architecture, numerical analysis, software engineering, operating systems, computer security, information management, artificial intelligence, robotics, and human and computer interactions.

Computer hardware engineers work specifically on the development and design of computers, from handheld computers to powerful supercomputers. They also develop embedded computers that are part of the devices that control aircraft, spacecraft, automation systems, or communication networks. In addition, these Computer Specialists are involved in designing the various parts that make up computers, such as circuit boards, processors, computer chips, networking boards, audio boards, and input tools.

Computer software engineers are involved in the research, production, and maintenance of software for aerospace products used in aviation and space exploration. Aerospace firms also employ software engineers to design different software systems used in scientific research, manufacturing, finance, human resources, management, and other areas of their companies.

Many aerospace firms employ computer systems analysts to help them achieve the maximum benefit from their investment in computer equipment, software, processes, and personnel. Systems analysts plan and design computer systems that fit a company's particular needs for business operations, payroll, accounting, engineering, manufacturing, and other purposes. They also coordinate tests and observe the initial use of the systems to ensure that they perform as planned.

Other Computer Specialists at aerospace firms are involved with writing, testing, and maintaining programs (or software) that instruct computers how to perform their functions. These specialists are known as computer programmers. They write programs from specifications developed by software engineers or systems analysts. This generally involves converting a design into a logical series of instructions, then coding it in a programming language such as Prolog, Java, or C++. Programmers may hold job titles that describe the programming language they use (such as Prolog programmer) or the function that they perform (such as database programmer).

In some companies, some Computer Specialists perform the job of both a computer systems analyst and a programmer. They are known as programmer-analysts.

Because companies have vast amounts of data stored on their computers, they employ Computer Specialists known as database administrators. They are responsible for ensuring that the various databases in their employer's computer systems are organized, managed, and stored efficiently. Other Computer Specialists, known as network administrators, are responsible for designing, installing, and maintaining their company's communication networks. These include such network systems as the company's local area network (LAN), the connection of computers within a company; wide area network (WAN), the connection to computers outside the company; and internetworks (such as the Internet), the connection of the company's computers to several communication networks at the same time.

Computer security is another job that some Computer Specialists perform for aerospace firms. Computer security specialists or information systems security specialists are responsible for safeguarding a company's information assets and computer-based information system from theft, tampering, accidental erasures, virus corruption, natural disasters, and so on. Their job involves coordinating, planning, designing, and implementing information security measures.

Many aerospace firms have Web sites on the World Wide Web as part of their marketing and sales strategies. They employ one or more Computer Specialists to create, design, and maintain Web sites. Some of these specialists are Webmasters, who oversee and manage company Web sites; Web designers, who create and design the Web pages; and Web site administrators, who keep Web sites running and updated.

Some Computer Specialists are responsible for providing technical assistance to computer users, who may be company employees or customers. They are usually known as computer support specialists and may also be known by such other job titles as help-desk technician, technical support specialist, and customer service representative. These Computer Specialists answer questions or troubleshoot problems that computer users might have about computer hardware, software, or computer systems.

Many Computer Specialists interact with coworkers—Computer Specialists as well as other employees—and customers. Computer engineers, programmers, and other specialists usually work as part of a team to develop, design, or install computer systems. Some Computer Specialists—such as systems analysts, database administrators, and network administrators—may work in any department within a company, including engineering, design, manufacturing, marketing, sales, business administration, and so on.

Computer Specialists typically work in offices or laboratories. They work a 40-hour week but sometimes put in additional hours to complete tasks or to resolve unexpected problems. Some Computer Specialists, such as computer security specialists, may be required to be on call 24 hours a day for emergencies.

Salaries

Salaries vary, depending on such factors as occupation, education, experience, employer, and geographical location. The U.S. Bureau of Labor Statistics, in its May 2003 *Occupational Employment Statistics* survey, reports the following estimated salary ranges for most of these computer professionals:

- research computer scientists and information scientists, $45,070 to $128,200
- computer hardware engineers, $48,210 to $117,170
- computer software engineers (systems software), $47,870 to $114,070
- computer software engineers (applications), $45,970 to $111,860
- network systems and data communications analysts, $35,320 to $93,100
- network and computer systems administrators, $35,740 to $88,440
- computer support specialists, $23,380 to $68,120

Employment Prospects

In addition to working in the private sector, Computer Specialists can find opportunities for working in aerospace technology with the federal government, private research institutions, and academic institutions. Some Computer Specialists are employed on a contractual basis as independent contractors or consultants.

In general, most opportunities become available as Computer Specialists retire, advance to higher positions, or transfer to other occupations. The Bureau of Labor Statistics reports that computer scientists, systems analysts, database administrators, software engineers, and computer hardware engineers are expected to be employed in the fastest growing occupations through 2010. Opportunities in the aerospace industry should be favorable for well-prepared Computer Specialists who have stayed up to date with technology.

Advancement Prospects

Computer Specialists with administrative and management ambitions can advance to become project managers, division directors, and executive officers. Those with entrepreneurial ambitions can start their own consulting firms.

Education and Training

The educational requirements vary for the different occupations. Minimally, Computer Specialists must possess a bachelor's degree, preferably in technical disciplines closely related to the work they wish to perform. For example, computer hardware engineers usually hold a bachelor's degree in electrical engineering, computer engineering, or a related field. Employers may hire Computer Specialists with a nontechnical degree, as long as they have qualifying computer training or experience.

To obtain research and management positions, Computer Specialists usually are required to possess a master's or doctoral degree. For example, employers prefer that robotics researchers possess a master's or doctoral degree in robotics, computer science, mechanical engineering, or another related field.

Throughout their careers, Computer Specialists enroll in training and continuing education programs to update their skills and keep up with technological advancements. They may complete courses, seminars, or workshops that are offered by employers, vendors, academic institutions, and professional computing societies.

Special Requirements

Computer hardware engineers and software engineers may be required by their employers to be licensed as Professional Engineers (P.E.) in the states where they practice. Engineers who offer their services directly to the public or perform work that affects the public safety and welfare are required to be licensed. For specific licensure information, contact the state board of examiners for professional engineers where you wish to practice.

Many computer engineers obtain P.E. licenses voluntarily to enhance their employability. Entry-level engineers may apply for the Engineer-in-Training licensure.

Experience, Special Skills, and Personality Traits

Applicants for entry-level positions need one or more years of work experience related to the jobs for which they are applying. Higher level positions typically require specialized experience or graduate-level training.

To perform well at their work, Computer Specialists must have strong analytical and problem-solving skills. In addition, they need adequate communication, interpersonal, and teamwork skills, as they must be able to work effectively with people from different backgrounds. Furthermore, they must have excellent self-management skills, including the ability to work independently, handle stressful situations, meet deadlines, and organize and prioritize tasks.

Being focused, detail oriented, logical, patient, persistent, ingenious, and imaginative are some personality traits that successful Computer Specialists have in common.

Unions and Associations

Computer Specialists join local, state, or national professional associations to take advantage of professional services and resources such as networking opportunities, education programs, and professional publications. Two major societies that offer programs for the various types of Computer Specialists are the Association for Computing Machinery and the Institute of Electrical and Electronics Engineers Computer Society.

Tips for Entry

1. Take advantage of internship or work-study programs while in college. If a company likes your work, it may offer you a full-time position after graduation. To learn about such programs, talk with your college adviser or a college career counselor.
2. Read job descriptions carefully, as job titles vary from company to company.
3. To enhance their employability, many Computer Specialists obtain professional certification from professional associations or other organizations.
4. To stay competitive, keep up with the latest technology.
5. Learn more about the various computer occupations on the Internet. To get a list of relevant Web sites, enter the name of the occupation, such as *computer software engineer* or *computer analyst,* into a search engine.

PRODUCTION MANAGER

CAREER PROFILE

Duties: Plan, direct, control, and coordinate the resources and activities required to produce finished products; perform duties as required

Alternate Title(s): Manufacturing Manager; Plant Manager; Production Supervisor; Operations Manager; Director of Operations

Salary Range: $41,000 to $120,000

Employment Prospects: Fair

Advancement Prospects: Fair

Prerequisites:

Education or Training—Bachelor's or master's degree in industrial engineering, industrial management, business administration, or another related field

Experience—Several years of experience in a manufacturing setting, preferably in the aerospace industry; an advanced degree may be substituted for one or more years of work experience

Special Skills and Personality Traits—Leadership, negotiation, interpersonal, problem-solving, planning, organizational, writing, communication, and computer skills; persuasive, well-rounded, analytical, detail-oriented, personable, flexible, self-motivated

CAREER LADDER

Plant Manager

Production Manager

Assistant Production Manager or Production Line Supervisor

Position Description

The ability of aerospace companies to operate at a profit—and by how much of a profit—depends on how much more efficiently they can manufacture their finished products than their competitors. It is the job of Production Managers to plan, direct, control, and coordinate the resources and activities required to produce finished products. They ensure that production programs are being completed on time and do not exceed the allocated budget. In addition, these managers are responsible for resolving any problems that occur within the manufacturing process.

Their primary responsibility is creating production plans that meet time and money constraints. They first review the production orders, scheduled delivery dates, and budgets upon which they determine completion dates for production programs. They prepare production schedules, which entails analyzing and forecasting the requirements for staffing, equipment, and supplies (or raw materials). They must take into consideration such questions as What machinery and equipment are needed? Will equipment need to be purchased? Will any machines need to be repaired? How much manpower is needed? Will extra shifts or overtime be required? Should the company hire additional staff? What supplies need to be purchased? If supplies are on back order, when are they expected to be delivered?

Aerospace Production Managers inform management if new equipment or additional manpower may be required. Additionally, they must be able to demonstrate to management that making investments of millions of dollars for production would, in the long run, be cost effective for their company.

Production Managers coordinate with program managers to implement production requirements, and monitor production on a regular basis to ensure that schedules are being met. If production is behind schedule, Production Managers determine whether overtime or additional work shifts should be required.

Another important duty of Production Managers is to monitor production standards. If products have been determined to be substandard, Production Managers are responsible for promptly investigating and recommending corrective actions. They look into various factors that may have contributed to poor quality, such as job performance, equipment performance, production methods, and substandard supplies. If the problem is found to be in the quality of job performance, then Production Managers might suggest that better training programs be implemented. If the problem is due to the quality of raw materials, then Production Managers might recommend finding new suppliers who have proven records of delivering quality materials.

In addition, aerospace Production Managers are responsible for ensuring that production departments comply with all policies, procedures, and practices regarding quality, safety, human resources, and manufacturing. This includes compliance with company protocols, aerospace industry standards, and governmental regulations. In some companies, Production Managers are also involved with planning training programs, hiring new production workers, and conducting job performance evaluations.

Furthermore, in an aerospace company, Production Managers are in charge of coordinating production activities with various departments. For example, Production Managers work with the procurement department to ensure that plant inventories are maintained, and they work with the purchasing department to make sure that a sufficient amount of supplies for production is ordered in a timely fashion. In addition, Production Managers work closely with the other department heads to plan and implement company goals, policies, and procedures.

These managers also work with production staff as well as with executive officers. Some Production Managers are designated the liaison between first-line supervisors and management.

Their job requires performing a variety of tasks each day, such as:

- setting work priorities
- analyzing production data
- monitoring production processes
- troubleshooting production problems
- attending departmental or program meetings
- preparing correspondence, memos, reports, documents, or other required paperwork
- providing verbal or written progress reports about production activities and resources to superiors
- maintaining accurate records and files

Production Managers usually report to the plant manager or the vice president for manufacturing. In aerospace manufacturing plants with several operations (such as machining or assembly), different Production Managers may be responsible for the different operations.

They are expected to stay abreast of new production technologies and management practices. They read professional and trade publications, attend trade shows, and aerospace industry conferences. They might also enroll in workshops, seminars, and continuing education courses.

Production Managers have a 40-hour work schedule, but most work additional hours, particularly when meeting production deadlines. Some Production Managers are on call on a 24-hour basis to handle emergencies as they occur.

Salaries

Earnings for Production Managers vary, depending on such factors as their experience, education, job responsibilities, employer, and geographical location. According to the May 2003 *Occupational Employment Statistics* survey (by the U.S. Bureau of Labor Statistics), the estimated annual salary for most Production Managers (in all industries) ranged from $41,270 to $120,080.

Employment Prospects

The U.S. Bureau of Labor Statistics reports that the job growth in the aerospace industry is expected to increase by 19 percent over the 2000–10 period. Factors that can affect positive or negative growth in this industry include commercial aircraft sales, federal defense expenditures, growth of telecommunications, and exports of products to other countries.

In general, Production Managers should not be greatly affected by layoffs or organizational restructuring because their positions are essential to efficient manufacturing operations. However, most job openings will become available as Production Managers retire or transfer to other occupations.

Advancement Prospects

Many Production Managers realize advancement by earning higher salaries, receiving more responsibilities, and gaining professional recognition. Some managers obtain jobs with other employers in order to earn higher pay and perform jobs with greater responsibilities or challenges.

Highly skilled and experienced Production Managers may be able to advance to management positions by becoming a plant manager or vice president for manufacturing. Production Managers can also pursue a career path as management consultants.

Education and Training

In general, Production Managers possess a bachelor's or master's degree in industrial engineering, industrial management, business administration, or another related field. Many employers seek job candidates who hold a bachelor's degree in engineering and a master's degree in business administration or industrial management.

Production Manager trainees who have been hired directly from college typically receive several months of extensive training. They learn about a company's production processes, company policies, and job requirements, as well as the functions of the various departments (such as purchasing) in which they would be working. Some companies place college graduates in positions as production line supervisors to gain experience before promoting them to management positions.

Experience, Special Skills, and Personality Traits

Requirements vary with the different employers. In general, many employers require that job applicants have five or more years of related experience in a manufacturing environment, preferably in the aerospace industry. They may have had previous experience as project engineers, program managers, or project administrators. Some employers allow candidates to substitute one or more years of experience for advanced degrees.

Production Managers must have excellent leadership, negotiation, and interpersonal skills, as well as problem-solving, planning, and organizational skills in order to handle and prioritize multiple tasks. Having strong writing, communication, and computer skills is also essential.

Some personality traits that successful Production Managers share are being persuasive, well-rounded, analytical, detail-oriented, personable, flexible, and self-motivated.

Unions and Associations

Production Managers might join professional management associations such as the American Management Association. These organizations offer various professional services, such as continuing education programs, professional certification, and networking opportunities.

Tips for Entry

1. Gain experience by obtaining internships with manufacturers, particularly in the aerospace industry.
2. Follow the instructions on job applications completely. For example, if you are asked to include your salary history, be prepared to provide such information.
3. Some Production Managers have worked their way up through the ranks. Most have earned college degrees and have completed company-sponsored management programs.
4. Employers may require that applicants be U.S. citizens or possess the proper documentation to work in the United States. Some employers also require that applicants pass a security clearance.
5. Check out Web sites of companies for which you would like to work. In addition to learning more about a company, you may find job postings there. Many companies also allow job applicants to post their résumés or apply for positions online.

AEROSPACE MACHINIST

CAREER PROFILE

Duties: Produce metal parts for aircraft, spacecraft, engines, and other products; operate lathes, drill presses, borers, and other machine tools; fabricate items according to job orders; perform duties as required

Alternate Title(s): A title such as Experimental Machinist that reflects a specialty

Salary Range: $20,000 to $49,000

Employment Prospects: Fair

Advancement Prospects: Fair

Prerequisites:

Education or Training—High school diploma; complete machinist training through apprenticeship programs, formal postsecondary programs, or on-the-job training

Experience—Experience working with machine tools; working in manufacturing settings generally preferred

Special Skills and Personality Traits—Mechanical aptitude; abstract reasoning and spatial relations proficiencies; teamwork, interpersonal, communication, decision making, problem-solving, and self-management skills; precise, detail-oriented, focused, practical, analytical

CAREER LADDER

Lead Machinist or Supervisor

Machinist

Apprentice or Trainee

Position Description

Aerospace Machinists are responsible for producing complex metal parts for aircraft, spacecraft, missiles, rockets, engines, and other products. They are highly skilled craftsmen whose jobs involve operating large, heavy, sophisticated machine tools such as lathes, borers, grinders, shapers, drill presses, and milling machines. Applying their knowledge of mechanics, the properties of metals (such as steel and titanium), machine shop mathematics, layouts, and machining procedures, Aerospace Machinists fabricate metal parts of precise specifications that range in size and shape from tiny and ultrathin to large and heavy.

Aerospace Machinists engage in different types of work. Many of them are engaged in the production of final products and are known as production machinists. Their job usually involves producing large quantities of one specific part. Production machinists may also be responsible for finishing, fitting, or assembling the finished part.

Some Aerospace Machinists are involved in the research and development of new or modified products. They are known as experimental machinists or prototype machinists, and they work closely with engineers and designers. Prototype machinists typically create one-of-a-kind items for experimental purposes, which include mechanisms, tools, and equipment. They also participate in developing procedures for improving manufacturing processes.

Other Aerospace Machinists, usually called maintenance machinists, are responsible for repairing and renovating industrial equipment and machinery at manufacturing plants. When engines or machines break down, these machinists may need to modify parts, or craft new parts, to replace broken ones.

Regardless of the type of work they do, Aerospace Machinists perform the same general tasks in completing a job. They start by carefully preparing and planning each job. They study blueprints and written instructions to determine how a workpiece will look, and what materials and machine tools are needed. They also calculate how the workpiece should be cut and at what rate it should be cut. In addition, Aerospace Machinists plan the sequence of the cutting and finishing steps they need to perform. They then gather their tools and materials, after which they create a layout on the metal stock to show where cuts should be made.

Once they have completed their preparations, Aerospace Machinists set up their machines and perform the machining operations. Production machinists usually do a trial run and make one workpiece to ensure the preciseness of their work.

Aerospace Machinists constantly monitor the feed and speed of their machines to make sure they are running properly. They also make sure that the metal stock is being well lubricated and cooled, as machining operations can generate a high amount of heat. They adjust cutting speeds to compensate for rising temperatures and vibrations, accordingly. After they have finished an item, they check the quality of the item. They make sure that it meets the requirements of the job order and that it is free of any defects.

Other tasks that Aerospace Machinists may perform include:

- cleaning, oiling, and maintaining machine tools to ensure that they are running at the maximum level of efficiency
- repairing or making new parts for lathes, grinders, and other machine tools
- maintaining logs and records, as required
- training and supervising lower-level Aerospace Machinists

Many Aerospace Machinists work with computer numerically controlled (CNC) machine tools (or machinery), which contain computers that direct a machine's operations. By programming a CNC machine tool, they are able to set up the machine to perform several operations, thus allowing them to produce parts with a very high level of precision. With these machines, Aerospace Machinists usually perform computer simulations instead of trial runs to check the accuracy of their programs. Some of them are responsible for writing programs for the machines, whereas others work with CNC programmers who perform that duty.

Aerospace Machinists generally work in clean, well-lighted, and ventilated machine shops. They wear protective clothing (such as safety glasses and earplugs) and follow strict safety procedures to reduce the risk of injury that may occur from sharp cutting tools, high-speed machinery, dust, flying metal chips, loud noise levels, and other hazards.

They also use various hand tools, equipment, and measurement instruments (such as micrometers and calipers) for setting up, repairing, and adjusting the metal-working machines. Some Aerospace Machinists are required to supply their own set of hand tools.

Their job involves frequent physical activity. Aerospace Machinists typically stand for long periods of time, as well as lift, push, pull, or carry heavy objects. They also bend, stretch, twist, and reach out, and repeat the same movements throughout the day. Their work requires them to hold their arms and hands steadily in one position and to repeat the same movements throughout the day.

Most Aerospace Machinists work a 40-hour week. They sometimes work overtime in order to meet production deadlines or to perform emergency repairs on machinery. In some companies, Aerospace Machinists are assigned to work shifts.

Salaries

Salaries vary, depending on such factors as education, experience, employer, and geographical location. According to the May 2003 *Occupational Employment Statistics* survey (by the U.S. Bureau of Labor Statistics), the estimated annual salary for most machinists, in all industries, ranged from $20,340 to $48,590.

Employment Prospects

Aerospace Machinists work for aerospace manufacturing companies and firms that offer machining services to aerospace companies.

Job opportunities are generally good for highly experienced Aerospace Machinists.The Bureau of Labor Statistics reports that the job market outlook for machinists, in general, is expected to grow slowly (between zero and 9 percent) through 2010. Most job openings become available as Aerospace Machinists retire or transfer to other positions or occupations.

Advancement Prospects

Aerospace Machinists can advance in several ways. With additional training, they can become CNC machinists or CNC programmers. Aerospace Machinists can also advance to supervisory or administrative positions in their firms. Those with entrepreneurial ambitions might eventually start their own machine shops.

Education and Training

Minimally, Aerospace Machinists should possess a high school diploma or general equivalency diploma.

Aerospace Machinists can learn their trade through one of the following programs:

- an apprenticeship program, which is usually three to four years long
- a certificate or degree program at a vocational school, trade school, or two-year college
- an employer's on-the-job training program
- a job training program offered by a military service

Many Aerospace Machinists enroll in training or continuing education programs to gain additional skills and knowledge, such as CNC programming.

Experience, Special Skills, and Personality Traits

Employers generally prefer that entry-level applicants have experience working with machine tools. They should also have previous work experience in manufacturing settings. For example, some Aerospace Machinists have previously been employed as machine setters, operators, or tenders.

Aerospace Machinists must have a mechanical aptitude and be proficient in abstract reasoning and spatial relations. They should also have teamwork, interpersonal, and communication skills. Having strong decision-making and problem-solving skills is also important. In addition, they need excellent self-management skills, which include the ability to work with minimal supervision, meet deadlines, understand and follow instructions, and prioritize multiple tasks.

Being precise, detail-oriented, focused, practical, and analytical are some personality traits that successful Aerospace Machinists share.

Unions and Associations

Many Aerospace Machinists belong to a union, such as the International Association of Machinists and Aerospace Workers. A union represents members in negotiations with their employers for contractual terms relating to pay, benefits, and working conditions.

Tips for Entry

1. Some high school subjects that can help you prepare for a career as an Aerospace Machinist include math, general science, computer science, metalworking, blueprint reading, and mechanical drawing.
2. To learn about job openings, check newspaper want ads, school placement offices, state employment offices, and local unions.
3. When you turn in your application, ask for the name and the phone number of the person whom you can contact about the status of your job application and job vacancies. Make a point of calling that person on a regular basis.
4. Apply directly to aerospace companies. Use the Internet to learn more about different companies. To find a particular Web site, enter the name of the company into a search engine.

PRECISION ASSEMBLER

CAREER PROFILE

Duties: Assemble, install, and test aerospace parts and materials; perform duties as required

Alternate Title(s): Assembly Technician; a title that reflects a specific job such as Airframe Assembler or Electromechanical Assembler

Salary Range: $16,000 to $57,000

Employment Prospects: Fair

Advancement Prospects: Fair

Prerequisites:

Education or Training—High school diploma; complete an employer training program

Experience—Previous work experience related to position for which one is applying; skilled in the hand tools, power tools, and equipment that would be used

Special Skills and Personality Traits—Manual dexterity; good eyesight for those working with small parts; teamwork, interpersonal, communication, self-management, writing, and reading skills; ability to read blueprints and graphic aids; detail-oriented, accurate, precise, methodical

CAREER LADDER

Senior Assembler

Precision Assembler

Trainee

Position Description

In the aerospace manufacturing industry, Precision Assemblers are highly skilled workers who play a valuable role in constructing complex products that are safe and efficient. They are responsible for assembling aerospace parts and materials, installing units or subassemblies, and handling finished products. Some Precision Assemblers are also responsible for fabricating parts from raw materials.

Precision Assemblers are involved in different types of assembly work in the aerospace industry. Many of them are aircraft assemblers who work in aerospace plants. They are responsible for the final assembly of aerospace vehicles—such as commercial airplanes, jet fighters, helicopters, satellites, or missiles. They assemble and install the structure, surfaces, rigging, and systems that make up aerospace vehicles. Other aircraft assemblers are trained to either put together, fit, fasten, or install various parts, such as tails, wings, fuselage, landing gear, rigging and control equipment, communication systems, or heating and ventilating systems.

Many Precision Assemblers work for companies that supply aerospace plants with specific types of units, subassemblies, components, or equipment for aerospace vehicles. Some of them are electrical and electronic equipment assemblers. Their jobs involve putting together and installing systems and support structures such as radar, control systems, computers, and radio equipment. Other Precision Assemblers are electromechanical equipment assemblers. They construct devices that contain electronic sensors that monitor, control, or activate mechanical operations—such as aircraft ejection seat mechanisms and devices used for aircraft radar, communication, and navigation systems.

Precision Assemblers perform routine and nonroutine tasks, which vary according to their particular positions. They are responsible for completing their intricate tasks precisely and accurately. For example, aircraft structure assemblers must be accurate about positioning and aligning structural parts or trimming the parts to fit before installing them.

Their jobs involve reading and interpreting various materials to determine the type and configuration of the parts, the relationship of the parts to assemble, assembly instructions, and so on. These materials may include work orders, engineering specifications, blueprints, schematic diagrams, manuals, and computer-aided drafting systems.

Precision Assemblers use various hand tools, power tools, and measuring instruments to complete their different tasks. For example, Precision Assemblers use power drills to make bolt holes in parts, soldering irons to connect electrical wiring, and precision measuring tools (such as calipers and micrometers) to measure parts to make sure they conform to specifications.

Precision Assemblers follow standard procedures to ensure the production of high-quality products. Additionally, they adhere to all safety requirements established by their employers. Precision Assemblers continually check the quality of their work and, if necessary, remove or disassemble parts to fix, repair, or rework them in order to fit specifications. They also use the appropriate test equipment to test the reliability of their finished work.

Precision Assemblers work in an assembly line environment. They are expected to maintain a steady work pace to ensure the even flow of work from one station to the next. In some companies, Precision Assemblers specialize in performing specific tasks. In other companies, Precision Assemblers are part of teams that perform a certain set of assembly tasks. All team members learn the different tasks and take turns performing them.

Some experienced Precision Assemblers are involved in product development at their companies. They assist engineers and technicians by assembling prototypes or test products, according to engineering specifications.

Working conditions vary for Precision Assemblers. Many of them must stand or sit for long periods of time. Some of them lift objects weighing up to 35 or 40 pounds. Electronic and electromechanical assemblers typically work in a clean, well-lit, and well-ventilated environment. Aircraft assemblers generally work in large, noisy facilities. Their jobs may involve working inside aerospace vehicles. Some aircraft assemblers operate hoists or cranes to position aircraft engines and other heavy parts.

Precision Assemblers may be permanent or temporary employees. Most assemblers work a 40-hour week and are expected to work overtime in order to meet production or customer deadlines. Many Precision Assemblers work shifts.

Salaries

Earnings for Precision Assemblers vary, depending on such factors as their experience, job position, type of assembly work, employer, and geographical location. According to the May 2003 *Occupational Employment Statistics* survey (by the U.S. Bureau of Labor Statistics), the estimated annual salary for most Precision Assemblers ranged as follows:

- aircraft structure, surfaces, rigging, and systems assemblers, $20,560 to $56,530
- electromechanical equipment assemblers, $16,860 to $40,460
- electrical and electronic equipment assemblers, $16,330 to $36,960

Employment Prospects

Precision Assemblers are employed by aerospace product and parts manufacturing companies. They work for large aerospace companies such as Boeing, Lockheed-Martin, and Cessna, which complete the final assembly of their aircraft. Precision Assemblers also work for small and midsize companies that fabricate engines and the parts that supply larger companies.

Most job openings become available as Precision Assemblers retire or transfer to other positions or occupations. Employers typically create additional positions—temporary or permanent—to fit their growing needs or to fulfill their customers' demands for their products.

In recent years, there has been a growing trend for U.S. aerospace companies to outsource assembly jobs to companies in other nations because the cost of labor is lower in those countries.

With additional education and training, Precision Assemblers can pursue other careers in aerospace manufacturing by becoming machinists, engineering technicians, or engineers.

Advancement Prospects

Most Precision Assemblers realize advancement by earning higher wages and being given more responsibilities. As Precision Assemblers gain experience and become more skilled, they can advance to become quality control inspectors and supervisors. Additionally, experienced Precision Assemblers may become members of research and development teams, which work on creating new or better products.

Education and Training

Most employers prefer to hire Precision Assemblers who hold high school diplomas or general equivalency diplomas. For electrical, electronic, or electromechanical equipment assembler positions, some employers require that applicants have completed postsecondary technical programs or equivalent military training.

Employers train new employees on the various assembly duties they will be required to perform. Trainees generally receive several weeks of instruction, which include both classroom and on-the-job training.

Experience, Special Skills, and Personality Traits

Requirements vary with the different assembly positions and various employers. Many employers prefer to hire Precision Assemblers who have one to two years of assembly experience related to the type of position for which they are applying. Employers also prefer Precision Assemblers skilled in using hand tools, power tools, and other equipment required for a particular position.

Precision Assemblers must have manual dexterity. Those who would be working with small parts need good eyesight (with or without glasses).

In general, Precision Assemblers should have strong teamwork, interpersonal, and communication skills. Additionally, they must have excellent self-management skills, such as the ability to work independently, meet deadlines, understand and follow instructions, and prioritize multiple tasks. Precision Assemblers must also have adequate writing and reading skills, as well as the ability to read blueprints and graphic aids such as schematic diagrams.

Being detail-oriented, accurate, precise, and methodical are some personality traits that successful Precision Assemblers possess.

Unions and Associations

Many Precision Assemblers are members of a labor union, such as the International Association of Machinists and Aerospace Workers or the International Brotherhood of Electrical Workers. A union represents members in negotiations with their employers for contractual terms relating to pay, benefits, and working conditions.

Tips for Entry

1. If job openings are unavailable at the company where you wish to work, you might consider applying for lesser-skilled jobs. Many Precision Assemblers are promoted from the ranks within their companies.
2. To learn about job openings for Precision Assembler positions, contact aerospace manufacturers as well as your local state employment office. You might also contact the local office for the union representing the workers at the companies where you would like to work.
3. Some Precision Assemblers find jobs through friends, family members, and others who work at aerospace manufacturing firms.
4. Another source for employment is employment agencies that seek temporary or permanent workers for employers in the aerospace industries.
5. Many companies post information about job vacancies on their Web sites. Some companies prefer applicants to apply for jobs through their Web site.

QUALITY SPECIALIST

CAREER PROFILE

Duties: Devise quality systems that ensure the finished products, the supplies used for producing them, and all manufacturing processes comply with company and industrial standards; perform duties as required for a position

Alternate Title(s): Quality Control Specialist; Quality Assurance Specialist; Quality Engineer

Salary Range: $25,000 to $100,000

Employment Prospects: Good

Advancement Prospects: Good

Prerequisites:

Education or Training—Bachelor's degree in an engineering or a science discipline; master's degree in business administration may be required

Experience—Previous work experience required

Special Skills and Personality Traits—Self-management, computer, math, writing, communication, interpersonal, and teamwork skills; flexible, meticulous, detail-oriented, observant

CAREER LADDER

Senior Quality Specialist

Quality Specialist

Quality Technician or Quality Analyst

Position Description

The success of aerospace manufacturing firms relies greatly on the quality of the products they sell. In manufacturing, the term *quality* refers to products having all the characteristics required to meet customer satisfaction and to products being free of any defects or deficiencies. Therefore, to guarantee the quality of their products, manufacturers employ quality professionals who are involved throughout all the stages of product development and production.

Among the various quality professionals are Quality Specialists. Their primary responsibility is to devise quality systems that ensure company and industrial standards are being met for:

- the finished products
- the supplies used to produce products
- the processes used to manufacture products

Most manufacturers have two or more Quality Specialists on staff. They work in either the quality control unit or the quality assurance unit. Although the terms *quality control* and *quality assurance* are often used interchangeably, the two quality units have different responsibilities. The quality control staff is involved in the day-to-day inspections of raw materials, products, or packaging during the production processes. If the materials or products are found to be unsatisfactory, they may be thrown out or the work is done over. The quality assurance staff, on the other hand, is responsible for the development and monitoring of quality policies, procedures, and programs.

Quality Specialists generally perform one or more primary activities. For example, Quality Specialists may be involved in monitoring the quality of supplies used in production; evaluating manufacturing processes; auditing the activities of production and quality control departments; improving the safety and reliability of products; or examining the quality of the various aspects of company performance, such as employee training programs, customer service, and information systems.

Some Quality Specialists have engineering backgrounds, and may hold specific job titles, such as quality assurance engineer, quality process engineer, or reliability engineer, that reflect their particular function.

Quality Specialists perform various duties that are specific to their primary functions. They also have responsibilities in common, performing such tasks as:

- collecting, evaluating, and analyzing information
- performing statistical analyses
- developing, performing, and evaluating quality inspections and tests
- developing, modifying, applying, and maintaining quality standards
- performing problem-solving and troubleshooting
- training other quality staff members
- preparing documentation and reports
- maintaining accurate and detailed records
- meeting deadlines
- staying up to date with laws and industry standards that regulate the quality of products their companies manufacture

Quality Specialists work in offices or at production sites. They generally work a 40-hour week. Many of them work evening or night shifts, which may include weekends.

Salaries

Salaries for Quality Specialists vary, depending on such factors as their education, experience, job responsibilities, employer, and geographical location. According to the online *Guide to Career Prospects in Virginia* (http://www.ccps.virginia.edu/career_prospects/), annual salaries for Quality Specialists generally start from the low to mid $30,000s, while experienced specialists can earn up to $60,000 or more. Directors of quality assurance departments can earn salaries ranging up to $100,000. Webfeet.com reports that annual salaries for quality control and quality assurance professionals range from $25,000 to $100,000.

Employment Prospects

Because quality is vital to aerospace manufacturing, Quality Specialists will continually be needed. However, most openings become available as Quality Specialists retire, advance to other positions, or transfer to other occupations. Employers will create additional jobs to fit growing needs as long as resources are available.

Advancement Prospects

As they gain experience, Quality Specialists can advance through the ranks to become senior quality specialists, managers, and directors. Promotional opportunities within a company may be limited; therefore Quality Specialists may need to seek managerial and administrative positions with other employers.

Education and Training

Minimally, Quality Specialists must have at least a bachelor's degree in an engineering or science field. Many employers require or strongly prefer to hire candidates with a master's degree in engineering or business administration, with an emphasis on quality management.

Employers typically provide training for new employees.

Experience, Skills, and Personality Traits

Requirements vary for the different positions, as well as from employer to employer. Aerospace manufacturers typically hire Quality Specialists who have several years of quality experience, particularly in the industry (such as aviation supplier industry) in which they would be working. Many Quality Specialists have risen through the ranks, starting as technicians or analysts. Some employers allow candidates to substitute college degrees for one or more years of work experience.

Quality Specialists must have excellent self-management skills, which include the ability to organize and prioritize tasks, meet deadlines, handle stressful situations, and work independently. Having strong computer, math, writing, and communication skills is also essential. In addition, they should have effective interpersonal and teamwork skills. Being flexible, meticulous, detail oriented, and observant are some personality traits that successful Quality Specialists share.

Unions and Associations

Many Quality Specialists in the aerospace manufacturing industry are members of the American Society for Quality or other professional associations that service quality professionals. These organizations offer various professional services and resources such as training programs, professional certification programs, current research data, and networking opportunities.

Tips for Entry

1. While in college, gain experience in the field of quality by obtaining a part-time job, summer job, or internship.
2. To enhance their employability and advancement prospects, some Quality Specialists have obtained professional certification through recognized organizations such as the American Society for Quality.
3. Take advantage of resources such as state employment offices, career centers, professional associations, and Internet job banks to learn about job openings.
4. Before taking a job offer, be sure you understand how the quality department is structured and what kind of career advancement opportunities are available to you. Be aware that organizational structure and advancement opportunities vary from one company to the next. Be sure to ask a prospective employer before taking any job offer.
5. Use the Internet to learn more about the quality control field. One Web site you might visit is the American Society for Quality, http://www.asq.org.

TEST PILOT

CAREER PROFILE

Duties: Conduct flight tests of experimental, prototype, modified, or newly built aircraft; analyze and evaluate flight test data; prepare written reports and oral briefings; perform other duties as required

Alternate Title(s): Experimental Test Pilot; Engineering Test Pilot; Research Test Pilot; Production Pilot

Salary Range: $53,000 to $147,000

Employment Prospects: Fair

Advancement Prospects: Fair

Prerequisites:

Education or Training—Bachelor's degree in engineering, physics, or another related field; complete a flight test-pilot training program

Experience—Be an experienced pilot; have at least one year of work experience in flight testing, as either a test pilot or test engineer; must have completed a minimum number of hours of flight time as pilot-in-command

Special Skills and Personality Traits—Leadership, teamwork, interpersonal, communication, writing, critical-thinking, and observation skills; level-headed, adventurous, brave, calm, adaptable, detail-oriented, self-motivated

Special Requirements—FAA commercial pilot or airline transport pilot (ATP) certificate with instrument rating and appropriate aircraft ratings; first-class FAA medical certificate

CAREER LADDER

Chief Pilot

Test Pilot

Test Pilot Trainee

Position Description

Test Pilots have a job that is unlike other pilot jobs. These men and women fly aircraft—airplanes, helicopters, seaplanes, jet airliners, fighter jets, and other aircraft—that have never been flown before. They are responsible for performing flight tests on experimental, prototype, or newly produced aircraft. They might also do flight tests on aircraft that have been modified with new computers, flight systems, or other components.

Test Pilots are highly skilled pilots who have completed intensive flight-test training. In addition, most Test Pilots have backgrounds as aeronautical engineers. Their combination of flying and engineering expertise provides researchers and designers with valuable insights for developing safe and efficient aircraft.

In aircraft manufacturing firms, some Test Pilots are involved in the research and development phase of creating new or improved aircraft. These pilots are known as experimental test pilots or engineering test pilots. They perform flight tests on experimental, prototype, and modified aircraft to evaluate whether they meet designers' standards.

Other Test Pilots at aircraft manufacturing plants are involved in performing flight tests on aircraft that have just been built. These Test Pilots are known as production Test Pilots. They assess that newly-produced aircraft meet the expected performance and standards.

Whether they are experimental or production pilots, all Test Pilots are responsible for the safe operations of flight tests. They simulate flights that the aircraft have been designed to perform while they evaluate the aircraft for such factors as airworthiness, design, performance, and reliability. They also make sure that the aircraft meet company and industry standards as well as customers' requirements.

The job of Test Pilots involves a high level of risk as they ensure that the aircraft are operating properly and safely. Test Pilots perform difficult and dangerous tasks, such as landing in short fields or refueling in the air, to rate how well an aircraft performs. They also execute various emergency situations, which could occur through pilot error or system malfunctions. For example, a Test Pilot might assess how well a jet airplane responds to the loss of an engine or to jammed landing gear while in flight. In addition, Test Pilots fly aircraft at varying high speeds and take them through precise aerobatic maneuvers, such as loops, spins, turns, and falls to see how aircraft behave.

All flight tests are carefully planned by flight engineers and Test Pilots. They spend several months developing flight test plans and organizing them. For example, they calculate how much fuel will be needed, what altitudes to fly, and how an aircraft should be loaded in order to fly safely. All aerobatic maneuvers are meticulously worked out and practiced repeatedly before Test Pilots perform flight tests.

Flight tests are conducted during the day as well as at night. While in flight, pilots use test instruments and make careful observations to check engines, controls, brakes, landing gear, and the various flight systems. Test Pilots may perform flight tests alone or with copilots.

Like other pilots, Test Pilots are responsible for preflight, flight, and postflight duties. Some of their tasks include:

- preparing flight plans, which outline their routes, and estimated times of departure and arrival
- filing flight plans with air traffic controllers
- gathering and analyzing weather forecasts for routes and areas where they plan to fly
- monitoring weather conditions during their flights
- calculating the amount of fuel needed for completing flights
- performing preflight and postflight checks to ensure that the aircraft and all its systems are in proper working order
- obtaining clearance and instructions from air traffic controllers for takeoffs and landings
- monitoring instruments, aircraft systems, and fuel during flights
- completing flight reports, pilot logbooks, and other required paperwork
- complying with all federal aviation regulations as well as their company's policies and protocols

Test Pilots generally fly fewer hours than airline or commercial pilots. They spend many of their work hours on the ground, performing various duties. For example, they might:

- analyze and evaluate the data about their flight tests
- prepare detailed written reports and oral briefings that are clear and easy to understand
- attend staff meetings to discuss test findings, safety issues, and other matters
- conduct tests on new software programs or cockpit controls on flight simulators
- assist flight test engineers in preparing master flight plans for testing purposes
- participate in the drafting of technical papers, aircraft specifications, or other materials about the operations and design of new aircraft
- deliver aircraft to customers or designated locations
- train customers in the operation of aircraft
- supervise and direct the work of subordinate staff members

Test Pilots generally work a 40-hour week.

Salaries

Salaries vary, depending on such factors as education, experience, job duties, size of employer, and geographical location. According to Salary.com, as of December 2003, the annual salary for Test Pilots (who have at least two years of experience) ranged from $53,336 to $65,141, whereas Test Pilots who have at least 10 years of experience earned annual salaries between $117,605 and $146,697.

Employment Prospects

Besides aircraft manufacturing companies, Test Pilots are employed by the airlines and the federal government, including the U.S. military, the Federal Aviation Administration (FAA), and the National Aeronautics and Space Administration (NASA).

Opportunities for Test Pilots generally become available as individuals retire or transfer to other positions. Employers will create additional positions to meet growing needs.

Advancement Prospects

In aircraft manufacturing companies, Test Pilots can advance to become chief test pilots. Most Test Pilots measure their success through job satisfaction, professional recognition, and higher earnings.

Depending on their interests, ambitions, and qualifications, Test Pilots can pursue pilot and nonpilot careers in aviation and aerospace industries. For example, they might pursue careers as astronauts, airline pilots, commercial pilots, flight instructors, aerospace engineers, professors, air traffic controllers, or aviation managers.

Education and Training

Employers generally require that Test Pilots possess at least bachelor's degrees in engineering, physics, mathematics, or another related field. Many Test Pilots hold advanced degrees in their fields.

Test Pilots must complete test-pilot training, either through the military or at a private flight school. Test-pilot training programs are usually one year long, and cover such topics as aircraft performance, aircraft stability and control, as well as systems testing. Training is intense, and includes both classroom instruction and hands-on practice exercises in airplanes or helicopters. Students receive training in a variety of aircraft.

Special Requirements

Depending on their employers, Test Pilots are required to hold either a commercial pilot certificate or airline transport pilot (ATP) certificate, both granted by the FAA. Pilots must also possess instrument ratings and other appropriate aircraft ratings. In addition, they must maintain a first-class FAA medical certificate in order to retain their jobs.

Experience, Special Skills, and Personality Traits

Test Pilots in the private sector have entered this field in various ways. Some gained entry by first working as engineers in research, design, flight testing, and other areas with aircraft companies. Others gained experience as Test Pilots, aeronautical engineers, or flight test engineers through the military, the FAA, or NASA.

Requirements vary from employer to employer. Minimally, job applicants should have at least three years of general experience as pilots-in-command or copilots. In addition, they should have at least one year of professional experience as flight-test pilots, flight test engineers, or aeronautical engineers in the private sector, military, or civil service. Their experience should include such duties as obtaining and evaluating flight data related to the performance of prototype or production aircraft. Furthermore, candidates must complete a minimum number of hours of flight time as pilots-in-command, as required by employers. For example, an aircraft manufacturer might require that job applicants have completed at least 1,500 hours of flight time as pilots-in-command.

To perform well at their job, Test Pilots need excellent leadership, teamwork, and interpersonal skills. They must also have superior communication and writing skills, as they must be able to provide oral and written reports that are clear, concise, and easily understood. Additionally, Test Pilots must possess strong critical-thinking and observation skills.

Being level-headed, adventurous, brave, calm, adaptable, detail-oriented, and self-motivated are some personality traits that successful Test Pilots have in common.

Unions and Associations

Many Test Pilots are members of professional associations such as the Society of Experimental Test Pilots, the American Institute of Aeronautics and Astronautics, or the American Helicopter Society (AHS) International. These organizations offer various professional services and resources, such as education programs and networking opportunities.

Tips for Entry

1. The following are some courses you might take in high school to prepare for a career as a Test Pilot: algebra, geometry, trigonometry, calculus, physics, computer science, English composition, technical drawing, and basic mechanics or auto shop.
2. Talk with former and current Test Pilots to get an idea of how they work and what steps they took to get into the field.
3. Use the Internet to learn more about the field of flight testing. Some Web sites you might visit are Society of Experimental Test Pilots, http://www.setp.org; National Test Pilot School, http://www.ntps.com; and Test Pilot Stuff, http://www.testpilots.com.

TECHNICAL COMMUNICATOR

CAREER PROFILE

Duties: Design and develop communication products for informational, training, and other purposes; prepare materials for publication; perform duties as required

Alternate Title(s): Communication Specialist; Information Developer; Documentation Specialist; a title that reflects a particular occupation such as Technical Writer, Technical Editor; Technical Illustrator; or Web Designer

Salary Range: $22,000 to $83,000

Employment Prospects: Good

Advancement Prospects: Good

Prerequisites:

Education or Training—Bachelor's degree in any field

Experience—Previous work experience or knowledge of subject matter preferred; one or more years of professional experience

Special Skills and Personality Traits—Writing, editing, information design, and project management skills; proficient with various software tools; communication, interpersonal, teamwork, and self-management skills; ethical, creative, diplomatic, analytical, organized, flexible, energetic, enthusiastic, quick learner, able to handle criticism

CAREER LADDER

Senior Technical Communicator or Independent Contractor

Technical Communicator

Junior or Assistant Technical Communicator

Position Description

Aerospace manufacturing companies employ Technical Communicators to create communication products that provide information about their employers' products, services, and policies. They are responsible for describing highly technical concepts accurately and clearly in language and visuals that can be understood by the intended audience, who are usually unfamiliar with the subject matter or are less technically minded. The audience may be professionals, technicians, employees, managers, executive officers, stockholders, customers, the media, or others.

Technical Communicators produce various types of communication products for aerospace manufacturing companies. The products may be in print, multimedia, or electronic form. The communication products are used for informational, reference, training, and other purposes. The following are a few examples of the materials that Technical Communicators create:

- user's guides and manuals for the installation, operation, or maintenance of products
- reference materials such as product specifications, parts lists, or assembly instructions
- company Web sites
- help systems that are integrated into software and Web sites to assist users
- policies and procedures manuals, employee handbooks, employee newsletters, and other company-related materials
- training materials, including workbooks, videotapes, audiotapes, tutorials (or lessons for developing work skills), and reference aids that workers can use on the job
- scientific or technical reports and articles for scientific, technical, and professional publications
- company proposals to bid for future jobs (as a supplier of products or services)
- printed or online catalogs, which describe the products a company offers for sale

- promotional materials such as brochures, press releases, newsletters, and e-zines, which provide news about company products, services, projects, employees, and so forth

Projects may take several days, weeks, or months to complete. Depending on the size of a project, Technical Communicators work alone or as part of a team. Technical Communicators are responsible for completing projects on schedule and within the allocated budget. They also keep all parties involved in the development of a communication project informed of its work status. On team projects, experienced Technical Communicators are usually designated project leaders.

Projects go through several phases. The first phase is planning the overall design of a product. Technical Communicators start to plan and organize their projects by answering such questions as What are the purpose and objectives of the product? Who is the audience? What information do they need? How should the content be sequenced? What types of visuals are needed? What medium should be used? What form shall it take? What formats and styles should be used?

Next is the development phase. Technical Communicators conduct research to learn about the subject matter. They interview subject-matter experts and review literature and data. If they are writing instructions about a product or procedure, they examine blueprints and specifications, observe how the product works, and sometimes learn how to use it themselves.

Technical Communicators organize information and determine which information is relevant and useful for the intended audience. They then write and edit manuscripts, following specific editorial guidelines. They make sure the information is technically accurate and correct and presented in a clear and logical manner. Technical Communicators also prepare or oversee the preparation of visual aids (such as illustrations, charts, photographs, and schematic diagrams) that help reinforce the information they are presenting. Throughout their projects, Technical Communicators meet with subject-matter experts and others to discuss ideas and clarify information.

Technical Communicators submit drafts of their works to their superiors and any interested parties for review. For example, a draft of a company brochure might be reviewed by a public relations officer or a marketing department head. Technical Communicators do one or more revisions to incorporate any changes that may be requested.

Once the works are finally approved, then Technical Communicators go into the final phase—production. That is, they prepare products for publication, which may be in print, multimedia, or electronic form. Copy is edited for grammar, spelling, and punctuation; after all corrections are made, copy is proofread for typographical errors. The final form of all visuals—illustrations, photographs, charts, and so forth—are produced. In addition, page layouts are designed and created.

When the final products are published, Technical Communicators may be involved in their maintenance. They might perform such activities as tracking the usability of communication products by users or updating information, by revising a user guide or a Web site, for example.

Some Technical Communicators specialize in creating specific types of communication products, such as user manuals, proposals, or training materials.

Many Technical Communicators specialize in performing one particular role. For example, they may work on projects as writers, editors, illustrators, graphic designers, or Web site designers. Some Technical Communicators are involved in education and training. Instructional designers develop training materials for employees, such as for those in the aerospace manufacturing industry. Still other Technical Communicators are educators who teach courses in the fields of technical communication.

Because the organizational structure varies from company to company, Technical Communicators are part of several departments. For example, different Technical Communicators might work for documentation, technical communication, product development, or marketing departments in various aerospace manufacturing firms.

Some Technical Communicators are independent contractors. Some of them work only in the aerospace manufacturing industry, whereas others work in other industries, such as computers, telecommunications, or pharmaceuticals.

Self-employed Technical Communicators are solely responsible for the daily management of their small businesses. They perform a variety of duties, such as bookkeeping, paying bills and taxes, negotiating contracts, billing clients, ordering office supplies, and maintaining their offices. In addition, they devote time in their schedule to finding future work. Independent contractors typically have flexible schedules. Depending on their projects, they may be required to travel to clients' offices and manufacturing plants for meetings and research purposes.

Technical Communicators, whether staff members or freelancers, usually work more than 40 hours a week to complete tasks and meet pressing deadlines.

Salaries

Salaries vary, depending on various factors, such as occupation, education, experience, size of employer, job responsibilities, and geographical location. According to the May 2003 *Occupational Employment Statistics* survey (by the U.S. Bureau of Labor Statistics), most of these occupations earned an estimated annual salary between the following ranges:

- technical writers: $30,600 to $83,360
- editors (including technical editors): $24,590 to $77,430
- graphic designers: $21,600 to $65,060

Depending on the project and client, freelancers may work on an hourly basis or for a flat fee. According to a 2001 salary survey by the Society for Technical Communication, the hourly rates for most independent contractors and temporary employees ranged between $32 and $72 per hour.

Employment Prospects

In the aerospace manufacturing industry, Technical Communicators may be employees or independent contractors. Some Technical Communicators work for contracting and consulting firms that offer technical communication services for hire.

The job market, in general, for Technical Communicators is strong and expected to continue throughout the decade due to technological advancements and the increase in global competition among businesses. Opportunities are more readily available for highly experienced and reputable Technical Communicators.

Due to the ease of communication and delivery of products via e-mail and the phone and fax, independent Technical Communicators are able to obtain projects from clients that are located in other cities, states, and even other countries.

Advancement Prospects

Technical Communicators can advance to supervisory and managerial positions as team leaders, project managers, and department supervisors. Technical writers and editors may advance to higher positions as senior writers or editors. The highest goal for some individuals is to become successful independent contractors or owners of communications firms. Some Technical Communicators desire to become consultants who provide advice and counsel on the development and design of projects.

Most Technical Communicators generally realize advancement by earning higher incomes, receiving more complicated assignments, and being recognized for the quality of their work.

Education and Training

Educational requirements vary with the different employers. Most employers prefer to hire Technical Communicators who have at least a bachelor's degree, which may be in communications, graphic design, English, engineering, computer science, physics, business, or another field.

Many Technical Communicators complete technical writing or technical communication programs sponsored by colleges, universities, continuing education programs, and professional societies. Depending on the program, they may earn a professional certificate, bachelor's degree, master's degree, or doctoral degree.

Experience, Special Skills, and Personality Traits

Typically, employers prefer to hire Technical Communicators experienced or knowledgeable in the subject matters about which they would be working. Many Technical Communicators in the aerospace manufacturing industry have previously worked in other occupations in the industry, as engineers, pilots, aircraft maintenance technicians, quality technicians, software developers, and training specialists. In addition, Technical Communicators have strong business sense.

Technical Communicators should have one or more years of professional experience in such fields as technical writing, illustration, or Web site design. They must have excellent writing, editing, information design, and project management skills. Additionally, they are proficient with various publishing, Web development, word processing, and other software tools.

Communication, interpersonal, and teamwork skills are essential for Technical Communicators to be successful. Furthermore, they should have strong self-management skills, such as the ability to work independently, handle stressful situations, meet deadlines, prioritize tasks, and understand and follow instructions.

Being ethical, creative, diplomatic, analytical, organized, flexible, energetic, and enthusiastic are some personality traits that successful Technical Communicators have in common. In addition, they are quick learners and able to handle criticism about their work.

Unions and Associations

Many Technical Communicators join professional associations to take advantage of networking opportunities, training programs, job listings, and other professional services and resources. Many of them belong to the Society for Technical Communication, which serves the general interests of Technical Communicators who practice in various fields.

Technical Communicators also join specific professional societies that serve their particular interests, such as the following organizations:

- National Writers Union
- American Institute of Graphic Arts
- International Association of Business Communicators
- American Society for Training and Development
- International Society for Performance Improvement
- Institute of Electrical and Electronic Engineers—Professional Communication Society
- Association for Computing Machinery—Special Interest Group for Documentation (SIGDOC)
- Editorial Freelance Association
- Association of Teachers of Technical Writing

Tips for Entry

1. To gain practical experience, consider working with temporary agencies.
2. Many Technical Writers learn about jobs through networking with colleagues at local or regional meetings of professional associations.
3. Create a portfolio that showcases samples of your work. Then bring the portfolio to your interviews to show prospective employers or clients.

4. Stay up to date with technological advancement in the aerospace manufacturing industry, as well as in aerospace technology in general.
5. Use the Internet to learn more about Technical Communicators in general. Two Web sites you might visit include EServer TC Library, http://tc.eserver.org, and Society for Technical Communication, http://www.stc.org. To get a list of other relevant Web sites, enter the keywords *technical communicators* into any search engine.

SPACE FLIGHT AND EXPLORATION

ASTRONAUT

CAREER PROFILE

Duties: Lead or crew space missions; operate flight and other systems aboard spacecraft; manage and perform scientific experiments; perform technical or management assignments between flight assignments; perform duties as required

Alternate Title(s): Astronaut-Pilot; Commander; Mission Specialist; Payload Specialist; ISS Commander; Flight Engineer; Astronaut Researcher

Salary Range: $44,000 to $82,000

Employment Prospects: Poor

Advancement Prospects: Fair

Prerequisites:

Education or Training—Bachelor's degree, but advanced degree more desirable; complete the astronaut-candidate training and evaluation program

Experience—At least three years of professional work experience; advanced degrees may be substituted for some or all experience; pilots need 1,000 hours of flight hours as pilots-in-command

Special Skills and Personality Traits—Teamwork, interpersonal, problem-solving, and communication skills; self-motivated, enthusiastic, adaptable, dedicated, decisive, curious, patient, hardworking

CAREER LADDER

Lead or Senior Astronaut

Astronaut

Astronaut Candidate

Position Description

Astronauts are highly experienced pilots, scientists, and engineers who are involved in space exploration. They also participate in scientific discoveries by conducting various research experiments in space to help earthbound scientists gain new scientific knowledge and understanding; find solutions to technical, medical, and environmental problems; or develop new commercial products and services.

The U.S. astronaut corps is part of the National Aeronautics and Space Administration (NASA), the federal agency that oversees the U.S. space exploration program. This corps is composed of both men and women. Some of them are U.S. military officers who have been detailed to NASA while serving duty as Astronauts.

Since the late 1950s, NASA Astronauts have been involved in many human space flights. They have orbited Earth thousands of times and have traveled to and from the moon. In addition to performing both flight and scientific research in space, Astronauts have completed missions in which they have deployed satellites and other spacecraft into space. Moreover, Astronauts have performed spacewalks, or extravehicular activities (EVAs), that require them to work outside their spacecraft. For example, some Astronauts have completed maintenance or repairs on satellites and space telescopes which orbit Earth.

Today the U.S. astronaut corps is involved in supporting two NASA space programs. One program is the International Space Station (ISS), which will be a permanent research facility with six state-of-the-art laboratories. It orbits about 220 miles over Earth while completing a full revolution every 90 minutes. Construction on the facility began in 1998 and is expected to be completed within the next few years. It is being built by the United States in collaboration with Canada, Russia, China, Japan, Brazil, and the European Space Agency (which is composed of Belgium, Denmark, France, Germany, Italy, the Netherlands, Norway, Spain, Sweden, Switzerland, and the United Kingdom). The ISS has been permanently staffed by an international crew of Astronauts since 2000.

NASA Astronauts also participate in the Space Shuttle program, which is currently America's major transport system between Earth and space. In little more than eight minutes, a space vehicle can take astronauts from a launch pad on Earth into orbit high above the planet. Space Shuttle Astronauts perform such missions as deploying spacecraft into Earth's orbit or into space, servicing and repairing satellites and space telescopes, conducting scientific research, assembling the ISS, and transporting crews and payload to and from the ISS.

NASA Astronauts perform one of two roles on a space flight. They serve as either pilots or mission specialists. Pilot-Astronauts are in charge of flight operations and the successful completion of their missions. They control and operate the spacecraft and are responsible for the safety of the crew and the spacecraft. They may also assist with the various tasks performed by the mission specialists.

Mission specialists are crew members aboard spacecraft. Their responsibilities include coordinating crew activity, as well as planning and managing fuel, water, food, and other consumables. Additionally, they manage and conduct the various onboard scientific experiments and perform spacewalks.

Three or more mission specialists are usually selected to serve as crew members on Space Shuttle missions. On the ISS, mission specialists may be known as astronaut researchers or by another title.

On occasion, U.S. space flights include Astronauts known as payload specialists. They perform specific tasks that have unique requirements related to the payload or other mission activities. Most of these specialists are scientists and technicians. They are nominated to these Astronaut positions by NASA or a payload sponsor, which may be a university, a private company, a research center, or even a foreign country.

Depending on the mission, Astronauts may be in space for a few days or several months. NASA usually makes flight assignments several years ahead of time. Astronauts generally train for a mission for one to two years. This includes training in simulators for the different phases of flight, from prelaunch to entry and landing. They also practice skills and tasks in full-size models of the spacecraft. If they will be performing EVAs, the Astronauts practice spacewalk maneuvers in huge swimming pools. Mission specialists spend time working and training with scientists whose experiments they would be performing. Furthermore, Astronauts simulate their mission with the flight control team who will be working with them.

In space, Astronauts follow flight plans, which are detailed time lines of what they must do on each day of their mission. Their activities are monitored on Earth by NASA flight controllers. Astronauts can directly communicate with flight controllers (as well as their family members) through radio, e-mail, and video.

Because of microgravity, Astronauts float in space. To perform their tasks, they fasten themselves to their workstations. When they work outside their spacecraft, Astronauts don specially crafted spacesuits. The spacesuits provide them with a controlled and regulated atmosphere for breathing. The spacesuits also protect Astronauts from the extreme temperatures of heat (from the sun) and cold (from space).

Upon completion of a mission, Astronauts usually spend several days in debriefings. They complete medical tests and are involved in discussions in which they recount their experiences. They also provide detailed accounts to the media.

Between flight assignments, Astronauts receive technical and management assignments that support the NASA space programs. For example, they may be involved in testing flight software, assisting with training flight crews, serving as flight controllers, or managing contractor activities. On launch days, novice Astronauts usually help flight-crew members prepare for their flight.

Astronauts work and train at the NASA Johnson Space Center in Houston, Texas. Space flights lift off from the NASA Kennedy Space Center in Florida.

Salaries

Earnings for NASA Astronauts vary, depending on their education, experience, and other factors. Civilian Astronauts earn salaries based on the federal government's General Schedule pay scale for grades GS-11 through GS-13. In 2004, the basic annual pay for federal employees at these grade levels ranged between $44,136 and $81,778. Military Astronauts continue to earn their military pay, which is based on their rank, pay grade, and years in service. They also continue to receive a housing allowance, sick leave, and other military benefits.

Employment Prospects

NASA accepts applications on a continual basis but generally selects candidates every two years, as needed.

Competition for Astronaut-candidate positions is very high. NASA usually receives several thousand applications, from which they select about 100 astronaut candidates for the astronaut training and evaluation program. Upon completion of the program, about 20 candidates are selected for pilot or mission specialist positions. They are expected to remain with NASA for at least five years. Civilian candidates who are not chosen to be astronauts may be offered other positions within NASA.

Interested military personnel submit applications through their military service. Each service has its own application procedures and requirements. In general, the military screens all applications, then submits the best ones to NASA for consideration.

To apply for the NASA Astronaut Candidate Program, individuals must meet the following minimum requirements:

- be a U.S. citizen
- pass a NASA space physical, which is similar to a military or civilian flight physical
- meet distance visual acuity standards, which varies for the pilot and mission specialist candidates (Note: Any type of surgery to improve visual acuity will disqualify candidates.)
- have blood pressure that measures no higher than 140/90 in a sitting position
- meet a height standard: between 64 and 76 inches for pilot candidates or between 58.5 and 76 inches for mission specialists

There are no minimum or maximum age restrictions.

Payload specialists must meet certain physical requirements and must pass NASA physical examinations.

Advancement Prospects

The ultimate career goal for Astronauts is to be selected for a mission. Some Astronauts have completed more than one mission.

Astronauts with managerial ambitions can pursue such positions within NASA.

After completing their tour of duty with NASA, military Astronauts continue their chosen path with their particular service.

NASA Astronauts typically start another career upon leaving the astronaut corps. Depending on their interests, skills, and ambitions, they pursue such careers as engineer, entrepreneur, management consultant, politician, and motivational speaker.

Education and Training

Minimally, astronaut candidates must possess a bachelor's degree from an accredited institution. The degree should be in the field of engineering, biological science, physical science, or mathematics. A degree in clinical psychology, physiological psychology, or experimental psychology is also acceptable. NASA does not consider a degree in any of the following fields as a qualification for the education requirement: technology (such as engineering technology); psychology (except for those mentioned above); nursing; exercise physiology or similar fields; social sciences; or aviation, aviation management, and similar fields.

It is generally more desirable that candidates have an advanced degree. Candidates may be able to substitute an advanced degree for part or all of the experience requirement. Most Astronauts hold a master's or doctoral degree in their field of interest.

Astronaut candidates go through a one- to two-year training and evaluation period, in which they participate in a basic astronaut training program. They acquire the knowledge and skills needed for formal mission training if they are selected to become Astronauts. During this period, Pilot-Astronaut candidates maintain flight proficiency by flying a minimum number of hours in NASA aircraft.

Successful Astronaut candidates become regular members of the U.S. astronaut corps. They continue with advanced training until they receive their flight assignments. Astronauts undergo intense, specialized training that prepares them for each mission.

Payload specialists are required to have the appropriate education and training related to the payload or experiment for which they would be responsible on each mission.

Experience, Special Skills, and Personality Traits

Astronauts are highly experienced and at the top of their fields in engineering or science. Pilot-Astronauts usually have military backgrounds, while mission specialists are mostly civilians.

Applicants for the NASA astronaut program must have at least three years of progressively responsible professional experience in their respective field. Advanced degrees may substitute for part or all of this experience requirement. Applicants for Pilot-Astronaut positions must have completed at least 1,000 hours as pilots-in-command of jet aircraft. It is desirable that candidates have flight test experience.

To perform their tasks effectively, Astronauts need excellent teamwork, interpersonal, problem-solving, and communication skills. Being self-motivated, enthusiastic, adaptable, dedicated, decisive, curious, patient, and hardworking are some personality traits that successful Astronauts have in common.

Unions and Associations

Astronauts might join the Association of Space Explorers, a professional and education organization composed of current and former Astronauts and cosmonauts. This professional association offers networking opportunities and other professional resources and services.

Astronauts might also belong to the American Institute of Aeronautics and Astronautics. In addition, they might join other professional associations that serve their particular fields. For example, Pilot-Astronauts are eligible to join the Society of Experimental Test Pilots and the Order of Daedalians.

Tips for Entry

1. If you are in high school, maintain good grades and develop strong study habits. Also begin developing teamwork and interpersonal skills by participating in

extracurricular activities such as sports, school clubs, and youth groups (for example, the Scouts or Civil Air Patrol cadet program).

2. Military personnel should contact the personnel center for their service for information about the application process for the NASA Astronaut Candidate Program.
3. NASA accepts civilian applications on a continual basis but establishes cut-off dates for recruitment cycles. All applications received after a cut-off date are considered for the next cycle.
4. If your application isn't accepted at first, keep trying. In the meantime, apply for another job with NASA to gain valuable experience working in the agency.
5. For further information about the NASA astronaut corps, check out these Web sites: NASA Astronaut Selection Homepage, http://astronauts.nasa.gov; NASA Human Space Flight, http://spaceflight.nasa.gov; NASA Johnson Space Center, http://www.jsc.nasa.gov; and NASA Astronaut Biographies Homepage, http://www.jsc.nasa.gov/Bio.

MISSION SPECIALIST

CAREER PROFILE

Duties: Conduct scientific experiments and perform payload activities and flight operation duties in space; perform technical or management assignments between flight assignments; perform duties as required

Alternate Title(s): Astronaut; Astronaut-Researcher

Salary Range: $44,000 to $82,000

Employment Prospects: Poor

Advancement Prospects: Fair

Prerequisites:

Education or Training—Bachelor's degree, but advanced degree more desirable; complete the astronaut-candidate training and evaluation program

Experience—At least three years of professional experience; advanced degrees may be substituted for some or all experience

Special Skills and Personality Traits—Teamwork, interpersonal, communication, and problem-solving skills; knowledgeable about cultures and being fluent in another language; enthusiastic, curious, patient, adaptable, dedicated, decisive, hardworking

CAREER LADDER

Lead or Senior Mission Specialist

Mission Specialist

Astronaut Candidate

Position Description

Mission Specialists are members of the U.S. astronaut corps, which is part of the National Aeronautics and Space Administration (NASA), the federal agency in charge of the U.S. space exploration program. Mission Specialists, along with pilot-astronauts, travel and work aboard spacecraft as they orbit Earth. The Mission Specialists serve as crew members, whereas the pilot-astronauts serve as the commanders of space flights.

Since the 1980s, NASA astronauts have participated in a variety of space missions. Some missions have involved deploying satellites, telescopes, or probes into space, whereas others required doing maintenance and repairs on satellites and space telescopes. In most, if not all, missions, astronauts are engaged in performing scientific research.

Mission Specialists are responsible for managing a variety of science experiments on space missions. Although they have extensive backgrounds as scientists and engineers, Mission Specialists do not perform their own research. Instead, they conduct experiments for earthbound scientists, including physicists, chemists, biologists, medical scientists, materials scientists, and geophysicists.

Because gravity is very low in space, researchers can study the fundamental conditions of matter in microgravity and the forces that affect those conditions. They can also examine the influence of gravity on physical processes and other phenomena. The science experiments performed by Mission Specialists can thus help earthbound scientists and technologists gain new scientific knowledge and understanding; find solutions to technical, medical, and environmental problems; or develop new commercial products and services.

Mission Specialists are also responsible for all payload operations, which may involve performing extravehicular activities (EVAs), or spacewalks, in space. For example, Mission Specialists might be assigned to replace parts on an orbiting satellite. In addition, Mission Specialists perform daily flight operations duties. They coordinate operations that involve crew activity planning, as well as manage consumable supplies such as food, water, and fuel. Additionally, they assist the pilot-astronauts with monitoring the spacecraft's operating systems.

For the next several years, the U.S. astronaut corps will support two NASA space programs. One program is the International Space Station (ISS), currently under construction, which orbits about 220 miles over Earth. This will be a permanent research facility with six laboratories. Construction on the facility began in 1998, and is expected to be completed before the end of the current decade. It is being built by the United States and its international partners—Canada, Russia, China, Japan, Brazil, and the European Space Agency. Astronauts from the partnering nations began staffing the ISS in 2000 to assemble the space laboratory as well as to conduct scientific experiments. Flight crews are rotated on a regular basis. On the ISS, Mission Specialists may be known by other job titles, such as astronaut researcher.

Secondly, Mission Specialists are involved in the Space Shuttle program, which is currently America's major transport system between Earth and space. Usually, three or more Mission Specialists are selected to serve as crew members on a Space Shuttle flight. Their missions include deploying spacecraft into space; servicing and repairing satellites and space telescopes; conducting scientific research; assembling the ISS; and transporting crews and payload to and from the ISS.

NASA generally makes flight assignments several years ahead of time. Space flights may last a few days or several months. Mission Specialists participate in one to two years of intensive training in preparation for each mission. Their training includes practicing in simulators for the different phases of flight, from prelaunch to entry and landing. They also practice skills and tasks in full-size models of the spacecraft. In addition, the flight crew simulates its mission along with the team of flight controllers who will be working with them on Earth.

If Mission Specialists will be performing EVAs, they rehearse spacewalk maneuvers in huge swimming pools. They also practice the tasks they will perform outside their spacecraft. For example, if they will be repairing hardware on a satellite, Mission Specialists are trained on the same hardware. These astronauts also spend time working and training with the scientists whose experiments they will perform.

Upon being selected as astronauts, new Mission Specialists serve in technical assignments until they are assigned to space flights. Mission Specialists also perform technical and management tasks between flight assignments. Their duties vary, depending on their expertise and skills. For example, some Mission Specialists might be involved in conducting basic research on rocket fuels, whereas others test flight software, create designs of future spacecraft, or participate in educational outreach activities. Mission Specialists may also assist with training flight crews and serve as flight controllers. Furthermore, novice astronauts typically assist flight crews to prepare for their flights on launch days.

Some Mission Specialists hold part-time faculty positions at nearby colleges and universities. Some of them also prepare papers for scientific journals and technical conferences.

The U.S. astronaut corps works and trains at the NASA Johnson Space Center in Houston, Texas. Space flights lift off from the NASA Kennedy Space Center in Florida.

Salaries

Earnings for Mission Specialists vary, depending on their education, experience, and other factors.

Civilian astronauts earn salaries based on the federal government's General Schedule pay scale for grades GS-11 through GS-13. In 2004, the basic annual pay for federal employees at these grade levels ranged between $44,136 and $81,778. Military astronauts continue to earn their military pay, which is based on their rank, pay grade, and years in service. They also continue to receive a housing allowance, sick leave, and other military benefits.

Employment Prospects

NASA accepts applications on a continual basis but generally selects candidates every two years, as needed.

Competition for astronaut positions is very high. NASA usually receives several thousand applications, from which they select about 100 astronaut candidates for the astronaut training and evaluation program. Upon completion of the program, about 20 candidates are selected for pilot or mission specialist positions. They are expected to remain with NASA for at least five years. Civilian candidates who are not chosen to be astronauts may be offered other positions within NASA.

Military personnel who are interested in applying to the NASA Astronaut Candidate Program must submit applications through their military service. Each service has its own application procedures and requirements. In general, the military screens all applications, then submits the best ones to NASA for consideration.

To apply for the NASA Astronaut Candidate Program, individuals must meet the following minimum requirements:

- be a U.S. citizen
- pass a NASA space physical, which is similar to a military or civilian flight physical
- meet the distance visual acuity standard which is 20/200 or better uncorrected, correctable to 20/20 in each eye (Note: any type of surgery to improve visual acuity will disqualify candidates.)
- have blood pressure that measures no higher than 140/90 in a sitting position
- meet the height standard, which is between 58.5 and 76 inches

There are no minimum or maximum age restrictions.

Advancement Prospects

The ultimate career goal for astronauts is to be selected for a mission. Some Mission Specialists have completed more than one mission.

Military astronauts are on detail from their military service. After completing their tour of duty with NASA, they continue their chosen path with the military.

Mission Specialists with management ambitions can pursue such positions within NASA.

Mission Specialists typically start another career upon leaving the astronaut corps. They pursue any number of careers, depending on their interests, skills, and ambitions. For example, they might become engineers, professors, management consultant, business executives, politicians, or motivational speakers.

Education and Training

Minimally, to apply for the NASA Astronaut Candidate Program, applicants must have earned bachelor's degrees from accredited institutions. Having advanced degrees is generally more desirable. NASA usually allows candidates to substitute advanced degrees for part or all of the experience requirement.

NASA accepts applicants with degrees in the fields of engineering, biological science, physical science, or mathematics. Degrees in clinical psychology, physiological psychology, or experimental psychology are also acceptable. NASA does not consider a degree in any of the following fields as a qualification for the education requirement: technology (such as engineering technology); psychology (except for those mentioned above); nursing; exercise physiology or similar fields; social sciences; or aviation, aviation management, or similar fields.

Most, if not all, Mission Specialists possess a master's or doctoral degree in their field of interest.

Astronaut candidates go through a one- to two-year training and evaluation period in which they participate in a basic astronaut training program. They acquire the knowledge and skills needed for formal mission training if they are selected to become astronauts. During this period, pilot-astronaut candidates maintain flight proficiency by flying a minimum number of hours in NASA aircraft.

Successful astronaut candidates become regular members of the U.S. astronaut corps. They continue with advanced training until they receive their mission assignments.

Mission Specialists undergo intense, specialized training that prepares them for each mission. This includes practicing skills in full-size models of the spacecraft in which they will be working, as well as practicing spacewalk maneuvers in huge pools. They also train in simulators for the different phases of flight, from prelaunch to entry and landing. In addition, astronauts simulate the mission with the flight control team that will be working with them in their flight.

Experience, Special Skills, and Personality Traits

Mission Specialists are highly experienced and at the top of their fields in engineering or science.

To apply for the NASA astronaut program, applicants must have at least three years of progressively responsible professional experience in their respective field. Advanced degrees may substitute for part or all of this experience requirement. However, to stay competitive, applicants with advanced degrees should have some experience. This may have been gained through internships, work-study programs, fellowships, summer employment, research projects, or other means.

Essential skills that Mission Specialists need are teamwork, interpersonal, communication, and problem-solving skills. Having knowledge about other cultures and being fluent in another language is desirable, as Mission Specialists often work with astronauts from other countries.

Being enthusiastic, curious, patient, adaptable, dedicated, decisive, and hardworking are some personality traits that successful Mission Specialists share.

Unions and Associations

Mission Specialists can join professional associations to take advantage of networking opportunities and other professional resources and services. Many of these astronauts belong to the American Institute of Aeronautics and Astronautics as well as the Association of Space Explorers, a professional and education organization composed of current and former astronauts and cosmonauts.

In addition, Mission Specialists might join professional associations that serve their particular fields in engineering and science. Some of these societies are:

- American Association for the Advancement of Science
- American Chemical Society
- American Institute of Physics
- American Mathematical Society
- ASM International—The Materials Information Society
- ASME International (American Society of Mechanical Engineers)
- Association for Computing Machinery
- Institute of Electrical and Electronics Engineers
- Society of Women Engineers

Tips for Entry

1. In high school, take college prep courses in science and math to help you prepare for your college program.
2. NASA offers various internship, fellowship, and research programs to undergraduate, graduate, and postdoctoral students at the Goddard Space Flight Center (GSFC). These programs are administered by the Office of University Programs at GSFC. You can learn more at the following NASA Web page: http://university.gsfc.nasa.gov.

3. Although a pilot's license is not required for Mission Specialist positions, having flying experience may enhance your employability.
4. Become physically fit and stay in shape. Learn how to swim if you haven't yet. Part of the basic astronaut training is to swim several lengths of a 25-meter pool in a flightsuit and shoes.
5. Learn more about human space flights on the Internet. Two Web sites you can visit are NASA Human Space Flight, http://spaceflight.nasa.gov, and Shuttle Online Press Kit, http://www.shuttlepresskit.com.

FLIGHT CONTROLLER (HUMAN SPACE FLIGHTS)

CAREER PROFILE

Duties: Monitor activities, operational systems, or other aspects aboard a human spaceflight; participate in training for an upcoming mission; perform technical duties related to human spaceflights; perform duties as required

Alternate Title(s): Flight Control Engineer; a title that reflects a specific position, such as Flight Director; Space Communicator; or Flight Surgeon

Salary Range: $31,000 to $92,000

Employment Prospects: Fair

Advancement Prospects: Fair

Prerequisites:

Education or Training—Bachelor's degree in an engineering or a science discipline; completion of a certified Flight Controller training program

Experience—One or more years of work experience

Special Skills and Personality Traits—Teamwork, interpersonal, communication, writing, organizational, and self-management skills; dedicated, responsible, confident, disciplined, persistent, innovative, alert

CAREER LADDER

Flight Director

Flight Controller (flight control room)

Flight Controller (back room)

Trainee

Position Description

Flight Controllers work closely with astronauts to ensure safe and successful human spaceflight missions. While astronauts are in space, they are monitored from Earth by Flight Controllers who use highly complex communication and computer systems to maintain a constant watch over the spacecraft and the crew's activities. Flight Controllers are ready to provide assistance to astronauts whenever major maneuvers, schedule changes, or unexpected problems or emergencies occur.

In the U.S. human spaceflight program, the National Aeronautics and Space Administration (NASA) houses its flight control operation at the Johnson Space Center in Houston, Texas. The operation is more commonly known as the Mission Control Center (MCC), which has been in charge of human space missions since 1965. At first, spacecraft were mostly controlled by Flight Controllers but, as technology advanced, spacecraft were designed so that flight crews became increasingly in control of spacecraft. Today, Flight Controllers help the flight crew manage the spacecraft systems by analyzing and evaluating data, giving them feedback about the various systems, and troubleshooting problems.

Currently, the MCC supports two human space programs. One program is the International Space Station (ISS), which is a research facility being built about 220 miles over Earth. The other program is the Space Shuttle, which is the main transport system between Earth and space. The Space Shuttle missions include deploying spacecraft into Earth's orbit or into space; servicing and repairing satellites and space telescopes; conducting scientific research; assembling the ISS; and transporting crews and payload to and from the ISS.

All NASA U.S. human space missions are launched from the Kennedy Space Center in Florida. Once a spacecraft lifts off, the MCC immediately becomes responsible for monitoring the spacecraft and its crew until it has re-entered

Earth's atmosphere and landed. Space Shuttle missions usually last a few days or a few weeks. The International Space Station mission, on the other hand, has had rotating crews since October 2000.

Many Flight Controllers work together to monitor the progress of a mission, and each Flight Controller is responsible for a specific activity. Some Flight Controllers keep track of certain systems, such as electrical systems, electrical power generation systems, communications systems, propulsion systems, navigation systems, life support systems, or robotics operations systems. Others are involved with watching over the flight crew's activities, which may entail completing routine operations, conducting experiments, performing spacewalks, and so on.

The lead Flight Controllers at the MCC work in large rooms known as flight control rooms. The Space Shuttle and ISS programs have their own main rooms. About 20 or more Flight Controllers work on a Space Shuttle mission, whereas 12 or fewer controllers are involved with the ISS missions.

The Flight Controllers perform their monitoring tasks in front of large consoles. The following are just a few of the different MCC Flight Controllers that work in flight control rooms during a mission:

- The flight director is responsible for managing the overall mission operations. He or she also supervises and directs Flight Controllers, as well as coordinates the planning and execution of all activities with Flight Controllers, payload customers, and others.
- The spacecraft communicator acts as the primary contact between the flight crew and the MCC. Usually, this controller is an astronaut.
- The flight dynamics officer is responsible for the planning and execution of the spacecraft's flight path, or trajectory, from its launch and as it orbits Earth, to its re-entry into Earth's atmosphere and its landing.
- The guidance officer, or guidance procedures officer, monitors the navigation and guidance computer software that is aboard the spacecraft.
- The data processing systems engineer monitors the onboard data processing system, which includes all the computer hardware, software, data lines, mass memory units, and timing units.
- The booster engineer monitors and evaluates the performance of the main engine, the rocket boosters, and the external tank during the prelaunch and ascent phases of the mission.
- The flight surgeon monitors the medical condition of the flight crew and keeps the flight director up to date on the crew's health status.
- The flight activities officer plans and monitors the activities, checklists, procedures, and schedules for the flight crew.
- The extravehicular activities systems engineer keeps track of astronauts and their spacesuits as they are performing spacewalks.
- The ground controller is responsible for maintaining voice and data communications between the MCC and the spacecraft.
- The public affairs officer provides the media and the public with current news about the mission.

Each Flight Controller in the flight control room is supported by a team of Flight Controllers who work in back rooms, which are also known as multipurpose support rooms. Those Flight Controllers usually have fewer years of experience in flight control. Their primary duties are to help monitor the spaceflight, analyze data, work out problems, and develop plans that support the main room Flight Controllers.

Furthermore, a wide network of engineering specialists are available to assist Flight Controllers. At any time, they can consult the engineering experts in NASA as well as the engineers who had helped build the systems aboard a spacecraft.

Monitoring human spaceflights is only a small part of a Flight Controller's job. Most of the time is spent in planning and organizing missions. Flight planning might begin two or more years before the mission takes place. Flight Controllers may have any number of duties, depending on their assignment, experience, and skills. For example, a Flight Controller could be involved with determining what activities would be performed by the flight crew, developing operational flight rules, writing technical procedures or manuals for Flight Controllers, designing software upgrades for MCC, or performing analyses of vehicle systems.

Another important duty of Flight Controllers is to train for each mission. They spend many hours studying the various systems aboard the spacecraft (such as the ISS) and practicing the tasks they would be performing during a mission. NASA has built a training room for Flight Controllers that resembles the flight control room in which they would be working. Here, Flight Controllers can practice their skills and how they would respond to various problems (such as a malfunctioning piece of equipment) and emergencies that could occur during a mission.

Flight Controllers also go through simulations with the flight crews of upcoming missions. Flight crews are trained in simulators that are replicas of the spacecraft they will be operating. These simulators are linked up to the Flight Controllers' training room, which provides Flight Controllers and flight crews the opportunity to practice working together before actual flights.

Flight Controllers generally work a 40-hour schedule and put in additional hours as needed to complete duties. During space missions, the Mission Control Center operates 24 hours, seven days a week. Flight Controllers are then assigned to work shifts.

Salaries

Salaries for Flight Controllers vary, depending on such factors as their education and experience. Information about actual earnings for Flight Controllers is unavailable.

Most Flight Controllers are engineers, and according to the May 2003 *Occupational Employment Statistics* survey (by the U.S. Bureau of Labor Statistics), the estimated annual salary for most engineers ranged between $30,870 and $92,040.

Employment Prospects

The following Flight Controller positions are filled by NASA employees—flight director, space communicator, and flight surgeon. The other Flight Controllers are usually employed by contractors that provide flight operations services to NASA. In 2004, many of the Flight Controllers in the NASA human spaceflight program were employed by the United Space Alliance or Barrios Technology, Inc., both of Houston, Texas.

Job opportunities typically become available as Flight Controllers retire or transfer to other occupations.

Flight Controllers also can seek employment as experienced engineers in other areas of aerospace technology, working for NASA, aerospace companies, academic institutions, research institutes, or other employers. The Bureau of Labor Statistics reports that the demand for engineers in the aerospace industry is projected to grow by 10 percent over the 2000–10 period. Replacements for a large number of engineers are expected to be needed, as many of them will be reaching retirement age within this period. Electrical and computer engineers are predicted to be most in demand by employers.

Advancement Prospects

Management opportunities in the Mission Control Center are limited. Flight Controllers may advance to become flight directors.

In general, Flight Controllers measure advancement through job satisfaction, by earning higher wages, and through gaining professional recognition. With additional experience and training, Flight Controllers might seek transfers to flight control positions that interest them. Flight Controllers might also pursue astronaut careers.

With their engineering backgrounds, Flight Controllers can obtain further education to pursue professional careers in such fields as medicine, law, politics, education, and business.

Education and Training

Minimally, Flight Controllers must hold a bachelor's degree in aerospace engineering, electrical engineering, mechanical engineering, computer engineering, computer science, mathematics, physics, or a related field.

New employees participate in a training program at the Johnson Space Center that leads them to become certified Flight Controllers. They learn the basic skills and knowledge they need to work in the Mission Control Center. Training may take several months or a few years, depending on the complexity of the position that Flight Controllers fill.

Experience, Special Skills, and Personality Traits

Depending on the position, job candidates for entry-level positions may be required to have one or more years of professional work experience in a technical field. Employers may hire recent college graduates if they have gained the appropriate experience through internships, work-study programs, part-time employment, or other means.

Flight Controllers who serve in the flight control rooms typically have had several years of experience working in flight control. After having completed their training, they usually serve first as Flight Controllers in multipurpose support rooms.

To perform their work effectively, Flight Controllers must have superior teamwork and interpersonal skills, as well as excellent communication, writing, and organizational skills. They must also have strong self-management skills, such as the ability to handle stressful situations, work independently, follow and understand directions, and prioritize tasks in order of importance.

Being dedicated, responsible, confident, disciplined, persistent, innovative, and alert are some personality traits that successful Flight Controllers share.

Unions and Associations

Many Flight Controllers join professional associations that serve the interests of their particular engineering or science fields. For example, Flight Controllers with computer engineering backgrounds might join the Association for Computing Machinery. By joining professional societies, individuals can take advantage of networking opportunities, publications, job listings, and other professional services and sources.

Tips for Entry

1. The United Space Alliance, the primary contractor to the NASA human spaceflight program, offers a cooperative education program to college students. Participants are given the opportunity to receive on-the-job training at NASA while completing their bachelor's degree. Students are given work assignments that are closely related to their academic programs. To be considered, students must be recommended by their institution's cooperative education program. For further information, contact your college career center. You can also contact the United Space Alliance Staffing Department at 600 Gemini Avenue, Houston, TX 77058-2783, or call them at (281) 282-4830, or fax them at (281) 282-3532. You can also visit the company's Web site at http://www.unitedspacealliance.com.
2. Having previous experience working in the space industry may enhance your employability.
3. Use the Internet to learn more about the U.S. human spaceflight program and the NASA Johnson Space Center, where the Flight Controllers work. You might start by visiting the Johnson Space Center at http://www.jsc.nasa.gov.

FLIGHT CONTROLLER (ISS PAYLOAD OPERATIONS CENTER)

CAREER PROFILE

Duties: Monitor research experiments and other payload activities aboard the International Space Station; participate in training for an upcoming mission; perform duties as required

Alternate Title(s): Technologist; Flight Control Engineer; Payloads Officer; a title that reflects a specific position, such as Payload Operations Director or Operations Controller

Salary Range: $31,000 to $92,000

Employment Prospects: Poor

Advancement Prospects: Fair

Prerequisites:

Education or Training—Bachelor's degree in an engineering or science discipline; completion of a certified Flight Controller training program

Experience—Previous work experience related to the duties of Flight Controllers preferred

Special Skills and Personality Traits—Teamwork, interpersonal, communication, writing, organizational, and self-management skills; dedicated, confident, disciplined, responsible, alert, persistent, innovative

CAREER LADDER

Payload Operations Director

Flight Controller

Trainee

Position Description

Many Flight Controllers at the U.S. National Aeronautics and Space Administration (NASA) are responsible for monitoring science experiments and other payload activities aboard the International Space Station (ISS). The ISS is a research facility that orbits about 220 miles above Earth. When it is completely assembled in the next few years, it will hold six state-of-the-art laboratories. Construction was begun in 1998 by the United States and it continues to be built by the United States and its international partners—Russia, Canada, China, Japan, Brazil, and the European Space Agency.

Since 2000, the ISS has been permanently staffed with an international crew of astronauts, which is rotated every few months. Each crew's mission is to conduct a variety of science experiments aboard the ISS in such areas as biomedicine, fundamental biology, biotechnology, fundamental physics, fluid physics, materials science, combustion science, earth science, space science, and advanced human support technology. The science experiments (also known as payloads) are sponsored by public and private enterprises from the partner nations.

NASA is responsible for overseeing the selection, processing, and monitoring of payloads that will be transported to the ISS. NASA's command post for the ISS payload operations is located at the Marshall Space Flight Center in Huntsville, Alabama. From there, all science experiments are monitored daily by Flight Controllers for onboard performance. The ISS payload operations center also maintains communication links with the Mission Control Center, in Houston, Texas, which has overall responsibility for the command and control of the ISS.

At the payload operations center, several Flight Controllers work together in a large room to monitor the daily progress of science experiments. They work at individual consoles that are linked to the International Space Station. They also monitor payload operations on the ISS through video systems.

The Flight Controllers lead teams composed of scientists, engineers, and others. The team members work in other rooms where they support the Flight Controllers by analyzing data, preparing procedures, troubleshooting, and monitoring onboard payload operations. The following are the various Flight Controllers who monitor the ISS payloads:

- The payload operations director leads, manages, and directs the day-to-day activities of the payload operations center. The director works closely with the flight director at the Mission Control Center.
- The operations controller monitors the daily work schedule to ensure that research activities are being done in a timely manner. This Flight Controller also makes sure that onboard resources (such as electrical power and equipment) are available to support science experiments.
- The payload communication manager is the main contact person with the ISS crew in regard to payloads. This Flight Controller answers questions about the various payloads and relays messages about experiments from earthbound scientists. This Flight Controller is also responsible for arranging video conferences between flight crew and scientists or payload system experts.
- The command and payload multiplexer/demultiplexer officer is responsible for maintaining the command link between the Payload Operations Center and the Mission Control Center in Houston. The Flight Controller also manages and monitors the command link with the various ISS nation partners and payload sponsors.
- The data management coordinator oversees and configures the ISS data systems for payload operations.
- The lead increment science representative monitors the status as well as accomplishments of payloads. In addition, this Flight Controller manages all research-related issues.
- The time line change officer manages and updates the daily schedule of science activities and work assignments.
- The safety coordination manager makes sure that science experiments on the ISS are being conducted according to safety regulations. This Flight Controller also ensures that all payloads and the support equipment comply with safety requirements.
- The shuttle operations controller keeps track of the ISS payloads as they are being transported to or from the ISS on the Space Shuttle. This Flight Controller makes sure that all payloads have been transferred between the Space Shuttle and the ISS.
- The payload rack officer monitors and configures the payload racks that support the science experiments aboard the ISS.
- The photo and TV operations manager oversees, configures, and coordinates the video system on board the ISS.

As the assembly of the ISS nears completion, new flight control positions will be added. For example, a data systems manager position is expected to be added as research activities increase. This Flight Controller will assist with the configuration of the ISS data system to ensure that data is being properly routed.

Flight Controllers prepare themselves for upcoming missions on the ISS. They undergo an intensive training program that includes being tested and evaluated on their performance in stressful flightlike simulations. Flight Controllers also spend time practicing simulations with the assigned flight crew members.

Flight Controllers perform other duties besides flight control. They may be involved in writing technical manuals for the payload operations center, developing operational rules or procedures, training new Flight Controllers, and so on.

The ISS Payload Operations Center is staffed 24 hours a day; therefore, Flight Controllers are assigned to one of three shifts.

Salaries

Salaries for Flight Controllers vary, depending on such factors as their education and experience. Information about actual earnings for Flight Controllers is unavailable. However, many Flight Controllers have engineering backgrounds. The estimated annual salary for most engineers ranged between $30,870 and $92,040, according to the May 2003 *Occupational Employment Statistics* survey (by the U.S. Bureau of Labor Statistics).

Employment Prospects

The Flight Controllers at the ISS Payload Operations Center are usually employees of companies that provide contractual services to NASA.

Job opportunities typically become available as Flight Controllers retire or transfer to other occupations.

Advancement Prospects

In general, Flight Controllers measure advancement through job satisfaction as well as by earning higher wages and by gaining professional recognition.

With additional experience and training, Flight Controllers can seek transfers to flight control positions that interest them. Flight Controllers can also pursue other careers with NASA by becoming trainers, researchers, astronauts, or managers.

Education and Training

Flight Controllers must possess at least a bachelor's degree in an engineering or science discipline. They may be required to have an advanced degree to hold management positions.

New employees must successfully complete a training program that certifies them for the desired flight control position.

Experience, Special Skills, and Personality Traits

Requirements vary for the different flight control positions. In general, applicants should have a few years of professional work experience that is relevant to the duties of Flight Controllers.

The job of Flight Controller requires excellent teamwork, interpersonal, and communication skills. Flight Controllers should also have strong writing and organizational skills, as well as superior self-management skills, such as the ability to work independently, handle stressful situations, and follow and understand directions.

Being dedicated, confident, disciplined, responsible, alert, persistent, and innovative are some personality traits that successful Flight Controllers share.

Unions and Associations

Flight Controllers are eligible to join professional associations that serve the interests of their particular engineering or science fields. By joining professional societies, individuals can take advantage of networking opportunities, publications, job listings, and other professional services and resources.

Tips for Entry

1. Keep up to date with the construction of the International Space Station and the variety of science research taking place on board. In addition to reading books and articles, you can check out relevant Web sites on the Internet. One source for current news is the NASA International Space Station Web site. The URL is http://spaceflight.nasa.gov/station.
2. While in college, gain experience working in the space industry by obtaining an internship or summer employment with NASA or private companies.
3. You can learn more about the ISS payload operations center and the ISS science operations on the Internet. Some Web sites you might visit are Payload Operations Center, http://www.scipoc.msfc.nasa.gov/payload.html; ISS Payload Information Source, http://stationpayloads.jsc.nasa.gov; and ISS Science Operation News, http://www.scipoc.msfc.nasa.gov.

NASA AEROSPACE TECHNOLOGIST (AST)

CAREER PROFILE

Duties: Conduct basic or applied research in space phenomena, aeronautics, or other area; perform duties as required of position

Alternate Title(s): Research Scientist, Engineer; a title that reflects a particular specialty, such as Materials Engineer; Chemist; or Astrophysicist

Salary Range: $30,000 to $114,000

Employment Prospects: Good

Advancement Prospects: Good

Prerequisites:

Education or Training—Bachelor's degree in an appropriate engineering, science, or mathematics discipline

Experience—At least one year of professional work experience for entry-level positions

Special Skills and Personality Traits—Research, writing, communication, teamwork, interpersonal, organizational, and problem-solving skills; enthusiastic, bold, innovative, creative, persistent, self-motivated, hardworking

CAREER LADDER

Senior Aerospace Technologist

Aerospace Technologist

Aerospace Technologist (entry-level)

Position Description

The U.S. space exploration program is managed and directed by the National Aeronautics and Space Administration (NASA), an independent federal agency. Since the 1950s, NASA scientists and engineers have made discoveries and built technologies that have led to human space travel and moon landings, the International Space Station, the Hubble Space Telescope, telecommunication satellites, and hundreds of robotic space probes that explore Mars and other celestial bodies in space. Furthermore, many of the technologies and products that NASA scientists and engineers have invented are now being used in medicine, construction, transportation, food manufacturing, firefighting, and other areas to make lives on Earth healthier and safer.

Scientists and engineers comprise more than half the professional workforce at NASA. They hold backgrounds in the various fields of science, engineering, and mathematics. NASA scientists include biologists, physiologists, psychologists, physicists, chemists, oceanographers, astronomers, space scientists, geophysicists, and meteorologists. Aerospace engineers, electrical engineers, mechanical engineers, materials engineers, and chemical engineers are just a few of the engineering specialists at NASA. In addition, many mathematicians, statisticians, computer scientists, computer hardware engineers, and software engineers from the mathematics and computer science disciplines are NASA employees.

Those NASA scientists and engineers who are involved in aerospace research and development at NASA are generally known as Aerospace Technologists (ASTs). ASTs may be engaged in conducting basic or applied research. ASTs conduct basic research to gain further understanding and knowledge about space phenomena and the science of aeronautics. For example, they investigate such subjects as the environment of interplanetary space, the physical characteristics of planets, the behavior of materials and structures in different environments, propulsion systems, the effects of microgravity on life systems, and the definition of life. Those ASTs involved in applied research are concerned with applying scientific knowledge to develop and design new or improved space vehicles, devices, instrumentation, products, and processes.

Aerospace research and development at NASA is generally divided into different subject areas, which are further subdivided into specialties. The following are a few of the subject areas in which ASTs work.

- Space sciences: Astronomers and space scientists are involved in the study of planets, moons, stars, and other celestial bodies, as well as the interplanetary space environment.
- Earth sciences: Physical scientists, geophysicists, oceanographers, and meteorologists examine the characteristics and phenomena of Earth and its atmosphere.
- Life sciences and systems: Physical scientists, biological scientists, and others are concerned with such diverse topics as the effects of space flight on the human body and mind; the requirements for life support and environmental control systems in space; the origin and evolution of biological processes, systems, structures, and species; and the means to detect life and life-related molecules on other planets.
- Fluid and flight mechanics: Engineers and others investigate, develop, test, and evaluate the fluid and flight mechanics that pertain to aircraft and space vehicles.
- Materials and structures: Engineers and scientists research, develop, design, manufacture, fabricate, process, test, and evaluate the many kinds of metallic and nonmetallic materials that may be used in aircraft and space vehicles.
- Propulsion and power: Engineers and scientists are concerned with studying, developing, designing, testing, and evaluating various propulsion systems (such as liquid, solid, chemical, nuclear, and antimatter) and aerospace power generation systems, along with their parts and subsystems.
- Data systems: Computer scientists, engineers, and mathematicians research, design, develop, test, and evaluate computer hardware and software systems for aerospace and aeronautical purposes.

ASTs collaborate on research projects, and each brings his or her scientific or engineering expertise to a project. In addition, ASTs work with technicians, research assistants, and others.

The work of NASA scientists and engineers varies each day, as they perform various tasks. For example, they might:

- conduct experiments
- analyze and interpret data
- conduct research on the World Wide Web
- read scientific journals and other research literature
- plan and organize their work schedules
- meet with colleagues to discuss projects
- prepare written reports
- supervise research assistants and technicians who provide administrative and research support

ASTs are expected to stay up to date with developments and technologies in their scientific disciplines. This involves various activities, such as reading professional journals and books, attending professional conferences, enrolling in education or training programs, and networking with colleagues.

They mostly work indoors in offices and laboratories. They generally work 40 hours a week but put in additional hours whenever necessary to complete various tasks. On occasion, they may be required to travel to other NASA research centers or laboratories to perform their duties.

Salaries

Salaries for NASA research scientists and engineers vary, depending on such factors as their education, experience, pay rank, and geographical location. In addition to their salaries, many federal employees receive locality pay to compensate for living in regions with higher costs of living.

Depending on their qualifications, entry-level NASA scientists and engineers usually receive starting salaries ranging from the GS-7 level to the GS-11 level. (GS stands for General Schedule, the pay schedule for most federal employees.) NASA researchers can advance to the GS-13 or GS-15 levels. In 2004, the annual basic pay for GS-7 to GS-11 employees ranged from $29,821 to $57,375. The annual basic pay at the GS-15 level ranged from $87,439 to $113,674.

Employment Prospects

Aerospace Technologists work in NASA centers and facilities that are located throughout the United States. Today, NASA's workforce is composed of more than 18,000 employees, and 60 percent of them are scientists and engineers.

Job prospects for NASA scientists and engineers are expected to be strong in the coming years due to the large number of employees who will soon become eligible for retirement. Some experts are concerned that NASA may experience a shortage of qualified candidates because fewer young people have been entering the fields of science and engineering. In addition, NASA must compete with the private sector, academic institutions, and other employers for the top candidates.

Some of the areas in which NASA particularly sees a need for skilled scientists and engineers are: nanotechnology, propulsion systems, systems engineering, advanced engineering technology, information technology, robotics, astrobiology, and fundamental space biology.

Advancement Prospects

NASA scientists and engineers can advance to lead, supervisory, and management positions. With additional training and experience, many seek transfers to positions that interest them.

Some ASTs with entrepreneurial interests may become consultants or business owners.

Education and Training

Minimally, NASA scientists and engineers must possess a bachelor's degree from an accredited college or university. Their major study must be in an appropriate field of engineering, physical science, life science, or mathematics. (Note: A bachelor's degree in engineering technology is unacceptable.) An advanced degree may be required for some research positions. In general, about half the scientists and engineers at NASA hold advanced degrees in their fields.

To qualify for entry-level positions at a higher pay, candidates usually must possess a master's or doctoral degree if they do not have the minimum number of years of professional experience.

Experience, Special Skills, and Personality Traits

To qualify for entry-level positions at the GS-7 level, job candidates must have at least one year of professional experience closely related to the desired positions. (Having a master's degree may be substituted for a candidate's work experience.) Work experience may have been gained through either paid or volunteer work experience, such as summer employment, internships, work-study programs, or research assistantships.

ASTs must have strong research, writing, and communication skills. Additionally, they need effective teamwork and interpersonal skills, as they must work well with colleagues, managers, and others from various backgrounds. Furthermore, they must demonstrate strong organizational and problem-solving skills.

Being enthusiastic, bold, innovative, creative, persistent, self-motivated, and hard working are a few personality traits that successful ASTs share.

Unions and Associations

Many ASTs are members of professional associations that serve their particular fields. By joining societies, they can take advantage of networking opportunities, continuing education programs, publications, job listings, and other professional services and resources. A few of the various professional associations that are available to scientists and engineers are:

- American Association for Artificial Intelligence
- American Association for the Advancement of Science
- American Chemical Society
- American Institute of Aeronautics and Astronautics
- American Institute of Physics
- American Mathematical Society
- ASM International—The Materials Information Society
- ASME International (American Society of Mechanical Engineers)
- Association for Computing Machinery
- Institute of Electrical and Electronics Engineers
- Society of Women Engineers

Tips for Entry

1. NASA has internship, cooperative education, and other programs that give college students the opportunity to gain experience working with the agency. For further information, check out the NASA Student Employment home page on the Internet. Go to http://www.nasajobs.nasa.gov/stud_opps/.
2. NASA visits colleges and universities to recruit for entry-level positions. To find out if NASA recruiters will be coming to your institution, or one nearby, contact your college career center.
3. Job applicants for NASA positions must be U.S. citizens. They must also be able to pass a security clearance.
4. Candidates are usually evaluated on the competencies they have that are directly related to the duties of the job. Therefore, carefully read the job announcement. Prepare your résumé so it demonstrates how your skills and experience match the job for which you are applying.
5. Learn more about NASA on the Internet. You might start by visiting NASA's Web site, http://www.nasa.gov. You might also check out these NASA Web pages: NASA Jobs, http://www.nasajobs.nasa.gov; Aerospace Technology Enterprise, http://www.aero-space.nasa.gov; and NASA Office of Space Flight, http://www.hq.nasa.gov/osf.

ASTRONOMER

CAREER PROFILE

Duties: Conduct research; design and conduct research projects; perform duties as required of the position

Alternate Title(s): Astrophysicist; Space Physicist, or other title that reflects a specialty

Salary Range: $42,000 to $131,000

Employment Prospects: Fair

Advancement Prospects: Good

Prerequisites:

Education or Training—Doctoral degree in astronomy or related field

Experience—Related work and research experience; postdoctoral experience

Special Skills and Personality Traits—Highly skilled in computers, computer programming, math, and statistics; analytical, problem-solving, observation, writing, communication, and interpersonal skills; patient, precise, determined, curious, self-motivated, imaginative

CAREER LADDER

Senior Astronomer

Astronomer

Postdoctoral Research Associate

Position Description

Astronomers (or astrophysicists) explore space from Earth. Using telescopes and other instruments on Earth and in space, these scientists are able to gather information about the stars, planets, asteroids, comets, and the black void, in the Milky Way and beyond. They seek to understand the physical nature, origin, and development of celestial bodies, galaxies, and the universe. They seek answers to such questions as How are stars born? How do they die? How far away are the nearest stars? Where do comets come from? What is the surface like on Mars? Does life exist elsewhere in the universe? How does a star system form? How did the universe begin?

Astronomy is an ancient science. Over centuries, this discipline has evolved from solely an observational science to a discipline that uses physics and mathematics to understand the phenomena of the universe. Today, astronomy is considered to be a subdiscipline of physics, and the terms *astronomy* and *astrophysics* are used interchangeably. In addition to studying the universe, Astronomers develop new and better techniques and instrumentation for conducting their research. They are also engaged in finding solutions to problems in such areas as space flight, navigation, and satellite communications.

Since astronomy is such a broad field, Astronomers typically focus their studies in a particular area. Some of these specialties include:

- cosmology—the study of the nature, origin, and evolution of the universe
- astrometry—the study of the positions of celestial bodies, their distances, and their movements
- celestial mechanics—the study of the motions of the celestial bodies, such as stars, planets, and comets, as well as the forces between celestial bodies
- solar astronomy—the study of the sun
- space physics—the investigation of the charged particles, magnetic fields, and other invisible phenomena that fill the region between the sun and the planets
- high-energy astrophysics—the study of high-energy events such as gamma ray bursts, black holes, and colliding stars that occur in the universe
- planetary geology—the study of the geology as well as the surface and interior processes of solid objects in the

solar system, including asteroids, comets, and the other planets, along with their moons and rings

- astrobiology—the study of life in the universe (Astronomers explore such subjects as the origin of the building blocks of life, how life affects, and is affected by, the environment in which it arose, and if life can expand beyond its planet of origin.)

Astronomers gather data about their subject matter by making direct observations of the skies or from information gathered by colleagues, amateur astronomers, and other scientists. In addition to supercomputers, Astronomers use various instrumentation to gather data about celestial bodies and phenomena. Some of these instruments are high-powered optical telescopes, radio telescopes, X-ray spectrometers, radar, magnetometers, special cameras, and so on. In addition, Astronomers obtain data from observations made by space telescopes (such as the Hubble Space Telescope), as well as from instrumentation aboard satellites and space probes traveling through the solar system.

Astronomers are often characterized by their methods of study—theoretical or observational. Theoretical Astronomers conduct much of their research on computers and develop theories based on observations made mostly by other Astronomers. Theoretical Astronomers usually create computer models (sets of mathematical equations), which they use to analyze data and interpret observations. Observational Astronomers, or Observers, analyze data based on the observations they gather from telescopes, as well as on observations gathered by spacecraft. Observers usually spend several days or weeks at a time making observations. This sometimes involves traveling to research facilities in remote areas, such as on mountaintops, and living and working there for the duration of their observing run.

Most professional Astronomers work in academic and government settings. Academic Astronomers normally research topics within their own interests, while most nonacademic Astronomers conduct research in areas that fulfill their employers' specific goals and missions. Astronomers from different work settings often collaborate on research projects. For example, academic Astronomers might assist other Astronomers as well as other scientists at the U.S. National Aeronautics and Space Administration (NASA).

Astronomers often work on several projects simultaneously, and sometimes collaborate on research projects. Most independent researchers are responsible for writing grant proposals and seeking out grants from the federal government or other sources to fund their research projects.

Most Astronomers have teaching, administrative, or other responsibilities in addition to their research work. Many Astronomers are employed as professors in colleges and universities. Their duties include planning and teaching astronomy courses to undergraduate and graduate students. Some professors also teach physics courses. Furthermore, they are responsible for advising students, supervising student research projects, writing scholarly works, performing administrative tasks, and fulfilling community service responsibilities.

All Astronomers are responsible for keeping up with the technology and new developments in their specialties as well as in the field of astronomy in general. Most Astronomers participate in scientific conferences to network with colleagues and to share research information. In addition, Astronomers write scientific papers about their research work and submit the papers to scientific journals for publication.

Astronomers divide their time by working in offices, laboratories, and observatories. Some travel to remote sites to make their observations. Many of them also travel to other cities in the U.S. and abroad to attend professional meetings and conferences.

Salaries

Salaries vary, depending on such factors as experience, employer, and geographical location. According to the May 2003 *Occupational Employment Statistics* survey (by the U.S. Bureau of Labor Statistics) the estimated annual salary for most Astronomers ranged between $42,120 and $130,740.

Employment Prospects

Most Astronomers are employed as faculty members at colleges and universities, particularly those with research and development laboratories and observatories. Some Astronomers work for NASA, the U.S. Department of Defense, and a few other federal agencies. Others are employed by commercial or nonprofit research laboratories. In addition, some Astronomers find private-sector employment in the aerospace, satellite communications, and other private industries.

In general, the turnover rate for jobs is small each year. Job openings become available as Astronomers retire or advance to other positions.

Advancement Prospects

Astronomers with managerial ambitions can become project leaders, program managers, and laboratory or observatory directors. As faculty members, Astronomers receive promotional rankings as assistant professors, associate professors, or full professors.

Most Astronomers measure their success by being able to conduct independent research, through making discoveries, and by earning professional recognition.

Education and Training

Most Astronomers possess a doctoral degree in astronomy, astrophysics, or physics. Individuals first earn a bachelor's degree in physics, astronomy, or another field. They then complete a master's program followed by a doctoral program. Altogether, graduate study may take between five to six years to complete. As part of their doctoral program, students conduct original research projects.

To conduct independent research, teach in universities and colleges, and hold top management positions, doctoral degrees are required.

Experience, Special Skills, and Personality Traits

Employers generally choose candidates who have work and research experience related to the desired position. Entry-level applicants may have gained relevant experience through research projects, internships, postdoctoral training, part-time employment, and so on.

Astronomers are highly skilled in computers, computer programming, math, and statistics. They also have excellent analytical and problem-solving skills, as well as good observation skills. In addition, they have proficient writing, communication, and interpersonal skills.

Being patient, precise, determined, curious, self-motivated, and imaginative are a few personality traits that successful Astronomers have in common.

Unions and Associations

Many Astronomers join professional associations to take advantage of networking opportunities, research, education programs, and other professional resources and services. The American Astronomical Society is one such professional society. Astronomers may also join such science associations as the American Institute of Physics and the American Geophysical Union.

They are also eligible to join professional societies that serve the interests of an academic faculty, such as the National Association of Scholars, the American Association for Higher Education, and the American Association of University Professors.

Tips for Entry

1. It is essential for you to have a solid foundation in physics and mathematics to become an Astronomer.
2. Join a local amateur astronomy club to learn more about stars and the universe. For example, you might join a branch of the American Association of Variable Star Observers. If none is available in your area, check out your school science club, a Scouts organization, or a nearby science museum.
3. You can gain many valuable experiences while you are in college. For example, you might work as a research assistant for an astronomy professor, or you can volunteer, intern, or work at an astronomy laboratory or observatory.
4. The U.S. National Aeronautics Space Administration (NASA) offers a variety of student programs that allow students to participate in space research. Each NASA field center manages its own programs. For information, contact a NASA office near you. You can also visit NASA's student opportunities Web page at http://www.nasajobs.nasa.gov/stud_opps.
5. Use the Internet to learn more about astronomy. Some Web sites you might visit are "American Astronomical Society," http://www.aas.org; "The Astronomy Cafe," http://www.astronomycafe.net; and "Science @NASA: Astronomy," http://science.nasa.gov/Astronomy.htm.

ROCKET SCIENTIST

CAREER PROFILE

Duties: Duties vary, depending on which function one performs, such as research, development, or design; perform duties as required of the position

Alternate Title(s): A title such as Aerospace Engineer or Chemist that reflects a disciplinary specialty; a title such as Propulsion Engineer that reflects a particular area of expertise; or a title such as Design Engineer or Research Scientist that reflects a particular function

Salary Range: $31,000 to $132,000

Employment Prospects: Fair

Advancement Prospects: Fair

Prerequisites:

Education or Training—Master's or doctoral degree preferred

Experience—Previous work experience generally required

Special Skills and Personality Traits—Problem-solving, communication, interpersonal, teamwork, and self-management skills; creative, imaginative, resourceful, curious, persistent, flexible, patient

CAREER LADDER

Senior Engineer or Senior Scientist

Engineer or Scientist

Engineer or Scientist (entry-level)

Position Description

Rocket Scientists are engineers and scientists who work in the aerospace industry. They may be aerospace engineers, electrical engineers, mechanical engineers, materials scientists, chemists, physicists, and so on. Their primary concern is with the creation of new and improved rockets to be used for military defense and space exploration. They work on the development and production of such rockets as:

- missiles, which are used in war
- launch vehicles, which are used to thrust manned or unmanned spacecraft into the solar system
- upper stages, which are used to launch spacecraft into higher orbits or further into space

The title *Rocket Scientist* is commonly used by the media and the general public. Indeed, many professionals refer to themselves by this title. However, in the workplace, Rocket Scientists have formal job titles that reflect a specialty, such as aerospace engineer or physicist, or a function, such as research scientist or design engineer.

Rocket Scientists work in many settings. Some work for the National Aeronautics and Space Administration (NASA), the federal agency in charge of the U.S. space exploration program. Others are employed by aerospace manufacturing companies and private research institutes. Some Rocket Scientists hold academic teaching positions at colleges and universities.

Most Rocket Scientists conduct research. Some, particularly those in academic settings, conduct basic research to gain further understanding and knowledge about the behavior of fuel, propulsion systems, fluid mechanics, the structural design of rockets, and other topics. Others conduct applied research. They work on the design and development of new or improved devices, products, or processes. For example, Rocket Scientists at a private company might be involved in finding ways to improve rocket designs.

Rocket Scientists also perform other functions in the development of rockets. They might be involved in designing products, testing rocket propulsion systems, developing launch operations, evaluating the quality of products, or various other activities.

Most Rocket Scientists collaborate on projects with other engineers and scientists. Many researchers share the results of their studies by writing scientific or technical papers, as well as by making presentations at scientific conferences.

Rocket Scientists' duties vary, depending on their position. For example, in addition to conducting research, college professors are responsible for teaching, advising students, performing community service, writing scholarly works, and performing administrative tasks.

Regardless of their particular function, most Rocket Scientists perform similar tasks. For example, they:

- develop work plans
- review and evaluate data
- troubleshoot problems
- create computer models, or simulations, to help them with their investigations
- write technical papers and other materials
- prepare correspondence, reports, proposals, and other documents
- attend meetings
- provide consultation to others
- supervise technicians and other staff members

Rocket Scientists are expected to stay current with new developments and technologies in their fields. They read professional journals and books, attend professional conferences, network with colleagues, and so on.

Rocket Scientists work in offices and laboratories. They normally work a 40-hour week. They sometimes work additional hours to complete tasks or meet deadlines.

Salaries

Salaries for Rocket Scientists vary, depending on their field, education, experience, employer, geographical location, and other factors. According to the May 2003 *Occupational Employment Statistics* survey (by the U.S. Bureau of Labor Statistics), these were the estimated annual salary ranges for most of the following scientists and engineers:

- aerospace engineers, $50,380 and $107,840
- chemical engineers, $48,600 and $109,670
- chemists, $31,220 and $93,100
- electrical engineers, $46,210 and $104,500
- materials scientists, $37,520 and $110,340
- mechanical engineers, $42,190 to $94,110
- physicists, $49,880 and $131,570

Employment Prospects

Rocket Scientists are employed by NASA as well as by aerospace companies (such as Boeing and Lockheed Martin). They also find employment with aerospace companies that provide contractual services to NASA. Some Rocket Scientists work in research institutions, and others hold teaching and research positions in colleges and universities.

The job market in the aerospace industry fluctuates with the economy. For example, when the economy is in a downturn, employers generally lay off employees and hire fewer new employees.

Job prospects for NASA scientists and engineers are expected to be strong in the coming years due to the large number of employees who will soon become eligible for retirement. Some experts are concerned that NASA may experience a shortage of qualified candidates because fewer young people have been entering the fields of science and engineering. In addition, NASA must compete with the private sector, academic institutions, and other employers for the top candidates.

Advancement Prospects

Depending on their interests and ambitions, Rocket Scientists can advance their careers in various ways. For example, they can seek positions in areas that interest them, such as design, process, technical support, or research. As they gain experience, Rocket Scientists can become team leaders and project managers. Those with administrative and management ambitions can rise through the ranks to executive director or executive officer positions. Doctoral degrees may be required for them to obtain top management positions.

Education and Training

Employers usually prefer that Rocket Scientists possess a master's degree in an appropriate field of physical science or engineering. To teach in four-year colleges and universities, to conduct independent research, or to hold top management positions, candidates are usually required to have a doctoral degree.

Rocket Scientists enroll in education and training programs throughout their careers to update their knowledge and skills.

Experience, Special Skills, and Personality Traits

Employers usually hire candidates who have work and research experience related to the desired positions. Their experience may have been gained through past employment, internships, fellowships, part-time employment, and so on. Ph.D. candidates for research scientist positions may be required to have several years of postdoctoral experience.

To work effectively at their jobs, Rocket Scientists must have excellent problem-solving, communication, interpersonal, and teamwork skills. They should have also strong self-management skills, such as the ability to work independently, organize and prioritize tasks, and meet deadlines.

Being creative, imaginative, resourceful, curious, persistent, flexible, and patient are some personality traits that successful Rocket Scientists share.

Unions and Associations

Many Rocket Scientists become members of professional associations to take advantage of professional services such as networking opportunities, continuing education programs, professional publications, and job listings. Some of the various scientific and engineering associations are:

- American Association for the Advancement of Science
- American Chemical Society
- American Institute of Aeronautics and Astronautics
- American Institute of Physics
- ASM International—The Materials Information Society
- ASME International (American Society of Mechanical Engineers)
- Association for Computing Machinery
- Institute of Electrical and Electronics Engineers

Tips for Entry

1. The ability to communicate clearly in writing and verbally is critical for Rocket Scientists. Therefore, in high school and college, develop your speaking and writing skills by taking such courses as English, speech, and journalism.
2. Take up rocketry as a hobby. To learn more about this hobby, check out the Web site for the National Association of Rocketry at http://www.nar.org.
3. Some employers visit college and university campuses to recruit for entry-level positions. To find out if an employer will be visiting your campus, contact your college career center.
4. Use the Internet to learn more about rocket science. To start, check out the following Web sites: NASA Stennis Space Center, http://www.ssc.nasa.gov; NASA White Sands Test Facility, http://www.wstf.nasa.gov; Rocket Science (by Paul Woodmansee), http://woodmansee.com/science/rocket/rocket-science.html; and Space-Travel: Your Portal to Space Flight (the rocket science section), http://www.space-travel.com/rocketscience.html.

APPENDIXES

APPENDIX I
PILOT CERTIFICATES AND RATINGS

This appendix will discuss the variety of pilot certificates and ratings that are required to operate civil aircraft in the United States.

FAA-ISSUED PILOT CERTIFICATES

In the United States, pilot certificates and ratings are granted by the Federal Aviation Administration (FAA), the federal agency in charge of enforcing civil aviation regulations. Pilots must possess the proper certification to operate airplanes, helicopters, gyroplanes, powered-lifts, gliders, airships, and balloons, for hire as well as for pleasure.

Pilots earn their certificates by successfully completing ground instruction and flight training provided by FAA-certified instructors. Pilots must also pass the appropriate set of tests—composed of written, oral, and flight exams—for each type of pilot certificate and rating they seek.

Except for the student pilot certificate, FAA-issued pilot certificates do not expire. Pilot certificates remain valid until pilots surrender them or until the FAA has suspended or revoked them.

STUDENT PILOT CERTIFICATE

The FAA student pilot certificate allows individuals to operate the aircraft they plan to fly, under the training and supervision of an authorized instructor. Once students have gained the proper training and endorsement by an instructor, they can fly solo. They continue their flight training to become eligible for a recreational pilot or private pilot certificate. The student pilot certificate expires 24 months after it has been issued.

To qualify for an FAA student pilot certificate, individuals must meet the following requirements:

- be at least 14 years old to operate a glider or balloon
- be at least 16 years old to operate an airplane, helicopter, or other aircraft that is not a glider or balloon
- be able to read, speak, write, and understand the English language

RECREATIONAL PILOT CERTIFICATE

The FAA recreational pilot certificate grants pilots limited flying privileges. They are allowed to fly during day hours and are only allowed to carry one passenger. They must usually stay within 50 nautical miles of the airport where they learned to fly. Recreational pilots cannot receive compensation for flying passengers or property.

To be eligible for an FAA recreational pilot certificate, individuals must meet the following requirements:

- be at least 17 years old
- be able to read, speak, write, and understand the English language
- hold a logbook endorsement from an authorized instructor, which certifies that the appropriate ground instruction has been completed
- complete at least 30 hours of flight training
- pass the required examinations—a written knowledge test and a practical test, which includes an oral exam and flight test

PRIVATE PILOT CERTIFICATE

The FAA private-pilot certificate grants pilots the privilege of acting as pilots-in-command of their aircraft. They may fly day or night. They may fly solo as well as carry passengers, as long as the pilots receive no compensation. With the appropriate ratings, private pilots may fly in poor weather conditions, such as fog, haze, or rain.

To qualify for an FAA private-pilot certificate, individuals must meet the following requirements:

- be at least 16 years old for a glider or balloon rating
- be at least 17 years old for a rating for any aircraft other than a glider or balloon.
- be able to read, speak, write, and understand the English language
- hold logbook endorsements from an authorized instructor, which certifies that the appropriate ground instruction and flight training have been completed
- complete a minimum number of flight hours (Note: the requirements differ for training that is being completed in FAA-approved flight schools as opposed to nonapproved flight schools.)
- pass the required knowledge and practical tests

COMMERCIAL PILOT CERTIFICATE

An FAA commercial-pilot certificate allows pilots to work for hire. They may receive compensation for their piloting services as employees or independent contractors. Commercial pilots work in a wide range of settings, such as air charter services, private companies, government agencies, nonprofit organizations, and aircraft manufacturing firms.

To qualify for an FAA commercial-pilot certificate, individuals must meet the following requirements:

- be at least 18 years old
- be able to read, write, speak, and understand the English language
- possess a private pilot certificate
- hold logbook endorsements from an authorized instructor, which certifies that the appropriate ground instruction and flight training have been completed
- complete a minimum number of flight hours
- pass the required knowledge and practical tests

AIRLINE TRANSPORT PILOT CERTIFICATE

The airline transport pilot (ATP) certificate is the most advanced pilot certificate that the FAA issues. It grants pilots the privilege of acting as captains, or pilots-in-command, of aircraft for commercial airlines.

To be eligible for an FAA ATP certificate, individuals must meet the following requirements:

- be at least 23 years old
- be able to read, write, speak, and understand the English language
- be of good moral character
- possess a commercial pilot certificate with an instrument rating, or have the appropriate military experience (Some foreign pilots may qualify, if they meet certain requirements.)
- complete at least 1,500 flight hours prior to applying for the practical test
- pass the required knowledge and practical tests

FLIGHT INSTRUCTOR CERTIFICATE

The FAA flight instructor certificate is an advanced pilot certificate that permits pilots to teach other pilots. They must also hold the appropriate flight instructor rating for each type of instruction—such as instrument, multiengine, glider, or helicopter instruction—they wish to offer.

Many pilots build up their flight time for pilot jobs with the airlines or other commercial operators by becoming flight instructors. Some of them are independent flight instructors, whereas others are employees of flight schools.

To become an FAA certified flight instructor (CFI), individuals must meet the following requirements:

- be at least 18 years old
- be able to read, write, speak, and understand the English language
- possess either a commercial pilot certificate with an instrument rating, or an air transport pilot certificate
- receive logbook endorsements from authorized instructors for having completed all required flight instructor training
- pass the required knowledge and practical tests

Flight instructors must obtain additional flight instructor ratings if they plan to offer instrument instruction (CFII) and multiengine instruction (MEI).

RATINGS

In addition to their pilot certificates, pilots earn FAA ratings, which state further privileges, conditions, or limitations under which pilots may operate aircraft. For example, pilots might seek:

- a multiengine aircraft rating
- an instrument rating (which is required to operate an aircraft using the aircraft's instruments)
- an aircraft rating for another type of aircraft they wish to fly as pilot-in-command

FAA MEDICAL CERTIFICATE

In addition to their pilot certificates, pilots must hold proper FAA medical certificates. A medical certificate demonstrates that a pilot has met certain medical standards.

The FAA issues three types of medical certificates: first-class medical certificate, second-class medical certificate, and third-class medical certificate. The first-class medical certificate is issued to pilots who have met the highest medical standards. This medical certificate is usually required by pilots who hold the ATP certificate.

FINDING MORE INFORMATION ON THE WEB

You can learn more about becoming a pilot on the Internet. Here are some Web sites you might visit to find more information:

- FAA: Information for Pilots and Aircraft Owners, http://www.faa.gov/AVR/afs/infoforpilotsowners/index.cfm
- Be a Pilot.com, http://www.beapilot.com
- The Student Pilot Network, http://www.studentpilot.net
- Pilot Resources (Thirty Thousand Feet—Aviation Directory), http://www.thirtythousandfeet.com/pilots.htm

APPENDIX II
EDUCATION AND TRAINING RESOURCES

In this appendix, you will find World Wide Web sources for education and training programs for some of the occupations in this book. To learn about programs for other occupations, talk with school or career counselors as well as with professionals. You can also look up schools in college directories produced by the Princeton Review or other publishers, which may be found in your school or public library.

Note: All Web site addresses were current at the time this book was written. If a URL is no longer valid, enter the title of the Web site or the name of the organization or individual into a search engine to find the new address.

GENERAL RESOURCES

The following Web sites provide links to various academic programs at colleges and universities in the United States.

- The Princeton Review, http://www.princetonreview.com
- "Web U.S. Higher Education," a listing of two-year and four-year colleges (maintained by the University of Texas at Austin), http://www.utexas.edu/world/univ
- GradSchools.com, http://www.gradschools.com

PILOT TRAINING

In the United States, individuals can earn FAA pilot certificates and ratings through one of the following ways:

- Obtain flight instruction through flight schools or independent flight instructors. The Student Pilot Network provides a listing of flight schools at http://www.studentpilot.net.
- Complete a two-year or four-year college degree program in aviation and pilot training. Along with obtaining pilot certificates and ratings, students earn associate's or bachelor's degrees.
- Receive pilot training through the military services. (For more information, read the profile on military pilots on page 192.)

Aerobatic Pilot Training

The International Aerobatic Club provides a listing of some aerobatic schools at http://www.iac.org/begin/schools.html.

Hang Gliding Pilot Training

For a listing of some hang gliding schools, visit one of the following Web sites:

- U.S. Hang Gliding Association, http://www.ushga.org/whereto.asp
- Air Sports Net Hang Gliding Database, http://www.usairnet.com/HangGliding/Training/HangGlidingSchools.html

Skydiving Training

For a listing of some skydiving schools and centers, visit one of the following Web sites:

- United States Parachute Association, http://www.uspa.org/dz/index.htm
- Skydiving School List, http://www.skydivinginfo.com

AVIATION

General Information

Thirty Thousand Feet.com, an aviation directory on the Web, provides listings of certificate and degree programs for flight training, aviation maintenance, aircraft dispatch, and other aviation fields. The Web page is http://www.thirtythousandfeet.com/training.htm.

Aviation Maintenance

The following Web sites provide listings for aviation maintenance programs:

- Directory of Aviation Maintenance Training Schools (posted by Aviation Today), http://www.aviationtoday.com/reports/avmaintenance/directory
- The Association for Women in Aviation Maintenance, http://www.awam.org/edtrainlink.htm

Collegiate Aviation

Aviation degree programs are offered at many two-year colleges, four-year colleges, and universities throughout the United States. Individuals can earn associate's or bachelor's degrees in such aviation fields as aviation technology, aviation maintenance, or aviation management. Some institutions also offer master's programs in aviation.

For listings of institutions that offer nonengineering aviation programs, check out *The Collegiate Aviation Guide,* which is compiled and published by the University Aviation Association. For further information, visit the society's Web site at http://uaa.auburn.edu, or contact the society by writing to 3410 Skyway Drive, Auburn, AL 36830, or phoning (334) 844-2434 or (334) 844-2432.

SCIENCE AND ENGINEERING

For education resources for doctoral students in science, engineering, and mathematics, visit the following Web site: PHDs.org (by Geoff Davis) at http://www.phds.org.

Astronomy

The American Astronomical Society provides a listing of astronomy programs at http://www.aas.org/education/deptaddress.html.

Computer Science

The Accreditation Board for Engineering and Technology provides a listing of computing science programs at http://www.abet.org/cac1.html.

Engineering

Listings of various engineering programs can be found at these Web sites:

- Accreditation Board for Engineering and Technology, http://www.abet.org/eac1.html
- Directory of Engineering Colleges, American Society for Engineering Education, http://www.asee.org/publications/colleges/default.cfm
- Graduating Engineer and Computer Careers Online, http://www.graduatingengineer.com

Engineering Technology

The Accreditation Board for Engineering and Technology provides a listing for engineering technology programs at http://www.abet.org/tac1.html.

Meteorology

The National Weather Association provides a listing of meteorology (or atmospheric science) programs at http://www.nwas.org/links/universities.html.

MEDICINE

The following Web sites provide listings of medical programs:

- Association of American Medical Colleges, http://www.aamc.org/medicalschools.htm
- The Princeton Review, http://www.princetonreview.com/medical/default.asp

For a listing of medical education programs and sponsoring institutions, visit the Accreditation Council for Graduate Medical Education Web site, http://www.acgme.org/adspublic.

LAW

The following Web sites provide listings of U.S. law schools:

- American Bar Association, http://www.abanet.org/legaled/approvedlawschools/approved.html
- Law School Admission Council, http://www.lsac.org
- Association of American Law Schools, http://www.aals.org/members.html

TECHNICAL COMMUNICATIONS

The Society for Technical Communication provides a database of academic programs in technical communication at http://www.stc.org/academic.asp.

MILITARY OFFICER TRAINING

Listed below is contact information for the U.S. military academies.

U.S. Air Force Academy
Colorado Springs, CO 80840
Phone: (719) 333-1110
http://www.usafa.af.mil

U.S. Coast Guard Academy
31 Mohegan Avenue
New London, CT 06320
Phone: (800) 883-8724 or (860) 444-8444
http://www.cga.edu

U.S. Military Academy at West Point
West Point, NY 10996
Phone: (845) 938-4011
http://www.usma.edu

U.S. Naval Academy
121 Blake Road
Annapolis, MD 21402
http://www.usna.edu

PAYING FOR YOUR EDUCATION

Scholarships, grants, student loans, and work-study programs are available to help students pay for their public or private colleges, universities, trade schools, or other postsecondary institutions. These financial aid programs are sponsored by government agencies, professional and trade associations, private foundations, businesses, and other organizations.

To learn more about available financial assistance programs, talk with your high school guidance counselor or college career counselor. Also, check out college catalogs, as they usually include financial aid information. You might also visit or contact the financial aid office at the college where you plan to attend or are attending now.

Many government agencies as well as professional and trade associations offer scholarships and other types of programs. For example, the National Business Aviation Association offers scholarships to college students who are interested in pursuing corporate pilot careers. Therefore, be sure to contact organizations that serve your particular interests. You can find contact information for many professional societies in Appendix III and information for some government agencies in Appendix IV.

Lastly, check out these Web sites for financial aid information:

- National Association of Student Financial Aid Administrators, http://www.nasfaa.org (click on the link *parents and students*)
- National Coalition for Aviation Education, http://www.aviationeducation.org/html/scholarshipsandawards/scholarshipsandawards.htm
- The Ninety-Nines, Inc.—Scholarship Listings, http://www.ninety-nines.org/scholar.html
- Student Aid on the Web (U.S. Department of Education Federal Student Aid), http://www.studentaid.ed.gov

APPENDIX III PROFESSIONAL ASSOCIATIONS AND UNIONS

In this appendix, you will find contact information and Web site addresses for the professional associations and unions that are mentioned in this book. Most of these organizations offer information about careers, job opportunities, training programs, educational resources, professional certification programs, and so on.

Many of these organizations have branch offices throughout the United States. Contact an organization's headquarters to find out if a branch is in your area. Other local, state, regional, and international professional associations are also available. To learn about other relevant professional organizations in your area, contact local professionals.

Note: All contact information and Web site addresses were current when the book was written. If you come across a URL that is no longer valid, you may be able to find an organization's new Web site by entering its name into a search engine.

PILOTS

Air Line Pilots Association, International
535 Herndon Parkway
Herndon, VA 20170
Phone: (703) 689-2270
http://www.alpa.org

Airborne Law Enforcement Association
P.O. Box 3683
Tulsa, OK 74101-3683
Phone: (918) 599-0705
Fax: (918) 583-2353
http://www.alea.org

Aircraft Owners and Pilots Association
421 Aviation Way
Frederick, MD 21701
Phone: (301) 695-2000
Fax: (301) 695-2375
http://www.aopa.org

Allied Pilots Association
O'Connell Building
14600 Trinity Boulevard, Suite 500
Fort Worth, TX 76155-2512
Phone: (817) 302-2272
http://www.alliedpilots.org

American Deputy Sheriffs' Association
702 S. Grand Street
Monroe, LA 71201
Phone: (800) 937-7940
Fax: (318) 398-9980
http://www.deputysheriff.org

American Federation of Police and Concerned Citizens
3801 Biscayne Boulevard
Miami, FL 33137
Phone: (305) 573-0070
Fax: (305) 573-9819
http://www.aphf.org/afp_cc.html

Associated Airtanker Pilots
P.O. Box 136
Woodacre, CA 94973
http://www.airtanker.com

Black Pilots of America
P.O. Box 7463
Pine Bluff, AR 71611
http://www.bpapilots.org

Federal Law Enforcement Officers Association
P.O. Box 326
Lewisberry, PA 17339
Phone: (717) 938-2300
Fax: (717) 932-2262
http://www.fleoa.org

Fraternal Order of Police
1410 Donelson Pike, Suite A-17
Nashville, TN 37217
Phone: (615) 399-0900
Fax: (615) 399-0400
http://www.grandlodgefop.org

Helicopter Association International
1635 Prince Street
Alexandria, VA 22314
Phone: (703) 683-4646
Fax: (703) 683-4745
http://www.rotor.com

International Society of Women Airline Pilots
2250 East Tropicana Avenue, Suite 19-395
Las Vegas, NV 89119-6594
http://www.iswap.org

National Agricultural Aviation Association
1005 E Street, SE
Washington, DC 20003-2847
Phone: (202) 546-5722
Fax: (202) 546-5726
http://www.agaviation.org

National Association of Flight Instructors
EAA Aviation Center
P.O. Box 3086
Oshkosh, WI 54903-3086
Phone: (920) 426-6801
Fax: (920) 426-6778
http://www.nafinet.org

National EMS Pilots Association
526 King Street, Suite 415
Alexandria, VA 22314-3143
Phone: (703) 836-8930
Fax: (703) 836-8920
http://www.nemspa.org

North American Wildlife Enforcement Officers Association
http://www.naweoa.org

Organization of Black Airline Pilots
8630 Fenton Street, Suite 126
Silver Spring, MD 20910
Phone: (800) JET-OBAP
http://www.obap.org

Professional Helicopter Pilots Association
P.O. Box 7059
Burbank, CA 91510-7059
Phone: (213) 891-3636
http://www.phpa.org

Seaplane Pilots Association
4315 Highland Park Boulevard, Suite C
Lakeland, FL 33813-1639
Phone: (888) SPA-8923 or (863) 701-7979
Fax: (863) 701-7588
http://www.seaplanes.org

Women in Aviation International
101 Corsair Drive, Suite 101
Daytona Beach, FL 32114
Phone: (386) 226-7996
Fax: (386) 226-7998
http://www.wiai.org

FLIGHT OPERATIONS

Airline Dispatchers Federation
2020 Pennsylvania Avenue, NW, Suite 621
Washington, DC 20006
Phone: (800) OPN-CNTL
http://www.flightdispatch.net

American Meteorological Society
45 Beacon Street
Boston, MA 02108
Phone: (617) 227-2425
Fax: (617) 742-8718
http://www.ametsoc.org

National Weather Association Aviation Weather Committee
http://www.nwas.org/committees/avn-wea.html

Professional Aviation Maintenance Association
717 Princess Street
Alexandria, VA 22314
Phone: (866) 865-PAMA or (703) 683-3171
Fax: (703) 683-0018
http://www.pama.org

CUSTOMER SERVICES IN AVIATION

Association of Flight Attendants, AFL-CIO
1275 K Street NW, Fifth Floor
Washington, DC 20005
Phone: (202) 712-9799
http://www.afanet.org

Association of Professional Flight Attendants
1004 West Euless Boulevard
Euless, TX 76040
Phone: (800) 395-2732 or (817) 540-0108
Fax: (817) 540-2077
http://www.apfa.org

Communications Workers of America
501 Third Street, NW
Washington, DC 20001-2797
Phone: (202) 434-1100
Fax: (202) 434-1279
http://www.cwa-union.org

International Brotherhood of Teamsters
25 Louisiana Avenue, NW
Washington, DC 20001
Phone: (202) 624-6800
http://www.teamster.org

Transport Workers Union of America
1700 Broadway
New York, NY 10019
Phone: (212) 259-4900
Fax: (212) 265-4537
http://www.twu.org

AIRCRAFT MAINTENANCE

Aircraft Mechanics Fraternal Association
67 Water Street, Suite 208 A
Laconia, NH 03246
Phone: (800) 520-2632 or (603) 527-9212
Fax: (603) 527-9151
http://www.amfanatl.org

Association for Women in Aviation Maintenance
P.O. Box 1030
Edgewater, FL 32132
Phone: (386) 424-4780
Fax: (386) 428-3534
http://www.awam.org

International Association of Machinists and Aerospace Workers
9000 Machinists Place
Upper Marlboro, MD 20772-2687
Phone: (301) 967-4500
http://www.goiam.org

International Brotherhood of Teamsters
25 Louisiana Avenue, NW
Washington, DC 20001
Phone: (202) 624-6800
http://www.teamster.org

Professional Aviation Maintenance Association
717 Princess Street
Alexandria, VA 22314
Phone: (866) 865-PAMA or (703) 683-3171
Fax: (703) 683-0018
http://www.pama.org

Transport Workers Union of America
1700 Broadway
New York, NY 10019
Phone: (212) 259-4900
Fax: (212) 265-4537
http://www.twu.org

AVIATION SAFETY

Aerospace Medical Association
320 South Henry Street
Alexandria, VA 22314-3579
Phone: (703) 739-2240
Fax: (703) 739-9652
http://www.asma.org

Air Traffic Control Association
1101 King Street, Suite 300
Arlington, VA 22314
Phone: (703) 299-2430
Fax: (703) 299-2437
http://www.atca.org

Aircraft Rescue and Fire Fighting Working Group
1701 West Northwest Highway
Grapevine, TX 76051
Phone: (817) 329-5092
Fax: (817) 329-5094
http://www.arffwg.org

Civil Aviation Medical Association
P.O. Box 23864
Oklahoma City, OK 73123
Phone: (405) 840-0199
Fax: (405) 848-1053
http://www.civilavmed.com

International Association of Fire Fighters
1750 New York Avenue, NW
Washington, DC 20006
Phone: (202) 737-8484
Fax: (202) 737-8418
http://www.iaff.org

International Society of Air Safety Investigators
Park Center
107 East Holly Avenue, Suite 11
Sterling, VA 20164
http://www.isasi.org

National Air Traffic Controllers Association
1325 Massachusetts Avenue, NW
Washington, DC 20005
Phone: (202) 628-5451
Fax: (202) 628-5767
http://www.natca.org

National Association of Air Traffic Specialists
11303 Amherst Avenue, Suite 4
Wheaton, MD 20902
Phone: (301) 933-6228
Fax: (301) 933-3902
http://www.naats.org

National Fire Protection Association
1 Batterymarch Park
Quincy, MA 02169
Phone: (617) 770-3000
Fax: (617) 770-0700
http://www.nfpa.org

Professional Airways Systems Specialists
1150 17th Street, NW, Suite 702
Washington, DC 20036
Phone: (202) 293-7277
Fax: (202) 293-7727
http://www.passnational.org

Professional Women Controllers, Inc.
P.O. Box 950085
Oklahoma City, OK 73195-0085
Phone: (800) 232-9792
http://www.pwcinc.org

AVIATION SECURITY AND LAW

American Bar Association (ABA)
740 Fifteenth Street, NW
Washington, DC 20005-1019
Phone: (202) 662-1000
or
321 North Clark Street
Chicago, IL 60610
Phone: (312) 988-5000
or
ABA Service Center
321 North Clark Street
Chicago, IL 60610
Phone: (800) 285-2221 or (312) 988-5522
http://www.abanet.org

American Bar Association—Aviation and Space Law Committee
(part of the Tort Trial and Insurance Practice Section)
321 North Clark Street
Chicago, IL 60610
Phone: (800) 285-2221 or (312) 988-5522
http://www.abanet.org/tips/aviation/home.html

American Bar Association—Aviation Litigation Committee
(part of the Litigation Section)
321 North Clark Street
Chicago, IL 60610
Phone: (312) 988-5662
Fax: (312) 988-6234
http://www.abanet.org/litigation/committee/aviation/home.html

American Bar Association—Forum on Air and Space Law
321 North Clark Street
Chicago, IL 60610
Phone: (312) 988-5660
Fax: (312) 988-5677
http://www.abanet.org/forums/airspace/home.html

American Federation of Government Employees
80 F Street, NW
Washington, DC 20001
Phone: (202) 737-8700
http://www.afge.org

American Federation of Police and Concerned Citizens
3801 Biscayne Boulevard
Miami, FL 33137
Phone: (321) 264-0911
http://www.aphf.org/afp_cc.html

Association of Trial Lawyers of America—Aviation Law Section
The Leonard M. Ring Law Center
1050 31st Street, NW
Washington, DC 20007
Phone: (800) 424-2725 or (202) 965-3500
http://www.atlanet.org/Networking/Tier3/Tier4AviationLaw.aspx

Federal Law Enforcement Officers Association
P.O. Box 326
Lewisberry, PA 17339
Phone: (717) 938-2300
Fax: (717) 932-2262
http://www.fleoa.org

Fraternal Order of Police
1410 Donelson Pike, Suite A-17
Nashville TN 37217
Phone: (615) 399-0900
Fax: (615) 399-0400
http://www.grandlodgefop.org

International Association of Airport and Seaport Police
Secretariat
111, B3–1410 Parkway Boulevard
Coquitlam, British Columbia
Canada, V3E 3J7
Phone: (604) 782-6386
Fax: (604) 945-6134
http://www.iaasp.net

International Association of Women Police
http://www.iawp.org

Lawyer-Pilots Bar Association
P.O. Box 685
Poolesville, MD 20837
Phone: (301) 972-7700
http://www.lpba.org

National Lawyers Association
17201 East 40 Highway, Suite 207
Independence, MO 64055
Phone: (800) 471-2994
Fax: (816) 229-8425
http://www.nla.org

National Transportation Safety Board Bar Association
P.O. Box 65461
Washington, D.C. 20036-5461
http://www.ntsbbar.org

AVIATION MANAGEMENT

Aircraft Owners and Pilots Association
421 Aviation Way
Frederick, MD 21701
Phone: (301) 695-2000

Fax: (301) 695-2375
http://www.aopa.org

American Association of Airport Executives
601 Madison Street
Alexandria, VA 22314
Phone: (703) 824-0500
Fax: (703) 820-1395
http://www.airportnet.org

American Management Association
1601 Broadway
New York, NY 10019
Phone: (800) 262-9699 or (212) 586-8100
Fax: (212) 903-8168
http://www.amanet.org

American Society for Training and Development
1640 King Street, Box 1443
Alexandria, VA 22313-2043
Phone: (703) 683-8100
Fax: (703) 683-8103
http://www.astd.org

National Business Aviation Association
1200 Eighteenth Street, NW, Suite 400
Washington, DC 20036-2527
Phone: (202) 783-9000
Fax: (202) 331-8364
http://www.nbaa.org

Professional Aviation Maintenance Association
717 Princess Street
Alexandria, VA 22314
Phone: (866) 865-PAMA or (703) 683-3171
Fax: (703) 683-0018
http://www.pama.org

Public Relations Society of America
33 Irving Place
New York, NY 10003-2376
Phone: (212) 995-2230
Fax: (212) 995-0757
http://www.prsa.org

AIRPORT ENGINEERING, PLANNING, AND MAINTENANCE

American Association of Airport Executives
601 Madison Street
Alexandria, VA 22314
Phone: (703) 824-0500
Fax: (703) 820-1395
http://www.airportnet.org

American Planning Association
122 South Michigan Avenue, Suite 1600
Chicago, IL 60603
Phone: (312) 431-9100
Fax: (312) 431-9985
http://www.planning.org

American Society of Civil Engineers
1801 Alexander Bell Drive
Reston, VA 20191
Phone: (800) 548-2723 or (703) 295-6300
Fax: (703) 295-6222
http://www.asce.org

Institute of Transportation Engineers
1099 Fourteenth Street, NW, Suite 300 West
Washington, DC 20005-3438
Phone: (202) 289-0222
Fax: (202) 289-7722
http://www.ite.org

National Association of State Aviation Officials
1010 Wayne Avenue, Suite 930
Silver Spring, MD 20910
Phone: (301) 588-0587
Fax: (301) 585-1803
http://www.nasao.org

National Society of Professional Engineers
420 King Street
Alexandria, VA 22314
Phone: (703) 684-2800
http://www.nspe.org

Professional Airways Systems Specialists
1150 Seventeenth Street, NW, Suite 702
Washington, DC 20036
Phone: (202) 293-7277
Fax: (202) 293-7727
http://www.passnational.org

Service Employees International Union
1313 L Street, NW
Washington, DC 20005
Phone: (202) 898-3200
TDD: (202) 898-3481
http://www.seiu.org

AVIATION TRAINING, EDUCATION, AND COMMUNICATIONS

Aircraft Owners and Pilots Association
421 Aviation Way
Frederick, MD 21701
Phone: (301) 695-2000
Fax: (301) 695-2375
http://www.aopa.org

American Association for Adult and Continuing Education
4380 Forbes Boulevard
Lanham, MD 20706
Phone: (301) 918-1913
Fax: (301) 918-1846
http://www.aaace.org

American Association for Higher Education
1 Dupont Circle, Suite 360
Washington, DC 20036
Phone: (202) 293-6440
Fax: (202) 293-0073
http://www.aahe.org

American Association of Airport Executives
601 Madison Street
Alexandria, VA 22314
Phone: (703) 824-0500
Fax: (703) 820-1395
http://www.airportnet.org

American Association of Museums
1575 I Street, NW, Suite 400
Washington, DC 20005
Phone: (202) 289-1818
Fax: (202) 289-6578
http://www.aam-us.org

American Association of University Professors
1012 Fourteenth Street, NW, Suite 500
Washington, DC 20005
Phone: (202) 737-5900
Fax: (202) 737-5526
http://www.aaup.org

American Aviation Historical Society
2333 Otis Street
Santa Ana, CA 92704
Phone: (714) 549-4818
Fax: (714) 549-3657
http://www.aahs-online.org

American Federation of Teachers
555 New Jersey Avenue, NW
Washington, DC 20001
Phone: (202) 879-4440
http://www.aft.org

American Helicopter Society (AHS) International
217 North Washington Street
Alexandria, VA 22314-2538

Phone: (703) 684-6777
Fax: (703) 739-9279
http://www.vtol.org

American Society for Training and Development
1640 King Street, Box 1443
Alexandria, VA 22313-2043
Phone: (703) 683-8100
Fax: (703) 683-8103
http://www.astd.org

American Society of Journalists and Authors
1501 Broadway, Suite 302
New York, NY 10036
Phone: (212) 997-0947
http://www.asja.org

Association for Women in Aviation Maintenance
P.O. Box 1030
Edgewater, FL 32132
Phone: (386) 424-4780
Fax: (386) 428-3534
http://www.awam.org

The Authors Guild
31 East Twenty Eighth Street, Tenth Floor
New York, NY 10016-7923
Phone: (212) 563-5904
Fax: (212) 564-5363
http://www.authorsguild.org

Experimental Aircraft Association
EAA Aviation Center
P.O. Box 3086
Oshkosh, WI 54903
Phone: (920) 426-4800
http://www.eaa.org

International Association of Business Communicators
One Hallidie Plaza, Suite 600
San Francisco, CA 94102
Phone: (800) 776-4222 or (415) 544-4700
Fax: (415) 544-4747
http://www.iabc.com

National Association of Flight Instructors
EAA Aviation Center
P.O. Box 3086
Oshkosh, WI 54903-3086
Phone: (920) 426-6801
Fax: (920) 426-6778
http://www.nafinet.org

National Association of Scholars
221 Witherspoon Street, Second Floor
Princeton, NJ 08542
Phone: (609) 683-7878
Fax: (609) 683-0316
http://www.nas.org

National Business Aviation Association
1200 Eighteenth Street, NW, Suite 400
Washington, DC 20036-2527
Phone: (202) 783-9000
Fax: (202) 331-8364
http://www.nbaa.org

National Education Association
1201 Sixteenth Street, NW
Washington, DC 20036
Phone: (202) 833-4000
Fax: (202) 822-7974
http://www.nea.org

National Writers Union
113 University Place, Sixth Floor
New York, NY 10003
Phone: (212) 254-0279
Fax: (212) 254-0673
http://www.nwu.org

The Ninety-Nines, Inc.
4300 Amelia Earhart Road
Oklahoma City, OK 73159
Phone: (800) 994-1929 or (405) 685-7969
Fax: (405) 685-7985
http://www.ninety-nines.org

Professional Aviation Maintenance Association
717 Princess Street
Alexandria, VA 22314
Phone: (866) 865-PAMA or (703) 683-3171
Fax: (703) 683-0018
http://www.pama.org

Professional Helicopter Pilots Association
P.O. Box 7059
Burbank, CA 91510-7059
Phone: (213) 891-3636
http://www.phpa.org

Public Relations Society of America
33 Irving Place
New York, NY 10003-2376
Phone: (212) 995-2230
Fax: (212) 995-0757
http://www.prsa.org

Soaring Society of America
P.O.Box 2100
Hobbs, NM 88241-2100
Phone: (505) 392-1177
Fax: (505) 392-8154
http://www.ssa.org

Society for Technical Communication
901 North Stuart Street, Suite 904
Arlington, VA 22203
Phone: (703) 522-4114
Fax: (703) 522-2075
http://www.stc.org

Society of Aerospace Communicators
P.O. Box 2356
Reston, VA 20195
http://saccom.org

University Aviation Association
3410 Skyway Drive
Auburn, AL 36830-6444
Phone: (334) 844-2434 or (334) 844-2432
http://uaa.auburn.edu/msie.htm

Women in Aviation International
101 Corsair Drive, Suite 101
Daytona Beach, FL 32114
Phone: (386) 226-7996
Fax: (386) 226-7998
http://www.wiai.org

AVIATION CONSULTING AND SALES

Aircraft Owners and Pilots Association
421 Aviation Way
Frederick, MD 21701
Phone: (301) 695-2000
Fax: (301) 695-2375
http://www.aopa.org

Airport Consultants Council
908 King Street, Suite 100
Alexandria, VA 22314
Phone: (703) 683-5900
Fax: (703) 683-2564
http://www.acconline.org

American Association of Airport Executives
601 Madison Street
Alexandria, VA 22314
Phone: (703) 824-0500
Fax: (703) 820-1395
http://www.airportnet.org

Aviation Insurance Association
14 West Third Street, Suite 200
Kansas City, MO 64105

Phone: (816) 221-8488
Fax: (816) 472-7765
http://www.aiaweb.org

Independent Insurance Agents and Brokers of America
127 South Peyton Street
Alexandria, VA 22314
Phone: (800) 221-7917 or (703) 683-4422
Fax: (703) 683-7556
http://www.iiaa.com

Institute of Management Consultants USA, Inc.
2025 M Street, NW, Suite 800
Washington, DC 20036-3309
Phone: (800) 221-2557 or (202) 367-1134
Fax: (202) 367-2134
http://imcusa.org

International Society of Air Safety Investigators
Park Center
107 East Holly Avenue, Suite 11
Sterling, VA 20164
http://www.isasi.org

National Aircraft Resale Association
4226 King Street
Alexandria, VA 22302
Phone: (703) 671-8273
Fax: (703) 671-5848
http://www.nara-dealers.com

National Association of Flight Instructors
EAA Aviation Center
P.O. Box 3086
Oshkosh, WI 54903-3086
Phone: (920) 426-6801
Fax: (920) 426-6778
http://www.nafinet.org

National Association of Sales Professionals
11000 North 130th Place
Scottsdale, AZ 85259
Phone: (480) 951-4311
http://www.nasp.com

National Business Aviation Association
1200 18th Street, NW, Suite 400
Washington, DC 20036-2527
Phone: (202) 783-9000
Fax: (202) 331-8364
http://www.nbaa.org

Professional Aviation Maintenance Association
717 Princess Street
Alexandria, VA 22314
Phone: (866) 865-PAMA or (703) 683-3171
Fax: (703) 683-0018
http://www.pama.org

AVIATION RECREATION, SPORTS, AND ENTERTAINMENT

Balloon Federation of America
P.O. Box 400
Indianola, IA 50125
Phone: (515) 961-8809
Fax: (515) 961-3537
http://www.Bfa.net

International Aerobatic Club
EAA Aviation Center
P.O. Box 3086
Oshkosh, WI 54903-3086
Phone: (920) 426-4800
http://www.iac.org

International Council of Air Shows
751 Miller Drive SE, Suite F-4
Leesburg, Virginia 20175
Phone: (703) 779-8510
Fax: (703) 779-8511
http://www.airshows.org

Motion Picture Pilots Association
7435 Valjean Avenue
Van Nuys, CA 91406
Phone: (818) 947-5454
http://www.moviepilots.com

U.S. Hang Gliding Association
P.O. Box 1330
Colorado Springs, CO 80901
Phone: (800) 616-6888 or (719) 632-8300
Fax: (719) 632-6417
http://www.ushga.org

United States Parachute Association
1440 Duke Street
Alexandria, VA 22314
Phone: (703) 836-3495
Fax: (703) 836-2843
http://www.uspa.org

MILITARY AVIATION

Aerospace Medical Association
320 South Henry Street
Alexandria, VA 22314-3579
Phone: (703) 739-2240
Fax: (703) 739-9652
http://www.asma.org

Air Force Navigator Observer Association
http://www.afnoa.org

American Helicopter Society (AHS) International
217 North Washington Street
Alexandria, VA 22314-2538
Phone: (703) 684-6777
Fax: (703) 739-9279
http://www.vtol.org

Commissioned Officers Association of the U.S. Public Health Service, Inc.
8201 Corporate Drive, Suite 200
Landover, MD 20785
Phone: (301) 731-9080
Fax: (301) 731-9084
http://www.coausphs.org

International Association of Military Flight Surgeon Pilots
http://www.geocities.com/iamfsp/index.html

The Order of Daedalians
P.O. Box 249
Randolph AFB, TX 78148-0249
http://www.daedalians.org

Professional Loadmaster Association
P.O. Box 4351
Tacoma, WA 98438
Phone: (800) 239-4524 or (253) 620-6768
http://www.loadmasters.com

Society of U.S. Air Force Flight Surgeons
P.O. Box 35387
Brooks AFB, TX 78235-5387
http://www.sousaffs.org

Society of U.S. Naval Flight Surgeons
P.O. Box 33008
NAS Pensacola, FL 32508-3008
http://www.aerospacemed.org

Women Military Aviators, Inc.
c/o Travel Soft, Inc
24 West Mall Drive
Huntington, NY 11743
Phone: (703) 644-1105 or (703) 644-7786
http://www.womenmilitaryaviators.org

AEROSPACE MANUFACTURING INDUSTRY

American Association for Artificial Intelligence
445 Burgess Drive
Menlo Park, CA 94025-3442
Phone: (650) 328-3123
Fax: (650) 321-4457
http://www.aaai.org

American Association for the Advancement of Science
1200 New York Avenue, NW
Washington, DC 20005
Phone: (202) 326-6400
http://www.aaas.org

American Chemical Society
1155 Sixteenth Street, NW
Washington, DC 20036
Phone: (800) 227-5558 or (202) 872-4600
Fax: (202) 872-4615
http://www.chemistry.org

American Helicopter Society (AHS) International
217 North Washington Street
Alexandria, VA 22314-2538
Phone: (703) 684-6777
Fax: (703) 739-9279
http://www.vtol.org

American Institute for Chemical Engineers
Three Park Avenue
New York, NY 10016-5991
Phone: (212) 591-7338
Fax: (212) 591-8897
http://www.aiche.org

American Institute of Aeronautics and Astronautics
1801 Alexander Bell Drive, Suite 500
Reston, VA 20191-4344
Phone: (800) 639-AIAA or (703) 264-7500; customer service (703) 264-7657
Fax: (703) 264-7551
http://www.aiaa.org

American Institute of Graphic Arts
164 Fifth Avenue
New York, NY 10010
Phone: (212) 807-1990
http://www.aiga.org

American Institute of Physics
One Physics Ellipse
College Park, MD 20740-3843
Phone: (301) 209-3100
Fax: (301) 209-0843
http://www.aip.org

American Management Association
1601 Broadway
New York, NY 10019
Phone: (800) 262-9699 or (212) 586-8100
Fax: 212-903-8168
http://www.amanet.org

American Mathematical Society
201 Charles Street
Providence, RI 02904-2294
Phone: (800) 321-4267 or (401) 455-4000
Fax: (401) 331-3842
http://www.ams.org

American Society for Quality
600 North Plankinton Avenue
Milwaukee, WI 53203
Mailing address:
P.O. Box 3005
Milwaukee, WI 53201-3005
Phone: (800) 248-1946 or (414) 272-8575
Fax: (414) 272-1734
http://www.asq.org

American Society for Training and Development
1640 King Street, Box 1443
Alexandria, VA 22313-2043
Phone: (703) 683-8100
Fax: (703) 683-8103
http://www.astd.org

ASM International—The Materials Information Society
9639 Kinsman Road
Materials Park, OH 44073-0002
Phone: (440) 338-5151 or (800) 336-5152 (in U.S. and Canada) or
(800) 368-9800 (in Europe)
Fax: (440) 338-4634
http://www.asm-intl.org

ASME International (American Society of Mechanical Engineers)
Three Park Avenue
New York, NY 10016-5990
Phone: (800) 843-2763 or (973) 882-1167
http://www.asme.org

ASME International—Aerospace Division
Mail Stop 22W3
Three Park Avenue
New York, NY 10016-5990
Phone: (212) 591-7797
Fax: (212) 591-7671
http://www.asme.org/divisions/aerospace

Association for Computing Machinery
1515 Broadway
New York, NY 10036
Phone: (800) 342-6626 or (212) 626-0500
http://www.acm.org

Association for Computing Machinery—The Special Interest Group on Documentation
P.O. Box 11315
New York, NY 10286-1315
http://www.acm.org/sigdoc

Association of Teachers of Technical Writing
http://www.attw.org

Editorial Freelancers Association
71 West Twenty-third Street, Suite 1910
New York, NY 10010-4102
Phone: (866) 929-5400 or (212) 929-5400
Fax: (866) 929-5439 or (212) 929-5439
http://www.the-efa.org

Institute of Electrical and Electronics Engineers
Corporate Office
Three Park Avenue, 17th Floor
New York, NY 10016-5997
Phone: (212) 419-7900
Fax: (212) 752-4929
Operations Center
445 Hoes Lane
Piscataway, NJ 08854-1331
Phone: (732) 981-0060
Fax: (732) 981-1721
www.ieee.org

Institute of Electrical and Electronics Engineers—Computer Society
1730 Massachusetts Avenue, NW
Washington, DC 20036-1992
Phone: (202) 371-0101
Fax: (202) 728-9614
http://www.computer.org

Institute of Electrical and Electronic Engineers—Professional Communication Society
IEEE Corporate Office
Three Park Avenue, 17th Floor
New York, NY 10016-5997
Phone: (212) 419-7900
Fax: (212) 752-4929
http://www.ieeepcs.org

Institute of Industrial Engineers
3577 Parkway Lane, Suite 200
Norcross, GA 30092
Phone: (800) 494-0460 or (770) 449-0460
Fax: (770) 441-3295
http://www.iienet.org

International Association of Business Communicators
One Hallidie Plaza, Suite 600
San Francisco, CA 94102
Phone: (800) 776- 4222 or (415) 544-4700
Fax: (415) 544-4747
http://www.iabc.com

International Association of Machinists and Aerospace Workers
9000 Machinists Place
Upper Marlboro, MD 20772-2687
Phone: (301) 967-4500
http://www.goiam.org

International Brotherhood of Electrical Workers
1125 Fifteenth Street, NW
Washington, DC 20005
Phone: (202) 833-7000
Fax: (202) 467-6316
http://www.ibew.org

International Federation of Professional and Technical Engineers
8630 Fenton Street, Suite 400
Silver Spring, MD 20910
Phone: (301) 565-9016
Fax: (301) 565-0018
http://www.ifpte.org

International Society for Performance Improvement
1400 Spring Street, Suite 260
Silver Spring, MD 20910
Phone: (301) 587-8570
Fax: (301) 587-8573
http://www.ispi.org

International Society of Allied Weight Engineers
P.O. Box 60024, Terminal Annex
Los Angeles, CA 90060
http://www.sawe.org

National Society of Professional Engineers
420 King Street
Alexandria, VA 22314
Phone: (703) 684-2800
http://www.nspe.org

National Writers Union
113 University Place, Sixth Floor
New York, NY 10003
Phone: (212) 254-0279
Fax: (212) 254-0673
http://www.nwu.org

Society for Industrial and Applied Mathematics
3600 University City Science Center
Philadelphia, PA 19104
Phone: (215) 382-9800
http://www.siam.org

Society for Technical Communication
901 North Stuart Street, Suite 904
Arlington, VA 22203
Phone: (703) 522-4114
Fax: (703) 522-2075
http://www.stc.org

Society of Experimental Test Pilots
44814 North Elm Avenue
Lancaster, CA 93534
Mailing address:
P.O. Box 986
Lancaster, CA 93584-0986
Phone: (661) 942-9574
Fax: (661) 940-0398
http://www.setp.org

Society of Flight Test Engineers
44814 North Elm Avenue
Lancaster, CA 93534
Mailing address:
P.O. Box 4037
Lancaster, CA 93539-4037
Phone: (661) 949-2095
Fax: (661) 949-2096
http://www.sfte.org

Society of Women Engineers
230 East Ohio Street, Suite 400
Chicago, IL 60611-3265
Phone: (312) 596-5223
Fax: (312) 596-5252
http://www.societyofwomenengineers.org

Women in Aerospace
P.O. Box 16721
Alexandria, VA 22302
Phone: (202) 547-9451
http://www.womeninaerospace.org

SPACE FLIGHT AND EXPLORATION

American Association for Artificial Intelligence
445 Burgess Drive
Menlo Park, CA 94025-3442
Phone: (650) 328-3123
Fax: (650) 321-4457
http://www.aaai.org

American Association for Higher Education
One Dupont Circle, Suite 360
Washington, DC 20036
Phone: (202) 293-6440
Fax: (202) 293-0073
http://www.aahe.org

American Association for the Advancement of Science
1200 New York Avenue, NW
Washington, DC 20005
Phone: (202) 326-6400
http://www.aaas.org

American Association of University Professors
1012 Fourteenth Street, NW, Suite 500
Washington, DC 20005
Phone: (202) 737-5900
Fax: (202) 737-5526
http://www.aaup.org

American Astronomical Society
2000 Florida Avenue, NW, Suite 400
Washington, DC 20009-1231
Phone: (202) 328-2010
Fax: (202) 234-2560
http://www.aas.org

American Chemical Society
1155 Sixteenth Street, NW
Washington, DC 20036
Phone: (800) 227-5558 or (202) 872-4600
Fax: (202) 872-4615
http://www.chemistry.org

American Geophysical Union
2000 Florida Avenue, NW
Washington, DC 20009-1277
Phone: (800) 966-2481 or (202) 462-6900
Fax: (202) 328-0566
http://www.agu.org

American Institute of Aeronautics and Astronautics
1801 Alexander Bell Drive, Suite 500
Reston, VA 20191-4344
Phone: (800) 639-AIAA or (703) 264-7500; customer service (703) 264-7657
Fax: (703) 264-7551
http://www.aiaa.org

American Institute of Physics
One Physics Ellipse
College Park, MD 20740-3843
Phone: (301) 209-3100
Fax: (301) 209-0843
http://www.aip.org

American Mathematical Society
201 Charles Street
Providence, RI 02904-2294
Phone: (800) 321-4267 or (401) 455-4000
Fax: (401) 331-3842
http://www.ams.org

ASM International—The Materials Information Society
9639 Kinsman Road
Materials Park, OH 44073-0002
Phone: (440) 338-5151 or (800) 336-5152 (in U.S. and Canada) or
(800) 368-9800 (in Europe)
Fax: (440) 338-4634
http://www.asm-intl.org

ASME International (American Society of Mechanical Engineers)
Three Park Avenue
New York, NY 10016-5990
Phone: (800) 843-2763 or (973) 882-1167
http://www.asme.org

Association for Computing Machinery
1515 Broadway
New York, NY 10036
Phone: (800) 342-6626 or (212) 626-0500
http://www.acm.org

Association of Space Explorers
1150 Gemini Avenue
Houston, TX 77058
Phone: (281) 280-8172
Fax: (281) 280-8173

Institute of Electrical and Electronics Engineers
Corporate Office
Three Park Avenue, Seventeenth Floor
New York, NY 10016-5997
Phone: (212) 419-7900
Fax: (212) 752-4929
Operations Center
445 Hoes Lane
Piscataway, NJ 08854-1331
Phone: (732) 981-0060
Fax: (732) 981-1721
http://www.ieee.org

The Order of Daedalians
P.O. Box 249
Randolph AFB, TX 78148-0249
http://www.daedalians.org

National Association of Scholars
221 Witherspoon Street, Second Floor
Princeton, NJ 08542
Phone: (609) 683-7878
Fax: (609) 683-0316
http://www.nas.org

Society of Experimental Test Pilots
44814 N. Elm Avenue
Lancaster, CA 93534
Mailing address:
P.O. Box 986
Lancaster, CA 93584-0986
Phone: (661) 942-9574
Fax: (661) 940-0398
http://www.setp.org

Society of Women Engineers
230 East Ohio Street, Suite 400
Chicago, IL 60611-3265
Phone: (312) 596-5223
Fax: (312) 596-5252
http://www.societyofwomenengineers.org

APPENDIX IV
FEDERAL GOVERNMENT AGENCIES

In this appendix, you will find contact information and Web site addresses for many of the U.S. government agencies that are mentioned in this book.

Note: All contact information and Web site addresses were current when the book was written. If you come across a URL that is no longer valid, you may be able to find an organization's new Web site by entering its name into a search engine.

FEDERAL AVIATION ADMINISTRATION (FAA)

The FAA is responsible for enforcing federal aviation regulations relating to civil aviation in the United States. It is an agency within the U.S. Department of Transportation.

FAA Headquarters
800 Independence Avenue, SW
Washington, DC 20591
http://www.faa.gov

FAA Flight Standards Service
800 Independence Avenue, SW, Room 822
Washington, DC 20591
http://www.faa.gov/avr/afs

FAA Flight Standards District Offices (FSDOs)
Listed below is the contact information for the various FSDO regional headquarters. Several district offices are within each FSDO region. To find out if a district office is near you, check your telephone directory or visit the regional office's Web site on the Internet.

Alaska Regional Headquarters
222 West Seventh Avenue
Anchorage, AK 99513
http://www.alaska.faa.gov

Central Region Headquarters
901 Locust Street
Kansas City, MO 64106
http://www.faa.gov/cen/index.cfm

Eastern Region Headquarters
One Aviation Plaza, Room 520
Jamaica, NY 11434
http://aea.faa.gov/aea200

Great Lakes Region Headquarters
2300 East Devon Avenue
Des Plaines, IL 60018
http://www.faa.gov/region/agl200

New England Region Headquarters
12 New England Executive Park
Burlington, MA 01803
http://www.faa.gov/region/ane/flightstandards/offices.cfm

Northwest Mountain Region Headquarters
1601 Lind Avenue, SW
Renton, WA 98055
http://www.nw.faa.gov

Southern Region Headquarters
1701 Columbia Avenue
College Park, GA 30281
http://www.faa.gov/fsdo/asoro/index.htm

Southwest Region Headquarters
2601 Meacham Boulevard
Fort Worth, TX 76137
http://www.faa.gov/asw/index.html

Western-Pacific Region Headquarters
1500 Aviation Boulevard
Lawndale, CA 90261
http://www.awp.faa.gov

NATIONAL TRANSPORTATION SAFETY BOARD (NTSB)

The NTSB is in charge of investigating aviation and other transportation accidents. It is an independent agency.

National Transportation Safety Board
Office of Public Affairs
490 L'Enfant Plaza, SW
Washington, DC 20594
http://www.ntsb.gov

NTSB Aviation
http://www.ntsb.gov/aviation/aviation.htm

U.S. NATIONAL WEATHER SERVICE (NWS)

The NWS is part of the National Oceanic and Atmospheric Administration (NOAA), which is a branch of the U.S. Department of Commerce.

NOAA National Weather Service
1325 East-West Highway
Silver Spring, MD 20910
http://www.nws.noaa.gov

Aviation Weather Center
NOAA National Weather Service
7220 NW 101st Terrace, Room 118
Kansas City, MO 64153-2371
http://aviationweather.gov

NOAA Marine and Aviation Operations
1315 East-West Highway
Silver Spring, MD 20910
http://www.nmao.noaa.gov

Aircraft Operations Center
NOAA Marine and Aviation Operations
P.O. Box 6829
MacDill AFB, FL 33608
Phone: (813) 828-3310
http://www.aoc.noaa.gov

U.S. DEPARTMENTS OF INTERIOR AND AGRICULTURE

Both these departments have subagencies that are responsible for managing forest fires that occur on federal lands.

USDA Forest Service
Fire and Aviation Management
3833 South Development Avenue
Boise, ID 83705
Phone: (208) 387-5100
http://www.fs.fed.us/fire

U.S. Bureau of Land Management
Office of Fire and Aviation
3833 South Development Avenue
Boise, ID 83705
Phone: (208) 387-5457
http://www.fire.blm.gov/index.htm

National Business Center Aviation Management
U.S. Department of the Interior
300 East Mallard Drive, Suite 200
Boise, ID 83706
Phone: (208) 433-5000
http://www.oas.gov

National Interagency Fire Center
3833 South Development Avenue
Boise, Idaho 83705
http://www.nifc.gov

U.S. DEPARTMENT OF DEFENSE (DOD)

The DOD is responsible for protecting the United States, its people, and its interests throughout the world.

Directorate for Public Inquiry and Analysis
Office of the Secretary of Defense (Public Affairs)
Room 3A750—The Pentagon
1400 Defense Pentagon
Washington, DC 20301-1400
http://www.defenselink.mil

Listed below are the military branches that are under the DOD.

U.S. Air Force
http://www.af.mil

U.S. Army
http://www.army.mil

U.S. Marine Corps
http://www.usmc.mil

U.S. Navy
http://www.navy.mil

U.S. Air National Guard
http://www.ang.af.mil

U.S. Army National Guard
http://www.arng.army.mil

U.S. DEPARTMENT OF HOMELAND SECURITY (DHS)

The DHS is responsible for the protection and security of U.S. borders. It was established in 2002 in response to the terrorist attacks that occurred in the United States on September 11, 2001. This department includes many federal law enforcement agencies, such as the Federal Air Marshal Service, the U.S. Secret Service, and the Immigration and Customs Enforcement.

U.S. Department of Homeland Security
Washington, DC 20528
http://www.dhs.gov

U.S. Coast Guard
http://www.uscg.mil

Transportation Security Agency
Mail Stop: TSA-6
400 Seventh Street, SW
Washington, DC 20590
http://www.tsa.gov

NATIONAL AERONAUTICS AND SPACE ADMINISTRATION (NASA)

NASA is responsible for overseeing the U.S. space exploration program. It is an independent federal agency.

NASA Home Page on the Web
http://www.nasa.gov

NASA Headquarters
Washington, DC 20546
http://www.hq.nasa.gov

NASA Centers
Listed below are NASA's research centers and facilities, which are located throughout the United States.

NASA Ames Research Center
Moffett Field, CA 94035
http://www.arc.nasa.gov

NASA Dryden Flight Research Center
P.O. Box 273
Edwards, CA 93523
http://www.dfrc.nasa.gov

NASA John H. Glenn Research Center
21000 Brookpark Road
Cleveland, OH 44135
http://www.grc.nasa.gov

NASA Goddard Space Flight Center
Code 130, Office of Public Affairs
Greenbelt, MD 20771
http://www.gsfc.nasa.gov

NASA Jet Propulsion Laboratory
4800 Oak Grove Drive
Pasadena, CA 91109
http://www.jpl.nasa.gov

NASA Johnson Space Center
2101 NASA Parkway
Houston, TX 77058
http://www.jsc.nasa.gov

NASA Kennedy Space Center
Public Inquiries
KSC, FL 32899
http://www.ksc.nasa.gov

NASA Langley Research Center
100 NASA Road
Hampton, VA 23681
http://www.larc.nasa.gov

NASA Marshall Space Flight Center
Huntville, AL 35812
http://www.msfc.nasa.gov

NASA Stennis Space Center
Public Affairs Office
Stennis Space Center, MS 39529
http://www.ssc.nasa.gov

NASA Wallops Flight Facility
Wallops Island, VA 23337
http://www.wff.nasa.gov

NATIONAL AIR AND SPACE MUSEUM

This museum is part of the Smithsonian Institution, a nationally owned museum based in Washington, D.C. The National Air and Space Museum has two locations. For general information, call (202) 357-2700 or visit the museum's Web site at http://www.nasm.si.edu.

on the National Mall:
National Air and Space Museum
Sixth & Independence Avenue, SW
Washington, DC 20560

near Dulles International Airport:
Steven F. Udvar-Hazy Center
14390 Air & Space Museum Parkway
Chantilly, VA 20151

U.S. BUREAU OF LABOR STATISTICS (BLS)

The BLS is part of the U.S. Department of Labor. Its mission is to conduct studies and prepare reports about labor economics and statistics. Many of its publications, such as the *Occupational Outlook Handbook,* can be accessed at its Web site.

U.S. Bureau of Labor Statistics
Postal Square Building
Two Massachusetts Avenue, NE
Washington, DC 20212
Phone: (202) 691-5200
Fax-on-demand: (202) 691-6325
http://www.bls.gov

U.S. OFFICE OF PERSONNEL MANAGEMENT (OPM)

This office is responsible for overseeing all personnel issues relating to the federal government's workforce. It also manages the job listings of all positions available at the different government agencies. OPM has branch offices throughout the United States.

OPM Headquarters
1900 E Street, NW
Washington, DC 20415
Phone: (202) 606-1800
TTY: (202) 606-2532
http://www.opm.gov

For information about federal employment, student opportunities, career development programs, and employment related information, visit these OPM Web pages:

Career Opportunities
http://www.opm.gov/Career_Opportunities/index.asp

USAJOBS
http://www.usajobs.opm.gov

APPENDIX V
RESOURCES ON THE WORLD WIDE WEB

In this appendix, you will find a listing of Web sites that may help you learn more about the various professions and fields in aviation and the aerospace industry. In addition, you will find some Web resources that offer career and job search information.

Note: All Web site addresses were current when this book was written. If a Web site address is no longer valid, you may be able to find the new address by entering the Web page title or the name of an organization or individual into a search engine.

GENERAL INFORMATION

Airports
by Federal Aviation Administration
http://www.faa.gov/arp

Aviation Links
by Kennon Aircraft Covers
http://www.kennoncovers.com/links/themeindex.html

Commission on the Future of the U.S. Aerospace Industry
http://www.aerospacecommission.gov

HowStuffWorks
http://www.howstuffworks.com

Thirty Thousand Feet—Aviation Directory
http://www.thirtythousandfeet.com

Wikipedia (the Free Encyclopedia)
http://www.wikipedia.org

World Book Reference Center Online
http://www.aolsvc.worldbook.aol.com

CAREER AND JOB INFORMATION

Airjobsonline.com—Aviation and Aerospace Jobs
http://www.airjobsonline.com

America's Job Bank
http://www.jobsearch.org

Aviation Employment.com
http://www.aviationemployment.com

California Occupational Guides
http://www.calmis.ca.gov/htmlfile/subject/guide.htm

Career Prospects in Virginia
University of Virginia
http://www.ccps.virginia.edu/career_prospects

CorporatePilot.com
http://www.corporatepilot.com

Global Aviation Human Resources
(specializing in flight crew and maintenance personnel)
http://www.makeitfly.biz

The High School Graduate.com
http://www.thehighschoolgraduate.com

Indiana Career and Postsecondary Advancement Center
http://icpac.indiana.edu

Monster.com
http://www.monster.com

NASA Jobs
http://www.nasajobs.nasa.gov

Occupational Employment Statistics
U.S. Bureau of Labor Statistics
http://www.bls.gov/oes

Occupational Outlook Handbook
U.S. Bureau of Labor Statistics
http://www.bls.gov/oco/home.htm

USA Jobs
U.S. Office of Personnel Management
http://www.usajobs.opm.gov

Virtual Skies
by NASA
http://virtualskies.arc.nasa.gov

WetFeet.com
http://www.wetfeet.com

AEROSPACE MANUFACTURING INDUSTRY

Aerospace Education Foundation
http://www.aef.org

Aerospace Industries Association
http://www.aia-aerospace.org

Aerospace Technology: The Web Site for the Aerospace Industry
http://www.aerospace-technology.com

Aerospaceweb.org
http://www.aerospaceweb.org

Aircraft Electronics Association
http://www.aea.net

General Aviation Manufacturers Association
http://www.generalaviation.com

IEEE Control Systems Society
http://www.ieeecss.org

Radical Departures
http://www.radical-departures.net

Society of Professional Engineering Employees in Aerospace
http://www.speea.org

AIR CARGO AGENT

Airforwarders Association
http://www.airforwarders.org

International Air Cargo Association
http://www.tiaca.org

AIRLINES

Airline Addresses
by Aviation Communications
http://www.flightinfo.com/airlineaddresses.asp

Airline Information Online on the Internet
http://airline.iecc.com

Air Transport Association
http://www.airlines.org/public/home/default1.asp

Aviation Communications
http://www.flightinfo.com

CrewStart—The Airline Crew Portal
http://www.crewstart.com

AIRPORT ENGINEER

Airport Engineering
The Civil Engineering Portal
http://www.icivilengineer.com/Transportation_Engineering/Airport_Engineering

CyberAir Airpark
http://www.cyberair.com

AIRPORT POLICE

Public Safety Training Center
Dallas/Ft. Worth International Airport
http://www.dfwairport.com/training

AIR TRAFFIC CONTROLLER

Air Traffic Cafe
http://www.airtrafficcafe.com

Professional Women Controllers
http://www.pwcinc.org

ASTRONAUT

Astronaut Scholarship Foundation
created by the Mercury 7 Astronauts
http://www.astronautscholarship.org

Encyclopedia Astronautica
http://www.astronautix.com

International Space Station
http://spaceflight.nasa.gov/station

NASA Astronaut Selection Home Page
http://astronauts.nasa.gov

ASTRONOMER

American Association of Amateur Astronomers
http://www.corvus.com

Ask a High-Energy Astronomer
http://imagine.gsfc.nasa.gov/docs/ask_astro/ask_an_astronomer.html

Ask an Astronomer at Cornell University
http://curious.astro.cornell.edu/index.php

Astronomical Observatory Links
http://www.ngcic.com/obs.htm

Astronomical Society of the Pacific
http://www.astrosociety.org

AVIATION CONSULTANT

Airport Consultants Council
http://www.acconline.org

Consultant and Professional Service Web Sites
Thirty Thousand Feet—Aviation Directory
http://www.thirtythousandfeet.com/consulta.htm

AVIATION EDUCATOR

National Coalition for Aviation Education
http://www.aviationeducation.org

AVIATION INSURANCE AGENT

Council of Insurance Agents and Brokers
http://www.ciab.com

Temple's Tips
Jerry Temple Aviation, Inc.
http://www.jtatwins.com/Tips%20Table%20of%20Contents.htm

AVIATION LAWYER

Aviation: An Overview
Legal Information Institute, Cornell Law School, Ithaca, New York
http://www.law.cornell.edu/topics/aviation.html

Aviation Law Corporation
by Phillip J. Kolczynski
http://www.aviationlawcorp.com

Aviation Law News
http://www.aviation-law-news.com

AVIATION MAINTENANCE

A&P.com: The Web Site for Aircraft Mechanics
http://aandp.com

AMT Online
http://www.amtonline.com

Jet Mex's Aviation Page
http://www.geocities.com/CapeCanaveral/Hangar/1982/index.html

AVIATION MANAGER

Airports Council International
http://www.aci-na.org

Fixed Base Operators
Thirty Thousand Feet—Aviation Directory
http://www.thirtythousandfeet.com/fbo.htm

AVIATION MEDICINE

Aerospace Medicine and Civil Aerospace Medical Institute
http://www.cami.jccbi.gov

FAA Aviation Medical Examiners Guide
http://www.cami.jccbi.gov/AAM-400/ameinfo.html

Naval Aerospace Medical Institute
http://www.nomi.med.navy.mil/NAMI/index.htm

Virtual Flight Surgeons
http://www.aviationmedicine.com

AVIATION METEOROLOGIST

Aviation Weather Center
NOAA National Weather Service
http://aviationweather.gov

Northwest Airlines Meteorology Portal
http://www.lattery.com/nwametro

AVIATION MUSEUM CURATOR

Flight-History.com—The Ghosts of Aviation
http://www.flight-history.com

Thirty Thousand Feet—Aviation Directory
http://www.thirtythousandfeet.com/museums.htm

AVIATION PROFESSOR

The Chronicle of Higher Education
http://chronicle.com

Preparing Future Faculty
http://www.preparing-faculty.org

AVIATION SAFETY—GENERAL RESOURCES

AirDisaster.Com
http://www.airdisaster.com

Aviation.org
by Aviation Safety Connection, Inc.
http://www.aviation.org

Aviation Safety Network
http://aviation-safety.net/index.shtml

FAA Office of Aviation System Standards
http://avn.faa.gov

Flight Inspections: International Committee for Airspace Standards and Calibration
http://avnwww.jccbi.gov/icasc/index.html

Flight Safety Foundation
http://www.flightsafety.org

Human Factors on Aviation Maintenance and Inspection
http://hfskyway.faa.gov

AVIATION SALES

Aircraftbuyer.com
Aviation Week's *A/C Flyer* magazine
http://www.aircraftbuyer.com

Aviation World Services
http://www.aviationworldservices.com

AVIATION TRAINING DEVELOPER

Aviation Training and Development Institute
http://www.iata.org/atdi/index

International Aviation Training Symposium
http://www.halldale.com/iats/about.asp

National Training Systems Association
http://www.trainingsystems.org

Neil Krey's Flight Deck
http://s92270093.onlinehome.us/fltdeck

COMPUTER SPECIALIST

ACM Career Resource Center
by Association for Computing Machinery
http://campus.acm.org/crc

Artificial Intelligence Depot
http://ai-depot.com/Main.html

Institute for Certification of Computing Professionals
http://www.iccp.org

MIT Laboratory for Computer Science
http://www.lcs.mit.edu

ENGINEERING—GENERAL RESOURCES

Discover Engineering Online
http://www.discoverengineering.org

The Junior Engineering Technical Society
http://www.jets.org

National Academy of Engineering
http://www.nae.edu

The Pre-Engineering Portal
http://www.engineerinyou.com

Schools of Engineering @ Purdue
https://Engineering.Purdue.edu/Engr

FLIGHT ATTENDANT

AirlineCareer.com
http://www.airlinecareer.com

Flight Attendant Corp of America
http://www.flightattendantcorp.com

Flight Attendants.org
http://www.flightattendants.org

Flight Attendants Resource
by Ken Turner
http://www.gofir.com/cater/index.htm

Skychick
http://www.skychick.com

HANG GLIDING INSTRUCTOR

The Hang Gliding Instructor's Forum
http://www.angelfire.com/ct/instructor

MACHINIST

American Machinist
http://www.americanmachinist.com

MILITARY AVIATION

Associations and Professional Societies
FAS Military Analysis Network
http://www.fas.org/man/assoc.htm

The Institute of Navigation
http://www.ion.org

Today's Military.com
by the U.S. Department of Defense
http://www.todaysmilitary.com

U.S. Navy—The Aircraft Carriers
http://www.chinfo.navy.mil/navpalib/ships/carriers

Women Military Aviators
http://www.militaryaviators.org

QUALITY SPECIALIST

CyberQuality Resource
by Bill Casti
http://www.quality.org

International Aerospace Quality Group
http://www.iaqg.sae.org/iaqg

PILOT—AEROBATICS

Aerobatics Server Home Page
by Dr. Gunther Eichhorn
http://acro.harvard.edu/ACRO

Aerobatic Pilot: World Airshow News
http://www.worldairshownews.com

FAA National Airshow Program
http://www.faa.gov/avr/afs/airshow

International Council of Air Shows
http://www.airshows.org

PILOT—AIR TANKER

Aerial Firefighting Industry Association
http://www.afia.com

ARFF.Info—Your Aircraft Rescue Fire Fighting Information Resource
http://www.arff.info

The Wildfire Page
by Thomas Eggleston
http://www.sonnet.com/usr/wildfire

PILOT—EMERGENCY MEDICAL SERVICE

Alliance of Emergency Medical Aviators
http://64.78.56.99/aema

Flight Web—For Air Medical Professionals
http://www.flightweb.com

PILOT—FLIGHT TESTING

Flight Test at Mojave Airport
http://www.mojaveairport.com/flight_test.htm

U.S. Navy Test Pilot School
http://www.usntps.navy.mil

PILOT—GENERAL RESOURCES

The Air Affair
by Ross Oliver
http://www.airaffair.com

Be a Pilot.com
http://www.beapilot.com

Civil Air Patrol Online
http://www.cap.gov

General Aviation
Aircraft Owners and Pilots Association
http://www.gaservingamerica.org

National Aeronautic Association
http://www.naa-usa.org

The Pilot Mentor Network
http://www.pilotmentors.homestead.com

Professional Air Sports Association
http://www.professionalairsports.org

The Student Pilot Network
http://www.studentpilot.net

Vertical Reference—Your Online Helicopter Resource
http://www.verticalreference.com

PILOT—HOT-AIR BALLOON

Hot-Air Ballooning
http://www.launch.net

National American Balloon Association
http://www.eballoon.com

TECHNICAL COMMUNICATOR

Association for Women in Communications
http://www.womcom.org

EServer TC Library
http://tc.eserver.org

Graphic Communicators Association
http://wwwidealliance.org

International Webmasters Association
http://www.iwanet.org

National Association of Government Communicators
http://www.nagc.com

World Organization of Webmasters
http://www.joinwow.org

SKYDIVING INSTRUCTOR

National Skydiving Association
http://www.skydivinginformation.com

SPACE FLIGHT AND EXPLORATION

The Astrobiology Web
http://www.astrobiology.com

Flight, FDO!
by former Flight Dynamics Officer Roger Balettie
http://space.balettie.com

Hubble Space Telescope Project
http://hubble.nasa.gov

NASA Aerospace Technology Enterprise
http://www.aerospace.nasa.gov

NASA Astrobiology Institute
http://nai1.arc.nasa.gov

NASA Human Space Flight
http://spaceflight.nasa.gov

NASA Imagine the Universe!
http://imagine.gsfc.nasa.gov

NASA Quest Biographies and Journals
http://questdb.arc.nasa.gov/bio_search.htm

International Space Station Information Payload
http://stationpayloads.jsc.nasa.gov

Rocket Section
Space Travel: Your Portal to Space Flight
http://www.space-travel.com/rocketscience.html

Science @ NASA
http://science.nasa.gov

Space Center Houston
http://www.spacecenter.org

GLOSSARY

A rating Airframe rating; an FAA rating that permits aircraft mechanics to perform the maintenance, repair, overhaul, and inspection of aircraft structures.

A&P mechanic An aircraft mechanic who holds both the airframe (A) and the powerplant (P) ratings, which are granted by the FAA.

aerobatic maneuver A precise spin, fall, roll, or other maneuver performed in the air by an airplane pilot after many hours of practice.

aerodynamics The study of the motion of air and other gases, as well as the motion of solid bodies, such as aircraft, in air.

aeronautics The science dealing with flight and the operation of aircraft.

aerospace The Earth's atmosphere and the space beyond Earth.

AFSS Automated Flight Service Station.

air ambulance An aircraft used to transport patients to medical facilities; it is equipped with medical equipment and staffed by medical professionals.

air cargo The mail and freight that is transported by air.

air carrier A commercial operator, such as an airline, that offers air transportation services.

air charter Air taxi.

aircraft A helicopter, airplane, balloon, or other device that is used for flying.

airframe All the parts and systems that make up an aircraft's structure, except for its propellers, engines, and aircraft instruments.

air navigation facility A navigational aid such as a ground-based navigational transmitter, instrument landing system, radar system, or global positioning system.

air show An exhibition of aircraft and the skills of pilots, skydivers, and other air performers.

airspace The space lying above a nation; all aircraft flying within a nation's airspace are under the jurisdiction of that nation.

air taxi A commercial operator who offers air transportation on an on-demand basis and usually operates aircraft that holds 30 or fewer passenger seats.

air traffic The flow of aircraft as they move through the air and on the airport grounds.

air traffic control A service that separates aircraft to ensure a safe and efficient flow of air traffic.

airway A designated air route equipped with navigational aids.

airworthy Having met the standard requirements for flight.

applied research Scientific studies that are conducted for practical purposes, such as developing new products, processes, or technologies.

apron Ramp or tarmac. (See: *ramp*)

ARTCC Air Route Traffic Control Center.

astronautics The science dealing with the construction and operation of spacecraft.

astronomy The study of the solar system and the universe; this discipline is also known as astrophysics.

atmosphere The gas that surrounds a planet, such as Earth.

ATP certificate Airline Transport Pilot certificate; the most advanced pilot certificate granted by the FAA.

aviation security The programs that airports, airlines, the FAA, or other organizations develop and implement to prevent dangerous activities, such as terrorist acts, from occurring in airports and aboard aircraft.

aviation The art or practice of operating, designing, developing, or manufacturing heavier-than-air craft.

avionics Electronics designed for aircraft or spacecraft.

basic research Scientific studies conducted to gain new knowledge and understanding about a particular subject.

BLS Bureau of Labor Statistics; an agency in the U.S. Department of Labor.

business aviation The segment of aviation that serves businesses and companies that have their own flight operations.

canopy A parachute.

captain The pilot-in-command of an aircraft or spacecraft.

cargo The mail and freight that is being transported in an aircraft.

cargo bay The cargo space of a transport vehicle.

celestial body A star, planet, comet, asteroid, or other body in space.

celestial mechanics The study of the motions of stars and other celestial bodies, as well as the forces between them.

CFI Certified (or Certificated) Flight Instructor; a pilot who has earned the FAA rating to give flight instruction.

copilot A pilot that assists the pilot-in-command of an aircraft or spacecraft.

collegiate aviation The segment of aviation that pertains to degree programs in aviation or aerospace technology that are offered at colleges and universities.

commercial airline An air carrier that offers service for scheduled flights on specific routes.

commercial operator Any individual or business that offers flight services for compensation.

communication skills The speaking and listening abilities workers need to perform their jobs.

control tower The building at an airport in which air traffic controllers work to direct air traffic in air near the airport, as well as on the ground.

corporate flight department The department that is responsible for a company's flight operations.

crew member A pilot, flight attendant, or other individual assigned to duty in an aircraft or space vehicle while in flight.

Crew (or Cockpit) Resource Management (CRM) The system by which flight crews work together to use the available resources in an efficient manner.

drop zone (DZ) A designated area where skydivers or objects will land.

en route On the way; in flight.

European Space Agency The organization in charge of the European spaceflight program. It is composed of Belgium, Denmark, France, Germany, Italy, the Netherlands, Norway, Spain, Sweden, Switzerland, and the United Kingdom.

experimental aircraft An aircraft that is still in the development stage.

expert witness An individual whom a court recognizes as having the required knowledge, expertise, and credentials to address specific issues in a court trial.

FAA Federal Aviation Administration

FBO Fixed Based Operator, an airport vendor that offers a variety of general aviation services, such as fuel, flight instruction, aircraft rentals, aircraft maintenance, and chartered flights.

federal aviation regulations (FARs) The body of U.S. rules and regulations that govern flying and flight training.

flight plan A statement that pilots file with air traffic control about their flight; it includes such information as their estimated departure and arrival times, their flight route, and the number of passengers being carried.

flight time The hours spent in flight.

fluid mechanics The study of fluids, such as fuel, in motion and at rest.

gates Where passengers board and disembark from aircraft in airport terminals.

general aviation The segment of aviation that serves all areas of flight operations except for military aviation and commercial airlines.

General Schedule (GS) The pay schedule used for most federal employees.

GIS Geographic Information Systems; the collection of geographic information that is stored in computer databases.

GPS Global Positioning System; the use of satellites to automatically pinpoint locations anywhere on Earth.

ground school A flight school where classroom instruction is provided.

hangar A building at an airport where aircraft are stored or repaired.

human factors An applied science that deals with designing and arranging objects, such as aircraft, so that people can interact more efficiently and safely with them.

human space flight A space flight in which humans operate the spacecraft.

Instrument Flight Rules (IFR) The set of FAA rules that govern flight when using the aircraft instruments to control the aircraft.

interpersonal skills The abilities a worker needs to communicate and work well with others on the job.

ISS International Space Station.

knowledge test The FAA written examination about the aeronautical knowledge pertinent to the specific pilot certificate or rating that an individual seeks.

layover One or more nights spent in the middle of a flight in a city other than the flight crew's home base.

lineperson A ramp service agent.

logbook A pilot's personal book in which he or she records his or her flight time.

mechanic certificate A document issued by the FAA that states an aircraft mechanic has met the standards to perform aircraft maintenance, repairs, overhauls, and inspections.

medical certificate A document issued by the FAA that states a pilot has met the medical standards to operate a particular aircraft.

meteorology The study of Earth's atmosphere.

microgravity A condition in space in which there is minimal gravity.

mission A specific task or flight operation.

NASA National Aeronautics and Space Administration.

NTSB National Transportation Safety Board.

oral exam A test that requires individuals to answer questions verbally.

orbit To move around a body in space, usually in an oval path.

parachutist A skydiver.

Part 121 The section of the federal aviation regulations that governs the operation of commercial air carriers that offer scheduled flights.

Part 135 The section of the federal aviation regulations that governs the operation of scheduled commuter air carriers and on-demand air taxi services.

Part 141 The section of the federal aviation regulations that governs FAA-approved flight schools.

Part 61 The section of the federal aviation regulations that governs pilot certification and training.

Part 91 The section of the federal aviation regulations that governs noncommercial operations, such as corporate flight departments.

passenger terminal A building at the airport where passengers begin and end their flights.

payload The commercial load (such as passengers, freight, or instruments) that an aircraft or spacecraft carries that is related to its flight mission.

pilot certificate A document issued by the FAA to pilots that permits them to operate specific aircraft under certain conditions.

pilot-in-command (PIC) Captain; the pilot in charge of an aircraft or space vehicle responsible for the overall safety and success of a flight.

postflight After a flight has landed.

practical exam The flight test a student must pass to demonstrate his or her skills to obtain a particular FAA pilot certificate or rating.

P rating Powerplant rating; an FAA rating that permits aircraft mechanics to perform the maintenance, repair, overhaul, and inspection on aircraft engines.

preflight Before a flight has taken off.

problem-solving skills The abilities a worker needs to analyze, interpret, and solve problems on the job.

production The manufacturing of goods.

Professional Engineer (P.E.) An engineer licensed in the state where he or she practices. He or she can perform engineering services that may involve the health, safety, and welfare of the general public.

prototype The original model of a new design or object, such as an aircraft, rocket, propeller, or engine.

quality Having all the required characteristics and being free of any defects or deformities.

ramp Apron or tarmac. The area at an airport where aircraft park to load and unload passengers and cargo, as well as to fuel and to receive maintenance.

rating A privilege, condition, or limitation that is added to a pilot certificate; for example, a private pilot may earn an instrument rating.

research and development The process of developing new products or improving existing products for commercial purposes.

runway A strip of land where airplanes take off or land.

satellite A moon or an artificial object that orbits around a planet.

second-in-command Copilot.

simulation The act of imitating a task or situation to evaluate how well an individual would perform the actual task or behave in the real-life situation.

solo Flying alone, without an instructor.

space probe An unmanned spacecraft that is launched into space to complete a specific exploratory mission.

tarmac Ramp or apron. (See: *ramp*)

taxi To move an airplane over the ground or water under its own power.

taxiway The area at an airport where aircraft move between the airport's runways and ramps or hangars.

teamwork skills The abilities a worker needs to work as part of a group on a job or on a work project.

technology The application of science for practical purposes.

TSA Transportation Security Administration.

Visual Flight Rules (VFR) The set of FAA rules that govern flight when using visual references to control the aircraft.

BIBLIOGRAPHY

In this section are some periodicals and books that can help you learn more about the various professions in this book.

Note: All web site addresses were current when this book was written. If a Web site address is no longer available, you may be able to find its new address by entering the name of the publication into a search engine.

A. PERIODICALS

Print and online publications are available for the various occupations that have been profiled in this book. These include magazines, journals, newspapers, newsletters, webzines, and electronic news services. Listed below are just a few publications that serve the different areas of aviation and the aerospace industry. You may be able to find some of the magazines at a public or school library, or at a magazine stand. Many of the print magazines also allow limited free access to their articles on the Web. Some of the Web-based publications are free, whereas others require a subscription to access current issues and other resources.

Air and Space Magazine
Smithsonian Institution
Circulation Department
P.O. Box 420113
Palm Coast, FL 32142
Phone: (800) 766-2149
Fax: (904) 447-2321
http://www.airandspacemagazine.com

Air Forces Monthly
Key Publishing Ltd.
P.O. Box 100
Avenel, NJ 07001
Phone: (800) 688-6247
http://www.keypublishing.com

Air Jobs Digest
http://www.airjobsdigest.com

Airliners: The World's Airline Magazine
Circulation Manager
P.O. Box 968
Sandpoint, ID 83864
Phone: (305) 477-7163
http://www.airlinersonline.com

Aviation International News
Subscriptions
81 Kenosia Avenue
Danbury, CT 06810
Phone: (203) 798-2400
http://www.ainonline.com

Aviation Today
http://www.aviationtoday.com

AvStop Magazine Online
http://www.avstop.com

AV Web: Internet Aviation Magazine and News Service
http://www.avweb.com

Aviation Week and Space Technology
http://www.aviationnow.com

Balloon Life
2336 Forty-seventh Avenue, SW
Seattle, WA 98116
Phone: (206) 935-3649
Fax: (206) 935-3326
http://www.balloonlife.com

Drop Zone.com
http://www.dropzone.com

Flight Web—For Air Medical Professionals
http://www.flightweb.com

Flying Magazine
http://www.flyingmag.com

Landings
http://www.landings.com

Plane and Pilot Magazine
P.O. Box 56381
Boulder, CO 80322
Phone: (800) 283-4330 or (850) 682-7654
Fax: (303) 604-7644
http://www.planeandpilotmag.com

Popular Science
Phone: (800) 289-9399
http://www.popsci.com

Private Pilot
Subscription Service Department
P.O. Box 68040
Anaheim, CA 92817-9800
Phone: (800) 999-9718
http://www.privatepilotmag.com

Professional Pilot
Thirty South Quaker Lane, Suite 300
Alexandria, VA 22314
E-mail: subscription@propilotmag.com
http://www.propilotmag.com

Scientific American
Phone: (800) 333-1199
http://www.sciam.com

Skydiving Magazine
1725 Lexington Avenue
Deland, FL 32724
Phone: (386) 736-4793
Fax: (386) 736-9786
http://www.skydivingmagazine.com

SpaceDaily.com: Your Portal to Space
http://www.spacedaily.com

Space Ref
http://www.spaceref.com

Space-Travel: Your Portal to Space Flight
http://www.space-travel.com

Sky & Telescope
49 Bay State Road
Cambridge, MA 02138
Phone: (800) 253-0245 or
(617) 864-7360
http://www.skypub.com

Universe Today
http://www.universetoday.com

US Aviation.com—America's Aviation Headquarters
http://www.usaviation.com

ZD Net—Info Resources for IT Professionals
http://www.zdnet.com

HOW TO FIND MORE PUBLICATIONS

Here are some things you might do to find publications that are specific to a profession in which you are interested.

1. Talk with librarians, professors, and professionals for recommendations.
2. Check out professional and trade associations. Many of them publish journals, newsletters, magazines, and other publications.
3. Visit an online bookstore, such as Amazon.com, to view the listings of magazines it has to offer for sale. Use such keywords as *aviation, pilot, flying, aerospace, astronomy,* or *engineering.* If the Web site does not have a particular search engine for magazines, be sure to add the word *magazine* to your keyword (for example: *aviation magazine*).
4. Visit the following Web pages to view a listing of various aviation publications:
   - Aero.com: Aviation Magazines, Newspapers, and Newsletters Worldwide, http://www.aero.com/publications/magazine.htm
   - Aviation Magazine Listing from Yahoo, http://dir.yahoo.com/Recreation/Aviation/Magazines
   - Landings.com—Magazines and Publications, http://www.landings.com/_landings/pages/publications.html
   - Thirty Thousand Feet.com—Aviation Magazines and Periodicals, http://www.thirtythousandfeet.com/magazine.htm

B. BOOKS

Listed below are some book titles that can help you learn more about careers in aviation and the aerospace industry. To find other books, ask a librarian for help. You might also ask professionals to recommend titles for you to read.

GENERAL INFORMATION

Grant, R. G., and John R. Dailey. *Flight: 100 Years of Aviation.* New York: DK Publishing, 2002.

Issacs, Alan, John Daintith, and Elizabeth Martin, eds. *A Dictionary of Science, 4th edition.* Oxford, England: Oxford University Press, 1999.

Nahum, Andrew. *Flying Machine.* New York: Dorling Kindersley Ltd., Alfred A. Knopf, Inc., 1990.

Winter, Frank H., and F. Robert Van Der Linden. *100 Years of Flight: A Chronology of Aerospace History, 1903–2003.* Reston, Va.: American Institute of Aeronautics and Astronautics, 2003.

CAREER INFORMATION

Carter, Sharon. *Careers in Aviation.* New York: Rosen Publishing Group, Inc., 1990.

Committee on Science, Engineering, and Public Policy, National Academy of Sciences, National Academy of Engineering, and Institute of Medicine. *Careers in Science and Engineering: A Student Planning Guide to Grad School and Beyond.* Washington, D.C.: National Academy Press, 1996. Available on the Web. http://www.nap.edu/readingroom/books/careers.

Editors of Ferguson Publishing Company. *The Top 100: The Fastest Growing Careers for the 21st Century.* Chicago: Ferguson Publishing Company, 1998.

Farr, J. Michael. *America's Fastest Growing Jobs, 5th ed.* Indianapolis, Ind.: JISTWorks, Inc., 1999.

Federal Aviation Administration Aviation Education Program. *Aviation Careers: The Sky's the Limit.* Washington, D.C.: Government Printing Office, 1995.

Hansen, Janet S., and Clinton V. Oster, Jr., eds. *Taking Flight: Education and Training for Aviation Careers.* Washington, D.C.: National Academy Press, 1997. Available on the Web. http://books.nap.edu/books/0309056764/html/index.html.

Krannich, Ronald, and Caryl Rae. *Best Jobs for the 21st Century, 3rd edition.* Manassas Park, Va.: Impact Publications, 1998.

Maples, Wallace R. *Opportunities in Aerospace Careers.* Lincolnwood, Ill.: McGraw-Hill Companies, 2003.

Pasternak, Ceel. *Cool Careers for Girls in Air and Space.* Manassas Park, Va.: Impact Publications, 2001.

U.S. Bureau of Labor Statistics. *Career Guide to Industries, 2002–03 Edition.* Washington, D.C.: Bureau of Labor Statistics, 2002. Available on the Web. http://www.bls.gov/oco/cg/home.htm.

U.S. Bureau of Labor Statistics. *Occupational Outlook Handbook 2002–2003.* Washington, D.C.: Bureau of Labor Statistics, 2002. Also available on the Web. http://stats.bls.gov/oco/home.htm.

U.S. Department of Labor Employment and Training Administration, *Dictionary of Occupational Titles, Vol. 1, Fourth Edition, Revised 1991.* Washington, D.C.: U.S. Department of Labor Employment and Training Administration, 1991.

Commercial and Public Service Pilots

Aviation Supplies and Academics, Inc. *FAR AIM 2003.* Newcastle, Wash.: ASA, Inc., 2002.

Bristow, Gary. *Ace the Technical Pilot Interview.* New York: McGraw-Hill Professional, 2002.

Cronin, John. *Your Flight Questions Answered by a Jetliner Pilot.* Vergennes, Vt.: Plymouth Press, Ltd., 1998.

Kershner, William K. *Student Pilot's Flight Manual, 9th ed.* Ames, Iowa: Iowa State Press, 2001.

Langewiesche, Wolfgang. *Stick and Rudder: An Explanation of the Art of Flying.* New York: McGraw-Hill Professional, 1990.

Machado, Rod. *Rod Machado's Private Pilot Handbook.* Seal Beach, Calif.: The Aviation Speakers Bureau, 1997.

Mark, Robert P. *Professional Pilot Career Guide.* New York: McGraw-Hill Companies, Inc., 1999.

McElroy, Ronald D., and Pam Ryan (ed.). *Airline Pilot Technical Interviews: A Study Guide, 3rd edition.* Englewood, Colo.: Cage Consulting, 1999.

Padfield, R. Randall. *Learning to Fly Helicopters.* New York: McGraw-Hill Professional, 1992.

Wells, Alexander T., and Seth Young. *Airport Planning and Management.* New York: McGraw-Hill Companies, 2003.

Flight Operations

Federal Aviation Administration. *Aviation Weather Services.* Newcastle, Wash.: Aviation Supplies & Academics, 2000.

Customer Services

Ferguson Publishing Editors. *Careers in Focus: Travel and Hospitality, 2nd edition.* Chicago: Ferguson Publishing Company, 2002.

Kirkwood, Tim. *Flight Attendant Job Finder and Career Guide.* River Forest, Ill.: Planning/Communications, 1999.

Paradis, Adrian A. *Opportunities in Airline Careers.* Lincolnwood, Ill.: VGM Career Horizons, NTC/Contemporary Publishing Company imprint, 1997.

Aircraft Maintenance

Carmody, Douglas. S. *Opportunities in Aircraft Maintenance.* Lincolnwood, Ill.: VGM Career Horizon, 1999.

Aviation Safety

Nolan, Michael S. *Fundamentals of Air Traffic Control, 4th edition.* Pacific Grove, Calif.: Brooks Cole, 2003.

Wells, Alexander T. (Editor). *Commercial Aviation Safety, 3rd edition.* New York: McGraw-Hill Professional, 2001.

Aviation Security and Law

Echaore-McDavid, Susan. *Career Opportunities in Law Enforcement, Security, and Protective Services.* New York: Checkmark Books, Facts On File, Inc., 2000.

Echaore-McDavid, Susan. *Career Opportunities in the Law and the Legal Industry.* New York: Checkmark Books, Facts on File, Inc., 2002.

Aviation Management

Richardson, J. D., Peggy Baty, and Julie F. Rodwell. *Essentials of Aviation Management: A Guide for Fixed Base Operators.* Dubuque, Iowa: Kendall/Hunt Publishing Company, 1995.

Sheehan, John J., and John W. Olcott. *Business & Corporate Aviation Management: On Demand Air Travel.* New York: McGraw-Hill Professional, 2003.

Airport Engineering, Planning, and Maintenance

Norman Ashford, Martin H. P. Stanton, and Clifton A. Moore (Contributor). *Airport Operations, 2nd edition.* New York: McGraw-Hill Professional, 1996.

Wells, Alexander, and Seth Young. *Airport Planning & Management, 5th edition.* New York: McGraw-Hill Professional, 2003.

Aviation Training, Education, and Communications

Brown, Gregory N., and Sean E. Elliott. *The Savvy Flight Instructor: Secrets of the Successful CFI.* Newcastle, Wash.: Aviation Supplies & Academics, 1997.

Echaore-McDavid, Susan. *Career Opportunities in Education.* New York: Checkmark Books, Facts on File, Inc., 2001.

Kershner, William K. *The Flight Instructor's Manual, 4th edition.* Ames, Iowa: Iowa State University Press, 2002.

Reis, Richard M. *Tomorrow's Professor: Preparing for Academic Careers in Science and Engineering.* New York: IEEE Press, 1997.

Aviation Consulting and Sales

Dolber, Rosyln. *Opportunities in Retailing Careers.* Chicago: VGM Career Books, 2003.

Hopkins, Tom. *Sales Prospecting for Dummies.* Foster City, Calif.: IDG Books Worldwide, 1998.

Karlson, David. *Consulting for Success: A Guide for Prospective Consultants.* Los Altos, Calif.: Crisp Publications, 1991.

Sindermann, Carl J., and Thomas K. Sawyer. *The Scientist As Consultant: Building New Career Opportunities.* New York: Plenum Press, 1997.

Aviation Recreation, Sports, and Entertainment

Buchanan, Tom. *JUMP!: Skydiving Made Fun & Easy.* New York: McGraw-Hill Professional, 2003.

Holmes, Len. *Fly the Wing: Hooking into Hang Gliding.* Southern Pines, N.C.: Carolinas Press, 2002.

Shenk, Ellen. *Outdoor Careers: Exploring Occupations in Outdoor Fields.* Mechanicsburg, Penn.: Stackpole Books, 2000.

Szurovy, Geza, and Mike Goulian. *Basic Aerobatics.* New York: McGraw Hill Professional Publishing, 1994.

Williams, Neil. *Aerobatics.* North Branch, Minn.: Specialty Press Publishers & Wholesalers, 1993.

Military Aviation

Bayne, Walter J. (Editor). *Air Warfare: An International Encyclopedia.* Santa Barbara, Calif.: ABC-CLIO, Inc., 2002.

Clancy, Tom, and Leon A. Edney. *Carrier: A Guided Tour of an Aircraft Carrier.* New York: Penguin USA, 2000.

Goodspeed, M. Hill (editor in chief), and Rick Burgess (editor). *U.S. Naval Aviation.* Pensacola, Fla.: Hugh Lauter Levin Associates, 2001.

Libal, Joyce. *Military and Elite Forces Officer.* Broomall, Penn.: Mason Crest Publishers, Inc., 2003.

Nicholas, John. *Army Air Support.* Vero Beach, Fla.: Rourke Enterprises, Inc., 1989.

Norman, C. J. *Aircraft Carriers.* London: Franklin Watts Ltd., 1986.

U.S. Department of Defense and JIST Publishing. *America's Top Military Careers: The Official Guide to Occupations in the Armed Forces.* Indianapolis, Ind.: JISTWorks, Inc., 2000.

Aerospace Manufacturing Industry

Anderson, John D., Jr. *The Airplane: A History of Its Technology.* Reston, Va.: American Institute of Aeronautics and Astronautics, 2003.

Bilstein, Roger E. *Enterprise of Flight: The American Aviation and Aerospace Industry.* Washington, D.C.: Smithsonian Institution Press, 2001.

Blatner, David. *The Flying Book: Everything You've Ever Wondered About Flying on Airplanes.* Vancouver, B.C.: Greystone Books, 2003.

Brandt, Steven A. (ed.), Randall J. Stiles, John J. Bertin, and Ray Whitford. *Introduction to Aeronautics: A Design Perspective.* Reston, Va.: American Institute of Aeronautics and Astronautics, August 1997.

Bristow, Gary V. *Encyclopedia of Technical Aviation.* New York: McGraw-Hill Professional, 2002.

Coe, Marlana. *Human Factors for Technical Communicators.* New York: John Wiley & Sons, 1996.

Echaore-McDavid, Susan. *Career Opportunities in Science.* New York: Checkmark Books, Facts on File, Inc., 2003.

Ferguson Publishing Editors. *Careers in Focus: Technicians.* Chicago: Ferguson Publishing Company, 2001.

Garner, Geraldine O. *Careers in Engineering.* Lincolnwood, Ill.: VGM Career Horizons, NTC Publishing, 1993.

Goldberg, Jan. *Careers for Scientific Types and Others with Inquiring Minds.* Lincolnwood, Ill.: VGM Career Horizons, NTC/Contemporary Publishing Group Inc., 2000.

Heppenheimer, T. A. *First Flight: The Wright Brothers and the Invention of the Airplane.* Hoboken, N.J.: John Wiley and Sons, Inc., 2003.

Rotman, Morris B., Luisa Gerasimo, and Robert W. Galvin. *Opportunities in Public Relations Careers.* Lincolnwood, Ill.: McGraw-Hill/Contemporary Books, 2001.

WetFeet.com. *WetFeet.com's Industry Insider Guide: The Inside Scoop on the Job You Want.* San Francisco, Calif.: Jossey-Bass, 2000.

Space Flight and Exploration

Baard, Erik, Bruce Grierson, Fenella Saunders, Wendy L. Schultz, and Jeffrey Winters. *Popular Science Space 2100: To Mars and Beyond in the Century to Come.* New York: Time, Inc., 2003.

Dyson, Marianne J. *Space Station Science: Life in Free Fall.* New York: Scholastic Inc., 1999.

Harrison, Albert A. *Spacefaring: The Human Dimension.* Berkeley, Calif.: University of California Press, 2001.

Hawking, Stephen W. *A Brief History of Time.* New York: Bantam Books, 1998.

Larson, Wiley J., and Linda K. Pranke. *Human Spaceflight: Mission Analysis and Design.* New York: McGraw-Hill, 1999.

Longuski, James. *Advice to Rocket Scientists: A Career Survival Guide for Scientists and Engineers.* Reston, Va.: American Institute of Aeronautics and Astronautics, 2003.

Maples, Wallace R. *Opportunities in Aerospace Careers.* Lincolnwood, Ill.: VGM Career Horizons, 1997.

Orange, Daniel, Ph.D., and Gregg Stebben. *Everything You Need to Know about Physics.* New York: Pocket Books, 1999.

Reichhardt, Tony, ed. *Space Shuttle: The First 20 Years—The Astronauts' Experiences in Their Own Words.* New York: DK Publishing, 2002.

Schulke, Flip, Debra Schulke, Penelope McPhee, and Raymond McPhee. *Your Future in Space. The U.S. Space Camp Training Program.* New York: Crown Publishers, Inc., 1986.

INDEX

J

L

M

N

O

P